MERCHANT FLEETS

MERCHANT FLEETS

ELLERMAN LINES

First published 1989

British Library Cataloguing Publication Data

Haws, Duncan
  Merchant Fleets 16
  Ellerman Lines
  1. Merchant Marine — History
  1. Title

  ISBN 0 946378 05 3

TEXT photoset in 9 on 10pt Times
by C. I. Thomas and Sons (Haverfordwest) Ltd.,
Merlins Bridge, Haverfordwest, Dyfed.
TCL Publications, Travel Creatours Ltd, 1 Meadowbank Rd, Hereford HR1 2ST.

CONTENTS

INTRODUCTION

As a Liverpool lad I was brought up within sound of the Mersey and spent my free time walking from Gladstone Dock, reached for one old penny by the lamented Overhead Railway, back to the Pier Head with a similar if less frequent expedition to the South Docks. The Ellerman ships were even then great favourites and have remained so. I am not by any means alone if the number of requests that this book be produced is anything to go by.

The number of ships involved plus the spread of companies and abetted by the oft-time changes in the managing firms has been a constant problem. One might say detective work more than research has often been the order of the day. In fact only a computer and a word processor make it possible adequately to store and retrieve. As always the experts can only reveal themselves after the work is printed; but I welcome with appreciation their additions and corrections. Such kindnesses mean that whenever a Merchant Fleets volume is re-printed it is brought up to date.

These works are more than anything else a compilation and an editing of numerous sources official and private. It is a pleasure to pay tribute to those who have been good enough to supply information, photographs and sketches. Thus my grateful thanks to: John Harrower, one of the foremost Ellerman experts, Lt. Cdr. A. Niblock RNR (Rtd), George Waring, David. E. Cope, Anthonly Blackler of the Department of Nautical Science at the College of Maritime Studies, Southampton, all of whom loaned their collections of photographs to enlarge or correct the illustrations as did James A. Stewart. To Alan J. Tennant, the U-boat expert, for filling in the U-boat gaps. To J. J. Bew; and George Monk for the list of all his Ellerman ships so that comparisons could be made. And at Lloyds: Barbara Jones.

Finally to Cunard-Ellerman themselves; Eric Flounders, Iain Kimberley and, especially, Noel Kent.

A considerable number of sources have also been consulted, chief among them being James Taylor's magnificent 'Ellermans — A Wealth of Shipping'; virtually with Lloyd's Register's Shipping Information Dept., the base document for this book. Sea Breezes 1946-88 including John Isherwood's splendid series and John McRoberts on Bucknall. World Ship Society's Marine News, Lloyd's Registers 1865-1988 and a whole host of works in my considerable library far too numerous to mention individually but which have contributed a strand here and there that together weave the whole fabric.

Duncan Haws

Hereford
November 1988

EXPLANATORY NOTES

The Ellerman Fleets are arranged in the order in which each joined the Group. The name of the concern is a heading across the top of all of the applicable pages.

The ships are arranged chronologically by date of build or acquisition except that sister ships are grouped together.

Tonnage: The method of calculation has changed several times since 1830. The gross and net figures given are generally those that applied when the vessel entered service.

Dimensions are 'between perpendiculars' unless otherwise specified.

Service speed is given. This is seldom the maximum speed attained on trials.

Abbreviations: To assist readers of all nationalities as few as possible have been used and short cuts aimed at saving print avoided.

ELLERMAN COMPANY ABBREVIATIONS

B & C	British & Colonial Steam Navigation Company.
BSSL	Bucknall Steamship Lines.
E & B	Ellerman & Bucknall.
ECL	Ellerman City Liners
E & P	Ellerman & Papayanni.
JRE	John Reeves Ellerman (I).
LL & O	London, Liverpool & Ocean S.S.Co.
M & W	Montgomerie & Workman.
W & L	Westcott & Laurence.
EHCL	Ellerman Harrison Container Line.

GENERAL

B	Built		**DD**	Dry dock
B	bridge deck		disp	displacement
bhp	Brake Horse Power		dwt	deadweight
Blr	boiler		**E**	East
C	Cargo		**E**/Eng	Engine/Engineering
Cabin	Cabin Class		exp	expansion
Co	Company		F/Fcsle	forecastle
Comp	compound		fwd	forward, forrard
cu m	cubic metre		4S,SA	four stroke single acting
cu ft	cubic feet		g	gross
cyl	cylinder		grt	gross registered tonnage
dbl	double		**H**	Hull
drg	double reduction geared		hp	horse power
Dft	Draught		ihp	indicated horse power
dk	deck		inv	inverted
D	Dimensions		kts	knots

lp	low pressure	rpm	revolutions per minute
Ltd	Limited	S	South
m	metres	SB	Shipbuilding
mp	medium pressure	scr	screw
M/v	maiden voyage	sgl	single
MOT	Ministry of Transport	Shg	Shipping
MOWT	Ministry of War Transport	shp	shaft horse power
n	net	SN	Steam Navigation
N	North	srg	single reduction geared
nhp	nominal horse power	SS	Steamship
oa	overall	S, S	Steam Ship
obb	over bulbous bow	stm	steam
Pad	Paddle	SV	sailing vessel
P	Passengers	**T**	Tons/tonnage
pd	per day	TEU	Twenty foot Equivalent Units
psi	pounds per square inch	tpd	tons per day
P	Poop	tpl	triple
PLC	Public Limited Company	Tst	Tourist class
Pty	Proprietary	Turb	Turbine
Q	quarter deck	tw	twin/two
quad	quadruple / four	2S,SA	two stroke single acting
ref	refrigerated	UAE	United Arab Emirates
r	registered	W	West
r/n	renamed	Wks	Works
Rly	Railway	WT	Water tube (boiler)

INDEX

For ease of cross-reference the complete book is numbered sequentially.
The fleets are in the order in which John Ellerman acquired them:
Where there is more than one ship of the same name the date of build is given.

11

City of Canterbury (I) 1875 226
City of Canterbury (II) 1922 269
City of Canterbury (III) 1964 618
City of Canterbury (IV) 1976 298
City of Canton (I) 1857   183
City of Canton (II) 1916   414
City of Cape Town (I) 1937 473
City of Cape Town (II) 1957 608
City of Cardiff (I) 1918   416
City of Cardiff (II) 1942   592
City of Cardiff (III) 1949   488
City of Carlisle (I) 1913   573
City of Carlisle (II) 1946   598
City of Carthage (I) 1873   225
City of Carthage (II) 1906 388
City of Cashmere   195
City of Chelmsford   593
City of Chester (I) 1910   393
City of Chester (II) 1944   476
City of Chicago   489
City of Christchurch   580
City of Christiania   444
City of Colchester   596
City of Colombo (I) 1909 391
City of Colombo (II) 1956 288
City of Corinth (I) 1870   216
City of Corinth (II) 1898   243
City of Corinth (III) 1913 405
City of Corinth (IV) 1918 423
City of Corinth (V) 1965   290
City of Cork   50
City of Coventry   486
City of Delhi (I) 1857   184
City of Delhi (II) 1867   210
City of Delhi (III) 1901   247
City of Delhi (IV) 1925   273
City of Delhi (V) 1956   495
City of Derby   585
City of Dieppe   274
City of Doncaster   594
City of Dover   212
City of Dublin (I)   181
City of Dublin (II)   238
City of Dundee (I) 1890   239
City of Dundee (II) 1921 458
City of Dundee (III) 1961 613
City of Dunedin   464
City of Dunkirk   402
City of Durban (I) 1921   462
City of Durban (II) 1953 607
City of Durban (III) 1978 300
City of Durham (I) 1911   396
City of Durham (II) 1947 131
City of Durham (III) 1955 138

City of Durham (IV) 1945 281
City of Eastbourne (I) 1923 449
City of Eastbourne (II) 1962 616
City of Edinburgh (I) 1852 177
City of Edinburgh (II) 1868 211
City of Edinburgh (III) 1876 230
City of Edinburgh (IV) 1899 246
City of Edinburgh (V) 1938 277
City of Edinburgh (VI) 1973 299
City of Ely (I) 1943   119
City of Ely (II) 1950   136
City of Evansville   447
City of Exeter (I) 1914   258
City of Exeter (II) 1952   605
City of Exeter (III) 1974   295
City of Famagusta   146
City of Florence (I) 1867   202
City of Florence (II) 1914 407
City of Florence (III) 1918 433
City of Florence (IV) 1970 154
City of Foochow   205
City of Genoa (I) 1906   441
City of Genoa (II) 1970   152
City of Glasgow (I) 1848   174
City of Glasgow (II) 1867 209
City of Glasgow (III) 1906 254
City of Glasgow (IV) 1920 443
City of Glasgow (V) 1958 499
City of Glasgow (VI) 1963 617
City of Gloucester (I) 1921 462
City of Gloucester (II) 1949 485
City of Gloucester (III) 1963 614
City of Guildford (I) 1919 436
City of Guildford (II) 1950 490
City of Guildford (III) 1957 497
City of Halifax   561
City of Hamilton   163
City of Hankow (I) 1869   214
City of Hankow (II) 1915 413
City of Hartlepool   303
City of Harvard   582
City of Hereford (I) 1927 467
City of Hereford (II) 1958 499

City of Hongkong   271
City of Hull (I) 1947   483
City of Hull (II) 1970   622
City of Ipswich   304
City of Istanbul   149
City of Izmir   143
City of Johannesburg (I) 1920   425
City of Johannesburg (II) 1947   484
City of Karachi (I) 1905   253
City of Karachi (II) 1937   276
City of Karachi (III) 1905 385
City of Karachi (IV) 1951 286
City of Keelung   576
City of Khartoum (I) 1913 571
City of Khartoum (II) 1946 478
City of Khios (I) 1878   228
City of Khios (II) 1925   452
City of Kimberley   586
City of Kobe   106
City of La Spezia   156
City of Lahore (I) 1864   204
City of Lahore (II) 1911   399
City of Lancaster (I) 1924 107
City of Lancaster (II) 1958 498
City of Leeds (I) 1956   141
City of Leeds (II) 1947   133
City of Leeds (III) 1944   597
City of Leeds (IV) 1950   490
City of Leicester (I) 1926 108
City of Leicester (II) 1956 140
City of Leicester (III) 1947 130
City of Lichfield (I) 1943 120
City of Lichfield (II) 1961 612
City of Lille   468
City of Limassol   294
City of Lincoln (I) 1911   398
City of Lincoln (II) 1938 591
City of Lisbon (I) 1970   151
City of Lisbon (II) 1977   302
City of Lisbon   649
City of Liverpool (I) 1948 487
City of Liverpool (II) 1970 620
City of Liverpool   656
City of London (I) 1851   176
City of London (II) 1876 229
City of London (III) 1906 255
City of London (IV) 1947 599
City of London (V) 1970 621
City of London   657
City of Lucknow (I) 1858 189
City of Lucknow (II) 1869 213
City of Lucknow (III) 1896 245

Duke of Argyll	166	Haddon Hall (II) 1895	363	Lorenzo	580
Duke of Athole	165	Hardwick Hall	364	Lotus	543
Duke of Connaught	190	Harriet Agnes	158	Lucian	127
Duke of Hamilton	168	Helena	309	Lusitania	504
Duke of Rothesay	164	Hermiston	419	Macedonia	9
Eaton Hall	340	Hero	103	Madrid	515
Echunga	312	Iberian See below	149	Magoola	317
Eden Hall	358	Ionia	7	Majestic	172
Egeria	320	Ionian (I) 1938	116	Malatian (I) 1914	78
Egypt	514	Ionia (II) 1947	131	Malatian (II) 1958	144
Egyptian (I) 1861	20	Italian (I) 1887	67	Malleney	328
Egyptian (II) 1891	50	Italian (II) 1899	82	Maltasian	137
Egyptian (III) 1920	99	Italian See below	149	Malvernian (I) 1924	106
Egyptian (IV) 1947	130	Johannnesburg	530	Malvernian (II) 1937	113
Elba	519	John Dixon	512	Manchurian	101
Elizabeth Fry	321	Joseph Dodds	513	Manica (I) 1892	529
Empire Clyde	628	Joshua Nicholson	44	Manica (II) 1900	539
Empire Comfort	625	Juan	168	Manica (III) 1901	541
Empire Faith	629	Kabinga	564	Manitoba	516
Empire Gauntlet	630	Kaffir	522	Maplemore	246
Empire Irving	631	Kafue	570	Mardinian (I) 1913	75
Empire Pendennis	632	Kalomo	561	Mardinian (II) 1919	92
Empire Rest	626	Kandahar	574	Marina	349
Empire Shelter	627	Kansas	567	Marine Raven	635
Empire Spartan	592	Karema	566	Maritzburg	554
Empire Viceroy	633	Karonga (I) 1907	562	Marlborough	335
Empire Wallace	634	Karonga (II) 1921	585	Marmorian See below	149
Estepona	334	Karroo	571	Maronian	77
Estrellano (I) 1910	70	Kasama	559	Mashona (I) 1892	528
Estrellano (II) 1920	97	Kasenga (I) 1907	565	Mashona (II) 1894	538
Estremadurian See below		Kasenga (II) 1899	579	Matoppo (I) 1904	555
	149	Kathlamba	573	Matoppo (II) 1905	556
Etona	520	Katuna	563	Mediterranean	149
Euphrates	547	Keelung (I) 1914	575	Melford Hall (I) 1911	400
Evorian See below	149	Keelung (II) 1919	576	Melford Hall (II) 1920	425
Fabian (I) 1881	29	Kentucky	569	Mercian	128
Fabian (II) 1919	88	Khersonese	319	Merida	517
Falernian (I) 1880	28	Kioto (I) 1910	568	Merton Hall (I) 1881	354
Falernian (II) 1914	76	Kioto (II) 1918	434	Merton Hall (II) 1889	374
Favonian	72	Kirby Hall	356	Merton Hall (III) 1905	437
Flaminian (I) 1880	30	Knaresboro'	587	Methley Hall	367
Flaminian (II) 1914	79	Knowsley Hall (I) 1873	341	Mexican	34
Flaminian (III) 1917	81	Knowsley Hall (II) 1903	375	Minho (I) 1890	33
Flaminian (IV) 1956	143	Koranna	557	Minho (II) 1970	150
Flavian	31	Kosmo	578	Mistley Hall	342
Florian (I) 1939	117	Laconia	3	Mistley Hall See below	431
Florian (II) 1955	142	Lancastrian (I) 1924	107	Mondego	157
Fort Constantine	638	Lancastrian (II) 1956	140	Morning Star	316
Fort Dunvegan	639	Langton Hall (I) 1905	379	Netherby Hall (I) 1890	360
Fort Edmonton	640	Langton Hall (II) 1918	416	Netherby Hall (II) 1905	380
Fort Kilmar	641	Lepanto	625	New Margaret	308
Fort Providence	642	Lesbian (I) 1874	23	Newby Hall	378
Fort St James	643	Lesbian (II) 1915	83	Ocean Spray	506
Fort Salisbury	494	Lesbian (III) 1923	98	Oporto (I) 1888	32
Fort Tadoussac	642	Lisbon (I) 1852	505	Oporto (II) 1928	111
Gascon	60	Lisbon (II) 1910	71	Orontes	6
Gerano	90	Lisbon (III) 1920	100	Orchis	40
Great Britain	310	Locksley Hall (I) 1869	338	Orestes	48
Grecian	135	Locksley Hall (II) 1888	368	Oriental	171
Grecian See below	149	Locksley Hall (III) 1893	373	Palm	17
Griqua	551	Locksley Hall (IV) 1903	383	Palmella (I) 1913	74
Gulf of Suez	43	Lord Clive	11	Palmella (II) 1920	96
Haddington	330	Lord Gough	12	Palmelian	129
Haddon Hall (I) 1868	337	Lord Palmerston	331	Pandorian	118

14

Pamelian	129	Saldanha	572	Tamega	152
Panola	314	Salerno	290	Tenedos	41
Parana	528	Salmo	289	Thermutis	332
Patrician	132	Samarina	119	Thessalia	2
Perim	42	Samboston	121	Thornton Hall	388
Persian (I) 1863	22	Samois	120	Tiber	155
Persian (II) 1891	522	Samtorch	123	Tigris	548
Pinemore	372	San Domingo	511	Torcello	104
Plantain	15	Sangro	293	Tomes	153
Plymothian	47	Sandon Hall (I) 1906	382	Trafford Hall	386
Pondo	527	Sandon Hall (II) 1921	458	Transvaal	524
Prome	373	Sardinia	58	Trentham Hall (I) 1876	346
Rapallo	294	Science	160	Trentham Hall (II) 1897	365
Ready	546	Scotia	336	Tronto	156
Rhone	159	Serbino	87	Truthful	14
Rialto	577	Sicilian	134	Tua	154
Rio Negro	584	Silvio	292	Urbino	624
Rio Pardo	583	Silvian See under	149	Vanguard	508
Robert Lees	325	Sorrento	291	Venetian (I) 1891	65
Rokeby Hall	339	Speke Hall	351	Venetian (II) 1947	133
Romeo	436	Spero See under	293	Vernon	333
Roumelia	13	Stanley Hall	362	Volta	65
Roumelian	80	Star of the South	315	Volturno	76
Ruby	507	Starlight	318	Walton Hall	389
Rufford Hall (I) 1888	370	Stewarts	306	Werneth Hall	355
Rufford Hall (II) 1903	384	Sutton Hall	381	Wharfedale	64
Rufford Hall (III) 1914	408	Swazi	549	Wistow Hall (I) 1878	352
Runnymede	329	Sydenham	510	Wistow Hall (II) 1890	361
Rydal Hall (I) 1871	344	Sylph	307	Worsely Hall	366
Rydal Hall (II) 1874	343	Tagus (I) 1872	509	Xantippi	169
Rydal Hall (III) 1878	350	Tagus (II) 1898	37	Zulu	486
Rydal Hall (IV) 1889	359	Tagus (III) 1970	151		
Rydal Hall (V) 1925	452	Taipooshan	636		

THE ELLERMAN LINE
JOHN REEVES ELLERMAN

1862 John Reeves Ellerman was born at 100 Anlaby Road, Hull, the third child and first son of Johann Herman Ellerman, a Lutheran German from Hamburg who had established himself in Hull as a corn merchant. His wife was Anne Reeves from whom the other christian name derives.

1869 Johann Ellerman died and the family went to live in Caen, Normandy, where JRE acquired not only the language but the French way of life which he so much liked. But his schooling was back in Birmingham at King Edward's School.

1876 At 14 John Ellerman left home and school and was articled to a chartered accountant, one William Smedly. A more than apt pupil his finals were passed brilliantly and with distinction. The youth had an acute and natural grasp of finance which never deserted him during the remainder of his life.

1884 JRE moved to London where he joined Quilter, Bell & Co in the City. After but two years he was made a junior partner at the age of 24.

1886 Clearly able to look after himself and a match for much older men in the profession he decided to launch out for himself; at still only 24 he established J. Ellerman & Co at 10 Moorgate, London.

1891 By now he had a branch office in Birmingham, which he regarded as his home town, and controlled the investments in four trust companies.

1892 On January 4 the flamboyant and mercurial shipowner Frederick Leyland collapsed and died on the platform at Blackfriars railway station leaving without a person in charge a shipping company which owned twenty-two vessels. JRE together with Christopher Furness and Henry O'Hagan put together a new company, Frederick Leyland & Co Ltd with a capital of £800,000 to purchase the ships from the executors; it was made up of £350,000 in 5% debenture stock to secure the mortgages on the ships, £250,000 7% debenture stock and £200,000 in ordinary shares. The plan succeeded and Christopher Furness, who had considerable connections in the shipping industry already, became the first caretaker Chairman and JRE Managing Director.

1893 The shareholders had complete confidence in the young man and JRE took over the Chair as well as remaining Managing Director. He was 31.

1899 His activities brought him into a number of non-shipping transactions among which was his purchase of Cambrian Collieries and Great Eastern Collieries. These he later used to bunker his vessels and also shipped out coal to the overseas depots whenever a ship was short of an outward cargo. His collieries established their main depots at Port Said and, key to the Persian Gulf and western India, at Karachi.

1900 The 20 ships, of 95,983grt, owned by the long established West India & Pacific SS Co Ltd were purchased for the Leyland Line. To accommodate them a new organisation was created: Frederick Leyland (1900) Ltd with a capital of £2,800,000.

1901 In the shipping world one of the most dramatic events of the new century was the creation by the American financier J. Pierpoint Morgan of the International Mercantile Marine Company (formalised Feb 4, 1902) with which he sought to buy up sufficient of the North Atlantic shipping concerns to make the United States pre-eminent in that field. The reason was that over the decades they had signally failed to establish even one front rank transatlantic line. Even now Mr. Morgan's purchases were so polyglot that no cohesive fleet was to emerge and the greater majority of his ships were not front rankers. However in 1901 he struck a deal with JRE whereby he purchased Frederick Leyland (1900) Ltd at £14.5 per share. A proviso was that JRE would not re-enter the North Atlantic business, excepting Antwerp-Montreal which, being Canada, was not covered by any IMMC deal, for a period of 14 years. A further deal was struck. IMMC did not require the Mediterranean ships owned by Leyland and so the Mediterranean, Portugal, Antwerp and Montreal serving ships with their routes and goodwill were excluded and £180,000 shares in IMMC were held by JRE in payment. Pierpoint Morgan also asked JRE to remain as Chairman of the Leyland concern to which he agreed. One aspect of the deal is interesting. Unlike other men JRE insisted upon cash for the purchase in place of shares in IMMC. He even refused other notes of credit. With the signing of the contract J. Pierpoint Morgan became the owner of 54 Leyland ships, including 18 which were former West India & Pacific vessels and out of which total JRE was to re-purchase the 20 excluded from the 14 year embargo.

In parallel to this JRE had to find a home for the 20 ships that he was now personally to own. To distinguish them from Leyland he added a blue band touching the black to their salmon pink funnels. In June negotiations with Nicholas Papayanni and his General Manager Graham Smith resulted in the addition of Papayanni's 8 ships at a total cost of £132,850 of which only £3,500 was goodwill. The fleet comprised 3 modern steamers and five old vessels, the eldest being 35. JRE now had a fleet of 28 ships and an organisation to operate them.

June 24: To accommodate the new entity he now formed the London, Liverpool & Ocean Shipping Company Ltd with a nominal capital of £1,300,000 consisting of 75,000 £10 4½% cumulative preference shares and 55,000 £10 ordinary shares. Only £120,000 was offered to the public. JRE held 29,000 ordinary and 21,000 preference shares. The blue band on the funnel was replaced with red (top), white and blue bands. The new company purchased the 20 Leyland ships with the 8 Papayanni still being owned personally by JRE. The directors of the new shipping company, with head office in Moorgate, London, were JRE Chairman, M. W. Mattinson and Val Prinsep — all former Leyland directors, Prinsep being Leyland's son-in-law and a noted artist. Their fees were a mere £100 per annum but each had to hold a minimum of £20,000 in qualifying shares. JRE's contract was that he was to manage the concern for a fee of 10% of the net profit in any year where a minimum 6% dividend was declared. Below that figure his fee was to be the £100.

JRE's ambitions extended beyond the Mediterranean and he sought to move into areas that were not closed to him by the IMMC deal. Being a financier rather than a creator he was looking for companies to buy. Two came to his notice and were the subject of his close scrutiny. His method was virtually unique. He asked what the seller wanted for his concern. If it fitted his view on the worth plus the potential of the purchase and he trusted the vendor he agreed there and then. He was even known to take out his cheque book and pay for it on the spot.

Sept 20: At the Annual General meeting JRE announced that negotiations were concluded to acquire for London, Liverpool & Ocean 50% of George Smith & Sons' City Line Ltd and, by October, 50% of the Hall Line. The other 50% of each being for JRE's personal account.

George Smith (III) had died in 1899 at the early age of 54. The family were therefore willing to sell. Robert Alexander who controlled the Hall Line was infirm and had no sons; to him selling to a man so pre-eminent in the business was to secure the future of his company.

The details of the transactions are recorded under the company histories of each. However the effect was to add 15 ships of 68,543grt and 11 ships of 41,636grt to the Ellerman fleet.

The next move planned by JRE was that, on the last day of the year, London, Liverpool & Ocean would acquire from him all his personally owned shipping interests consolidating them into one group. JRE taking the value in shares not cash.

Dec 23: An Extraordinary General Meeting of London, Liverpool & Ocean increased the capital to £1,470,000 by means of 16,990 £10 ordinary shares and 100 £1 Management shares; these repeated the 10% of net profit subject to 6% or more as a dividend. Thus 10 shares were equivalent to 1% of the net profit of the concern. All of the new issue were allocated to JRE.

A further resolution was that the name of London, Liverpool & Ocean be changed to Ellerman Lines Ltd. The effective date for the change to be December 31 (but actually Jan 22 1902). On this day JRE also resigned from Leylands in order to devote his time, as Chairman, to Ellermans.

While all this had been going on the L,L & O purchased three steamers with which to carry horses and mules to the Boer War. They were William Johnston's *Pinemore* (372) and *Maplemore* (246) plus Patrick Henderson's *Prome* (373).

1902 January 22: Ellerman Lines Ltd was incorporated and one of the greatest shipping lines in the world was officially born. The directors were the same as those of London, Liverpool & Ocean plus F. G. Burt. Papayanni & Co operated separately under Frank Swift who came across from Leyland; he replaced Papayanni's General Manager Graham Smith who became JRE's deputy. The whole fleet consisted of forty-nine ships plus 8 Papayanni.

The business to the Mediterranean of Ellerman Lines with Papayanni & Co was all from the West coast of Britain. London was not served and was well covered by existing lines. In the JRE mould purchase not invasion was the way in.

The family firm of Westcott & Laurence operated 9 ships out of London. Initially they were disinclined to sell but under a deal whereby William Westcott and his brother John were to remain as managers with JRE as Chairman they sold out for £67,000 plus a further £17,000 for Westcott & Flint, their Antwerp subsidiary. The arrangement worked very successfully.

A further transaction was the purchase for Papayanni of Palgrave, Murphy & Co's Oporto trade together with the two ships, coincidentally already bearing 'city' names, *City of Cork* and *City of Amsterdam* (51-52). The cost was £22,000.

The fleet that had been put together contained a few Atlantic carriers employed on the Antwerp-Montreal service. They did not fit in with Ellerman's plans and it was decided to withdraw; JRE therefore sold back to Frederick Leyland (1900) Ltd, for £216,678, *Albanian, Almerian, Belgian,*

Mexican (34-36) and *Pinemore (Oxonian)* plus the rights and goodwill of the service.

May 21: The Boer War ended with the signing of the Treaty of Vereeniging. The ending of hostilities produced over capacity. Ellerman Lines with Thos & Jas Harrison entered into an agreement with Cayzer Irvine's Clan Line to join the South African Conference. There were to be 108 sailings per annum with Clan having 78, Hall Line 15 and Harrison 15. In addition Hall undertook not to enter the passenger business for which Union-Castle paid Hall £60 per sailing. Clan was to benefit for allowing the newcomers in by receiving for three years 5 shillings per ton on freight earning more than 25 shillings per ton.

1903 The profit on trade to India was deteriorating due to a price war which followed the incursion of Frank Strick who had expanded his Persian Gulf activities to include west coast Indian ports; he was also providing sailings from Newport, South Wales. Attempts, in retaliation, to enter the Persian Gulf trade could only be done by undercutting Strick and to drive him away from India required even greater reductions in the rates. Two years of manoeuvring and bickering followed. It ended with Strick berthing out of London and Newport only.

May 3: Hall Line entered the South American trade in partnership with the Allan Line who were the Glasgow agents for George Smith & Son's City Line (the Allans were relatives by marriage). Allans were members of the River Plate Conference and, using Hall ships 24 sailings per annum were planned. The other members did not like this move but the balance was upset when R. P. Houston came onto the route. The effect was to be consistently unprofitable round voyages.

1904 Oct 10: The present Ellerman funnel was adopted. JRE did not like the existing colours. He admired that worn by the Liverpool based Alexandra Towing Co and sought and was given their permission to copy it. There is one minor difference; Alexandra have a pin stripe black band between the buff and white. Ellerman do not. The other change was that the blue JRE pennant was to be worn above the houseflags of the constituent fleets although Ellerman Lines and Papayanni vessels flew only the pennant.

1905 Feb: Val Prinsep died and his place was taken by Francis Speed. By the King's birthday honours JRE was created a Baronet. Also in February a new Ellerman-Strick route was opened to Marmagoa.

Dec: The Glen Line, owned by McGregor, Gow & Co, were unable, for financial reasons, to contribute sufficient ships to take up their share of the Far East Conference. JRE arranged for four Hall ships to be 'sold' to Glen, renamed and operated by Glen but with Hall crews. The deal was 1/64 share of each ship was sold to Glen and 63/64ths were managed by them. Financially Hall Line was to receive 2/5ths of the Glen's share of the trade for seven years. *Netherby Hall* (380) became *Glenearn* and *Branksome Hall* (377) *Glenavon*. No others were renamed.

1906 Jan 15: *Glenearn* took the first sailing under the scheme.

1907 The Glen Far East venture was yielding poor results.

1908 Oct: Hall Line withdrew from the Glen scheme but the vessels remained on charter. Hall also came off the South American route. Allan continued alone selling out to Donaldson in 1913.

1908 The Bucknall Steamship Lines were experiencing the severe financial difficulties set out in their historical chronology on page no. 163 and John Ellerman took effective control of the company.

1909 March: Bucknalls, the West Hartlepool S.N.Co. and Strick had a Persian Gulf trading agreement that had its beginnings back in 1903. West Hartlepool now withdrew from its share of the commitment to supply sailings and John Ellerman, somewhat unexpectedly, entered into an arrangement that left Frank Strick, a man with whom he could not get on, in virtual control with Ellerman vessels interlocking with Strick ships upon Frank Strick's say so but with the undertaking that it would be 'fair shares for all'. The explanation was really that in this way Ellerman fully occupied Strick with the Persian Gulf, which was his main area anyway, and thus kept him out of the developing India trade — or at least made it that much easier to resist him if he tried.
Dec 21: A son also named John Reeves Ellerman was born.

1910 June: Ellerman with Clan and Thos. & Jas. Harrison inaugurated a new joint service from the west coast of the UK via the Red Sea to East Africa. A route hitherto not served from Liverpool and the west UK. The first sailing was in fact taken by Harrison's *Traveller*. Beira became the terminal port and at Mombasa A.M. Jeevanjee became the agent.

1912 The lifeblood South African mail contract was held by Union-Castle, which was at that time owned by the Royal Mail S.P.Co. with Sir Owen Philipps (Lord Kylsant) as chairman. 1912 was renewal year but there was a serious difficulty. In the previous year the South African government had passed an act which made discounting illegal for mail carriers. Rebates, discounts, were part of the South African Conference system of rewarding loyal customers who stuck to the conference vessels when cheaper charter opportunities inevitably arose from time to time. The dilemma was that legally Union-Castle could not bid for the contract and equally, legally, they could not break the conference rules. The impasse was finally settled by all members cancelling their rebate terms across the board and having to live with the fillip given to outside shipping companies.

A further difficulty which arose during the year was that the Balkan crisis (Serbia, Bulgaria and Greece were enlarged at the expense of Turkish Europe) led in turn to the temporary cancellation of Papayanni sailings to Greece, Turkey and the Black Sea.

1913 The East African Conference was formed with Ellerman as a founder member.

1914 The Ellerman & Bucknall Steamship Co Ltd was formed. Into it was transferred all the Bucknall vessels, their routes and the goodwill of their trade. It commenced a seemingly endless series of transfers to and from their colours; frequently for a single voyage. South Africa became their prime area of activity until the mid-twenties.

Aug 4: Saw the outbreak of World War I. It was initially seen to be a land war centred on the Central Powers with the French Army being the Allied dominant partner to the British Expeditionary Force. But a blockade of Germany led to the growth of unrestricted submarine warfare with catastrophic results for Allied, and outstandingly, British shipping. Because of its sheer numerical size the ships of the Ellerman group suffered alarmingly.

Aug 5: *City of Winchester* (411) became the Company's first casualty when she was taken by the German cruiser *Koenigsberg* although *City of Khios* (228) probably deserves this dubious distinction having been already seized by the Turks at Smyrna. These were the only two 1914 losses.

1915 Commerce continued despite the war, indeed some routes prospered because of the re-channelling of demand away from war closed areas. E & B now joined the Far East Conference and were also admitted to the Rangoon Homeward Conference. *City of Sparta* (242) took the first sailing. In November the Manchester-USA service was started in conjunction with the White Star Line and Lamport & Holt.

To increase cargo carryings out of Burma control of the Arracan Company was obtained. Ellerman thereby became the owners of the Arracan Flotilla of river steamers. From the Receiver of Enemy Property came the German Diekman's Mills which were renamed Ellerman Rice Mills (Burma) Ltd, later the whole was renamed Ellerman's Arracan Rice & Trading Co.

War losses were six ships of which two were by marine hazard.

1916 June: The chance for Papayanni to serve Marseilles and Italy from Manchester was taken by the acquisition, with Cunard, of the Watson Steamship Company's business.

However, the outstanding achievement of the year was the acquisition by John Ellerman personally of the firm of Thomas Wilson, Sons & Co of Hull. For £4,100,000 he bought the Company and its 68 ships. To it he gave the name Ellerman's Wilson Line (The history of this concern and of its fleet is not covered in this work).

War losses amounted to seven ships but out of this number three were by marine hazard.

1917 The U-boat campaign reached its peak and the blockade of Great Britain was close to success. The Ellerman group, alone, lost a staggering 39 ships of which three were wrecked and one went missing in the non-war zone Pacific. Losses were Papayanni/Ellerman Line 15, City 5, Hall 9 and Bucknall 10.

By now the Mediterranean, with its Austro-Hungarian submarine bases in Dalmatia (particularly Cattaro where 20 submarines were based), was as dangerous as the Atlantic — some say more so. The Allies, in 1916, had divided the sea into two zones. The western being under a French Admiral and the eastern under the command of Flag officer Malta. There were no convoys and varying but pre-set steamer routes were laid down, these being patrolled by armed trawlers. Thus the enemy had only to track the trawler's path and then wait for the merchantman to come along. As so often in war there was a lack of co-operation across the two areas and even complaints when a U-boat was chased into the other's zone. Eventually convoys had to be organised, escorted by additional destroyers (19 in 1917 plus 106 scouting seaplanes based at Malta) and, in an attempt to bottle up the enemy the infamous Otranto net barrage was laid. This absorbed the depot ship *Blenheim*, 30 destroyers, 36 American submarine chasers, 30 hydrophone trawlers, 109 drifters, 4 kite balloon ships and 40 motor launches plus 15 patrolling submarines between it and Malta. U-boat losses were in no way commensurate with the effort; it was the convoy system which produced results. In the 12 months following their introduction only seven outbound and seven inbound ships were lost out of 285 and 329 ships convoyed.

1918 Up to the end of the war, on Nov 11, ten ships were lost — one being wrecked. The toll of destruction was:

Ellerman Line and Papayanni	22 sunk	4 lost	=	26
City	7		=	7
Hall	16	5	=	21
E & B	11	2	=	13
	56	11		67

(Ellerman's Wilson lost 49)

1919 The Bucknall American & Indian Line, New York-India, restarted with *City of Benares* (249) taking the first sailing. The service was basically winter only and the sailings were far from regular.

1920 Montgomerie & Workman, the London agents were amalgamated into the Group under the title Montgomerie & Workman (1920) Ltd See page 71.

An irritant at the time was the purchase, for post-war fleet rebuilding, of the West Hartlepool shipbuilding firm of William Gray & Co Ltd which was done with Lord Inchcape and Frank Strick. When Lord Inchcape withdrew it left the quarrelsome pair John Ellerman and Frank Strick to argue about how best to deal with the investment. Many Ellerman ships were perforce built at Gray's but the standard of construction was superb.

1921 During the period of postwar fleet replenishment 40 secondhand vessels were purchased.

1927 In order to strengthen their presence in South Africa a new concern, Ellerman & Bucknall (Proprietary) Ltd, was formed with head office at Cape Town and a branch at Durban.

1928 In April Lord Kylsant purchased JRE's 46% stake in Shaw, Savill & Albion. Sir John foresaw trouble for the Kylsant group, the largest shipowners in the world (with Royal Mail, Union-Castle, P.S.N.C, Nelson and Elder Dempster) when the price of £994,000 was met by the issue of White Star shares based on intercompany loans and not reserves. Furthermore Lord Kylsant did not need the 46%; he already had control. JRE at once converted these shares into cash.

The Polish-British Shipping Co was formed by the Wilson side of the house. 75% Polish capital and 25% Ellerman's Wilson. Four ships were sold to the Company for £290,000 and passed under the Polish ensign. It lasted until 1939.

E & B ended the carriage of passengers on their Far East route.

1932 When John Ellerman founded his empire the Rufford Street Liverpool office ran the Mediterranean ships of Ellerman Lines Ltd, The Ellerman Line, and Papayanni. They were now combined into the new concern of Ellerman & Papayanni Lines Ltd.

1933 July 16: Sir John Reeves Ellerman, Bart, Companion of Honour, aged 71, died of a heart attack while on holiday at Dieppe. He left a fortune of £40 million and one of the largest shipping organisations ever. His son, also John Reeves Ellerman, was 23 and too young to inherit his father's mantle. Sir Miles Mattinson took over the chair and an executive committee was formed to run the group. F. T. L. 'Thoby' Prinsep was Managing Director, the others were H. H. Heron, H. S. Holden (of the Wilson Line), F. G. Burt and Wm Cox.

1935 H. S. Holden became Managing Director following the death of Thoby Prinsep.

1936 Jan 1: Montgomerie & Workman ceased to be shipowners and their five vessels (The Cities of *Auckland* (465), *Bagdad* (261), *Hankow* (413) and *Oran* (259) and *Volturno* (76)) were absorbed into Ellerman Lines Ltd.

City of Benares (275) was the outstanding addition to the fleet; the only two funnelled ship ever built for Ellerman, or his predecessors. She was undeniably the 'flagship'.

The M.A.N.Z. (Montreal, Australia, New Zealand) service started with NZSCo and Port Line.

1939 April: Hall Line signed an exclusive agreement with the Mogul line for the carriage of cotton between Port Sudan and Bombay outside of the Hadj season.

Sept 4: World War II broke out. The slaughter at sea commenced immediately. The High command of the Kriegsmarine knew that the submarine could stifle the British war effort. And within months, after the fall of France, they pinned their hopes on starving the British into surrender. Had not Adolf Hitler been so obdurate (and Chamberlain so successful in gaining a year's stay of war) there is little doubt that the U-boat would have succeeded. Future history will record that World War II was factually lost to the Axis in 1936 when a boastful Hitler ordered British-matching battleships and an aircraft carrier (plan Z) instead of meeting Grand Admiral Raeder's demand for submarines. The German high seas fleet was to be as unsuccessful during this war as had their counterparts been in the previous one. Submarines were quite a different matter.

The Ellerman fleet stood, at this time at 105 ships of 919,969 dwt. E & P owned 25 ships, City 18, Hall 49, E & B 12 and W-L 1.

Oct 17: *City of Mandalay* (273) became the first Company loss, followed by three E & P ships.

1940 Feb 1 saw the introduction of the Shipping General Requisitioning Scheme. An immediate effect was the formation of an All India Conference. The Moorgate HQ was evacuated to Cobham.

Fourteen ships were lost: E & P 5, City 4, Hall 3, E & B 2.

1941 Eleven vessels were destroyed. E & P 6, City 2, Hall 3.

1942 War losses peaked at 15 ships, of which two were wrecked and one sunk by convoy collision. They were spread: E & P 2, City 13.

1943 Again a tragic year with 14 losses including one wreck and one collision. E & P 4, City 2, Hall 4 and E & B 4.

As a note of interest this year saw the start of Wilson's famous and daring Swedish ball bearing dash using converted Motor Gun Boats.

1944 Feb: Chairman Sir Miles Mattinson died and H. S. Holden took his place. E. A. Lloyd moved onto the Board.

City of Adelaide (422) became the final Ellerman war loss.

1945 Fleet losses during the war totalled 58 vessels (plus 2 managed ships *Cap Padaran* (646) and *D'Entrecasteaux* (648)) excluding 25 of Ellerman's Wilson. The break-down was E & P 19, City 9, Hall 24, B & B 5, W-L 1. 153 awards were made to Ellerman staff.

1946 H. S. Holden died; his place as Chairman was taken by E. A. Lloyd.

1947 Aug 15: India and Pakistan became independent members of the British Commonwealth. This was the start of far reaching and fundamental changes for the City and Hall fleets. The independent countries passed Acts aimed at setting up their own merchant fleets. These Acts were based on the concept of 'half the trade in out bottoms'; furthermore there were aspects that were protectionist by preventing foreigners from controlling the fledgling companies. Demand to join the Conferences with equal rights as to sailings had to be met. Both the India Steamship Co and Scindia SS Co were admitted on this basis. Flag discrimination came into being. Thus from this date the slow inexorable decline in the fortunes of City and Hall began. Of course from the other point of view City and Hall Lines had held a privileged exploiting position which had now ended. The true position is really one of world evolution and at sea containerisation was soon to upset the apple cart again.

1948 There were 95 ships, of 614,174grt, in the combined fleets (excepting Wilson) of which 56 carried some passengers with 22 under construction. Four were Passenger liners, *City of Paris* (268), *City of Hongkong* (271), *City of Exeter* (258) and *City of Canterbury* (269). The remainder had accommodation for 12 or less.

1950 Chairman E. Aubrey Lloyd died and his place was taken by Wilson's J. W. Bayley but within a few months he too deceased and A. F. Hull took over command in the final month of the year.

On the South African routes two indigenous companies joined the South African Conference. They were South African Marine and South Africa Lines — yet further biting into the trade available to Ellerman vessels.

The 'fifties were an era of dock side labour troubles and ships were held up for weeks, or even months, waiting for a berth. Australia was particularly badly affected and London commenced to decline so that eventually the unthinkable happened and it actually ceased to be a port.

1952 For the South African passenger route of Ellerman & Bucknall four new passenger ships of the *City of Port Elizabeth* (604) class were built. In Burma a policy of withdrawal from contact with the West and reliance upon the homeland led to the cessation of all trade and Ellerman withdrew entirely; including their interest in the Arracan Flotilla which was nationalised.

1953 All Ellerman passenger services to India ceased. The British Military and Civil servants who had once used the service were gone under nationalisation and the businessmen were using air.

1954 The effects of the changes in trading led to the decision to phase out 19 of the older ships over a three year period. Furthermore the fleet needs were assessed as being met by 70 ships. Even this was to turn out to be optimistic.

A new sphere of trade was attempted with the Ellerman Great Lakes service which was not a success and lasted but five years.

1955 The fleet numbered 94 ships.

1957 A Board decision was to dispose of the 12 Liberty ships as and when buyers could be found. There was still a lively demand as tramps for these economic heavy capacity war-horses. They lasted until they failed their respective third special surveys after which renewal, modification and especially insurance tended to be prohibitive.

1958 Oct: Ellerman & Papayanni acquired the Mossgiel S.S.Co to give them a further slice of the Mediterranean trade; this time out of Glasgow.

1960 Nov: Pakistan Steamship Lines joined the All India Conference.

1961 The fleet stood at 82 ships. At this time City Line was still resident at 75 Bothwell Street, Glasgow.
Oct: The USA-India service was withdrawn.

1965 The locations of the Companies were as follows:
At 12/20 Camomile Street, London: Ellerman & Bucknall, City and Westcott & Laurence.
At Tower Buildings, Water Street, Liverpool: Ellerman & Papayanni and Hall.

1966 In January Ellerman, Blue Star, Ben Line, Port Line and Thos. & Jas. Harrison met and agreed to form a container line which became Associated Container Transportation Ltd — or ACT for short. Orders for ships were to be placed.

An agreement was entered into with Container Services Inc to supply containers to E & P for the Lisbon route. *Catanian* (145) and *Malatian* (144) were adapted to carry 24 each. The change was a success. An addition to the fleet was the purchase from Sweden of *Cortian* (147); she was a palletised cargo carrier for the Oporto service which could not then take containers. She had the attraction, economically, of being worked with fewer crewmen and a study of her was made. There could be no compromise on safety but enhanced in port handling allied to a more self contained engine room were seen to provide better voyage profits when faced with the fierce competition provided by the larger, very fast and still growing in size container ships which were able to berth, drop a batch of containers and speed onto their next drop. These new generation ships struck at the very heart of the dedicated ship trade whereby a ship served between set ports for the whole of her active life. At the year end the fleet comprised 64 ships.

1967 April: A. F. Hull died and Dennis F. Martin-Jenkins became Chairman. July: Ellerman, Blue Star and Port Line formed Associated Container Transportation (Australia) Ltd — ACTA. They were joined by the Australian National Line — ANL.

Prior to sailing from London to Beira the *City of Port Elizabeth* class (604) undertook mini-cruises Middlesbrough-Continental ports - London.

1968 Feb: Ellerman & Ben Line integrated their Europe-Far East services on a joint basis. Ellerman ceased independent sailings to Indonesia. Five Ellerman ships; Cities of *Khartoum* (478), *Newcastle* (494) *Poona* (481) *Swansea* (480) and *Winchester* (603) were transferred and renamed. A clause gave Ellerman the right to re-purchase them at the end of five years.

1969 March: *ACT 1* entered service for ACT.

Minho (150) was the first of the Hustler class of eight small container ships which were built by Sea Containers Inc and taken onto demise charter.

1970 Six of the eight ships of the new 'Hustler' class of compact container ship were now on bare-boat demise charter for Ellerman & Papayanni services which were thereby totally containerised.

1971 East and West Pakistan were formed by civil war in which India intervened. Further disruption followed. Hostility towards India was such that Indian Ellerman crew were interned at Karachi.

The Canadian City Line was formed and the three ships transferred from the Australian routes were given the names of Canadian cities.

1972 May: Ellesmere Port replaced Liverpool as the container terminal for E & P vessels.

1973 Jan 1: Ellerman City Liners was formed and except for the three ships owned by HLL (Cities of *Hull, Liverpool* and *London* (622-4)), the other 33, spread across all the group including Ellerman's Wilson, excepting 3 Scandinavian ferries, were transferred. For several months a committee had reviewed the future of the group. They recommended that three Divisions be created. Ships, all but the Scandinavian services, should go into one, Ellerman City Liners being the vehicle, the second named EWL should cover the Scandinavian and road transport side and a third Ellerman Travel & Leisure should act as its name suggested. The whole to be administered by a specialist unit with another small team to deal with finance, taxation etc. The whole being owned by Ellerman Lines Ltd. The Board had accepted the recommendations and they now took effect. The Company capital structure was most unusual. 79% was held by two charitable trusts (the Moorgate and Audley Trusts; ie JRE's two London addresses) set up by Sir John Ellerman (I) and 31% was owned by a Luxembourg company wholly owned by Lady Ellerman. This was merged into one Trust. In the middle of all this Sir John Ellerman (II) died on July 17 — he was 63. However penal death duties had been avoided.

The effect of all this was to end the histories of Papayanni, Westcott & Laurence, Hall and Ellerman & Bucknall. Only City now remained, Montgomerie and Workman having gone in 1936. Even so these dramatic changes were to be only the beginning of yet a further decade when the fleet numbers were destined to decline.

Nov 9: *City of Edinburgh,* (299) 58,440grt, 2,800 TEU's came into service for Ben Line's Ben Line Containers on the Ben-Ellerman berth. She joined her sisters *Benalder* and *Benavon.* Ellerman City had only a share in her despite the name. The ship was a member of the Trio consortium to the Far East.

1974 As an extension of the policy of the previous year all the ships of Ellerman City Liners were given City names although they remained registered where they were. Thus some 'City boats' now had Hull as their home port.

A mail contract UK-Lisbon was obtained. Letters went by air but bulk was containerised.

1975 In January the fleet numbered 36 ships plus 3 EWL vessels. The decline in British shipowning was now a matter of national concern. The UK merchant fleet was down to 1,614 vessels of 50 million dwt tonnes. The modern trend was for shipowners to charter ships for seasonal services and to transfer all conventional services to the growing breed of large, fast and quick servicing container ships.

1978 By the year end the conventional cargo vessel had been phased out and replaced by container, part container and palletised ships. *City of Durban* (300) entered service for Ellerman-Harrison Container Line (EHCL). For the Mediterranean the *City of Plymouth* class (301) started to come into service; they progressively released the smaller 'Hustlers'.

1982 This was the final profitable year of the Ellerman family regime. By November the UK merchant fleet had shrunk to 893 ships of 23.5 million dwtonnes; half the 1975 figure. Of this number 13% were unemployed. The Ellerman City Liners fleet now stood at six ships. All, with the exception of *City of York* (297), being of the *City of Plymouth* (301) class of container ships with the container giant *City of Durban* (300) operating under the Ellerman-Harrison Container Lines banner.

1983 With the agreement of the shareholders the Group, with losses of £9 million, was put up for sale. The two hotelier brothers David and Frederick Barclay were the purchasers. They paid £47 million for the entire Ellerman group which included such non shipping activities as brewing and printing. They formed Ellerman Holdings plc.

1984 When the Isle of Man opened its shipping register the fleet was re-registered at Douglas, Isle of Man.

It is interesting that of the six ships still managed by Ellerman City Liners only *Bakkafoss (City of Oxford)* (305) was owned by Ellerman Lines plc. The other five were on charter from finance houses. However it would give the wrong impression if one did not realise that Ellerman were heavy participators in Associated Container Lines as well as both the Harrison and Thompson container activities.

1985 At the beginning of the year City of London banks and the finance companies, who owned all but one of the Ellerman fleet of five ships *(City of York* (297) having been sold), put together the money needed for a Management buy-back from the Barclay brothers of Ellerman Holdings Ltd. Anthony Cooke became chairman.

1986 The first buy-back year ran for 16 months to Dec 31 and a profit of £5.2 million was recorded on a turnover of £68.2 million. The assets stood at £17.3 million. Five ships were in the fleet and shares were held in ten others across the container industry.

1987 Trafalgar House plc, which made a profit of £145.8 million in the previous year, the owners of Cunard, purchased the Ellerman shipping interests for £24.1 million. This sum was raised by an issue of new shares worth £22.5 million. The remainder by unsecured loan stock held by finance houses. Ellerman Holdings retained 3,750,000 shares and 5,480,000 were placed on the market, through Kleinwort Benson, at £3.83 per share. The cargo activities of Cunard were thereupon merged with the new purchase and Cunard-Ellerman was created. Alan Kennedy, of Cunard, became chairman with Anthony Cooke as his deputy and chief executive.

1988 At the year end Cunard-Ellerman, still at 12/20 Camomile Street, London, through their involvement in other consortia, have interests in:
  Associated Container Transportation (ACT and ACTA)
  Atlantic Container Line
  Ben Line Containers
  Cunard Steam-Ship Co (three H.E. Moss tankers)
  Ellerman Harrison Container Line

A total of 19 ships.

ROUTES

( ) = optional or alternative ports. (date) = Commencement.
It is impractical to attempt to list every route or port of call because they varied by voyage, season and commercial need.
It is best done by illustrating the growth of John Ellerman's routage through his acquisitions.

ELLERMAN LINE (1901-1973)
Liverpool-Portugal-Gibraltar-North Africa-Spain (homewards only). (Glasgow)-Liverpool-(South Wales)-Marseilles-Malta-Alexandria-Cyprus-Israel-Lebanon-Syria-Malta-Spain-(South Wales)-Liverpool-(Glasgow).
(1918) Liverpool-Manchester-Syria-Cyprus.
(1976) Garston-La Spezia.

PAPAYANNI & CO (1855-1973)
Liverpool-Malta-Greece-Levant-Turkey-Black Sea-Constanza-Danube ports.
Dublin-Oporto (1901-1973).
(1916) Manchester-Marseilles-Italian ports.
(1954-59) UK-Great Lakes-US Atlantic ports-Mediterranean-UK.

WESTCOTT & LAURENCE (1863-1973)
Duplicated out of London the Liverpool Mediterranean services.
(1971) London-Israel.

CITY LINE (1840-1973)
Sailing ships: Glasgow-Indian ports direct via the Cape of Good Hope. They also traded occasionally to the West Indies and to South America, Valparaiso terminal. More frequently to Australia and New Zealand or Calcutta-New York-Glasgow.
Steamers:
Glasgow-Liverpool-Port Said-Suez-Bombay-Karachi-Kathiawar ports-various routes inbound including East and South Africa-Continent-UK ports-Glasgow.

Glasgow-Suez Canal-Aden-Vizagapatam-Chalna (founded 1950)-Calcutta-Colombo-UK and Contintental ports-Dundee-Glasgow.

HALL LINE (1860-1973)
Sailing vessels: India-Cape-India direct.
Liverpool-USA-India-Liverpool.
Liverpool-Australia.
Steamers:
Duplicated out of Liverpool the India routes of City Line.
(1915) Liverpool-Suez Canal-Colombo-(Madras)-(Calcutta)-Rangoon. Liverpool-Cape of Good Hope-South and East Africa-Mauritius-Suez Canal-Liverpool or reverse.

Homebound frequently Calcutta-Madras-East and South Africa-Las Palmas-Liverpool.

Liverpool-Red Sea Ports-East Africa.

Liverpool-Suez Canal-Madras coast-Calcutta.

Brazil Steamship Co 1903: Liverpool-Las Palmas-South American ports.
(1905-1939) Calcutta-Rio de Janeiro-Santos-Montevideo-Buenos Aires-Calcutta or UK.
Liverpool-Suez Canal-Rangoon-Burma ports.
(1915-34) Manchester-New York.

ELLERMAN & BUCKNALL (1880-1973)
Glasgow/Liverpool/London, variously-South and East African ports-Beira (terminus)-(Mauritius)-(Madagascar).
(1895-1912) Passengers: London-Cape Town-India-Suez Canal-London.

Liverpool-Panama Canal-North Pacific ports-Puget Sound or Vancouver (during the Yukon gold rush: Puget Sound-Skagway).
UK-Suez Canal-Red Sea ports-Persian Gulf.

(1915) UK-Marseilles-Suez Canal-Malaya-Singapore-Philippines-Hong Kong-Shanghai-Japan (on this route ships of City and Hall were frequently used).

Manchester-Liverpool-Panama Canal-Australia-New Zealand.

Manchester-Liverpool-Panama-Los Angeles-Dutch East Indies-Philippines-China-Japan-Dairen (some of these routes combined on the same vessel to provide a round the world service; they were also used to position or relieve crews — especially at New York).
(1921) Middlesbrough-Gdynia-Hamburg-Antwerp-London-Malaya-Hong Kong-Shanghai-Japan.

Ellerman & Bucknall and Norton, Lilly & Co, New York (1893-1930).
American & Indian Line: New York-Cape-Calcutta.
American & African Steamship Line: New York-South Africa.
American & Manchurian Line: New York-Philippines-China-Japan-Dairen.
American & Australian Line: New York-Australia-Hobart-New Zealand.
American, Mediterranean & Levant Line: New York-as title.
These services continue, without passengers, as follows: Canada-USA-Alexandria-Port Said-East Africa-Karachi-Bombay-Colombo-Madras-Calcutta.

(1920) Montreal-USA-Port Sudan-Bombay-Colombo-Calcutta-Rangoon-Singapore-Batavia-Samarang-Sourabaya.

(1926) Montreal-USA-Port Sudan-Bombay-Colombo-Calcutta-Rangoon-Singapore-Batavia-Samarang-Sourabaya.

(1926) Montreal-USA-South and East Africa-Mauritius-Réunion-Madagascar.

(1926) Montreal-USA-Mediterranean ports-(Black Sea ports)-Red Sea ports-Persian Gulf.

(1936) M.A.N.Z. service: Montreal-Australia-New Zealand. Australia-Java-Singapore-Australia.

Australia-South and East Africa-Mauritius-(Madagascar)-Australia.

ELLERMAN CITY LINERS (1973-1987) then CUNARD-ELLERMAN
London or Ellesmere Port-Rotterdam-Oporto-Lisbon.

Hull-London-Rotterdam-Gibraltar.

Ellesmere Port-Dublin-Gibraltar.

Ellerman Strath Container Service: Ellesmere Port-Malta-Piraeus-Limassol-Beirut-Tartous-Iskenderun-Salerno-Cartagena-Ellesmere Port.

Ellerman Prince Container Service: Hull-Esbjerg-Rotterdam-London-Malta-Iskenderun-Tartous-Beirut-Limassol-Piraeus-La Spezia-Cartagena.

Ellerman Prince Moss-Hutchison Zim: London or Ellesmere Port-Ashdod-Haifa.

ELLERMAN HARRISON CONTAINER LINE (1978-1989)
Southampton-Hamburg-Bremerhaven-Rotterdam-Zeebrugge-Le Havre-Cape Town-Port Elizabeth-Durban.

TRIO CONTAINER SERVICE
Comprising: Ben Line Containers Ltd in which Ellerman have a share through *City of Edinburgh* (299), Hapag-Lloyd A.G., NYK, Mitsui-OSK and Overseas Container Ltd (19 vessels).
Southampton-Le Havre-Rotterdam-Bremerhaven-Hamburg-Singapore-Hong Kong (with trans-shipment to the Philippines)-Taiwan-South Korea-Kobe-Tokyo.

ELLERMAN LINES LTD.
Livery

Funnel	1901-	Ex-Leyland ships. Pink with broad blue band touching a black top.
	1901-1903	Buff, some were still pink, red, white and blue bands with red touching the black top.
	1904	Buff, thinnish white band touching the black top; usually half black top depth.
	1946	The white band was doubled in width.
Hull	1901-1921	Black. The bridge deck was sometimes white; especially with passenger berths.
	1921-1988	Dove grey with white strake to main deck bulwark top. Some ships carried black hulls until the mid-thirties; mainly Hall and Bucknall lines. These ships usually had white castles and almost invariably a white bridge deck.
	1946	The white strake was carried down to main deck level.
Waterline		Red. When grey hulls were introduced the colour became red-lead.
Uppers	1901-1914	The Ships bore the upperworks colouring of the parent owner viz buff deck deck houses or upper-half white deck house sides. Because photographs are never dated it is not possible to isolate these correctly.
	1921-1988	White.
Masts	1901-1914	Brown.
	1921-1939	Biscuit buff. Darkish.
	1946-1970	Biscuit buff with a tinge of pink to them.
	1970-1988	White.
Ventilators		Black was phased out after 1921 and replaced by funnel buff. Except around the funnel white predominated. Insides: red.
Lifeboats		White.

PAPAYANNI & COMPANY
Chronological history

1832 Georges Michael Papayanni came to London to establish a Greek commodity house dealing mainly in the import of dried fruit. He however exported British goods which increasingly came from the industrial north of England.

1844 The business was transferred to Liverpool which served his exports better than London without interfering with his Greek imports. He still worked mainly with Greek owner captains and the vessels were generally sail. In order to ensure continuity of trade he frequently took shares in the ships but did not control them. His brother Basilio acted as his Piraeus agent and fixed most of the charters.

1846 Steam was developing to the Mediterranean. *Rattler*, owned by Vianna, Jones & Chapple having inaugurated sailings in the previous year. Now Georges Papayanni commenced to charter space, as opposed to whole ship, on the steamers.

1850 The Papayanni business was now chartering whole ships and these were almost always British and increasingly steam driven. It was now that the firm officially became Papayanni and Mussabini. Pierre Mussabini was a Liverpool based Levant and Turkey merchant as well as being Turkish vice-consul.

1852 G. M. Papayanni was naturalised and became British and the firm became Papayanni, Mussabini & Company. He was a well respected Liverpool merchant, Greek consul and prominent in philanthropic society. It was said that he was, like so many anglophiles, more English than the English themselves.

1855 Basilio, the chartering expert, joined his brother in Liverpool. The reason was that they had decided that it would be prudent to protect their business by owning steamers. Already the parallel Liverpool competition was thriving and the shipowning merchants were forcing prices down which left less for anyone paying the voyage profit eroding charter rates. Another aspect was that the ships would fly the British flag which was beneficial at a time when there was much mutual hostility between Greece and Turkey with consequent difficulties in the ports of call. The partnership gave the firm even stronger connections in the eastern Mediterranean and the Black Sea.

   Five ships were planned for regular route sailings. Their size represented the needs of the trade in which each was to be employed.

1862 Pierre Mussabini retired from the partnership and the firm became Papayanni & Company.

1861 In January seven American states had voted for secession from the United States and the civil war began. This soon stopped the cotton exports to Lancashire. To offset this trade to Egypt was developed and Papayanni entered into the Egyptian cotton business.

1866 When the aftermath of the Civil War subsided Papayanni & Co continued in the Egyptian cotton trade but additionally, during the season, loaded cargoes from the southern US cotton ports.

1870 G. M. Papayanni retired from the day to day business but remained in financial control. His place in the office was taken by his son Michael, who was already a trader in his own right. Basilio continued to superintend the shipping line.

1871 With the intention of extending their Transatlantic interests *Lord Clive* (11) was built. She spent her life on that ocean but not for Papayanni who realised that resources could not match those of his likely competitors (nevertheless G. M. Papayanni, Papayanni & Co built a sister eight years later for the same charter trade).

1870s The fleet continued at an average of nine ships which met the firm's needs. No attempt was made to expand the family concern beyond its chosen parameters.

1897 The organisation was incorporated as The Papayanni Steamship Company Ltd but still as a family concern. There were nine ships in the fleet most of them in need of replacement before the end of the century. On Sept 29 Basilio Papayanni died. His place was taken by his elder son, also Basilio, who had spent some years in the business. His death had the effect of spreading the shares across the family (two sons and three daughters) and thus, without capital injection by the shareholders, preventing the implementation of a rebuilding programme.

1901 June 17: After negotiations with Nicholas Papayanni, the second son, John Reeves Ellerman purchased the Company's shares and with them the eight ships of the fleet:

Agia Sofia (4),   *Britannia* (16),
Adalia (19)   *Laconia* (3),
Anatolia (18),   *Plantain* (15) and
Ararat (10),   *Roumelia* (13).

The price was £108,250 for the three modern ships and the goodwill plus an agreed £24,500 for the five older vessels which it was proposed to replace — although *Britannia* was to last until the war.

1902 Jan 22: Owned by Ellerman Lines Ltd, who as Ellerman Lines operated the ex-Leyland ships, but who continued to operate Papayanni as a separate entity at Rumford Street, Liverpool.

PAPAYANNI BROTHERS
ELLERMAN & PAPAYANNI
Livery

Funnel	1855-1901	Pale pink (almost white), black top, copper steam pipes.
	1901-1904	Pink, blue band, black top.
	1904-1973	Ellerman Livery.
Hull	1855-1901	Black, red waterline.
	1901-1922	Several ships had white bridge decks — but by no means all. No pattern.
	1922-1973	Ellerman.
circa	1950-1960	The ships on refrigerated service had white hulls.
Uppers	1855-1914	Dull brown. Some facings were white.
	1920-1973	White.
Masts	1855-1901	Brown.
	1901-1973	Ellerman livery.
Ventilators	1855-1901	Black, decks brown. Interiors Greek blue.
	1901	Then moved across to Ellerman.
Lifeboats		White.

WESTCOTT & LAURENCE
As Ellerman & Papayanni in general. Funnel black, ventilators had red interiors.

MONTGOMERIE & WORKMAN
As Papayanni (1855-1901). They owned no steamers prior to the Ellerman take over.
House flag: White St Andrew's cross on blue but hoist and fly segments red.

Illustrated Fleet List

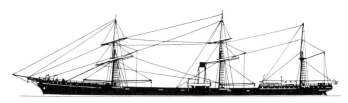

ARCADIA, THESSALIA, LACONIA

1 ARCADIA
B 1855 J & G Thompson, Glasgow. **T** 1,901g, 1,221n.
D 303.8/92.6 x 31.7/9.66 x 27.4/8.35.
E Sgl scr, 2 cyl, simple. 9 kts. By builder.
H Iron. 2 dks. **P** 32 1st. Crew 18 including 1 steward.
1855 Completed as a brig for Georges Michael Papayanni. His first ship after years of chartering. Liverpool-Mediterranean service with Constantinople as terminus.
1875 Lengthened by Thompson & Co, Newcastle, to the above dimensions and tonnage, power was doubled by the installation of a second single expansion engine and new boilers were fitted. She emerged with three masts, as drawn.
1898 Broken up by Thos W. Ward at Preston.

2 THESSALIA
As 1. **T** 1,857g, 1,206n.
1855 Delivered. Owned by Basilio Papayanni.
1875 Lengthened to 303.2/92.41 and modified like her sister by Fawcett & Preston, Liverpool. 3 masts.
1881 Sold. Trace lost, presumed broken up.

3 LACONIA
As 1 except **B** 1856. **T** 1,982, 1,295.
1856 Completed.
1870 The first of the trio to be rebuilt as detailed in 1 but by Fawcett, Preston & Co, Liverpool; the engines were also compounded. **D** 314.3/95.8. Three masts.
1874 Mar 13: Enroute Alexandria-Algiers when nearing Tunis with returning Mecca pilgrims 278 were washed overboard by a freak wave. Incredibly only 9 were drowned.
1901 June 17: Transferred with the fleet to J. R. Ellerman.
1902 March: Broken up at Genoa being too old for his use.

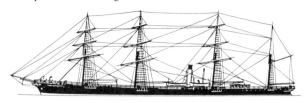

4 AGIA SOPHIA
B 1857 J & G Thompson, Glasgow. **T** 1,437g, 977n.
D 259.3/79.02 x 34.6/10.55 x 22/6.71.
E Sgl scr, 2 cyl comp inv. 9 kts. By builder.
H Iron. 3 dks. Barque rig.
1857 Entered service. Name means Queen Sophia.
1872 Lengthened to 338.4/103.14 x 35.5/10.8 (new section width). Twinned engine and new boilers by Fawcett & Preston, Liverpool. **T** 2,593g, 1,654n. Emerged as a 4 masted barque rig.
1901 June 17: Acquired by J. R. Ellerman. Too old for his intentions.
1902 Sold to Italy. R/n *Tripoli*.
1903 Broken up at Livorno.

5 BOETIA
B 1855 T. D. Marshall & Co, South Shields. **T** 951g.
D 220.1/67.09 x 29.4/8.96 x 22.7/6.92.
E Sgl scr, 2 cyl simple exp. **H** Iron. 2 dks.
1855 Built for J. Dudgeon, London. Mediterranean trade.

1858 Acquired by Basilio Papayanni. Same name.
1859 Sold to J. Bibby, Sons & Co, Liverpool.
1864 Became *Barbadian* of West India & Pacific S.N. Co, Liverpool.
1865 Dec: Lost on the Blackwater Bank.

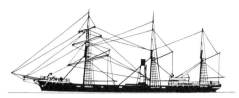

6 ORONTES
B 1851 Archibald Denny, Dumbarton. **T** 701n, 436n.
D 187.1/57.02 x 27.4/8.35 x 17/5.18.
E Sgl scr, 2 cyl simp inv, 98 hp, 8 kts. By B. Hick & Son, Belfast.
H Iron. 1 dk.
1851 Completed for Moss S.S.Co, Liverpool. She is not in the Denny lists of ships built. There are early gaps in the records.
1859 Acquired by Papayanni Bros, same name.
1861 Sold to Henry W. Withers, Liverpool.
1878 Sold to George P. Forward, Liverpool. Same name. Operated to Morocco by the Mersey S.S.Co. Foundered at sea this year.

---

7 IONIA
B 1856 T. D. Marshall & Co, South Shields. **T** 1,388g.
D 244.4/74.49 x 32.1/9.78 x 25.9/7.89.
E Sgl scr, 3 cyl simple exp. 9 kts. **H** Iron. 2 dks.
1856 Built for Papayanni Bros. Her appearance was undoubtedly similar to *Boetia* from the same yard.
1861 Sold to J. Bibby, Sons & Co. Same name.
1870 Owned by the Anglo-Egyptian Navigation Co.
1872 Lengthened to 303/92.35. Compounded, new boilers. **T** 1,758g.
1875 Dec: Lost in the River Congo.

8 AMALIA
B 1860 J. & G. Thompson, Glasgow. **T** 1,825g, 1,284n.
D 277.7/84.64 x 37/11.28 x 25.6/7.8.
E Sgl scr, 2 cyl simple expansion. 9 kts. By builder.
H Iron. 2 dks. Fcsle and poop.
1860 Dec: M/v Clyde-Mediterranean. Thereafter out of Liverpool. Bell topped funnel.
1866 Foundered in the Bay of Biscay.

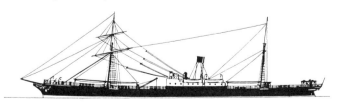

9 MACEDONIA
B 1867 Thos. Vernon & Son, Liverpool. **T** 1,732g.
D 288.6/87.96 x 35.3/10.76 x 22.9/6.98.
E Sgl scr, 2 cyl simple inv. 10 kts. By Fawcett, Preston & Co, Liverpool.

H Iron. 2 dks.
1867 Jan: Delivered.
1875 2 x 2 cyl engine conversion by G. Forrester & Co, Liverpool.
1881 Lengthened to 348.1/106.1. **T** 2,853g, 1,866n.
1899 Broken up in Italy.

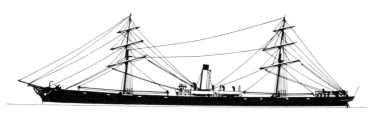

10 ARARAT
B 1871 Liverpool S.B.Co, Liverpool. **T** 2,016g, 1,305n.
D 323.4/98.57 x 33.4/10.18 x 26/7.92.
E Sgl scr, 2 cyl comp inv. 9½ kts. By Forrester & Co, Liverpool.
H iron 2 dks.
1871 Built for Papayanni Bros.
1901 June 17: Sold to J. R. Ellerman. Too old; sold for £3,900 and broken up in Italy.

LORD CLIVE, LORD GOUGH

11 LORD CLIVE
B 1871 R. & J. Evans, Liverpool. **T** 3,386g, 2,206n.
D 381/116.13 x 40.1/12.22 x 26/7.92.
E Sgl scr, 2 cyl comp inv. 10 kts. By G. Forrester & Co, Liverpool.
H Iron. **P** First and third.
1871 Oct 28: Launched for G. M. Papayanni. It was his intention to operate her Liverpool-Boston. She spent all her career on the North Atlantic.
1872 Chartered to the Dominion Line. Apr 15: First sailing Liverpool-Quebec-Montreal.
1875 Operated by the American Line. Dec 15: On Liverpool-Philadelphia service.
1888 Sold to Lord Clive S.S.Co, Liverpool, owned by the American Line. Emigrant traffic Liverpool-Philadelphia. British flag.
1896 Sold to Gastaldi & Co, Genoa. British flag. R/n *Clive*. New York-Genoa-Naples route. Chartered to Furness, Withy & Co. Nov 8: New York-Naples-Genoa service.
1897 April: Withdrawn; the route being sold to Prince Line. Made a few cargo voyages Liverpool-Boston.
1898 April: Broken up.

12 LORD GOUGH
As 11 except: **B** 1879 Laird Bros, Birkenhead. **T** 3,655g, 2,370n.
D 382.8/116.68. **E** By builder.
1878 Nov: Launched for G. M. Papayanni to go on charter to American Line.
1879 April: M/v Liverpool-Philadelphia, American Line.
1888 Sold, with her sister. Lord Gough S.S.Co, Liverpool.
1895 March: Withdrawn.
1896 Sold to Aberdeen Atlantic Line; same name. Emigrant service to New York.
1898 July: Withdrawn and finally sold for scrap.
1899 Jan: At Genoa for breaking up.

13 ROUMELIA

B 1877 Thos. Royden & Sons, Liverpool. **T** 2,158g, 1,384n.
D 320.7/97.75 x 35.4/10.79 x 25.5/7.71.
E Sgl scr, 2 x 2 cyl comp inv, 260 nhp. 10 kts. By G. Forrester, Liverpool. **H** Iron 2 dks. **P** 19.
1877 Built for Basilio Papayanni.
1901 June 17: Sold to J. R. Ellerman with the fleet of eight.
1905 April: Sold to Parr's Bank Co and broken up at Garston.

14 TRUTHFUL

B 1877 Barrow S. B. Co, Barrow-in-Furness. **T** 956g, 600n.
D 240.2/73.21 x 30/9.14 x 16.1/4.91.
E Sgl scr, 2 cyl comp inv, 160 nhp, 70 psi. 9 kts. By builder.
H Iron. 1 dk. F 42/12.8. B 60/18.29. P 53/16.15.
1877 Nov: Delivered to F. H. Powell, Liverpool. As drawn.
1880 Owned by J. Ellis, Liverpool.
1883 Acquired by Papayanni & Co. This ship, same name, was later put on the Greek register. She had been built for coastal services and was unsuited for the long Bay of Biscay passages. Employed in the Aegean.
1886 Out of the register.

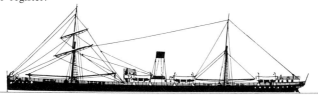

15 PLANTAIN

B 1879 Thos. Royden & Sons, Liverpool. **T** 2,117g, 1,360n.
D 315.6/96.19 x 35.2/10.73 x 25.8/7.86.
E Sgl scr, 'Siamese' tandem, 2 x 2 cyl comp inv, 300 nhp, 75 psi. 9½ kts. By G. Forrester & Co, Liverpool.
H Iron 2 dks. Brig rig. **P** 28.
1879 Sept: Completed for G. H. Horsfall & Co, Liverpool, red funnel, black top.
1886 Acquired by Papayanni S.S.Co Ltd with Papayanni & Co as managers.
1901 June 17: Transferred to Ellerman ownership.
1903 Broken up by Robert White & Sons, Glasgow.

---

16 BRITANNIA

B 1885 Thos. Royden & Sons, Liverpool. **T** 3,129g, 2,041n.
D 353/107.59 x 39.3/11.99 x 28.1/8.56.
E Sgl scr, 2 cyl comp, 280 nhp, 75 psi, 10 kts. By G. Forrester & Co.
H Iron. 2 dks. 4 masted barque. **P** 25.
1885 Built for Papayanni S.S.Co.
1901 June 17: Taken over with the fleet by J. R. Ellerman.
1917 Apr 2: Torpedoed by *U-65* off Pantelaria, mid-Mediterranean.

---

17 PALM

B 1869 McNab & Co, Greenock. **T** 1,826g, 1,394n.
D 299.5/91.29 x 31.8/9.69 x 25.8/7.86.
E Sgl scr, 2 cyl comp, 140 hp. 9 kts. By builder.
H Iron. 2 + awning dk. Brig rig.
1869 Built for G. H. Horsfall & Co, Liverpool. His ships were called after tropical trees.
1885 Acquired by Papayanni S. S. Co with, as usual, Papayanni & Co as managers.
1898 Scrapped.

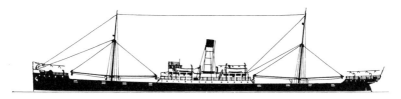

ANATOLIA, ADALIA

18 ANATOLIA

B 1898 Sir James Laing & Sons, Sunderland. **T** 3,848g, 2,490n.
D 360/109.73 x 46/14.02 x 17.6/5.36.
E Sgl scr, 3 cyl tpl exp. 406 nhp, 180 psi. 10 kts. By G. Clark & Co, Sunderland.
H Steel. 1 + spar dk. F 37/11.28. B 102/31.09. P 29/8.84.
1898 Dec: Delivered. For a period she was placed on the Hall Line India berth and was managed by Robert Alexander & Co.
1901 June 17: Transferred to Ellerman ownership. Hall Line managers.
1917 June 25: Sunk off Genoa by *UC-35*.

19 ADALIA

As 18 except: **B** 1899. **T** 3,847g, 2,482n. **D** 360.5/109.8. **H** P 35/10.67.
1899 Aug: Delivered to Papayanni S. S. Co but instead of Papayanni & Co being managers she followed her sister into Robert Alexander & Co's management.
1901 June 17: Purchased with the fleet by J. R. Ellerman. Hall Line managers; same name.
1917 Apr 29: Became a stores ship to the 16th Squadron, Russian Forces. July 29: Captured by *U-94* and sunk by gunfire 53 miles east of Muckle Flugga, Unst, Shetland Islands. 1 dead when the ship's radio installation was hit by a silencing shell.

TWENTY EX-LEYLAND SHIPS

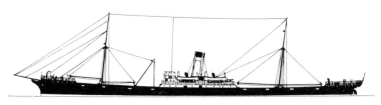

EGYPTIAN (I), ARABIAN (I)

20 EGYPTIAN (I)

B 1861 E. J. Harland, Belfast. **T** 1,986g, 1,356n.
D 335/102.1 x 34.2/10.42 x 24/7.32.
E Sgl scr, 2 cyl simple exp. 9 kts. By J. Jack, Rollo & Co, Liverpool.
H Iron. 1 dk. Three pole masts, no yards, fore and aft sails only.
1861 Built for John Bibby, Sons & Co, Liverpool. The first of the long ships that had greater length than usual compared with the beam. Rolled a great deal; said by some owners to be unsafe. Nicknamed 'Bibby's coffins'.
1873 Sold with 20 other ships to Frederick Leyland & Co when Bibby withdrew from shipowning. Same name.
1879 Compounded by G. Forrester, Liverpool. Emerged with two masts as drawn.
1889 Reboilered.
1901 Apr 25: Frederick Leyland & Co (1900) Ltd was taken over by J. Pierpoint Morgan to become part of the International Mercantile Marine Company (yet to be formed). May 26: J. Pierpoint Morgan sold to John Ellerman the 20 Mediterranean and Antwerp-Montreal trading vessels of the fleet of Frederick Leyland & Co (1900) Ltd. The ships were then transferred to the newly formed London, Liverpool & Ocean Shipping Co Ltd which then, Dec 31, had its name changed to Ellerman Lines Ltd. The eight Papayanni ships were personally owned by John Ellerman.
1902 Jan 22: All ships were transferred to Ellerman Lines Ltd and remained under the management of the group's constituent companies but with *Egyptian* and the 19 others under Frederick Swift's management as the "Ellerman Line'. The eight Papayanni ships remained separate but all 28 were managed from 11 Rumford St, Liverpool.
1903 Scrapped.

21 ARABIAN (I)
As 20 except: **B** 1862 Harland & Wolff (just formed), Belfast. **T** 1,995g.
1862 April: Delivered to John Bibby, Sons & Co.
1871 Compounded by G. Forrester. Two masts.
1872 Transferred to Frederick Leyland & Co.
1901 Bought by JRE. Owned by Ellerman Lines Ltd.
1902 Under Fred Swift's Papayanni management. Broken up.

22 PERSIAN (I)
B 1863 Harland & Wolff, Belfast. **T** 2,075g, 1,396n.
D 361.8/110.28 x 34/10.36 x 24.3/7.41.
E Sgl scr, 2 cyl, comp inv. 10 kts. By J. Jack, Rollo & Co, Liverpool.
H Iron. 2 dks.
1863 Built for Bibby; their first straight stem. A 'long ship'.
1873 Taken over by Frederick Leyland & Co.
1901 May 26: Taken over by JRE.
1902 Jan 22: Fred Swift of 'Ellerman Line' as manager. July: Scrapped.

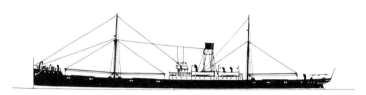

LESBIAN (I), ATHENIAN (I)

23 LESBIAN (I)
B 1874 Thos. Royden & Sons, Liverpool **T** 1,559g, 1,019n.
D 302.3/92.14 x 31.2/9.51 x 23.2/7.07.
E Sgl scr, 2 cyl comp inv. 9 kts. By J. Jack, Rollo & Co, Liverpool.
H Iron. 2 dks.
1874 Completed for Frederick Leyland & Co.
1901 May 26: Purchased by JRE.
1902 Jan 22: To Fred Swift, 'Ellerman Line' as manager.
1903 Broken up in Italy.

24 ATHENIAN (I)
As 23. **T** 1,619g, 1,057n.
1875 Built for Frederick Leyland & Co. Had a tall single derrick post aft.
1901 May 26: To JRE.
1902 Jan 22: Owned by Ellerman Lines Ltd with Fred Swift, 'Ellerman Line' as manager.
1906 Broken up.

25 ALGERIAN (I)
B 1876 Bowdler, Chaffer & Co, Seacombe. **T** 1,757g, 1,152n.
D 312/95.1 x 31.2/9.51 x 23.9/7.28.
E Sgl scr, 2 cyl comp inv, 220 hp. 9 kts. By J. Jones & Sons, Liverpool.
H Iron. 1 dk. F 28/8.53.
1876 Delivered to Frederick Leyland & Co.
1901 May 26: Taken over by JRE.
1902 Jan 22: Owned by Ellerman Lines Ltd. Fred Swift, Ellerman Line, as manager.
1903 A number of the ex-Leyland ships had their funnels heightened to improve the boiler draught.
1904 Inbound crossing the Bay of Biscay in a gale the funnel went overboard. A 10ft/3.05 canvas replacement was rigged which had to have a hose playing on it to prevent fire. Unable to maintain the steam pressure the ship could make only 5 knots and arrived over 2 days late at Liverpool where she was feared lost.
1906 Broken up out of lay up.

26 ALSATIAN
As 25 except: **B** 1877. **T** 1,765g, 1,158n.
1876 Laid down.
1877 Due to a strike over pay the ship was towed away from Seacombe and finished in the adjacent Birkenhead docks by Leyland.
1901-2 As *Egyptian* (20).
1907 Broken up.

27 ANDALUSIAN (I)
As 25 except: **B** 1877. **T** 1,763g, 1,158n.
1876 Laid down by Bowdler, Chaffer.
1877 Completed, like her sister, by Frederick Leyland & Co.
1901-2 As *Egyptian* (20).
1909 Scrapped.

---

28 FALERNIAN (I)
B 1880 Oswald Mordaunt & Co, Woolston, Southampton. **T** 2,252g, 1,479n.
D 343.4/104.67 x 34.5/10.52 x 23.5/7.16.
E Sgl scr, 2 x 2 cyl comp, 288 nhp, 9½ kts. By Fawcett, Preston & Co, Liverpool.
H Steel. 2 dks. F 33/10.06.
1880 Built for Frederick Leyland & Co.
1894 Reboilered.
1901-2 As *Egyptian* (20).
1911 Nov: Broken up by J. J. King & Sons, Garston.

29 FABIAN (I)
As 28 except: **B** 1881. **T** 2,248g, 1,476n.
1881 Completed for Frederick Leyland & Co.
1901-2 As *Egyptian* (20).
1916 Oct 26: Attacked by submarine gunfire in St. George's Channel. Hit several times, with one death, before escaping.
1917 Sept 20: Torpedoed by *UB-50* off Cape Spartel, near Tangier.

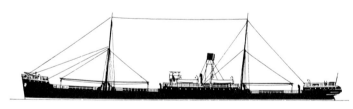

FLAMINIAN (I), FLAVIAN

30 FLAMINIAN (I)
B 1880 Palmers Co, Newcastle. **T** 2,131g, 1,381n.
D 333/101.5 x 33.3/10.15 x 23.6/7.19.
E Sgl scr, 2 cyl comp inv, 208 nhp. 9½ kts. By builder.
H Iron. 2 dks. Whale backed F, B & P.
1880 Delivered to S. S. Flaminian Co Ltd with Leylands as managers.
1895 Reboilered.
1901-2 As *Egyptian* (20).
1912 Late: Sold with *Flavian* to G. Longueville and broken up in France.

31 FLAVIAN
As 30. **T** 2,139g, 1,387n.
1880 Completed for S. S. Flavian Co Ltd. with Leylands as managers.
1896 Reboilered.
1901-2 As *Egyptian* (20).
1913 Early: Delivered to G. Longueville and scrapped.

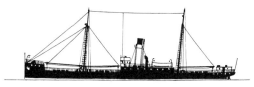

OPORTO (I), MINHO (I)

32 **OPORTO (I)**
B 1888 Charles J. Bigger, Londonderry. **T** 739g, 460n.
D 212/64.61 x 27.1/8.26 x 16.8/5.12.
E Sgl scr, 2 cyl comp. 80 rhp, 10 kts. By D. Rollo & Sons, Liverpool.
H Iron. 2 dks. F 23/7.01. B 59/17.98. (Both whale backed).
1888 June: Entered Leyland service to Iberian Peninsula ports.
1901-2 As *Egyptian* (20).
1918 Sold to Bombay S.N.Co for coastal services. Red funnel black top.
1925 Broken up at Bombay.

33 **MINHO (I)**
B 1890 J. Jones & Sons, Liverpool. **T** 825g, 510n.
D 211.1/64.34 x 27/8.23 x 16.8/5.12.
E Sgl scr, 2 cyl comp. 9 kts. By builder.
H Iron. 2 dks. F 29/8.84. B 55/16.76.
1890 May: Completed for Leyland.
1901-2 As *Egyptian* (20).
1913 Sold to J. B. Pla, Valencia. R/n *Manuela Pla*.
1916 Sold to Dutrus & Carsi, Valencia. Same name.
1924 Fabregas y Garcias became her managers; same owners.
1929 No owners recorded and deleted from the register in 1931. Scrapped.

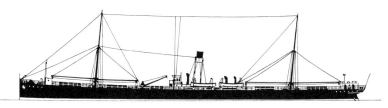

34 **MEXICAN**
B 1891 Naval Construction & Armament Co, Barrow-in-Furness. **T** 3,488g, 2,270n.
D 360/109.73 x 43.2/13.17 x 26.6/8.11.
E Sgl scr, tpl exp, 399 nhp, 10 kts. By builder. **H** Steel. 2 dks.
1891 Oct: Completed for West India & Pacific S. S. Co, Liverpool.
1900 Jan 1: The fleet of 18 ships was taken over by Frederick Leyland & Co.
1901-2 History as *Egyptian* (20). Placed on the Antwerp-Montreal route.
1903 Re-sold to Leyland for the Antwerp-Montreal route.
1913 R/n *Messicano*, De Gregori & Gennaro, Genoa.
1918 Lost in the Mediterranean, a marine casualty not a war loss.

35 **ALMERIAN (I)**
B 1897 Robert Thompson & Co, Sunderland. **T** 2,984g, 1,910n.
D 351.5/107.14 x 42.2/12.86 x 23.3/7.1.
E Sgl scr, tpl exp, 284 nhp, 200 psi, 10 kts. By G. Clark, Sunderland.
H Steel. 2 dks. F 36/10.97. B 106/32.31. P 37/11.28.
1897 Completed for Leyland.
1901-2 As *Egyptian* (20).
1903 Re-sold to Frederick Leyland.
1918 Oct 19: With less than a month to the end of the four years of war *Almerian* was sunk by a mine 13 miles west by south of Licata, Sicily. Laid by *UC-52*.

36 ALBANIAN
As 35 except: **B** 1898. **T** 2,930g, 1,876n.
1898 Completed.
1901-2 As *Egyptian* (20).
1903 Re-sold to Leyland.
1921 Sold to Oughtred & Harrison, Hull, as managers of the Hull Beacon Shipping Co. Same name.
1928 Became *Burgandrea* owned by V. Saglimbene, Catania, Sicily.
1933 Broken up in Italy.

37 TAGUS (II)
B 1898 Caledon S. B. & E. Co, Dundee. **T** 937g, 509n.
D 220/67.08 x 28.7/8.75 x 16.3/4.97.
E Sgl scr, 2 cyl comp, 88 rhp, 160 psi, 1 sgl blr. 9½ kts. By builder.
H Steel. 2 dks. F 33/10.06. B 79/24.08.
1898 Oct: Completed for Leyland.
1901-2 As *Egyptian* (20).
1916 Sept 6: Captured 35 miles north-east of Ushant by *UB-39* and sunk by bombs.

38 DOURO (I)
As 37 except: **B** 1900. **T** 1,028g, 638n. **D** 235/71.63 x 30.7/9.36.
H F 37/11.28. B 82/25.
1900 Built as a slightly larger version of *Tagus*.
1909 Wrecked at Oporto.

39 BELGIAN
B 1900 Sir James Laing & Sons, Sunderland. **T** 3,657g, 2,364n.
D 382.3/116.53 x 45.3/13.82 x 25.9/7.87.
E Sgl scr, tpl exp, 366 nhp, 200 psi, 11 kts. By T. Richardson & Sons, Hartlepool.
H Steel. 2 dks. F 43/13.11. B 132/40.23. P 40/12.19.
1900 Oct: Completed for Frederick Leyland & Co. The last vessel before the IMMC purchase. Intended for the Antwerp-Montreal service but entered service to Halifax (St Lawrence frozen up).
1901-2 As *Egyptian* (20).
1909 Re-sold to Frederick Leyland & Co (1900) Ltd. Atlantic routes.
1917 May 24; Torpedoed by *U-57* 50 miles from Fastnet, 2 killed.
Amazingly *Belgian* struggled to port but her back was broken and the ship was scrapped.

**THIS IS THE END OF THE LEYLAND SHIPS TAKEN OVER
THE NINE WESTCOTT & LAURENCE SHIPS WERE NEXT**

40 ORCHIS
B 1870 J. G. Lawrie & Co, Glasgow. **T** 1,765g, 1,138n.
D 280.5/85.5 x 33.8/10.3 x 24.9.
E Sgl scr, 2 cyl comp inv. 187 nhp, 2 dbl blrs. 9 kts. By J. Howden & Co, Glasgow.
H Iron. 2 dks. Brig rig.
1870 Nov: Completed as *Orchis* for Wm. Johnson, Liverpool.
1884 Sold to Hornstedt & Carthorne, Liverpool. Re-boilered there.
1889 Acquired by Westcott & Laurence. London-Mediterranean services.
1901 Aug: The 9 ships owned by Westcott & Laurence joined the Ellerman group but remained totally under the control of that company with John Ellerman as Chairman.
1913 Sold to A/S Brunkeberg; r/n *Birka* with Moller & Perrson as managers.
1916 Jan: Wrecked.

41 TENEDOS
B 1873 London & Glasgow Eng. & Iron S. B. Co, Glasgow. **T** 1,280g, 953n.
D 241.7/73.67 x 32.3/9.84 x 22.7/6.92.
E Sgl scr, 2 cyl comp, 162 nhp, 60 psi, 2 sgl blrs. 9 kts. By builder.
H Iron. 2 dks.
1873 Nov: Completed for the Globe Steamship Co, London. M/v Clyde-India then London-India.
1889 Acquired by Westcott & Laurence.

1901 Aug: Owned by Ellerman, managed W. & L.
1904 Sold to Scounaki, Ibrahim & Co, Salonika (then Turkish). R/n *Salonique*.
1917 Scrapped. (She is also recorded as being broken in 1955 at Savona but this is not confirmed in Lloyd's Register — unless she was hulked.)

42 PERIM
B 1877 London & Glasgow Eng. & Iron S. B. Co, Glasgow. **T** 1,348g, 1,016n.
D 241.3/73.55 x 32.6/9.94 x 22.7/6.92.
E Sgl scr, 2 cyl comp, 118 nhp, 65 psi, 2 sgl blrs. 9 kts. By builder.
H Iron 2 dks. B 24/7.31.
1877 April: Built for R. W. Cousins & Co, London.
1891 Feb: Acquired by Westcott & Laurence.
1901 Aug: Owned by Ellerman; W & L managers. Her donkey boiler flue was painted in funnel colours; she was jokingly called 'the two funneller'.
1917 Oct 21: Sank after a collision off Tarragona.

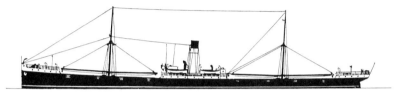

43 GULF OF SUEZ
B 1880 Wm. Gray & Co, West Hartlepool. **T** 1,608g, 1,014n, 2,480dwt.
D 260/79.25 x 34/10.36 x 21.7/6.61.
E Sgl scr, 2 cyl comp, 170 nhp, 80 psi, 2 blrs. 9 kts. By Blair & Co, Stockton (before Gray set up Central Marine Engine Works). Coal 221 tons.
H Iron. 2 dks. F 35/10.62. B 61/18.59. P 38/11.58. C 120,000/3,398 cu g. **P** 6.
1880 May: Delivered as *Gulf of Suez* to Greenock S. S. Co, Greenock; the Gulf Line (As drawn).
1887 Tripled by Blair & Co, Stockton-on-Tees.
1897 Acquired by Westcott & Laurence.
1901 Aug: Acquired by Ellerman; W & L managers. Owned by the Gulf of Suez S. S. Co.
1924 Feb: Sold to A. Coker & Co, Liverpool and broken up.

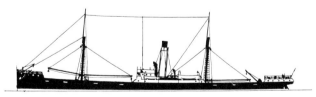

44 JOSHUA NICHOLSON
B 1880 Tyne Iron S. B. Co, Wilmington-on-Tees. **T** 1,853g, 1,196n.
D 270/82.29 x 35/10.67 x 24.5/7.47.
E Sgl scr, 2 cyl comp, 160 nhp, 90 psi. 2 blrs. 9½ kts. By R. & W. Hawthorn, Newcastle.
H Iron. 2 dks. F 32/9.75. B 75/22.86. P 33/10.06.
1880 Oct: Built for Charles Tully & Co, North Shields.
1886 Late: Tully went out of business. The fleet was laid up for disposal. Owned by Joshua Nicholson S. S. Co.
1889 Bought by Stephens & Mawson; later Stephens, Sutton Ltd.
1894 Tripled by Palmers' Co, Jarrow. 160 nhp, 180 psi, a doubling of the steam pressure to give no greater hp but a 45% saving on fuel.
1898 Bought by Westcott & Laurence. Joshua Nicholson S. S. Co. Black fcsle.
1901 Aug: To Ellerman, W. & L. managers.
1917 March 18: Enroute London-Alexandria torpedoed by *U-70* off Wolf Rock Light; all 26 lost.

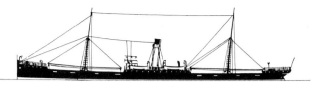

45 CEDARDENE

B 1881 Bartram, Haswell & Co, Sunderland. **T** 2,197g, 1,437n.
D 285.5/87.02 x 37.2/11.34 x 24.4/7.44.
E Sgl scr, 2 cyl comp, 300 nhp, 90 psi, 2 brs. 10 kts. By R. & W. Hawthorn, Newcastle.
H Iron. 2 dks. F 35/10.67. B 70/21.34. P 33/10.06.
1881 Nov 8: Launched. Nov: Completed as *Clan Monroe,* Clan Line.
1892 Converted to quad exp by Westray, Copeland, Barrow.
1897 Sold to Dene Steam Shipping Co Ltd, Newcastle, J. T. Lunn managers.
1899 Acquired by Westcott & Laurence. Black Sea trade.
1901 Aug: To Ellerman. W. & L. managers. Owned by Cedardene S. S. Co.
1903 Feb 24: Wrecked, en-route Clyde-Alexandria, north of Azile, Morocco.

46 AVOCA

B 1883 Strand Slipway Co, Sunderland. **T** 1,539g, 995n.
D 250/76.2 x 35.2/10.73 x 18/5.49.
E Sgl scr, 2 cyl comp inv. 9 kts. By North East Marine Eng. Co, Sunderland.
H Iron. 1 dk. F 28/8.53. B 52/15.85. Q 92/28.04.
1883 March: Completed for Westcott & Laurence. London-Antwerp-Mediterranean service. W. & L. now had an Antwerp office.
1901 Aug: Taken over with the fleet.
1906 Sold to Capt. J. R. Laurence, commanded by him. Owned by London Avoca S. S. Co; managed by W. & L.
1908 Sold to Brodrene Biornstad's Acties Avoca. R/n *Christiania.*
1912 Owned by A. H. Arvesen. Same name.
1913 Wrecked.

47 PLYMOTHIAN

B 1883 C. S. Swan & Hunter, Wallsend, Newcastle. **T** 1,626g, 1,053n.
D 260.5/79.4 x 36/10.97 x 18.5/5.64.
E Sgl scr, 2 cyl comp, 198 nhp, 85 psi, 2 sgl blrs. 9 kts. By Wallsend Slipway Co, Newcastle.
H Iron. 1 dk. F 28/8.53. B 52/15.85. Q 98/29.87.
1883 Completed for Port of Plymouth S. S. Co, Bellamy & Co, managers.
1894 Purchased by Westcott & Laurence.
1901 Aug: To Ellerman with W. & L. managers.
1906 R/n *Marika* by G. Andrada, Piraeus.
1908 Owned by Domestinis, Oeconomou, Piraeus. The Bank foreclosed.
1909 Taken over by the Bank of Athens; A. Sachtouri & G. Andreon managers.
1913 Sold to George Coulouras, Andros. Same name.
1917 Out of register.

48 ORESTES

B 1888 Schlesinger Davies & Co, Newcastle. **T** 1,779g, 1,434n.
D 260/79.25 x 36.3/11.06 x 19.3/5.88.
E Sgl scr, 2 cyl comp, 207 nhp, 2 sgl blrs. 9 kts. By Black, Hawthorn & Co, Gateshead.
H Iron. 1 dk. F 32/9.75. B 50/15.2. Q 101/30.78. P 30/9.14.
1888 Dec: Completed as *Orestes* for H. Collings & Co, London.
1894 Acquired by Westcott & Laurence. Same name.
1901 Aug: Taken over by Ellerman; W. & L. managers. Owned by Orestes S. S. Co.
1907 Renamed *Kingsdyke.* Owned by Kingsdyke S. S. Co, managed by Ross, Allan & Johnston, Glasgow.
1917 Sold to the Lowland Steam Shipping Co; J. Crass & Co, Glasgow managers.
1918 Jan 17: Torpedoed by *UB-80* 20 miles north east of Cape Barfleur. 16 dead.

49 BARCELONA

B 1882 James Laing & Co, Sunderland. **T** 2,307g, 1,506n.
D 295.7/90.13 x 37.9/11.55 x 20/6.1.
E Sgl scr, 2 cyl comp inv, 261 nhp, 115 psi, 2 sgl blrs. 9 kts. By North East Marine Eng Co, Sunderland.
H Iron. 1 + spar dk.
1882 Jan: Delivered as *Friary* to Jones Bros. & Co, Newport.
1899 Owned by Friary S. S. Co, H. W. Hartmann & I. Howard Jones.
1900 Feb: Renamed *King Edward VII,* same owner.
1903 Sold to Rabassa, Montevideo. R/n *Barcelona.*
1904 May: Bought by Westcott & Laurence. This ship was not one of the original nine that were purchased by John Ellerman.
1912 Nov 30: Foundered.

50 EGYPTIAN (II)

B 1891 Russell & Co, Port Glasgow. **T** 2,923g, 1,934n.
D 311.5/94.95 x 41.3/12.51 x 20.2/6.16.
E Sgl scr, tpl exp, 246 nhp, 160 psi, 2 sgl blrs. 10 kts. By Blackwood & Gordon, Port Glasgow.
H Steel 1 dk. F 33/10.06.
1891 Built as *Cynthiana.* Owned by Cynthiana S. S. Co, with McLean & Sutherland as managers.
189? Owned by British Maritime Trust, London.
1899 Sold to T. Ronaldson & Co. Renamed *Saxon King.*
1904 Acquired by Ellerman Lines Ltd; Westcott & Laurence managers. R/n *Egyptian.*
1912 Wrecked by Great Yarmouth.

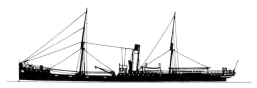

51 CITY OF CORK

B 1870 T. R. Oswald & Co, Sunderland. **T** 1,001g, 622n.
D 229.5/69.95 x 30/9.14 x 17.2/5.24.
E Sgl scr, 2 cyl simple, 129 nhp, 60 psi, 2 blrs. 9 kts. By T. Richardson & Son, Hartlepool.
H Iron. 1 dk F 34/10.36. P 115/35.05.
1870 Built for Palgrave, Murphy & Co, Dublin as *Marquess of Lorne,* as drawn. Dublin-Liverpool service.
1877 Compounded and new higher pressure boilers fitted by engine suppliers. R/n *City of Cork,* Dublin-Oporto service.
1902 Acquired by Ellerman Lines Ltd together with *City of Amsterdam* (52) when the Dublin-Oporto trade was purchased from Palgrave, Murphy. Fred Smith manager.
1906 Sept: Scrapped.

52 CITY OF AMSTERDAM

B 1877 Richardson, Duck & Co, Stockton-on-Tees. **T** 823g, 503n.
D 220.5/67.21 x 30.2/9.2 x 15.6/4.75.
E Sgl scr, 2 cyl comp, 129 nhp, 60 psi, 2 blrs. 9 kts. By T. Richardson & Son, Hartlepool.
H Iron. 1 dk. F. 29/8.84. P 33/10.06.
1877 May: Completed for Palgrave, Murphy & Co, Dublin.
1902 Acquired with her consort. Fred Smith manager.
1908 Owned by Bravo S.S.Co., G. Smith manager. City Line routes.
1913 Owned by Asia Minor S.S.Co.; same manager but Papayanni berthed.
1913 March: Wrecked.

ARABIAN (II) See Bloemfontein (1), Bucknall 526.

PERSIAN (II) See Kaffir, Bucknall 522.

53 ASSIOUT

B 1889 Harland & Wolff, Belfast. **T** 3,146g, 1,994n.
D 345.6/105.34 x 40.9/12.47 x 26.7/8.14.
E Sgl scr, tpl exp, 305 nhp, 180 psi, 2 dbl blrs. 11½ kts. By builder.

H Steel. 2 dks (1 iron). F 43/13.11. B 88/28 82. P 33/10.06.
1889 April: Built as *British Empire*, British Shipowners Co Ltd, Liverpool.
1901 Purchased by Ellerman Lines Ltd. Fred Swift manager. R/n *Assiout*.
1914 Her management was now by Graham Smith. Aug: Sunk by Turkish naval forces.

54 AUSTRIAN
B 1894 Wm Denny Bros, Dumbarton. **T** 3,127g, 2,028n.
D 316.8/96.56 x 40.2/12.25 x 19.3/5.88.
E Sgl scr, tpl exp, 278 nhp, 160 psi. 11 kts. By builder.
H Steel. 1 + spar dk. F 45/13.72. B 86/26.21. P 39/11.89. Crew 42.
1894 Aug 6: Launched. Sept 11: Delivered as *Bhamo* to British & Burmese S.N.Co, P. Henderson & Co, Glasgow. Cost £32,469.
1901 Acquired by Ellerman Lines Ltd, Fred Swift manager. R/n *Austrian*.
1921 Sold to Ognam Shipping Co, London. Same name.
1926 Arrested in Italy for debt. Sold by Italian Admiralty court order.
Aug: Broken up at Preston by Thos. W. Ward.

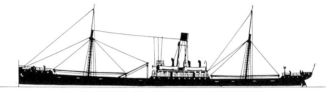

BELGRAVIAN (1), BOSNIAN, BULGARIAN (1)

55 BELGRAVIAN (I)
B 1891 Wm. Doxford & Sons, Sunderland. **T** 2,521g, 1,592n.
D 312/95.1 x 39/11.89 x 23.5/7.16.
E Sgl scr, tpl exp, 305 nhp. 11 Kts. By builder.
H Steel. 2 dks. F 40/12.19. B 74/27.56. P 31/9.45.
1891 Feb 14: Launched. March: Delivered to Clan Line as *Clan McNeil* as drawn.
1902 Acquired. Fred Swift manager. R/n *Belgravian*.
1922 Sold to Kenneth Saunders, Glasgow. Same name.
1929 Broken up in Italy.

56 BOSNIAN
As 55. **T** 2,507g, 1,576n.
1891 March 25: Launched. May: Completed as *Clan Macleod*, Clan Line.
1902 Acquired. Fred Swift as manager. R/n *Bosnian*.
1922 Became *Psara*, M. Basiliades, Chios.
1929 Broken up.

57 BULGARIAN (I)
As 55. **T** 2,515g, 1,613n.
1891 Apr 28: Launched. June: In service as *Clan MacIntyre*, Clan Line.
1902 Acquired. Fred Swift as manager. R/n *Bulgarian*.
1917 Jan 20: Torpedoed by *U-84* in the Atlantic en route Cartagena-Liverpool. 14 lost.

58 SARDINIA
B 1888 Hawthorn, Leslie & Co, Hebburn. **T** 2,474g, 1,500n.
D 310/94.49 x 40.3/12.28 x 22.6/6.89.
E Sgl scr, tpl exp, 361 nhp, 170 psi, 3 sgl blrs. 10 kts. By Blair & Co, Stockton.

H Steel. 2 dks. F 83/25.3. B 78.23.77. P 82/25. **P** 20.
1888 Aug: Built as *Gulf of Corcovado*, Greenock S.S.Co, the Gulf Line.
1899 Owners became Gulf Line Ltd. D. McDougall manager.
1900 Sold to P. Viale di G.B, Genoa, r/n *Paolo V*.
1902 Acquired. R/n *Sardinia*. Noted for her tall funnel.
1908 Nov 25: Sailed from Malta for Alexandria with 152 deck passengers, mainly pilgrims for Mecca. One mile offshore, probably due to embers from a pilgrim's cooking brazier, fire broke out in the nitrate in no. 2 hold which quickly took hold. The engineroom was abandoned and the ship steamed in circles. All the boats were ablaze and those aboard had to jump into the sea. The ship then went ashore on Ricasoli Rocks and burned out. 120 were lost: 16 crew including the captain, 5 European passengers and an estimated 100 pilgrims.

---

59 ALEXANDRIA
B 1890 James Laing & Sons, Sunderland. **T** 3,501gn, 2,194n.
D 365/111.35 x 42.2/12.86 x 19/5.79.
E Sgl scr, tpl exp, 387 nhp, 180 psi. 10 kts. By G. Clark & Co, Sunderland.
H Steel. 1 + spar dk. 3 masts. F 37/11.28. B 82/12.86. P 42/5.79.
1880 Built as *Ville de Paris* for Cie. Havraise Peninsulaire de Nav. a Vapeur, Le Havre.
1902 Acquired. R/n *Alexandria*.
1914 Broken up by J. J. King & Co, Garston, Liverpool.

CITY OF CAMBRIDGE	see City of Cambridge (II),	City Line 236
CITY OF KHIOS	see City of Khios,	City Line 228
CITY OF VENICE	see City of Venice,	City Line 227
CITY OF OXFORD	see City of Oxford,	City Line 236
CITY OF DUNDEE	see City of Dundee,	City Line 239

1906 ELLERMAN & PAPAYANNI CO LTD FORMED. THE SHIPS WERE ELLERMAN LINE OWNED AND PAPAYANNI MANAGED.

60 GASCON
B 1890 S. McKnight & Co, Ayr. **T** 1,106g, 683n.
D 230/70.6 x 31.1/9.48 x 16.5/5.03.
E Sgl scr, tpl exp, 181 nhp, 160 psi, 1 dbl blr. 9½ kts. By D. Rowan & Co, Glasgow.
H Steel. 2 dks. F 26/7.92. B 88/13.41. P 88/26.82. 3 masts.
1890 April: Completed as *Gascony* for Moss S.S.Co, Liverpool. Her sister was *Guienne*.
1904 Sold to J. McCormick & Co, Leith. R/n *Gascon*. Her sister became *Teuton*.
1906 Acquired. Same name.
1909 Dec 23: Lost at Douro. Went aground in the estuary as she was leaving the river for Liverpool.

---

61 AVON
B 1880 James Laing & Sons, Sunderland. **T** 2,199g, 1,395n.
D 283.3/86.35 x 35.2/10.73 x 29.3/8.93.
E Sgl scr, 2 cyl comp inv, 200 nhp, 75 psi, 1 dbl blr. 9 kts. By North East Marine Engineering Co, Sunderland (note: they had also a works at Newcastle). **H** Iron. 2 dks.
1880 Built for Royal Mail Steam Packet Co's continental feeder network.
1903 Acquired. Same name.
1916 April: Sunk in fog by collision in the River Mersey.

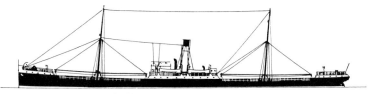

BAVARIAN, ALGERIAN (II)

62 BAVARIAN
B 1895 Sunderland S.B.Co, Sunderland. **T** 3,012g, 1,950n.
D 343/104.55 x 41.1/12.53 x 26/7.92.
E Sgl scr, tpl exp, 326 nhp, 160 psi, 2 sgl blrs. 10 kts. By North East Marine Eng Co, Sunderland.
H Steel. 1 + spar dk. F 42/12.8. B 78/23.77. P 38/11.58.
1895 Jan: Built as *Merionethshire* for the Shire Line of Jenkins & Co, London. One of a series built for Jenkins by Sunderland S.B.Co. over seven years. The later ones being slightly larger. Drawing is from *Denbighshire* of 1899.
1907 Acquired by Ellerman Lines Ltd, Fred Swift manager. R/n *Bavarian*. Royal Mail acquired the remainder of the fleet.
1928 Aug: Sold for £6,000 and scrapped. Breaker's name given as Cohen but their yard was at Smyrna.

63 ALGERIAN (II)
As 62 except: **B** 1896. **T** 3,837g, 2,404n. **D** 364/110.95 x 45.2/13.78.
E 344 nhp. **H** B 80/24.38.
1896 June: Delivered as *Flintshire* for Jenkin's Shire Line.
1907 Taken over by Royal Mail Steam Packet Co. Same name and service.
1913 Acquired by Ellerman to join her sister. R/n *Algerian*. Fred Swift manager.
1916 Jan 12: Sunk by a mine laid by *UC-52* 2½ miles from the Needles, Isle of Wight.

---

64 WHARFEDALE / ARCADIAN (I)
B 1891 Short Bros, Sunderland. **T** 2,855g, 1,833n.
D 320/97.54 x 42/12.8 x 17.8/5.42.
E Sgl scr, tpl exp, 254 nhp, 160 psi, 3 sgl blrs. 9 kts. By W. Allan & Co, Sunderland.
H Steel. 1 + spar dk F 34/10.36. B 59/17.98.
1891 May: Built as *Nerano* for Columbia S.N.Co. Ltd, Sunderland, W. & T. W. Pinkney, managers.
1903 Renamed *Alangüeta* by Cia. Algortena de Nav, Bilbao.
1904 Bought by Sir James Laing & Sons. R/n *Wharfedale*.
1908 Acquired. Fred Swift as manager, initially registered as *Wharfedale* but then r/n *Arcadian*.
1910 Jan 2: Sunk in collision with Turnbull Martin's *Ayrshire* in thick fog off Tuskar Rock, near Rosslare and 20 miles north of the Smalls. *Arcadian* was en route London-Glasgow to complete loading before proceeding to the Persian Gulf for City Line. She was struck on the starboard side abaft the bridge and sank quickly. Out of 51 aboard 12, all Lascars, were drowned.

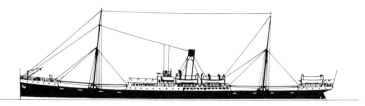

65 VOLTA / VENETIAN (I)
B 1891 Naval Construction & Armament Co, Barrow. **T** 2,734g, 1,723n.
D 327.6/99.85 x 39.4/12.01 x 22/6.71n.
E Sgl scr, tpl exp, 253 nhp, 160 psi, 2 sgl blrs. 10½ kts. By builder. Coal 201 tons at 26 pd.
H Steel 3 dks. F 42/12.8. B 108/32.92. P 40/12.19. C 171,540/4,857.4 cu g. **P** 44 1st, 14 2nd.
1891 Aug 8: Launched. Sept: Delivered to British & African S.N.Co, Elder Dempster & Co, Liverpool as managers. Her sisters were *Bonny* and *Loanda*.
1908 Acquired. Fred Swift as manager. Initially as *Volta* but then given a Papayanni 'ian' name: *Venetian*.
1916 Transferred to Papayanni & Co who advertised as 'Papayanni Line'.
1924 June: Broken up at Alblasserdam, Netherlands.

66 CASTILIAN (I)
B 1890 Wm Gray & Co, West Hartlepool. **T** 1,923g, 1,232n.
D 270.4/82.42 x 37.5/11.43 x 16.2/4.94.
E Sgl scr, tpl exp, 232 nhp, 150 psi, 2 sgl blrs. 10½ kts. By Central Marine Eng. Wks, West Hartlepool.
H Steel. 1 + spar dk. F 21/6.4. B 26/7.92. P 51/15.54.
1890 March: Completed as *Umbilo* for Bullard, King & Co, London. African services.
1903 Re-boilered.
1909 Acquired. R/n *Castilian*; Fred Swift as manager. Papayanni routes.
1917 Apr 18: Torpedoed by *U-61* 110 miles from Tory Head, Ireland.

67 ITALIAN (I)
B 1887 Wigham Richardson & Co, Newcastle. **T** 2,581g, 1,645n.
D 330/100.58 x 38.3/11.67 x 18.7/5.7.
E Sgl scr, 346 nhp, 160 psi, 3 dbl blrs. 10½ kts. By builder.
H Steel. 1 + spar dk. 3 masts. **P** 1st (Saloon) and 3rd.
1887 Dec: Completed as *Port Fairy* for William Milburn & Co's Anglo-Australasian S.N.Co, London.
1888 Jan 2: M/v London-Melbourne-Sydney.
1892 With the decision to withdraw from passenger carrying the applicable ships were disposed of. R/n *Dona Maria*, J. H. Andressen Successores, Oporto.
1907 Sold to Booth Steamship Co (1901) Ltd. R/n *Port Fairy*. Aug 17: First sailing Liverpool-Manaus.
1909 Sold to shipbreakers but acquired by Ellerman Lines. R/n *Italian*. Fred Swift manager.
1913 Broken up by Thos. W. Ward at Preston.

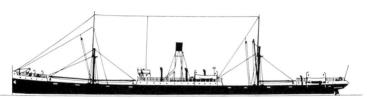

68 ASTURIAN
B 1890 Chas. Connell & Co, Glasgow. **T** 3,193g, 2,070n, 4,479dwt.
D 350/106.68 x 40/12.19 x 20.2/6.16.
E Sgl scr, tpl exp, 315 nhp, 160 psi, 2 dbl blrs. 10 kts. By J & J Thompson, Glasgow.
H Steel. 1 dk. F 40/12.19. B 81/24.69.
1889 Building as *Capella* for Rathbone Bros.' Star Line but purchased on the stocks when Thos. & Jas. Harrison took over the five Rathbone ships.
1890 Jan: Completed for TJH. Liverpool-West Indies route.
1899 Reboilered.
1910 March: Acquired. R/n *Asturian*, Fred Swift manager.
1917 Feb 18: Attacked by submarine gunfire in the Mediterranean saved by a warship which arrived to drive off the aggressor.
1921 Sold for £5,500 to the Franco-British S.N.Co; same name.
1922 Sept: During the Greco-Turkish hostilities after the Turkish victory at Dumlu Punar (Dumlupinar) *Asturian* evacuated Greeks from Smyrna (captured Sept 9) to Piraeus. Nov 10: Ran out of coal 260 miles west of Ushant during a gale. She was towed into Corcubion by *Admiral Cochrane*, Byron S.S.Co.
1923 Laid up at Queens Dock, Cardiff. Sold for £5,500 and broken up in Germany.

69 DOURO (II)
B 1881 Wm. Doxford & Sons, Sunderland. **T** 1,603g, 1,022n.
D 255/7.77 x 34.6/10.55 x 22.9/6.98.
E Sgl scr, tpl exp, 192 nhp, 150 psi, 2 sgl blrs. 9½ kts. By G. Clark & Co, Sunderland.

H Iron. 1 + spar dk.
1881 Dec: Completed as *Congella*, Bullard, King & Co, London.
1910 Acquired. R/n *Douro*, Fred Swift manager.
1915 Sept 5: Captured and sunk by gunfire from *U-20* 75 miles southwest of Bishop's Rock to become E & P's first loss of the war.

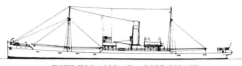

ESTRELLANO (I), LISBON (II)

70 **ESTRELLANO (I)**
B 1910 Ramage & Ferguson, Leith. **T** 1,161g, 703n.
D 230.1/70.13 x 34.8/10.61 x 16.5/5.03.
E Sgl scr, tpl exp, 132 nhp, 150 psi. 10½ kts. By builder.
H Steel. 2 dks. F 26/7.92. B 71/21.64. P 12/3.66.
1910 The first ship built for the Papayanni services since the Ellerman take over. Manager Fred Swift.
1917 Oct 31: Torpedoed by *UC-71* off Pillier Island, Greece. 3 dead.

71 **LISBON (II)**
As 70 except: **B** 1910 W. Harkess & Co, Middlesbrough. **T** 1,203g, 724n.
D 231.5/70.56x 35.7/10.88. **E.** Richardsons, Westgarth & Co, **H** P 14/4.27.
1910 Completed. Fred Swift manager.
1917 May 30: Mined off the Royal Sovereign Lightship. Laid by *UC-62*.

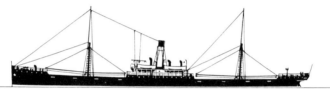

72 **FAVONIAN (II)**
B 1894 Tyne Iron S.B.Co, Newcastle. **T** 3,039g, 1,957n.
D 320.2/97.6 x 41.6/12.68 x 25.9/7.89.
E Sgl scr, tpl exp, 287 nhp, 160 psi, 2 sgl blrs. 12 kts. By J. Dickinson, Sunderland.
H Steel. + spar dk. F 34/10.36 B 78/23.77. P 29/8.84.
1894 Feb 6: Launched. March: Completed as *Alnwick* for Norwick S.S.Co.; Hunting & Sons managers.
1910 Acquired for £9,000 by Ellerman. R/n *Favonian*, Westcott & Laurence as managers and therefore London based.
1916 Aug 4: Torpedoed by *U-35* 24 miles southwest of Planier Island, Mediterranean.

73 **ANDALUSIAN (II)**
B 1911 W. Harkess & Co, Middlesbrough. **T** 2,349g, 1,452n.
D 298.5/90.98 x 40.5/12.34 x 22.7/6.92.
E Sgl scr, tpl exp, 304 nhp, 215 psi, 2 sgl blrs. 10½ kts. By Richardsons, Westgarth & Co, Middlesbrough.
H Steel. 2 dks. F 30/9.14. B 94/28.65. P. 27/8.23.
1911 June: Delivered to Ellerman. Fred Swift manager.
1915 March 12: Captured by *U-29* 25 miles from Bishops Rock. Scuttled.

EDEN HALL See *Eden Hall*, Hall Line 358

74 **PALMELLA (I)**
B 1913 Ramage & Ferguson, Leith. **T** 1,352g, 759n.
D 232.8/70.96 x 37.1/11.31 x 16.6/5.06.
E Sgl scr, tpl exp, 192 nhp, 220 psi, 2 sgl blrs. 10 kts. By builder.
H Steel. 2 dks. F 23/7.01. B 77/23.47. P 29/8.84.
1913 Feb: Delivered to Ellerman Lines with Fred Swift as manager.
1915 Graham Smith took over as manager.
1918 Aug 22: Torpedoed by *UB-92* 25 miles northwest of South Stack. All 28 aboard were lost.

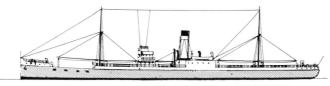

MARDINIAN (I), FALERNIAN (II) / VOLTURNO

75 MARDINIAN (I)
B 1913 W. Harkess & Co., Middlesbrough. **T** 3,322g, 2,125n.
D 313/95.4 x 42.4/12.92 x 21.6/6.58.
E Sgl scr, 344 nhp,215 psi,3 sgl blrs. 10½ kts. By Richardsons, Westgarth & Co, Middlesbrough.
H Steel. 1 dk F 41/12.5. B & P 203/61.87.
1913 Aug: Completed for Ellerman Lines, Fred Swift manager. The first Papayanni trades ship with a cruiser stern.
1914 Graham Smith took over from Fred Swift as manager of the Papayanni group of ships.
1917 May 19: Torpedoed by *U-34* 4 miles west of Tabraca Island, Mediterranean.

76 FALERNIAN (II) / VOLTURNO
As 75 except; **B** 1914. **T** 3,419g, 2,917n. **D** 318/96.93. **H F** 40/12.19. **P** 205/62.48
1914 July: Delivered. M/v to the Black Sea. Aug 4: In port in Turkey at the outbreak of war. The ship was detained being unable to leave. Sept: Arrested for debt. Oct 29: Turkey entered the war and the ship was seized.
1919 Reverted to Ellerman.
1928 The ship was in port damaged when she was sold to E. Cesano. R/n *Bosforo*. Repaired and repurchased. R/n *Volturno* by Ellerman & Papayanni. Later transferred to Montgomerie & Workman management.
1943 June 23: Bombed by German aircraft off Cape St Vincent, southern Portugal. Sank next day.

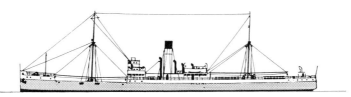

77 MARONIAN
B 1913 Earles S.B. Co, Hull. **T** 3,385g, 2,182n, 5,000dwt.
D 318.9/97.2 x 42.4/12.92 x 21.8/6.64.
E Sgl scr, tpl exp, 343 nhp, 215 psi, 3 sgl blrs. 10½ kts. By builder.
H Steel. 1 dk. F 39/11.89. B & P 207/63.09. 5 hatches.
1913 Delivered.
1938 Sold for £19,500 to E. Szabados, Venice. R/n *Luciano*.
1941 Apr 15: Sunk by Allied air attack off Valona.

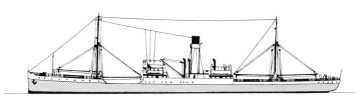

MALATIAN (I), FLAMINIAN (II)

78 MALATIAN (I)
As 77 except: **B** 1914. **T** 3,427g, 2,224n. **D** 323.8/98.45. **H F** 74/22.55. B & P 216/65.83. **P** 42.
1914 Jan: Completed.
1925 Operated in Bucknall livery, including a black hull, on the Australia-Dutch East Indies route.
1936 Nov: Renamed *Santa Maria*, Cia Ligure di Navegazione, Genoa.
1943 Sept: Taken over by the Germans and operated by Mittelmeer Reederei GmbH, the company that operated all the assorted vessels that had been seized or, in the case of Italy, taken over on war-charter.
1944 Oct: Sunk at Venice by Allied air attack.

79 FLAMINIAN (II)
As 78 except: **B** 1914. **T** 3,439g. **D** 323.8/98.45 x 42.2/12.86.
1914 Completed.
1915 March 29: Captured by *U-28* 50 miles southwest of the Scilly Isles and sunk by gunfire.

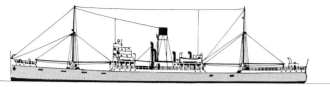

ROUMELIAN, FLAMINIAN (III)

80 ROUMELIAN
B 1914 Palmers' Co, Newcastle. **T** 2,687g, 1,710n.
D 312/95.09 x 43/13.11 x 23.8/7.25.
E Sgl scr, tpl exp, 331 nhp, 220 psi, 2 sgl blrs. 11 kts. By Richardsons, Westgarth & Co, Newcastle.
H Steel. 2 dks. F 32/9.75. B 103/31.39. P 71/21.64.
1914 Delivered. A handy and sturdy vessel that had one look-alike sister; Papayanni seemed to settle down to no set design.
1936 Dec: Sold to Soc. Anon di Nav. Transmediterranea, Sicily. R/n *Drepanum*.
1942 Taken over by the Germans. Operated by 'Neptun' Dampschiffahrts Ges., Bremen.
1943 Nov 20: Lost by collision off Gothenburg.

81 FLAMINIAN (III)
As 80 except: **B** 1917 W. Harkess & Son, Middlesbrough. **T** 3,227g, 2,068n.
D 315/96.01 x 42.4/12.92. **E** 226 nhp. **H** F 33/10.05. B 140/42.67. P 73/22.25.
1917 Completed. Entered commercial service on the Mediterranean routes. Manager Graham Smith.
1939 Sept: Taken over by the Admiralty. R/n *Empire Flaminian*, Ellerman Papayanni as managers.
1946 She ended the war as the Royal Engineers depot ship at Southampton. Returned to Papayanni. Reverted to *Flaminian*.
1950 July 21: Arrived for scrapping by Dover Industries, Dover.

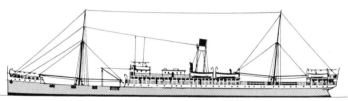

82 ITALIAN (II)
B 1899 Barclay, Curle & Co, Glasgow. **T** 3,648g, 2,302n.
D 345/105.15 x 44/13.41 x 14.2/4.33.
E Tpl exp, 370 nhp, 180 psi, 4 sgl blrs. 12½ kts. By builder.
H Steel. 1 + spar dk. F 41/12.5. B & P 226/68.88.
1899 April: Built as *Fantee* for African S.S. Co, Elder Dempster & Co, managers. Her sister was *Sobo*.
1901 Holed by a submerged rock and put out of action at Cape Palmas, Liberia. Until the arrival of HMS *Dwarf* she was being looted by the locals.
1904 May 3: Aground at Douala, Cameroon but assisted off by Elder, Dempster's *Egga*.
1913 Acquired by Ellerman; Graham Smith manager but registered in London. R/n *Italian*. She also served on the Ellerman & Bucknall routes during the war.
1921 Transferred to Ellerman's Wilson Line, Hull, R/n *Rollo*. **P** 40 1st.
1932 Sept: Broken up at Copenhagen.

83 LESBIAN (II)
B 1915 W. Harkess & Son, Middlesbrough. **T** 2,555g, 1,625n.
D 305.3/93.06 x 42.2/12.86 x 23.2/7.07.
E Sgl scr, tpl exp, 226 nhp, 180 psi, 2 sgl blrs. 11 kts. By Richardsons, Westgarth & Co, Middlesbrough.
H Steel. 2 dkrs. F 33/10.06. B 97/29.56. P 70/21.33.
1915 Built for Ellerman Lines; Graham Smith manager.
1917 Jan 5: captured and sunk by gunfire from *U-35* 125 miles east of Malta. As often happened the master was taken prisoner.

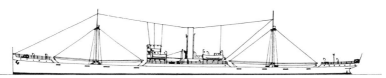

84 BORDER KNIGHT

B 1899 D. & W. Henderson & Co, Glasgow. **T** 3,774g, 2,394n.
D 360/109.72 x 46/14.02 x 25.7/7.83.
E Sgl scr, tpl exp, 325 nhp, 160 psi, 3 sgl blrs. 10 kts. By builder.
H Steel. 2 dks. F 43/13.11. B 92/28.04. P 44/13.41.
1899 July: Completed for Border Union S.S. Co, J. Little & Co, Liverpool, as managers.
1917 Acquired as a war loss replacement but to no avail.
Nov 14: Torpedoed by *UC-17* 1½ miles off the Lizard, Cornwall. 1 killed.

BORDERER see *Borderer*, Hall Line 420.

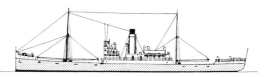

85 DARINO

B 1917 Ramage & Ferguson, Leith. **T** 1,349g, 830n.
D 236.3/72.02 x 36.5/11.12 x 17.1/5.21.
E Sgl scr, tpl exp, 203 nhp, 210 psi, 2 sgl blrs. By builder.
H Steel. 2 dks. F 26/7.92. B 79/24.08. P 33/10.06.
1917 Oct: Completed for Ellerman Lines with Graham Smith as manager.
1939 Nov 19: Torpedoed by *U-41* off Spain. 16 killed.

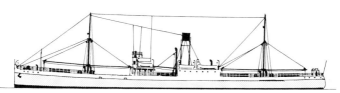

86 ANDALUSIAN (III)

B 1918 Earles S.B. Co, Hull. **T** 3,074g, 1,907n.
D 321.5/98 x 45.2/13.78 x 24.2/7.38.
E Sgl scr, tpl exp, 241 nhp, 11 kts. By builder.
H Steel. 2 dks. F 83/25.3. B 108/32.92. P 73/27.25.
1918 Completed. Graham Smith as manager.
1940 June 20: Attacked by *U-51* but the torpedo exploded before reaching the ship; the Germans were having considerable trouble with malfunctions which they put down to sabotage but there was a design fault if the torpedo porpoised out of the water. On re-entry it detonated. Nevertheless very few such explosions were reported by Allied ships. Sabotage came much later when foreign workers were employed.
1941 Mar 17: Torpedoed by *U-106* in the Atlantic.

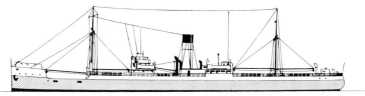

87 SERBINO

B 1919 Ramage & Ferguson, Leith. **T** 4,080g, 2,636n.
D 342.4/104.36 x 46/14.02 x 24.8/7.56.
E Sgl scr, tpl exp, 388 nhp, 220 psi, 2 sgl blrs. 11 kts. By builder.
H Steel. 2 + shelter dk. F 39/11.89. B & P 262/79.86.

1919 May: Delivered to Ellerman & Papayanni.
1922 Transferred to Hall Line Ltd as managers. Ellermans Lines Ltd owners.
1933 Moved back to E & P.
1914 Oct 21: Torpedoed by *U-82* in convoy SL 89. Cunard's *Aurania* was sunk in this same attack.

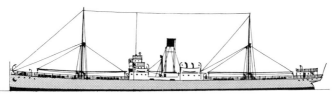

88 FABIAN (II)

B 1919 Wm. Gray & Co, West Hartlepool. **T** 3,059g, 1,861n.
D 331.2/100.95 x 46.8/14.26 x 23.2/7.07.
E Sgl scr, tpl exp, 407 nhp, 180 psi, 3 sgl blrs. 11 kts. By Central Marine Eng. Wks, West Hartlepool.
H Steel. 1 + shelter dk.
1919 Sept: Delivered.
1940 June 17: Carried 1,000 troops and civilians St Nazaire-UK. Nov 16: Torpedoed by *U-65* in the Atlantic 02.49N,15.29W.

89 BULGARIAN (II)

B 1904 Flensburger S.G., Flensburg. **T** 2,064g, 1,268n.
D 292.5/89.15 x 41.2/12.56 x 18.8/5.73.
E Sgl scr, tpl exp, 200 nhp, 170 psi, 2 sgl blrs. 10 kts. By builder.
H Steel. 1 dk. F 34/10.36. B 174/53.03. P 17/5.18.
1904 Built as *Marie Menzell* for Menzell & Co's Hanseatische Dampfer. Ges, Hamburg. The firm was later re-titled Menzell Linie GmbH.
1915 Became *Otto Kalthoff*, owned by Vulkan Reederei 'Otto Kalthoff' GmbH, Hamburg, Germany.
1918 Nov: Managed by N. V. Handel & Maats. 'Vulcaan', Rotterdam.
1919 Ceded to Great Britain. Became *Bulgarian*, Westcott & Laurence.
1936 Apr 24: Stranded but salvaged and broken up by W. Arnott Young at Dalmuir.

90 GERANO

B 1914 Stettiner Oderwerk, Stettin. **T** 2,080g, 1,289n.
D 258.3/78.73 x 40.5/12.34 x 16.2/4.94.
E Sgl scr, tpl exp, 156 psi, 1 sgl blr. 10 kts. By builder.
H Steel. 1 dk. F & B 164/48.99. Q 75/22.86. P 32.9.75.
1914 Built as *Stern*, Rudolf Christian Gribel manager.
1919 Ceded to Great Britain; Westcott & Laurence as managers.
1920 They then acquired her. R/n *Gerano*. The ship also served with Ellerman's Wilson according to need; but out of London to Scandinavia.
1935 Broken up.

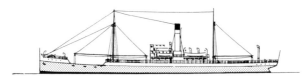

91 CRESSADO

B 1913 Henry Koch A.G., Lubeck. **T** 1,227g, 717n.
D 241.4/73.58 x 36.2/11.03 x 15.9/4.85.
E Sgl scr, tpl exp, 154 nhp, 200 psi, 2 sgl blrs. 9½ kts. By Ottsener Maschinen Fabrik, Altona, Hamburg.
H Steel. 1 dk. F 34/10.36. B & P 186/56.69.

1913 Completed as *Cressida* for Adolf Kirsten, Hamburg.
1919 Ceded to Great Britain.
1920 Acquired by Westcott & Laurence and owned by Gulf of Suez S.S. Co, London. R/n *Cressado*.
1938 Transferred to Ellerman & Papayanni as managers. Based Liverpool.
1942 May 8: Sank after colliding with HMS *Pozarica* (McAndrews) off the Skerries.

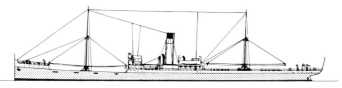

92 **MARDINIAN (II)**
B 1919 S.P. Austin & Son, Sunderland. **T** 2,434g, 1,426n.
D 303.2/92.41 x 43/13.11 x 20.8/6.34.
E Sgl scr, tpl exp, 266 nhp, 180 psi, 2 sgl blrs. 10 kts. By Richardsons, Westgarth & Co, Sunderland.
H Steel. 1 dk. F 32/9.75. B & P 233/71.02.
1919 Aug: Completed for Ellerman Lines Ltd. Until her eventual transfer to Ellerman & Papayanni she was under no specific manager.
1940 Sept 9: Torpedoed by *U-28* in convoy SC.2 in the Atlantic, 56.37N,09W. 31 survivors picked up by HM trawler *Apollo*. This convoy, in which four ships were sunk, revealed a weakness in that no one was responsible for recording ships lost. In fact *Apollo* came upon *Mardinian's* boats by accident although she had been seen to fall out of line. The convoy system was changed. A maroon was fired by any ship seeing another hit and the nearest escort fired a rocket of acknowledgement; all escorts recorded the rocket count. Star shells were then fired outwards by all escorts in order to turn night into day around the convoy so that the surfaced submarines could be seen. They had to surface to keep up and often fired torpedoes from the surface. Forcing them to dive enabled depth charges to become effective as well as helping the convoy to escape.

RIO PARDO See Bucknall 583

RIO NEGRO See Bucknall 584

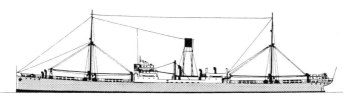

93 **CASTILIAN (II)**
B 1919 Sir Raylton Dixon & Co, Middlesbrough. **T** 3,067g, 1,849n.
D 331.3/100.98 x 46/8/14.26 x 23.2/7.07.
E Sgl scr, tpl exp, 310 nhp, 2,580 ihp, 180 psi, 2 sgl blrs. 10 kts. Richardsons, Westgarth & Co, Middlesbrough.
H Steel. 2 dks F 29/8.84. B 98/29.87. P 33/10.06.C 327,715/9,280cu g.
1919 Delivered to Ellerman Lines Ltd; Westcott & Laurence managers.
1937 Owned by Westcott & Laurence Ltd, London.
1943 Feb 12: Wrecked en route Manchester-Lisbon, in fog, at night, on the East Platters by the Skerries Light, Anglesey.

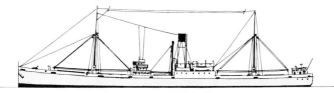

DESTRO / DESTRIAN, DIDO (II)

94 **DESTRO / DESTRIAN**
B 1920 Dunlop, Bremner & Co, Port Glasgow. **T** 3,553g, 2,177n. 5,050dwt.
D 314/95.7 x 45.2/13.78 x 28.7/8.75.
E Sgl scr, tpl exp, 240 nhp, 180 psi, 2 blrs. 10½ kts. By builder.

H Steel. 1 + shelter dk. Flush.
1920 July 18: Completed as *Destro* for Ellerman's Wilson but served on Ellerman & Papayanni's Mediterranean route.
1926 Transferred to Ellerman Lines.
1940 The ship had an amazing war record. June 12: After Italy came into the war (June 10) attacked by Italian bombers off Milos; no damage.
1941 Served as a supply ship in the Mediterranean to such places as Tobruk and Bardia. April: Took part in the Greek campaign including the evacuation of Crete. Survived over 50 bomb attacks some of which were directed at her specifically.
1942 Mar 27: Damaged by bombs at Tobruk. She suffered 68 air raids in two weeks.
1946 March 19: Renamed *Destrian* when she returned to Ellerman & Papayanni service. The mushroom vents at her foremast became cowl.
1948 Jan: Sent out a distress signal during a gale. Other ships stood by but were not needed.
1950 Sold for £25,000 to Bock, Goddefroy's Deutsche Levant Linie; R/n *Pergamon*.She had a poop by now.
1956 Taken over with the line by Rudolf A. Oetker's Hamburg Sud-Amerika group.
1964 Broken up at Bremerhaven.

95 DIDO (II)
As 94 **T** 3,554g, 2,175n.
1920 Built for Ellerman's Wilson.
1922 Placed on Ellerman & Papayanni routes but Wilson owned.
1932 Laid up at London.
1941 Nov: Seized in drydock at Brest by the Germans after they entered un-occupied France. R/n *Dorpat*. Operated by Leth & Co, Hamburg.
1943 Apr 11: Mined and sunk at Aarhus; raised.
1945 May 3: Bombed by Allied aircraft in the Great Belt off Langeland. Sold to Finland. R/n *Leila*, owned by W. Rostedt, Abo. Varnstamo Rederi.
1963 Sept: Scrapped.

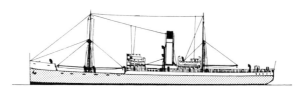

PALMELLA (II), ESTRELLANO (II), LESBIAN (III)

96 PALMELLA (II)
B 1920 Ramage & Ferguson, Leith. **T** 1,568g, 978n.
D 245.9/74.95 x 38.2/11.64 x 16.9/5.15.
E Sgl scr, tpl exp, 210 nhp, 220 psi, 2 sgl blrs. 10 kts. By builder.
H Steel. 1 dk. F 59/17.98. B & P 156/47.55.
1920 May: Completed for Ellerman Lines Ltd, Liverpool. Operated on the Papayanni services.
1941 Dec 1: Torpedoed by *U-37* off Portugal.

97 ESTRELLANO (II)
As 96 except: **B** 1920 Hall, Russell & Co, Aberdeen. **T** 1,963g, 1,226n.
D 250.8/76.44. **E** 230 nhp. By builder. **H** F 27/8.23. B & P 157/47.85.
1920 Nov: Delivered to Ellerman Lines.
1941 Feb 9: Torpedoed by *U-37* off Portugal in convoy HG 53 (Home-Gibraltar). Over a two hour period *Estrellano, Courland* (Currie) and *Brandenburg* (Currie) were all sunk.

98 LESBIAN (III)
As 96 except: **B** 1923 Swan, Hunter & Wigham Richardson, Newcastle.
T 2,532g, 1,460n. **D** 272.1/82.94 x 41.7/12.71 x 19.9/6.06.
E 274 nhp; by Wallsend Slipway Co. **H** F 31/9.45. B & P 172/52.42.
1923 Sept: Completed Ellerman Lines.
1940 June 23: Detained at Beirut by the French after the fall of France.
1941 June: When British and Free French forces were later involved in conflict with the Vichy French in Syria and in the Lebanon the ship was destroyed.

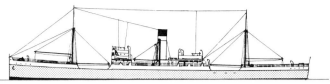

99 **EGYPTIAN (III)**
B 1920 W. Harkess & Son, Middlesbrough. **T** 2,866g, 1,806n.
D 316.3/96.41 x 44.1/13.44 x 23.3/7.1.
E Sgl scr, tpl exp, 233 nhp. 220 psi, 2 sgl blrs. 11 kts. By Richardsons, Westgarth & Co, Middlesbrough.
H Steel. 2 dks. F 73/22.25. B 102/31.09. P 72/21.94.
1920 Completed.
1943 Mar 6: Torpedoed by *U-230* in convoy SC 121 in the Atlantic.

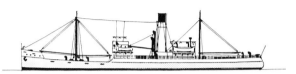

100 **LISBON (III)**
B 1920 Hall, Russell & Co, Aberdeen. **T** 1,964g, 1,242n.
D 250.8/76.44 x 38.2/11.64 x 17.1/5.21.
E Sgl scr, tpl exp, 230 nhp, 220 psi, 2 sgl blrs. 11 kts. By builder.
H Steel. 1 dk. F 27/8.22. B & P 157/47.65.
1920 Sept: Delivered.
1940 Oct 29: Wrecked on Rattray Head, east coast of Scotland.

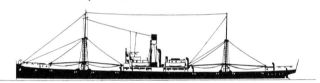

101 **MANCHURIAN**
B 1905 A. G. Neptun, Rostock. **T** 2,819g, 1,760n.
D 292.1/89.03 x 41.3/12.59 x 25.7/7.83.
E Sgl scr, tpl exp, 229 nhp, 185 psi, 2 sgl blrs. 9½ kts. By builder.
1905 Built as *Tilly Russ,* Ernst Russ, Hamburg. T 2,775g. Derricks high on masts.
1919 Transferred to the Shipping Controller.
1920 Acquired. R/n *Manchurian.*
1934 Nov: Scrapped at Milford Haven by Thos. W. Ward.

CITY OF ALEXANDRIA see *City of Alexandria* Bucknall 583

CITY OF PALERMO see *City of Palermo* Bucknall 584

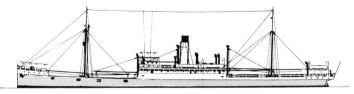

102 **ASSYRIAN**
B 1914 Blohm & Voss, Hamburg. **T** 2,962g, 1,761n.
D 332/101.19 x 44.8/13.65 x 23.1/7.04.
E Tw scr, oil; 2 x 2 stroke. dbl acting diesels, 1,660 IHP. 10 kts. By builder.
H Steel. 2 dks. F 35/10.67. B & P 212/64.62. **P** 9.
1914 Feb 24: Launched as *Fritz* for Woermann Line. Aug: Entered the West African service. The first motor vessel on the route.
1919 Nov 13: Ceded to Great Britain; the Shipping Controller.

1920 March: Renamed *Assyrian*, Ellerman Lines, Graham Smith manager. Factually the Company's first motor ship. Maintaining the German metric engine proved difficult; no spares were then available.
1923 Converted to steam by Cooper & Greig Ltd, Dundee. 2 x tpl exp, 280 nhp each, 180 psi, 2 sgl blrs.
1932 Laid up at London.
1940 Oct 19: Torpedoed by *U-101* in the calamitous convoy SC 7. *Assyrian* was the commodore lead ship (Admiral Lachlan MacKinnon) in the fifth column and at one stage in the attack she chased the periscope of a U-boat so closely that the submarine dared not sheer to port or starboard but had to out-run her pursuer. During the two day attack 8 U-boats fired 32 torpedoes and sank 23 ships. *Assyrian's* survivors were picked up by the sloop *Leith*.

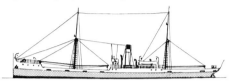

103 **HERO**

B 1895 Earles, Hull. **T** 775g, 331n.
D 216.5/65.99 x 30/9.14 x 13.6/4.14.
E Sgl scr, tpl exp, 239 nhp, 2 sgl blrs. 9 kts. By builder.
H Steel. F 29/8.84. B 55/16.76. Q 61/18.59.
1895 June: Built for Thos. Wilson, Sons & Co. As drawn. She had no sisters.
1905 Transferred to Wilson's N. E. Rly. Shipping Co, Hull. Same name.
1916 Sold to General Steam Navigation Co, G.S.N.C.
1923 Went back to Wilson's N. E. Rly. Shg. Co, then to Ellerman Lines.
1926 Again owned by G.S.N.C. as *Hero*.
1933 Scrapped.

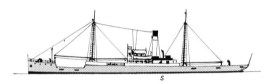

104 **TORCELLO**

B 1911 Stettiner Oderwerke, Stettin. **T** 1,479g, 875n.
D 231.7/70.62 x 36.4/11.09 x 14.7/4.48.
E Sgl scr, tpl exp, 105 nhp, 185 psi, 2 sgl blrs. 9½ kts. By builder.
H Steel. 1 dk. F 29/8.84. B 101/30.78. Q 75/22.86.
1911 Completed as *Stahlhof* for Neue Dampfer-Cie A. G., Stettin.
1919 Nov: Transferred to the Shipping Controller.
1920 Acquired by Ellerman's Wilson. R/n *Torcello*.
1923 Transferred to Ellerman Lines, Graham Smith as manager.
1938 Sold at Liverpool to African & Continental S.S. Co. R/n *Lutine*. Sept: Renamed *Zenobia Martini* by Piero & Mario Martini; operated by Cia. Italian Commerciale Marittima, (CICOMA), Genoa.
1943 March 23: Torpedoed by HM Submarine *Unseen* in the Gulf of Gabes, Tunisia.

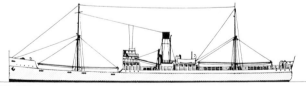

105 **ALGERIAN (III)**

B 1924 Barclay, Curle & Co, Glasgow. **T** 2,305g, 1,441n.
D 295/89.91 x 43.7/13.32 x 21/6.4.
E Sgl scr, tpl exp, 300 nhp, 225 psi, 2 sgl blrs. 11 kts. By builder.
H Steel. F 31/9.45. B & P 184/56.08.
1924 May: Completed.
1943 Requisitioned. One of ten assorted sized ships converted for the laying of the 'Pipeline Under The Ocean', better known as Pluto, used to carry petrol to the Normandy invasion areas. The conversion work was carried out by Green & R. H. Silley Weir, Thames. *Algerian* was fitted to carry 30 nautical miles of 3 inch/7.62 cm (internal size) 'Hais' pipe in two cable tanks. Rollers were fitted on her bows with deck rollers to pay out the extremely heavy pipe. Pay-out and Pick-up gear was fitted fore and aft

capable of handling 30 tons at a speed of 1 knot. There were two types of cable: 'Hammel', of flexible steel, necessitated a minimum 30ft/9.14m drum and was the type payed out from a 48ft/14.63m towed floating drum, known as a Conun. 'Hais' was a hollow submarine cable type of pipe.

1944 June - July: *Algerian*, plus her consorts, laid two pipes Sandown-Cherbourg and, later, as the Germans retreated from the French coast, 11 from Dungeness to Boulogne. The 'Conundrums' laid the Normandy beach head pipes.
1946 Returned to Ellerman.
1957 Dec 12: Sold for breaking up.

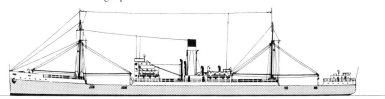

106 **MALVERNIAN (I) / CITY OF KOBE**
B 1924 Ramage & Ferguson, Leith. **T** 4,373g, 2,743n.
D 367.1/111.89 x 49.7/15.15 x 27.4/8.35.
E Sgl scr, tpl exp, 301 nhp, 180 psi. 4 blrs. 12 kts. By builder.
H Steel. 1 dk. F 80/24.38. B 162/49.38. P 37/11.28.
1924 Completed for Ellerman Lines and placed with Papayanni management.
1925 Transferred to Hall Line as managers.
1927 Renamed *City of Kobe*. Hall Line. Her funnel was now taller.
1939 Dec 19: Mined off Great Yarmouth.

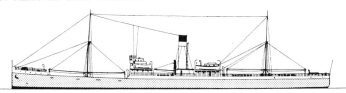

107 **CITY OF LANCASTER (I) / LANCASTRIAN (I)**
B 1924 Palmers' S.B.Co., Jarrow. **T** 3,040g, 1,923n.
D 330.2/100.64 x 45/13.72 x 22.8/6.89.
E Sgl scr, tpl exp, 362 nhp, 225 psi, 3 sgl blrs. 12 kts. By builder.
H Steel. 1 dk. F 41/12.5. B & P 219/66.75.
1924 Feb: Completed. Mediterranean service of Papayanni but owned by Ellerman Lines Ltd.
1929 Lengthened to 335.2/102.17 with the fitting of a new forefront.
1940 June 16: Aided in the evacuation of troops and civilians from St Nazaire. The ship was adjacent to Cunard's *Lancastria* when she was hit by bombs and sunk with appalling loss of life. She brought back 2,500 persons to Plymouth but without food for the voyage except soup and hot drink.
1943 Jan: On a voyage to Lisbon she took the British spy Edward Chapman, code named zigzag, back to Europe. Chapman, an ex-guardsman and safe blower was captured by the Germans in the Channel Islands and trained by them as a spy. He parachuted with a wireless into Britain where he at once reported to the British secret service and from then on worked under their control. He wirelessed his intention of travelling in *City of Lancaster* and for the journey, and unknown to the crew, the ship was 'protected' by the enemy. This was done by knowing from him the sailing date and destination; all U-boats were alerted to sink no ships along the projected route area for 72 hours. A whole convoy sailed with *City of Lancaster* safely through this gap.
1947 Renamed *Lancastrian*.
1953 Dec: Broken up by BISCO at Troon.

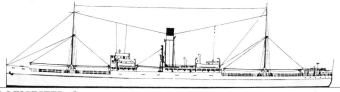

108 **CITY OF LEICESTER (I)**
B 1926 Wm. Gray & Co, West Hartlepool.**T** 3,351g, 1,994n.
D 345/105.16 x 47.5/14.48 x 23.6/7.19.
E Sgl scr, tpl exp, 389 nhp, 220 psi, 2 sgl blrs. 11½ kts. By Central Marine Eng. Wks, West Hartlepool.

H Steel. 1 + shelter dk.
1926 Jan: Delivered to Ellerman Lines, Graham Smith as manager.
1937 Apr 20: Transferred to Hall Line.
1942 Jan 6: Transferred to Westcott & Laurence ownership.
1952 Aug 9: Arrived at Troon and broken up by BISCO.

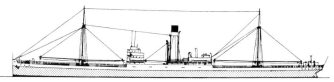

109 CITY OF OXFORD (III)
B 1926 Swan, Hunter & Wigham Richardson, Wallsend. **T** 2,759g, 1,633n.
D 326.7/99.58 x 46.4/14.14 x 20.9/6.37.
E Sgl scr, tpl exp, 306 nhp, 185 psi, 3 sgl blrs. 11 kts. By Wallsend Slipway Co, Wallsend.
H Steel. 1 + shelter dk.
1926 Dec: Completed for Ellerman Lines, Graham Smith as manager.
1942 June 15: 0430 hrs, off the Azores, hit in the forward hold by a torpedo from *U-552*. The ship, enroute Huelva-Garston in convoy HG 84, continued steaming and rolled over onto her side and dived under. *U-552* sank 5 ships in the convoy including Ellerman's Wilson's *Thurso*. It could have been worse. *U-575* fired four torpedoes into HG 84. Three missed but the fourth struck a ship but it was a dud.

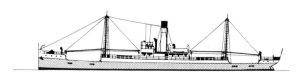

110 COMO
B 1910 Earles S. B. & E. Co, Hull. **T** 1,246g, 706n.
D 250/76.2 x 35.2/10.73 x 15.7/4.78.
E Sgl scr, tpl exp. 116 nhp, 2 sgl blrs. 10 kts. By Amos & Smith Ltd, Hull.
H Steel. 1 dk. F 31/9.45. B 136/41.45. P 16/4.87.
1910 Completed for Thos. Wilson, Sons & Co, Hull. Her sisters were *Castro* and *Hydro*.
1914-18 Remained in commercial service mainly Kirkwall-Norway.
1916 Nov 15: Purchased personally by John Ellerman, with the fleet of 69 ships. New owners became Ellerman's Wilson Line Ltd.
1921 Served under the Westcott & Laurence banner.
1926 Transferred to Ellerman Lines Ltd, Graham Smith manager.
1930 Reverted to Ellerman's Wilson. Still as *Como*.
1945 Owned first by Lenaghans, Belfast. Then sold to John Carlblom & Co, Hull. R/n *Nelkon*.
1948 R/n *Kerempe* by Vapurcul Kollektif Sirketi, Istanbul.
1954 Broken up.

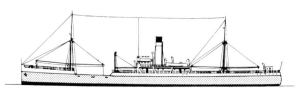

111 OPORTO (II)
B 1928 Ramage & Ferguson, Leith. **T** 2,352g, 1,437n.
D 270.6/82.48 x 40.2/12.25 x 18.4/5.61.
E Sgl scr, tpl exp, 269 nhp, 220 psi, 2 sgl blrs. 10½ kts. By builder.
H Steel. 1 dk. F 51/15.54. B & P 178/54.25.
1928 July; Completed.
1943 Mar 12: One of four ships torpedoed by *U-107* in convoy OS 44 bound UK-Freetown but with *Oporto* to split off for Gibraltar.

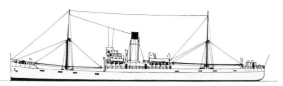

112 **ANATOLIAN (I)**

B 1932 Swan, Hunter & Wigham Richardson, Wallsend. **T** 1,944g, 1,138n.
D 266.2/81.65 oa, x 40/12.19 x 19.5/5.94.
E Sgl scr, tpl exp. 1,600 ihp, 200 psi, 2 sgl blrs. 12 kts. By builder.
H Steel. 1 dk. F 29/8.84. B 70/21.34. Q 72/21.94. P 26/7.92.
1932 March: Completed. A refrigerated vessel and with a quarterdeck hull that was different from the normal Ellerman trader. Trade was being hit by the world wide depression.
1933 Jan: Sold to Cie. Generale d'Armaments Maritimes, a subsidiary of the French Line who were also managers. R/n *Grande-Terre* (as drawn). Banana carrier French Antilles-France.
1939 Sold to Norway. R/n *Pasat* by Skibs A/S Pasat, Oslo, T. B. Torgersen, manager.
1940 Became *Koa Maru*, Kyukyo Hogei K.K., Tokio. War loss.

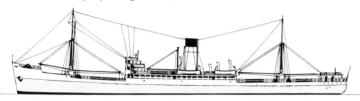

MALVERNIAN (II), BELGRAVIAN (II), CORINTHIAN, IONIAN (I)
FLORIAN (I), PANDORIAN

113 **MALVERNIAN (II)**

B 1937 Wm. Gray & Co, West Hartlepool. **T** 3,133g, 1,397n.
D 345.6/104.34 x 50.1/15.27 x 20.7/6.31.
E Sgl scr, tpl exp + LP turb dbl reduction geared and hydraulic coupling, 606 nhp, 225 psi, 3 sgl blrs. 13 kts, by Central Marine Eng. Wks, West Hartlepool.
H Steel. 1 + shelter dk. F 29/8.84.
1937 June: Completed for Ellerman & Papayanni Lines Ltd.
1940 Requisitioned by the Admiralty and armed for use as the ocean boarding vessel HMS *Malvernian*.
1941 July 19: Sank after being bombed by German aircraft off Spain; set on fire and put out of action.
July 21: 32 crew reached Corunna and 25 landed at Vigo next day. The remainder, 107 out of 164, were captured by German minesweepers when nearing land.

114 **BELGRAVIAN (II)**

As 113.
1937 Delivered to E & P.
1941 Aug 5: Torpedoed by *U-372* in convoy SL 81 enroute to the UK. The convoy was attacked 10 times by *U-372*, *U-75* and *U-204* and 6 ships were lost.

115 **CORINTHIAN**

As 113 except: **B** 1938. **T** 3,198g, 1,342n. **D** 358.7/109.33 oa. **H** F 30/9.14.
1938 Aug; Delivered to E & P.
1963 Apr 4: Arrived at Dalmuir and broken up by W. Arnott Young.

116 **IONIAN (I)**

As 113 except: **B** 1938. **T** 3,114g.
1938 Nov: Delivered to E & P.
1939 Nov 29: Enroute London-Hull struck a mine 3½ miles from Newarp Light vessel, North Sea. Despite attempts to reach port the ship had to be abandoned and sank.

117 **FLORIAN (I)**

As 113 except: **B** 1939. T 3,174g.
1939 Completed for E & P.
1941 Jan 18: Left Oban, she was routing Hull-New York in ballast.
Jan 20: Torpedoed by *U-94* in the North Atlantic. She was seen to sink in 42 seconds and did not even have time to send out a distress signal. All her crew of 44 were lost. A naval convoy rescue trawler sighted floating wreckage and found an empty lifeboat.

118 PANDORIAN

As 113 except: **B** 1940 Swan, Hunter & Wigham Richardson, Newcastle. **T** 3,146g, 1,306n.
D 359.5/109.57 oa. **E** By builder. **H** F 24/7.31.
1940 March: Completed for E & P.
1963 Jan 10: Sold to T. N. Epiphaniades, Greece. R/n *Kyrakali*.
1964 Bought by Bluesky Corp., Monrovia. R/n *Bluesky*.
1969 Sold to Nereus Maritime Co. Ltd, Cyprus. R/n *Varosi*.
1970 Mar 28: Arrived at Shanghai from Kuwait for scrapping.

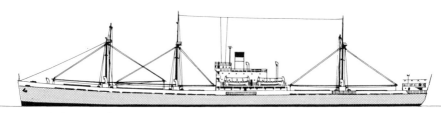

SAMARINA / CITY OF ELY (I), SAMOIS / CITY OF LICHFIELD (I)
SAMBOSTON / CITY OF ROCHESTER, BEN H. MILLER / CITY OF SHREWSBURY,
SAMTORCH / CITY OF STAFFORD

119 SAMARINA / CITY OF ELY (I)

B 1943 Bethlehem Fairfield Corp, Baltimore. **T** 7,258g, 4,473n.
D 441.7/134.63 oa, 423.7/129.14 x 57/17.37 x 34.8/10.61.
E Sgl scr, tpl exp, 2,500 bhp at 76 rpm. 240 psi, 2 wt blrs. 11 kts. By General Machy. Corp, Hamilton, Ohio. **H** Steel. 2 dks.
1943 Launched as *James Blair*. Sept: Completed as *Samarina* for the US War Shipping Administration on bare boat charter to M.O.W.T. (as were all the transferred Liberties) with Westcott & Laurence as managers.
1946 Her charterers renamed Ministry of Transport (M.O.T.).
1947 Acquired by Ellerman & Bucknall. R/n *City of Ely*.
1961 Sold to Trader Line Ltd, London. R/n *Paget Trader*.
1965 Nov 2: Cargo on fire. Put into Singapore. Nov 6: At Singapore.
1966 Jan: Laid up at Hong Kong. Aug: Broken up at Kaohsiung.

120 SAMOIS / CITY OF LICHFIELD (I)

As 119 except: **T** 7,263g, 4,448n. **E** By Worthington Pump and Machinery Corp, Harrison, N. J.
1943 Launched as *Samuel H. Ralston*. Nov: Completed as *Samois*, M.O.W.T. with Westcott & Laurence as managers.
1946 To M.O.T.
1947 Aug: R/n *City of Lichfield* by Ellerman & Bucknall.
1959 Became *Camerona* of Panamanian Oriental Steamship Co; Wheelock, Marden & Co, owners. Panama flag.
1961 R/n *Chee Lee*, Eddie Steamship Co, Keelung.
1963 Owned by the Far Eastern Nav. Corp, Taiwan.
1967 April: Broken up at Kaohsiung.

121 SAMBOSTON / CITY OF ROCHESTER

As 119. **T** 7,265g, 4,453n.
1943 Launched as *Willis J. Abbot*. Dec: Completed as *Samboston* M.O.W.T. with Ellerman Papayanni as managers.
1946 M.O.T. charterers.
1947 Jan: Managed by Ellerman & Bucknall. June: Acquired. R/n *City of Rochester*.
1962 Became *Fotini Xilas* of Sirikari Cia Nav S. A, Piraeus.
1964 R/n *Resolute II* by Cardinal Shipping Corp, Monrovia.
1967 Dec 4: At Kaohsiung and broken up by Kuang I Enterprises.

122 BEN H. MILLER / CITY OF SHREWSBURY

As 119. **T** 7,262g, 4,468n. **E** By Worthington Pump & Machy. Corp, Harrison, N. J.
1943 Dec: Built as *Ben H. Miller* on bareboat charter to M.O.W.T. with E. & P. as managers.
1946 M.O.W.T. became M.O.T.
1947 Acquired. R/n *City of Shrewsbury* by Ellerman & Bucknall.
1959 Apr 30: Sold to Cia de Nav Arcoul, Beirut. R/n *Marucla*.
1969 Broken up in Japan.

123 SAMTORCH / CITY OF STAFFORD
As 119 except: **B** 1944. **T** 7,208g, 4,715n. **E** By Ellicott Mchy. Corp, Baltimore.
1944 May: Completed as *Samtorch* on charter to M.O.W.T. with E. & P. as managers.
1946 To M.O.T.
1947 Acquired by Ellerman. R/n *City of Stafford*. Ellerman & Bucknall managers.
1961 Oct 6: Sold to Stuart Navigation (Bahamas) Ltd., Nassau. R/n *Kuniang*.
1962 Owned by Sygiamore S. S. Co, London. Same name.
1963 Her owners became Sycamore S. S. Co, Hong Kong, of the World-Wide Shipping Group.
1965 Sold to Jupiter Shipping Co, Hong Kong. Same name.
1966 R/n *Prospect* by Trefoil Nav. Inc, Monrovia.
1967 Apr 13: Arrived at Kaohsiung. Broken up.

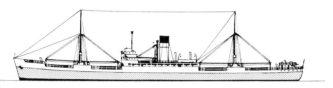

124 ANGLIAN
B 1947 Wm Gray & Co, West Hartlepool. **T** 2,219g, 867n.
D 306.7/93.48 oa, 295/89.9 x 46.2/14.08 x 17.9/5.45.
E Sgl scr, tpl exp + LP turb. 225 psi, 2 sgl blrs. 12 kts. By Central Marine Eng. Wks, West Hartlepool.
H Steel. 1 + shelter dk. F 26/7.92.
1947 June: Delivered to Ellerman & Papayanni Lines. Made one voyage to Alexandria and then chartered to Ellerman's Wilson for the Hull-Sweden service.
1963 Sold to African Coasters (Proprietary) Ltd, Durban. Grindrod, Gersigny & Co. (Pty), R/n *Bulwark*.
1968 Became *Aroma* Amenkroog Marine Corp, Panama.
1970 Sold to Formosa Navigation Inc, r/n *Froma*.
1973 Broken up.

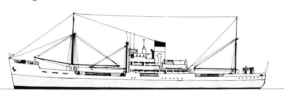

CROSBIAN, DARINIAN, LUCIAN, MERCIAN, PALMELIAN

125 CROSBIAN
B 1947 Wm Gray & Co, West Hartlepool. **T** 1,518g, 647n.
D 272/82.9 oa, 259/78.94 x 42.2/12.86 x 14.9/4.54.
E Tw scr, oil, 2 x 6 cyl by British Polar Diesels, Glasgow. 12 kts.
H Steel. 1 dk. F 30/9.14.
1947 Aug: Delivered to E. & P. All four for Liverpool-Oporto-Lisbon run.
1963 Transferred to the subsidiary company Mossgiel S. S. Co Ltd, John Bruce (Shipping) Co, managers.
1967 Aug 29: Sold for about £40,000 to Davao Reawood Corp, Davao, Philippines. R/n *Mabuhay*.
1978 Sold to Solid Shipping Corp, Philippines. Same name.
1980 Nov 11: Delivered at Manila for breaking up by Mascor Marketing Corp, Makati.

126 DARINIAN
As 125 except: **B** 1947 Henry Robb Ltd, Leith. **T** 1,533g, 644n. **D** 273/83.3 oa.
1947 Nov: Delivered to E. & P. Also operated for Westcott & Laurence out of London.
1970 June 24: Sold to Cia. Naviera Evdelia S. A. Panama. R/n *Kostandis Fotinos*.
1971 Sold to Rosade Lines S. A. L. Lebanon. R/n *Tania Maria*.
1973 Became *Nektarios*, Koutourada Shipping Co Ltd, Cyprus.
1978 Apr 16: Wrecked on Perim Island out of Aden and abandoned. 12 crew were picked up by the Indian freighter *Jag Deesh*, Great Eastern Shipping, Bombay.

127 LUCIAN
As 125 except: **B** 1948. **T** 1,516g, 647n.
1948 Feb: Completed. Had a white hull at one stage. Served also London-Oporto.
1964 May 14: Sold at London to Seaways Inc, Panama. R/n *Amorgos*. Her first voyage was Liverpool-Ellesmere Port-Piraeus.

1970 Sold to Amorgos Shipping Co S. A., Panama. Later transferred to the Greek flag. Same name.
1974 Owned by Ligeas Shipping Co, Greece. Same name.
1975 Her owners were Viadoro Cia. Naviera S. A. Greece. Sold to Antilles Marine Cargo Ltd, Liberia still as *Amorgos*.
1976 Owned by Kadi Cia. Nav S. A., Greece. R/n *Yashoo*. Still with a grey hull and only the white band removed from her funnel.
1979 Sold to Crystal Star Cia. Naviera S. A., Greece. Same name.
1986 Broken up.

128 MERCIAN
As 125 except: **B** 1948 Swan, Hunter & Wigham Richardson, Newcastle. **T** 1,517g, 657n. **H** F 28/8.53.
1948 March: Delivered to Westcott & Laurence Line Ltd. Later transferred to E. & P. White hulled at one period.
1970 Aug 18: Sold to Canopus Shipping S. A. Famagusta. R/n *Rinoula*.
1971 Owned by Rigel Shipping Co Ltd, Famagusta; same name.
1974 Sold to Kamara Cia Nav S. A., Panama. Same name.
1975 Became *Gabriella* of Adnamar S. A., Panama.
1977 Sold to Caobamar S. A., Panama. R/n *Donatella 1*.
1978 Owned by Rotary Traffic S.p.A.di Nav., Italy. R/n *Stabia 1*.
1979 Jan 4: Inbound from Bahia, Brazil, she was driven onto the rocks at Salerno during a storm and became a total loss. All saved.

129 PAMELIAN/PALMELIAN
As 125 except: **B** 1948 Henry Robb & Co, Leith. **T** 1,535g, 644n. **D** 273/83.21 oa.
1948 March: Launched by error as *Pamelian*. Completed for E. & P. as *Palmelian*. Ice strengthened.
1970 July 11: Sold for £30,000; arrived at Bilbao and broken up by Algonso & Fernadez.

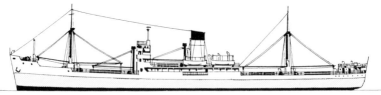

EGYPTIAN (IV) / CITY OF LEICESTER (III), IONIAN (II) / CITY OF DURHAM (II), PATRICIAN, VENETIAN / VENETIAN (II) / CITY OF LEEDS (II), SICILIAN, GRECIAN

130 EGYPTIAN (IV) / CITY OF LEICESTER (III)
B 1947 J. & L. Thompson & Sons, Sunderland. **T** 3,607g, 1,452n.
D 373/113.69 oa, 356.5/108.56 x 50.9/15.51 x 21.7/6.61.
E Sgl scr, 3 stm turbs LP and MP sgl, HP dbl reduction geared, 3,775 shp. 12½ kts. By Wallsend Slipway Co, Wallsend.
H Steel. 1 + shelter dk. F 29/8.84. C 5 hold/hatches. 273,711/7,750.6cu g. + 10,8603,310cu ref.
1947 Jan: Delivered to Ellerman & Papayanni Lines.
1964 Renamed *City of Leicester;* same owners.
1965 Sold to Gardenia Shipping Co, S. A., Piraeus. R/n *Gardenia*.
1966 Became *Chung Hsin* of the Great Pacific Nav. Co, Panama. Resold to Chung Lien Navigation Co, S. A., Panama.
1967 Broken up at Taiwan.

131 IONIAN (II) / CITY OF DURHAM (II)
As 130. **T** 3596g, 1,442n.
1947 March: Completed for E. & P.
1964 Replaced *Anatolian* (138). Renamed *City of Durham*, same owners. Transferred to Indian services. Oct 20: Sold for £48,000, R/n *Angelica N.* by Eurata Shipping Co, S. A. Greece.
1968 Owned by Theresia Ltda, S. A., Panama. R/n *Eliza*.
1971 Feb 17: Grounded at Abijan and sustained severe bottom corrugation. The voyage continued to Amsterdam where the damage was assessed as beyond economical repair. Sold to Eisen and Metall. A. G. Hamburg. Mar 29: Arrived at Hamburg for breaking up.

132 PATRICIAN
As 130. **T** 3,604g, 1,457n.
1947 June: Delivered to E. & P.
1963 July 8: Sank in the Strait of Gibraltar after collision with the American Liberty ship *Santa Emilia*, Liberty Nav. & Trading Co, Wilmington.

133 VENETIAN (II) / CITY OF LEEDS (II)

As 130. **T** 3,578g, 1,433n.

1947 August: Completed for Westcott & Laurence, managed by E. & P.

1964 Renamed *City of Leeds*. Transferred to Ellerman & Bucknall.

1965 May 7: Sold to Orizon Shipping Co Ltd, Monrovia. R/n *Catrina P,* also recorded as *Katrina P*. Her owners then became Papank Shipping Co S. A.

1966 Became *Transrodopi III*. One of four vessels operated by Transrodopi S. A., Piraeus but this ship was owned by Kyriacos Shipping Corp.

1968 All four Transrodopi ships were sold to Navigation Maritime Bulgare, Varna, and given names commencing with 'A'. R/n *Acrux*.

1970 Renamed *Silistra*. Same owners.

1975 Sold to Brodespas for scrap. Dec 28: Arrived at Split.

1976 June 30: Breaking up commenced.

134 SICILIAN

As 130 except: **B** 1948. Ailsa S. B. Co, Troon. **T** 3,351g, 1,426n.
D 361/110.03 oa, 346.1/105.49 x 50.1/15.27 x 20.8/6.34. **E** Differed in that the turbine was LP only and dbl reduction geared through a hydraulic coupling. By builder. **H** F 28/8.53.

1948 Oct: Completed for E. & P., a slightly smaller member of the class. Identical except that all her deck vents were mushroom not cowled. Also her funnel was half the white band thickness taller.

1964 Nov 6: Sold to Bluesea Corp, Monrovia. R/n *Bluesea*.

1970 Owned by Nereus Maritime Co Ltd, same name.

1971 July 15: Left Singapore Roads for Shanghai and breaking up.

135 GRECIAN

As 130 but a sister to *Sicilian*. **B** 1949 Ailsa S. B. Co, Troon. **T** 3,347g, 1,517n.

1949 June: Delivered to E. & P.

1966 Feb 9: Sold to Astropropicio Cia Nav S. A., R/n *Alexandra*.

1969 May 26: Arrived at Split for breaking up by Brodospas.

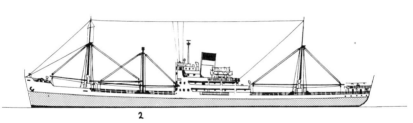

2

ANDALUSIAN (IV) / CITY OF ELY (I), MALTASIAN / CITY OF NORWICH (II)

136 ANDALUSIAN (IV) / CITY OF ELY (II) / ANDALUSIAN

B 1950 Wm Gray & Co, West Hartlepool. **T** 3,913g, 1,964n, 5,330dwt.
D 374.8/114.24 oa, 360/109.73 x 53.1/16.18 x 21.1/6.43.
E Sgl scr, tpl exp with LP turb dbl reduction geared by hydraulic coupling, 225 psi, 2 sgl blrs. 13 kts. By Central Marine Eng Wks, West Hartlepool.
H Steel. 1 + shelter dk. F 30/9.14.

1950 June: Completed for E. & P.; a new look design that spread over nine ships before engines - aft took over.

1962 Renamed *City of Ely*. Same managers.

1964 Reverted to *Andalusian* without further change.

1966 Aug 28: Sold to Aghia Barbara Cia Nav S. A., Panama. R/n *Capetan Andreas P*. She was later transferred to Ezkos Maritime Technical Co, Panama.

1973 Jan: Disabled at Constanza by a boiler-room fire and broken up there.

137 MALTASIAN / CITY OF NORWICH (II) / MALTASIAN

As 136. **T** 3,910g, 1,955n.

1950 Sept: Delivered to Westcott & Laurence with E. & P. as managers.

1962 Renamed *City of Norwich;* same managers. Both City and Hall routes.

1964 Reverted to *Maltasian*.

1967 Jan 25: Sold for about £100,000 to Kallisto Cia. Maritima S. A., Panama. R/n *Capetan Christos P*.

1975 Sold to Conga Marine Nav S. A., Greece. R/n *Aias* for voyage to the breakers.

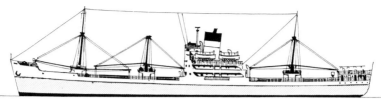

ANATOLIAN (II) / CITY OF DURHAM (III), CASTILIAN (III) / CITY OF PETERBOROUGH,
LANCASTRIAN (II) / CITY OF LEICESTER (II), ALMERIAN (II) / CITY OF LEEDS

138 ANATOLIAN (II) / CITY OF DURHAM (III)

B 1955 Wm. Gray & Co, West Hartlepool. **T** 3,799g, 1,637n, 5,300dwt.
D 376.9/114.88 oa x 53.3/16.25 x 22/6.71.
E Sgl scr, tpl exp + LP turb dbl reduc geared with hydraulic coupling, 225 psi, 2 sgl blrs. By Central Marine Eng. Wks.
H Steel. 1 + shelter dk. Crew 40.
1955 Nov: Delivered to E. & P. The class was soon outmoded by the oil engines of the sixties: economical and needed about 20 less crew.
1963 R/n *City of Durham;* same managers. Hall Line's Indian service.
1964 Reverted to *Anatolian.* Her place was taken by *Ionian* (131).
1966 Apr: Chartered to Cunard S. S. Co for the Liverpool-Chicago service. R/n *Ascania.* E. & P. remained managers. Sept: Reverted to *Anatolian.*
1968 The same arrangement was repeated for Cunard. Again r/n *Ascania.* Dec 11: As *Anatolian* sold to M. J. Lemos & Co. (Agents), London. R/n *Agia Sophia.* Owned by Gulf Shipping Corp, Cyprus. Replaced by *Mediterranian* (149).
1970 Owned by Wavecrest Shipping Co, Famagusta.
1971 R/n *Fulka* by Millwala & Sons (England) Ltd, London. Pakistan owners.
1974 Became *Khalid,* Arabian Gulf Trading Co, Sharjah, United Arab Emirates. The first ship to hoist the Sharjah ensign.
1975 Sold to Sharjah Shipping Co Ltd, Sharjah. R/n *Gulf Unity,* her ninth and final renaming.
1977 Owned by Gulf Shipping Lines, Sharjah. Same name.
1978 Feb 19: At Gadani Beach for breaking up.

139 CASTILIAN (III) / CITY OF PETERBOROUGH

As 138 except: **B** Alex Stephen & Sons, Glasgow. **T** 3,803g, 1,619n.
D 377.2/114.97. **E** As *Anatolian.*
1955 July: Completed for Westcott & Laurence with E. & P. as managers.
1963 R/n *City of Peterborough.*
1964 Reverted to *Castilian.*
1966 Chartered to Cunard for the summer Great Lakes service. R/n *Arabia.* E. & P. managers.
1967 Off charter. R/n *Castilian.*
1971 Feb 15: Sold to Maldivian Nationals Trading Corp (Ceylon) Ltd, Colombo. R/n *Maldive Freedom,* Maldives Shipping Ltd, managers.
1977 Jan 31: Aground enroute Aqaba-Straits of Tiran. Feb 6: Refloated. Mar 17: Arrived Karachi for breaking up. May: Scrapped at Gadani Beach.

140 LANCASTRIAN (II) / CITY OF LEICESTER (II)

As 138 except **B** 1956. **T** 3,799g, 1,641n.
1956 Feb: Delivered to E. & P.
1962 R/n *City of Leicester.* The anticipatory press announced the change as *City of Lancaster* and then corrected it. Hall Line routes.
1964 Reverted to *Lancastrian.*
1966 Apr: Chartered to Cunard S. S. Co, R/n *Alsatia.* Oct: *Lancastrian,* off charter.
1969 Apr 9: Sold to M. J. Lemos & Co (Agents), London. R/n *Theokrates,* owned by Ionian Shipping Co Ltd, Famagusta, Cyprus.
1974 R/n *Khorfaken* by Sharjah Sea Transport Co, Sharjah, U.A.E.
1975 Feb 2: Driven ashore in a gale at Sharjah. Became a total loss.

141 ALMERIAN (II) / CITY OF LEEDS (I)

As 138 except: **B** 1956 Caledon S. B. & E. Co, Dundee. **T** 3,649g, 1,519n.
D 377.1/114.94. **E** As *Anatolian.*
1956 Oct: Completed for Ellerman & Bucknall with E. & P. as managers; the final steam ship for Ellerman.
1962 R/n *City of Leeds.*

1964 Reverted to *Almerian.*
1966 Chartered to Cunard S. S. Co, r/n *Assyria.* Great Lakes service. Oct: Reverted to *Almerian.*
1967 Again used by Cunard. R/n *Asia.* Autumn: reverted to *Almerian.*
1969 Dec 18: Sold to Galaction Shipping Co Ltd, Famagusta. R/n *Theokletus.*
1974 Sold to Marcoroma Cia Naviera, Panama. Same name. May 5: Left Singapore Roads and broken up in China.

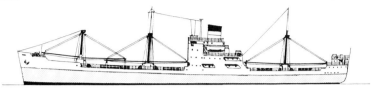

FLORIAN, FLAMINIAN (IV) / CITY OF IZMIR

142 FLORIAN
B 1955 Wm. Gray & Co, West Hartlepool. **T** 3,134g, 1,126n.
D 351.3/107.08 oa, 325/99.06 x 52.3/15.94 x 20.3/6.19.
E Sgl scr, oil. 8 cyls 2S.SA, Clark-Sulzer, 3,850 bhp. 13½ kts. By Sulzer, Winterthur.
H Steel. 1 + shelter dk. F 31/9.45. P 26/7.92. C 211,385/5,985.8cu g + 23,590/668cu ref. 12 derricks.
1955 May: Delivered to E & P.
1956 May: In dock at Liverpool when a fire broke out in her cotton cargo; she suffered buckled deck plates. Dec: She had another fire, also cotton, in the same hold; again had to have the deck plating renewed.
1971 Dec 20: Sold to Maldive Shipping Ltd, Male. R/n *Maldive Loyalty.*
1982 Oct 5: Arrived at Gadani Beach for breaking up.

143 FLAMINIAN (IV) / CITY OF IZMIR
As 142 except: **B** 1956 Henry Robb & Co, Leith. **T** 3,100g, 1,115n.
E Sulzer type fitted by Geo. Clark & N. E. Marine (Sunderland) Ltd.
1956 Feb: Entered service for Westcott and Laurence.
1965 Sept: Collided off Gibraltar with the French tanker *Floreal,* Soc. des Transports Maritimes Petroliers. *Flaminian* was set on fire by burning fuel but it did not enter the holds and was extinguished.
1969 Transferred to Ellerman & Papayanni management.
1973 Jan 1: All ships were moved into Ellerman City Liners Ltd.
1974 R/n *City of Izmir* when all the fleet were given 'City' names.
1975 April: Became *Climax Pearl,* Climax Shipping Corp, Maldives.
1981 R/n *Maldive Pearl;* same company but owned by Maldive Shipping Ltd.
1984 Apr 3: Arrived at Gadani Beach and scrapped there.

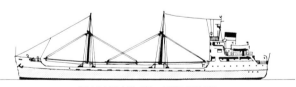

MALATIAN (II), CATANIAN

144 MALATIAN (II)
B 1958 Henry Robb & Co, Leith. **T** 1,407g, 597n.
D 269.9/82.26 oa, 250/76.2 x 42.9/13.06 x 14.8/4.51.
E Sgl scr, oil; 7 cyl Sulzer, 2S.SA, 2,100 bhp. 12½ kts. By G. Clark & N. E. Marine (Sunderland) Ltd, Sunderland.
H Steel. 2 dks. F 25/7.62. P 68/20.73.
1958 May: Completed for Westcott & Laurence with E & P as managers.
1969 Transferred to E & P ownership.
1971 Nov 18: Became *Maldive Victory,* Maldive Shipping Ltd, Male.
1981 Feb 13: Inbound from Singapore struck a reef while entering Male harbour and sank in shallow water. Total constructive loss.

145 CATANIAN
As 144. **T** 1,408g. **H** 1 + shelter dk.
1958 Aug: Completed for E & P.
1972 Feb 14: Sold for about £80,000 to Pacific Ocean Lines Ltd, Male, Maldive Islands. R/n *Ocean Glory.*

1977 Sold to Gala Shipping Ltd, Male. R/n *Ocean Glory No 6*. They owned no ships numbered 1-5.
1986 Renamed *Ocean Glory;* owned by Century Shipping Corp, Panama.
1987 Jan 1: Arrived at Gadani Beach for demolition.

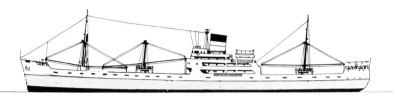

ARCADIAN (II) / CITY OF FAMAGUSTA
146 ARCADIAN (II)/CITY OF FAMAGUSTA
B 1960 Henry Robb & Co, Leith. **T** 3,402g, 1,419n.
D 366.9/111.83 oa, 340/103.63 x 54.4/16.58 x 21/6.4.
E Sgl scr, oil; 7 cyl Sulzer 2S.SA, 3,500 bhp. 14 kts. By Fairfield S.B.Co., Glasgow.
H Steel. 1 + shelter dk + pt 3rd. F 30/9.14. P 29/8.84. 5 holds/hatches.
1960 July: Delivered to E & P.
1973 Jan 1: Transferred with all ships to Ellerman City Liners.
1974 R/n *City of Famagusta.*
1977 May: Sold with *City of Limassol (294)* to Associated Levant Lines S.A.L., Beirut, T Gargour & Fils. R/n *Batroun.*
1986 Dec 18: Arrived at Gadani Beach for scrapping.

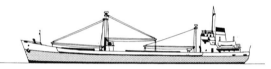

147 CORTIAN
B 1962 A/B Lodose Varv, Lodose, Sweden. **T** 537g, 279n.
D 234.3/71.41 oa, 213.8/70.65 x 34.2/10.42 x 12.55/3.82.
E Sgl scr, oil; 8 cyl 4S.SA, 1,200 bhp. 11 kts. By Motoren Werke, Mannheim.
H Steel. 1 + shelter dk. F 27/8.23.
1962 Apr: Completed as *Cortia*, Erik Kekonius, Skarhamn, Sweden.
1966 Managed by Lars Johansson, Skarhamn. Acquired by E & P. R/n *Cortian.*
1968 Transferred to Mossgiel S.S.Co., John Bruce (Shipping) Co. as managers. Same name. She remained on E & P berthings out of Glasgow.
1971 Sold to Capt. Folke Patriksson, Sweden. Reverted to *Cortia;* she was then owned by Anders F. Partriksson Partrederi.
1974 Sold to Cala d'Olivio S.p.A., Italy. R/n *Austerity*. Converted into a livestock carrier.
1978 R/n *Bruno Alphina* by Neptune S.p.A., Palermo.
1986 Became *Siba Foggia* for SIBA S.p.A., Brescia. Siba= Societe Importazione Bestiame Allevamento. Owned by Balzarini, Corvi & Cia.
1989 Still in service.

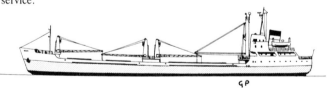

GP

148 ATHENIAN (II) / CITY OF VALETTA
B 1966 Henry Robb & Co, Leith. **T** 2,702g, 1,432n.
D 307.9/93.84 oa, 282.1/85.98 x 45.7/13.93 x 22/6.71.
E Sgl scr, oil; 6 cyl 4S.SA, 2,580 bhp. 13 kts. 14 kts. By Mirrlees National Ltd, Stockport. Controllable pitch propeller.
H Steel. 2 dks. F 36/10.97. P 69/21.03.
1966 July: Built for Westcott & Laurence with E & P as managers.
1973 Jan 1: To Ellerman City Liners.
1974 R/n *City of Valetta.*
1980 Sold to Pacific International Lines (Pte), Singapore. R/n *Kota Jade.*
1989 Still in service.

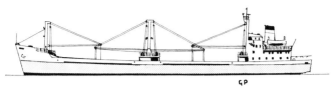

149 MEDITERRANIAN / CITY OF ISTANBUL
B 1968 Henry Robb & Co, Leith. **T** 1,460g, 730n, 2,600 dwt.
D 309.2/94 oa, 280/85.34 x 47.9/14.6 x 16.7/5.09.
E Sgl scr, oil; 6 cyl 4S.SA, 2,580 bhp. 13 kts. By Mirrlees National Ltd, Stockport. Controllable pitch propeller.
H Steel. 2 dks. F 40/12.19. 2 holds/hatches. C 190/600/58,094.9 cu g.
1968 Oct: Completed for E & P. Note the spelling of the name. She was the last ship to be built for Ellerman & Papayanni.
1973 Jan 1: Transferred to Ellerman City Liners.
1974 R/n *City of Istanbul*. E & P managers.
1978 Became *Fenchurch*, Gracechurch Shipping Ltd, Newcastle.
1983 Sold to Angelopoulos & Sarlis, Greece. R/n *Pelor*.
1989 Still in service.

WET-BOAT CHARTERS WHICH WERE GIVEN ELLERMAN & PAPAYANNI NAMES AND LIVERY
(Although some were handled out of Hull by Ellerman's Wilson)
ESTREMADURIAN
B 1958. **T** 1,921g. Ex-*Varodd*, Nils Naesheim A/S.
1968 Chartered by E & P. Liverpool-Oporto. Carried 56 containers. Was the first vessel to berth at Gladstone Dock Container Terminal.
1970 Off charter; reverted to *Varodd*.

IBERIAN, EVORIAN, ITALIAN

IBERIAN
B 1964. **T** 455g. **B** as *Yuki Hansen* for Knud Hansen A/S, Copenhagen.
1966 R/n *Iberian*. Hull-Oporto.

EVORIAN
B 1963. **T** 455g. Built as *Karin Smits* for M. Smits, Netherlands.
1969 R/n *Evorian* on charter. Hull-Oporto trade. Reverted to *Karin Smits* off charter.

ITALIAN
B 1963. **T** 454g. **B** as *Dita Smits* (II) for M. Smits.
1968 R/n *Italian*.
1971 Off charter; became *Duel*, H. Rasmussen, Denmark.

GRECIAN
B 1966. **T** 1,450g. **B** as *Andromeda* for M. Moermaus, Netherlands.
1969 R/n *Grecian* on 5 year charter.
1974 Off charter; became *Sela*, Hafskip H/f Island, Iceland.

MARMORIAN
B 1966 **T** 1,174g. **B** as *Marmorhav* for Hvide & Schjott, Norway.
1967 R/n *Marmorian* on charter.
1968 Off charter; reverted to *Marmorhav*.

ANGLIAN
B 1966. **T** 499g. **B** as *Wilhelm S* for Tim Schepers & Sohne, Germany.
1968 R/n *Anglian*. Hull-Oporto.
1970 Reverted to *Wilhelm S* off charter.

SILVIAN
B 1956. **T** 1,877g. B as *Transsylvania*. **1971** R/n *Stahleck*, D.D.G. 'Hansa'.
1971 R/n *Silvian* on charter.
1972 Off charter. Became *Kathy*, Katrien N.V., Netherlands Antilles.

SEA CONTAINERS INC. DEMISE CHARTERS

MINHO (II) / CITY OF MILAN (II), TAGUS (III) / CITY OF LISBON (I)
TAMEGA / CITY OF GENOA (II), TORMES / CITY OF OPORTO,
TUA / CITY OF FLORENCE (IV), TIBER / CITY OF NAPLES (II),
TRONTO / CITY OF LA SPEZIA, MONDEGO / CITY OF VENICE (IV)

150 **MINHO (II) / CITY OF MILAN (II)**
B 1969 A. Vuijk & Zonen, Capelle, Rotterdam. **T** 1,578g, 892n.
D 279.9/85.31 oa, 258.7/78.85 x 45.1/13.75 x 13.7/4.17.
E Sgl scr, oil; 6 cyl, 4S.SA, 3,200 bhp at 512 rpm drg to 275 rpm. 13 kts. By N. V. Werkspoor, Amsterdam. Lips type controllable pitch propeller.
H Steel. 2 dks. F 23/7. Raised fore dk 49/14.93. 2 holds, 7 pontoon hatches. 120-150 20ft/6.09 containers (48 below and 72 on deck).
1969 Oct 10: Launched. Dec: One of the 'Hustler' Class of 17, of which 15 were built in the Netherlands and two in Spain, owned by Sea Containers Inc., New York, proprietor J. B. Sherwood, and placed on demise charter with E & P, General Steam Nav Co. and Currie.
1970 Eight bare-boat contracted to E & P. Placed on Liverpool-Oporto route. Crewed by Ellerman.
1974 R/n *City of Milan* when all the fleet were given 'city' names.
1978 The delivery of the five ships of the larger and faster *City of Plymouth* class (301) released the eight 'Hustler' class which all came off charter contract; they were released back to Sea Containers Inc. as each charter contract ended although the owners took back the unexpired portions of some; viz 151.
1979 Sold. R/n *Eco Mondego* by Ope Investment & Marine Co. S.A., Panama.
1989 Still in service.

151 **TAGUS (III) / CITY OF LISBON (I)**
As 150 except:
B 1970 Astilleros del Cadagua, Bilbao.
1970 Jan 7: Launched. March: On charter to E & P.
1972 She was the first ship to berth at Seaforth container terminal.
1974 R/n *City of Lisbon*. When Ellerman Container Line obtained the contract to carry the parcel mail UK-Lisbon she became the first to fly the Royal Mail pennant.
1979 Became *Cape Hustler*, Sea Containers Inc., registered at Hamilton, Bermuda. Based South Africa.
1983 Apr 9: Sustained engine damage enroute Durban-Cape Town. Put into Port Elizabeth and up for sale 'as is'.
1985 Purchased by Bona Mercantile Co. Ltd, Honduras. R/n *Cape*.
1989 Still in service.

152 **TAMEGA / CITY OF GENOA (II)**
As 150 except: **B** 1970.
1970 Sept: Completed. On charter to E & P.
1974 R/n *City of Genoa*.
1982 Became *Hustler Ebro*, Sea Containers Inc, Bermuda flag.
1983 R/n *Bermudiana*. Same owners.
1989 Still in service.

153 **TORMES / CITY OF OPORTO**
As 150 except: **B** 1970 Zaarndamsche Schips. Maats., Amsterdam.
1970 April: Launched. June: Delivered.
1974 R/n *City of Oporto*.
1980 Joined her sister *City of Milan* (150) and became *Eco Guadiana* with Ope.
1989 Still in service.

154 TUA / CITY OF FLORENCE (IV)
As 150 except: **B** 1970. **T** 1,599g, 909n.
1970 Aug 18: Launched. Nov: Delivered.
1974 R/n *City of Florence.*
1983 Oct: Became *Hustler Fal,* Sea Containers Inc., Laid up at Manchester.
1984 Sold to Seaco Holdings, Cyprus. R/n *Confrigo 1.*
1989 Still in service.

155 TIBER / CITY OF NAPLES (II)
As 150 except: **B** 1970 Zaarndamsche Schips. Maats, Amsterdam.
1970 Oct 2: Launched. Dec: On demise charter to E & P.
1974 R/n *City of Naples.*
1979 Reverted to *Tiber,* Sea Containers Ltd, Liverpool. Sold to Atlantic Clipper Ltd, Cayman Islands; r/n *Atlantic Clipper*
1984 Sold to Hyde Shipping Corp, Cayman Islands. R/n *Hybur Clipper.*
1986 Owned by Bay Island Shipping Ltd, Georgetown, Grand Caymen.
1989 Still in service.

156 TRONTO / CITY OF LA SPEZIA
As 150 except: **B** 1971. **T** 1,559g, 909n.
1971 Laid down as *Tigris.* Oct 16: Launched. Jan (1972): Delivered.
1974 R/n *City of La Spezia.*
1979 Reverted to *Tronto* and Sea Containers Chartering Ltd, Liverpool.
Sold to Atlantic Intrepid Ltd, r/n *Atlantic Intrepid,* Cayman Islands.
1984 Sold to Bahia Shipping Ltd, Grand Cayman. R/n *Hybur Intrepid.*
1989 Still in service.

157 MONDEGO / CITY OF VENICE (IV)
As 150 except: **B** 1972 Astilleros de Atlantico, Santander. **T** 1,559g, 909n.
1972 June 10: Launched. Dec: Delivered.
1974 R/n *City of Venice* (IV).
1980 Reverted to owner's Sea Container Chartering Ltd. Became *Atlantic Resolute,* Sea Containers Ltd, Hamilton, Bermuda.
1982 Her owners were again Sea Containers Chartering Ltd, Liverpool. R/n *Hustler Indus,* chartered to Sea Containers Inc. Laid up in the USA then placed on the Jacksonville-Bermuda container service.
1989 Still in service.

WESTCOTT & LAURENCE

1857 Stephenos Xenos, formerly a Piraeus general shipping merchant who, a few years earlier, had established himself in the Greek ship handling business in London, now formed the Greek & Oriental Steam Navigation Company. His financial partner was George Lascaridi who was domiciled in London as a banker and shipowner. To establish the G. & O.S.N. Co. Lascaridi contributed his steamers *Aleppo* and *Beirut* while Xenos medium term chartered two vessels *James Brown* and *Britannia*.

1858 Although profits were good Xenos fell out with George Lascaridi because his handling charges were unrealistically high. He was, clearly, trying to make a killing.

1859 Stephenos Xenos sought the assistance of the bankers Overend, Gurney & Co to buy out Lascaridi which he did and then went on to borrow money with which he extended his fleet to no fewer than 24 ships all of which were pledged to the bank against the loans; the terms of which turned out to be too high.

1863 Xenos was bankrupt and the ships reverted to Overend, Gurney who then acquired the Greek & Oriental S.N. Co for £2,500. It so happened that one of the Xenos captains was George Westcott, of the *Admiral Miaoulis*, then aged 33. He was in his ship at Malta, where he was well known for his shrewd integrity, when the news broke. With the backing of a Valetta businessman named Gollcher the ship was bunkered and returned to London where Westcott set up in business and was joined by another Xenos employee Robert Simpson Houseden. They established themselves as Westcott & Houseden and operated as ship charterers. Westcott captained and Houseden managed the business end. Their efforts were continuously successful and the number of ships which they berthed grew annually.

By way of a historical note: Overend & Gurney changed the name of G & OSN to Black Sea & Levant Steam Navigation Company and continued to operate the ships which they had inherited to the area in the title. The mistake that had been made was that the Greeks were the principal traders in the area whereas the company name was Turkish orientated. Within two years the whole concern had gone.

1867 Westcott & Houseden purchased their first steamer the *Harriet Agnes*.

1869 To manage their Continental business Westcott & Flint was established at Antwerp.

1871 Robert Houseden died. His place in the partnership was taken by Charles James Laurence and the name was changed to Westcott & Laurence.

1879 The *Harriet Agnes* was replaced by the steamer *Rhone* whose captain was the founder's son John Richard Westcott.

1889 Charles Laurence died and his place was taken by George Westcott's eldest son William George Westcott. John Richard was also made a partner but his income derived from his ownership of *Rhone*.

1901 May: George Westcott died. The fleet now stood at nine vessels:
Avoca (46)
Cedardene (45)
Gulf of Suez (43)
Joshua Nicholson (44)
Orchis (40)
Orestes (48)
Perim (42)
Plymothian (47)
and *Tenedos* (41)

Dec: These were sold to John Ellerman thereby giving him his London-Mediterranean trade with which to complement the Liverpool based ships. The arrangement was that he be Chairman of Westcott & Laurence Ltd. but that the management of the fleet was to remain in London untouched. An arrangement which worked extremely well over the years.

WESTCOTT & LAURENCE — EARLY SHIPS

158 **HARRIET AGNES**
B 1865 Sweden. **T** 624g 473n.
D 195/59.44 x 26/7.92 x 15.2/4.63.
E Sgl scr 2 cyl comp inv. 120 nhp. 9½ kts.
H Iron 3 masts F 19/5.79 P 102/31.1.
1865 Built.
1867 Acquired by Westcott & Houseden. Their first ship.
1878 Owned by W. G. Westcott.
1879 Sold to R. Fell, junior, London.
1886 The final entry in Lloyd's Register.

RHONE, SCIENCE

159 **RHONE**
B 1868 W. Pile & Co Sunderland. **T** 1,343g 868n.
D 249.6/76.07 x 30.1/9.17 x 17.6/5.36.
E Sgl scr 2 cyl simple.
H Iron. 1 + spar dk.
1868 Feb: Launched as *Rhone* (as drawn) for the Ryde Line, (Ryde & Co), London. London (Millwall Docks)-Antwerp-Falmouth-Rio de Janeiro-Montevideo-Buenos Aires service.
1871 Lengthened as above. Compounded by Millwall Dock Eng.
Wks, London. 200 nhp, 56 psi. 11 kts.
1879 Acquired by Westcott & Laurence; same name. Mediterranean service.
1898 Sold to Soc. Anon. Belge de Nav. a Vap. Schaldis, Antwerp with De Clerck & Van Hemelryk as managers.
1904 Sold to G. Lauro, Naples. Same name.
1906 Sold to L & G Agarinis, Venice. Broken up in the same year.

160 **SCIENCE**
Sister to *Rhone*. **T** 1,348g 873n.
1868 March: Launched as *Richard Cobden* for the Ryde Line.
1871 Lengthened and compounded like her sister.
1874 Her terminal port was extended via the Straits of Magellan to Valparaiso.
1876 Became *Vidal Sala* owned by Sala y Vidal, Barcelona.
1876 R/n *Lys* by Cie. Gantoise de Nav., Ghent.
1889 Purchased by Westcott & Laurence. R/n *Science*.
1899 Mar 26: Sunk in a collision of Cape St Vincent.

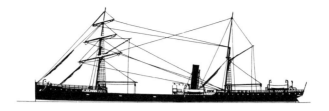

161 **JUAN**
B 1864 A. Leslie & Co Hebburn-on-Tyne. **T** 1,585g, 1,020n.
D 270.6/82.48 x 33.1/10.09 x 23.1/7.04.
E Sgl scr 2 cyl comp inv, 200 nhp, 30 psi. 10 kts. By Maudsley, Son & Field, London.
H Iron. F 47/14.3 P 92/28.04. Barquentine rig.
1864: Built as *Galileo* (I) for Lamport & Holt, Liverpool. Traded as the Liverpool, Brazil and River Plate Nav. Co.
1869 Sold to T. H. Jackson & Co, Liverpool. R/n *Juan* (Pronounced Jewan not Hwan).
1874 Purchased by J. Jack & Co Liverpool re-engined as above. On charter thereafter.
1878 Sold to J. B. Palmer, London.
1882 Owned by Wm. Banks, London. South American service.
1884 Purchased by T. A. Hinton, London. still as *Juan*.
1888 Acquired by Westcott & Laurence. Same name.
1898 Sold to H. Diedrichsen, Kiel, who traded along the China coast from an office in Hong Kong. Same funnel: black.
1898 Aug 26: Left Hong Kong for Kiaochow and posted missing.

MONTGOMERIE & WORKMAN

1849 Captain Alexander Greenhorne, one of the Allan Line masters, met in Montreal, and became friends with Edmonstone Montgomerie where he was a partner in Edmonstone, Allan & Co shipping merchants. Greenhorne was also a relative of the George Smith & Sons family and he and they were also related by marriage to the Allans.

When the Smiths decided to appoint a permanent London agent it was suggested that 'being family' Greenhorne and Montgomerie might take up the appointment; which they did. They were encouraged to indulge in every facet of the business including ship owning with the proviso that it be out of London and that overseas handling be with Smith's agents. Indeed George Smith looked upon the London office as a City line offshoot and took shares in some of the vessels managed by Greenhorne & Montgomerie. The principal area of trade, however, was Canada with which both men had had wide experience.

1855 Ship owning commenced based on the 64ths system with themselves also as brokers, insuring agents and managers. *City of Quebec* was one ship operated by the partners and Smiths had a share in her but she was not a part of their Glasgow based fleet; nor does she occur in their fleet lists.

1865 The sailing ships owned or managed were mainly 'Dukes': *Abercorn, Argyll, Athole, Connaught, Hamilton & Rothesay.*

1866 Another City, *City of Hamilton,* indicated another close link with George Smith & Sons but once again she was not one of their ships even though they had an investment in her.

1877 Alexander Greenhorne died. Another 'family' nominee took his place and the advent of Henry Workman produced Montgomerie & Workman.

1901 When John Ellerman took over the City Line Montgomerie & Workman remained the London agents and went about their business as before. JRE introduced steamships into the fleet.

1913 The firm became Montgomerie & Workman Ltd with Ellerman nominee directors added to the board. On Dec 31 City Line took over the limited company as a wholly owned subsidiary and appointed William E. Montgomerie and Robert A. Workman to manage the London office as Montgomerie & Workman.

1920 The London office was amalgamated into that of the City Line but ships were still registered in the name of Montgomerie & Workman Ltd.

1936 Jan: Shipowning ceased with the transfer of *City of Auckland* (465), *City of Bagdad* (261), *City of Hankow* (413), *City of Oran* (259) and *Volturno* (76) to Ellerman Lines Ltd with operating management vested in their constituent firms.

MONTGOMERIE & GREENHORNE
MONTGOMERIE & WORKMAN
Early ships

\ Sister to *City of Manchester* (179)

162 CITY OF QUEBEC
B 1855 Robert Steele, Greenock. **T** 729g, 708n.
D 184.4/56.2 x 30.6/9.33 x 20.1/6.13. **H** Iron. 2 dks. F 22/6.7. P 29/8.84.
1855 June: Completed for Montgomerie & Greenhorne; their first ship. She worked, virtually, as a member of George Smith's 'City' line.
1877 Her owners became Montgomerie & Workman.
1895 Sold to Berneaud & Cia, Para, Brazil. Hulked.

---

163 CITY OF HAMILTON
B 1850 Aberdeen. **T** 524g, 517n.
D 127.7/38.92 x 26.3/8.02 x 19/5.79. **H** Wood. 1 dk Ship rig.
1850 Built.
1856 Owned by Montgomerie & Greenhorne.
1865 Her owners were Edmonstone, Allen & Co. The ship operated London-USA.
1872 Sold to Gillespey & Co. Same name and service.
1874 Lost at sea.

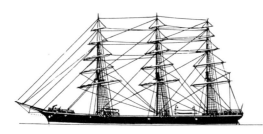

DUKE OF ROTHESAY, DUKE OF ATHOLE, DUKE OF ARGYLL

164 DUKE OF ROTHESAY
B 1864 Denny & Rankin, Dumbarton. **T** 999.
D 199.7/60.87 x 33.4/10.18 x 20.9/6.37.
H Iron. 2 dks. Ship rig.
1864 Nov. Built for Montgomerie & Greenhorne.
1866 Lost.

165 DUKE OF ATHOLE
Sister of *Rothesay* except: **B** 1865. **T** 963.
D 199.2/60.72 x 33.2/10.12.
1865 Feb: Completed for Montgomerie & Greenhorne.
1877 Owned by Montgomerie & Workman.
1878 The first sailing ship to transit the Suez Canal, under tow.
1880 Sold to Devitt & Moore, London.
1889 German owned.
1897 Abandoned at sea.

166 DUKE OF ARGYLL
Sister of *Rothesay* except: **T** 960.
1865 Oct: Completed for Montgomerie & Greenhorne.
1877 Owned by Montgomerie & Workman.
1896 Sold to Georg T. Monsen, Stavanger. R/n *Signe* (as drawn).
1904 Owned by A. Bech, Tvedestrand. Same name. Trace lost.

167 DUKE OF ABERCORN
B 1869 Chas. Connell & Co Glasgow. **T** 1,096g.
D 212/64.62 x 35.1/10.7 x 20.5/6.25.
H Wood. Iron frames. 2 dks. Ship rig. F 30/9.14. P 47/14.33.
1869 Oct: Built for Montgomerie & Greenhorne. Australia and China trade.
1877 Owned by Montgomerie & Workman.
1892 Lost en-route Cardiff-Callao with coal.

168 DUKE OF HAMILTON
B 1850 **T** 524 **H** Wood. 1 dk.
1850 Built for Edmonstone, Allan & Co. London registry.
1868 Acquired by Montgomerie & Greenhorne.
1871 Sold.
1876 Disappeared en route Philadelphia-Hamburg with cased petrol.

DUKE OF CONNAUGHT See *City of Madras* (190)

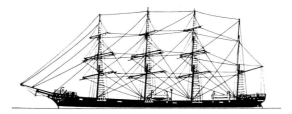

169 XANTIPPI
B 1893 Workman, Clark & Co., Belfast. **T** 972.
D 211.3/64.4 x 35.3/10.76 x 17.3/5.27.
H Iron 2 dks F 21/6.4. P 29/8.84.
1893 June: Built for Montgomerie & Workman. The only four masted barque in this book. Registered at Belfast.
1895 Disappeared at sea.

GEORGE SMITH & SONS
THE CITY LINE

1777 George Smith the line's founder was born at Stevenston, Ayrshire. He was by trade a weaver.

1799 His bride of this year was Margaret Workman whose family were to become closely involved with George Smith's future business.

1801 Son Robert was born.

1803 The second son of the title, George, was born.

1810 The family moved to Belfast in order to take advantage of the government subsidies granted to Irish manufactured goods. They were followed by two of Margaret Workman's relatives, John and Robert, who were in due course to become founders of the shipbuilding firm of Workman, Clark & Co at Belfast.

1820 Following the death of Margaret Smith the family, with the exception of elder son Robert, returned to Glasgow. George Smith had not found Ireland a happy place but a good level of business in the cotton manufacturing trade had been established and it was to superintend this that he caused Robert to remain. Later the Workmans took over the management of the business freeing Robert also to return to Glasgow.

Back in Glasgow George Smith, now 43, looked for other interests to occupy his time. He commenced to take 64th shares in a number of small trading vessels and spent his spare time studying their financial worth and the trades which produced the most satisfactory returns on his investments. He established that the best results were to be found from trade with the East — India and the 'Spice Islands' of the Dutch East Indies. Ships, in fact, became his passion and helped to fill the gap left by the death of his wife.

1826 The two brothers Robert and George jnr joined forces and with the backing of their father set up as George Smith & Sons, warehousemen, with premises at 91 Candleriggs, Glasgow.

1833 The exclusive right of the Honourable East India Company, nicknamed the John Company, to trade with British India was rescinded and the markets were opened to all. There had been some independent traders who flaunted the monopoly but now others commenced to send venture ships to the ports of the Deccan. George Smith was one such backer; he found that jute for making sacks, at that time as universal as cardboard is today, was in growing demand.

1840 Smith decided to go into ship-owning by taking up the majority share-holding and permitting relatives and friends to subscribe to a minority holding. The Glasgow Herald of March 13 contained a 'For Sale' advertisement for a Canadian built barque named *Constellation* (170) which was discharging her cargo of timber on the south side of the Clyde. George Smith and his two sons bought her and the City Line was born — not though, at this stage, known as such.

Constellation's first voyage was to Calcutta; it was almost a disaster. Her captain, Robert Service, died on the voyage out. Homeward bound the mate was drowned shortly after leaving Calcutta and the ship was somewhat perilously brought to the Clyde by the young novice second mate. But nevertheless it was profitable.

1843 A second ship, *Oriental* (171), was bought while fitting out at Ayr.

1846 Two ships were now ordered to the specifications laid down by George Smith and based upon his experience in the Indian trade. It was to become one of the Company's strengths that their ships were built for what are now called 'liner trades' — set services to set ports of call. The two new ships were named *Majestic* (173) and *Asia* (172).

1848 Smith went to Barclay Curle for his fourth ship; larger than her predecessors she was named *City of Glasgow* (174) as a tribute to his home town. But within months the effect on his clients was such that he decided that a sister ship should be ordered and given the name *City of Calcutta* (175).

1850 Saw the advent of *City of Calcutta* and from this date the advertisements commence to refer to the City Line. However as the fleet expanded many voyages to destinations like Valparaiso were fixed and loaded under the names of such firms as P. Henderson & Co. or Donaldson Brothers with the City vessel filling the berth. They were not chartered. It was probably at this juncture that grey hulls with a white strake and black painted ports were introduced; paintings of the earliest Smith vessels are black with strake and ports.

1852 For Scotland an innovation was introduced when George Smith began to advertise set dates of sailing regardless of the volume of cargo aboard ship. His friends thought him crazy; his shippers were delighted for the long wait before a ship sailed tied up their goods (and capital) for many weeks and delayed the resultant payment. Even the warehousemen awaiting goods from the East hailed the new concept. To the confounding of his critics the scheme was a success — soon to be copied by others who joined with City Line to provide regular monthly sailings.

1854 George Smith went to that most celebrated of builders Robert Steele for six ships larger than any so far but noteworthy in that they introduced iron hulls into the fleet. With one exception, *Ballengeich* (185), iron hulls were to become standard.

1855 It was now 15 years since *Constellation* was bought and the fleet stood at 12 Clyde built, reliable and sturdy ships.

1863 A regular monthly service to Bombay was inaugurated; until now the Calcutta bound ships had visited the port — and others such as Madras — en route. There was still no deep water quays there and the ships anchored in the vast island dotted roadstead and discharged their cargoes into barges and coastal dhows. The first steam tugs were in use. The voyage time was 75-80 days.

1865 Karachi was added to the ports of call — again the City Line worked ship to shore.

1866 This year became significant in the history of the firm because the shipping and the merchandising cum textile activities were now split into two separate sections. Shipping came under the banner of George Smith & Sons while the remainder was renamed Smith, Sons & Laughland. The Laughland was Andrew who had married Ellen Workman, sister of William Service Workman, who was named after Robert Service the relative who died in Constellation during her first voyage to Calcutta. William Workman, who was a nephew of George Smith's late wife, was later to become managing director of City Line. With the split George Smith III, then aged 21, elected to join the shipping side in preference to the merchandising. Once again, as happened so frequently in British shipping, the concern was tightly family run with a hierarchy headed by the founder; public limited companies were yet to come.

1867 April 15: The founder George Smith died at the age of 90.

1869 On Nov 17 the Suez Canal was opened thereby converting the Mediterranean from an inland sea into a throughway to the East, cutting the voyage time for a steamer down to 35 to 40 days; roughly half that of a sailing ship. Although having taken 9½ years to build there were few ship-owners who had planned ahead to capitalise on this short cut. The reason was the economics of sail versus the small but coal hungry steamers. Sail was predominant. Nevertheless City Line at once planned to build steamers.

1870 The first steamer, *City of Oxford* (220), entered service. The success of this vessel and her three sisters led to the decision to concentrate on steam and to run down the sailing fleet. So dramatic was the effect of the Canal and the steamships that several steamers were chartered to maintain the faster services to India while sail continued around the Cape of Good Hope. Many City ships were also to be found on spot voyages to South America and, quite widely, to New Zealand or Australia.

1873 In July Robert Smith died aged 72.

1875 Aug: In order to curb the spread of over competition and largely at the behest of the Company the Clyde shipowners agreed a uniform tariff to Indian ports with through freight prices to inland destinations such as Benares. They also agreed upon the number of annual sailings for each participant. City, for example, were allocated 26 to Calcutta to give them twice monthly sailings, and to Bombay and Karachi 13 each. In all 52 Clyde clearances yearly. This was the commencement of the Conference system which later went further and regulated carryings, this was to prevent very large ships being built which would keep to the annual allocated voyages but would clear the market for those who next followed.

1876 George Smith II died, also aged 72.

1877 Robert Smith Allan, son of Robert Allan founder of the Allan Line, became a partner. He was 'Family' in that his wife was Jane Smith daughter of Robert Smith, George senior's elder son.

1880 The fleet stood at 25 sailing ships and 12 steamers.

1882 The final pair of sailing ships, and the largest, *City of Benares* and *City of Madras* (233-34) entered service. No sailing vessels had been built since 1869, 13 years ago. Why they were built is not clear; one supposition was that they were used to train crews and that they were used on routes, such as New Zealand, not yet fully converted to steam.

1890 Dec 7: The Company became City Line Limited. The authorised capital was £750,000 divided into £10 shares. 400,000 were issued fully paid. Sixty percent went to George Smith (III) and the remainder was allocated to George Smith (IV) and other members of the family. The first directors were George Smith, Chairman, W. S. Barr, Robert Clark, J. P. Kerr, George Smith (IV), H. Workman and W. S. Workman (managing director). A 4½% debenture stock was issued to cover the preference shares (also debentures) held by some shareholders in respect of certain of the steamers. The managers of the City Line Ltd remained George Smith & Sons.

In practice City Line Ltd owned all the steamers except those covered by the debentures, while George Smith & Sons remained the proprietors of the sailing ships.

1893 All 14 steamers were owned and valued at £650,000.

1894 Trading conditions were not buoyant and the £10 shares were quoted at £8.14 each.

1895 Trade worsened and no dividend was paid. The family members were all wealthy and willingly agreed to retaining the sums earned for use in the Company.

1899 In October the fighting in the Boer War began and City ships were used to carry troops and horses from India to South Africa as well as from the UK. Trade was such that a dividend of 8% was declared. On November 2 George Smith (III) died aged only 54 and his untimely death left the company without the experience and drive that was needed at the commencement of the twentieth century. His place was taken by his son George Smith IV.

1901 August: The family decided to accept the offer of £1,000,000 for the Company, and its fifteen ships, from John Reeves Ellerman.

The ships that came under Ellerman control were:
City of Athens (244), *City of Bombay* (247), *City of Calcutta* (232), *City of Cambridge* (236), *City of Corinth* (243), *City of Delhi* (210), *City of Dundee* (239), *City of Khios* (228), *City of Lucknow* (245), *City of Madrid* (248), *City of Oxford* (235), *City of Perth* (240), *City of Sparta* (242), *City of Venice* (227), *City of Vienna* (241).

Livery

Sailing Ships	1840	Black hulls, white strake and painted gun ports. Black waterline. Masts: Varnish but with white fittings. Lifeboats white inside and out.
	1846	Grey hulls with a white strake and 12-14 black gun ports. Red waterline. Masts: varnished brown. Lifeboats: white.
	1850	The upper grey strake was painted black.
Steamers		
Funnel	1870-1901	Dark buff with black top.
	1901-1904	Buff, black top, red, white and blue bands.
	1904-1988	Ellerman colours.
Hull	1870	Black with white band at main deck level.
	1875	The white band was discontinued.
	1919	Black.
	1930	Grey, Ellerman colours. The change to grey was progressive and even then revertible, viz on Bucknall service.
Masts and derricks	1870-1914	Chocolate brown. Quite dark. Some early photographs have the lower part of the main/mizzen mast white.
	1920s	Ellerman buff.
	1970	White.
Upperworks	1870-1914	Mahogany brown.
	1919-1988	White.
Ventilators	1870	Black; red interiors. These remained until Ellerman colours were adopted.
Lifeboats		Always white but interiors seemed to vary; some were buff; some even red ochre.

CITY LINE
Illustrated Fleet List

CONSTELLATION, ORIENTAL

170 CONSTELLATION
B 1839 at Quaco, New Brunswick. **T** 334.
D 100.6/32.49 x 23.9/7.28 x 16.9/5.15. Barque. **H** Wood. 1 dk.
1839 Aug: Launched. On completion loaded with timber and sent to the Clyde where she was advertised for sale.
1840 Acquired for £4,000 by George Smith & Sons, Glasgow. Clyde-Calcutta for one voyage.
1841 Traded to the USA and to South and the South Africa for guano from Itchboe Is.
1848 Sold to Capt P. McPhee.
1854 Owned by J. Loveday, West Hartlepool.
1864 Nov 5: Lost.

171 ORIENTAL
B 1843 at Ayr. **T** 346.
D 109.3/33.31 x 23.8/7.25 x 17.8/5.42. Barque rig. **H** Wood. 1 dk.
1843 Purchased while fitting out. Calcutta service.
1846 Sold to Capt. J. Neill, who later joined Thomas Dunlop as a partner (see *City of Perth* 186). Clyde-West Indies service.
1865 Owned by Morris & Co, Rhyl, North Wales. Berthed out of Liverpool.
1868 Wrecked.

172 MAJESTIC
B 1846 Robert Steele & Co, Grenock **T** 565g, 458n.
D 125.3/38.19 x 25/7.62 x 19/5.79. Ship rig. **H** Wood 1 dk.
1846 Built for George Smith & Sons. Calcutta service.
1860 Sold to R. & J. Craig, Glasgow. Clyde-Java service.
1868 Condemned and broken up.

173 ASIA
B 1846 A. McMillan & Son, Dumbarton. **T** 450. Ship rig. **H** Wood. 1 dk.
1846 Built for George Smith & Sons, Glasgow.
1862 Jan 25: Foundered off the Cape of Good Hope.

CITY OF GLASGOW (I), CITY OF CALCUTTA (I), CITY OF LONDON (I)
CITY OF EDINBURGH (I)

174 CITY OF GLASGOW (I)
B 1848 Barclay, Curle & Co, Glagow. **T** 509.
D 127.7/38.92 x 26.6/8.11 x 19.9/6.1. **E** Ship rig. **H** Wood.
1848 Built for George Smith & Son, Glasgow and introduced the name 'City Line' which became the banner under which the sailings from Glasgow were announced in the press. The choice of name was intended as a compliment to the city and not a naming policy. There are two paintings of this ship one with and one without the stern gallery.
1866 Sold to Connell & Co, Glasgow.
1872 Nov: Owned by John Wright & Sons, Glasgow.
1873 Abandoned at sea enroute Greenock-Pensacola.

175 CITY OF CALCUTTA (I)
Sister to 174. **B** 1850. **T** 541.
1850 Entered service to Calcutta. It was this choice of a 'City' name for this vessel that caused ships to be given City names.
1859 Aug: Lost on the George and Mary Shoal, Calcutta. The ship had loaded her cargo and was to sail next morning when the tide race caused her to touch bottom and roll over onto her side. All the crew scrambled onto her side but one passenger below decks was drowned.

176 CITY OF LONDON (I)
As 174 except: **B** 1851. **D** 133.5/40.69 x 29/8.9.
1851 Completed.
1867 Sold to Hendry & Co, Greenock.
1870 Wrecked in the Solway Firth.

177 CITY OF EDINBURGH (I)
As 174 except: **B** 1852. **T** 599g, 549n. **D** 139/42.37 x 26.1/7.95.
1852 Entered service to India.
1867 Sold to J. McAlister. Same service for City Line.
1869 Wrecked in the Bay of Bengal.

Appearance as 174 *City of Glasgow* except no verandah deck aft.

178 CITY OF BENARES (I)
B 1853 Barclay, Curle & Co, Glasgow. **T** 692.
D 163.8/49.93 x 27.4/8.35 x 20.9/6.37. **E** Ship rig. **H** Wood 1 dk.
1853 Delivered. East Indies trade.
1865 Jan 31: Destroyed by fire at Calcutta, 'burnt to the water's edge.'

CITY OF MANCHESTER (I), CITY OF MADRAS (I), CITY OF DUBLIN (I)
CITY OF TANJORE, CITY OF CANTON (I), CITY OF DELHI (I)

179 CITY OF MANCHESTER (I)
B 1854 Robert Steele & Co, Greenock. **T** 766g, 686n.
D 165.5/50.44 x 27.1/8.26 x 21.1/6.43. **E** Ship rig. **H** Iron. 2 dks.
1854 Completed. Robert Steele built six sisters which introduced iron hulls into the fleet. As so often happened the dimensions differed even though the appearance was the same.
1871 Sold to J. McAlister to replace his lost *City of Edinburgh* (177).
1874 Owned by W. Kenneth & Co, Glasgow. Same name.
1876 Reported lost in a cyclone off the Arracan coast — but arrived damaged at Rangoon.
1883 Broken up. It is at once apparent for how much longer an iron hulled ship might see service compared with her wooden hulled bretheren. The extra initial cost was worth the fifteen extra years of trading life.

180 CITY OF MADRAS (I)
As 179 except **B** 1855. **T** 800g.
D 200.3/61.05 x 30.2/9.2 x 20.7/6.31.
1855 Completed.
1856 Mar 1: Wrecked in a gale off Corsewell Point, near Stranraer.

181 CITY OF DUBLIN (I)
As 179 except: **B** 1855. **T** 813g. **D** as 169.
1855 Entered service.
1878 On her outward leg she did London-Port Chalmers in 93 days. She then left New Zealand in ballast for the USA. Oct 15: Wrecked at Portland, Oregon, on the Columbia River bar.

182 CITY OF TANJORE
As 179 except: **B** 1855. **T** 799g. **D** 194.1/59.16 x 28.7/8.75 x 20.7/6.31.
1855 Entered service to India.
1879 Sold to T. C. Guthrie later Guthrie, McDonald & Hood & Co, Glasgow.
1880 Became *Suzanne Boulet*, Prentout-Leblond & E. Boniface, Rouen.
1891 Sold to Capt. J. Gilhoux, Redon.
1895 Became the Norwegian *Nor;* owned by A. Melling, Stavanger.
1897 Sold to Pangani Gesellschaft, Berlin. A new concern to trade with the German East African Colony, now Tanzania. R/n *Deutschland*.
1898 On her first voyage, when on tow up the Pangani River, the rope snapped and she went ashore. Salved. Sold to Zanzibar.
1904 Broken up at Bombay.

183 CITY OF CANTON (I)
As 179 except: **B** 1857. **T** 908g. **D** 197.4/60.17 x 31.2/9.51 x 20.8/6.34.
H 1 dk. **F** 35/10.67. **P** 36/10.97.
1857 Aug: Entered service.
1877 Sold to J & R Wilson, Glasgow.
1892 Became *Ffynone* owned by M Tutton, Swansea.
1903 Renamed *Undal* by J. M. Thomsen, Norway.
1906 Lost in the North Atlantic.

184 CITY OF DELHI (I)
As 179. **B** 1857. **T** 813g. **D** 178.7/54.47 x 31.9/9.72 x 21.8/6.64.
1857 Oct: Completed.
1867 Jan: Wrecked on Dungenness Point, Straits of Dover.

---

185 BALLENGEICH
B 1849 Barclay, Curle & Co, Glasgow. **T** 478.
E Ship rig. **H** Wood 1 dk.
1849 Built for J. Tod for Clyde-USA-Calcutta route.
1851 Clyde-Australia with emigrants.
1855 Acquired by Smith & Son. Same name. Few Scottish sailing ships had their names changed after purchase; it was said to be unlucky. Calcutta service.
1859 May: Wrecked on the Madras coast. City's first loss.

CITY OF PERTH (I), CITY OF YORK (I)

186 CITY OF PERTH (I)
B 1857 Barclay, Curle & Co, Glasgow. **T** 466g.
D 155.4/47.37 x 27.4/8.35 x 18.3/5.58. **E** Ship rig. **H** Wood, iron beams.
1857 Delivered. A composite ship; wood and iron.
1867 Sold to Capt. McPhail, Connell & Co, Glasgow.
1872 Owned by Thomas Dunlop and John Neil, Glasgow. Same name. She replaced their first ship *Wye* but never became a part of the fleet of Dunlop & Sons who used 'Clan' prefixes until 'Queen' was introduced in 1884 to avoid confusion with the Clan line.

1876 Sold to A. Benecke, London, who promptly re-sold her to French interests. No new name or owner recorded. Being 21 years old she was either hulked or scrapped.

187 CITY OF YORK (I)
As 186. **B** 1859. **T** 569. **D** 156/47.55 x 29.2/8.9 x 19.2/5.85.
1859 Delivered.
1865 Lost enroute Calcutta-Glasgow.

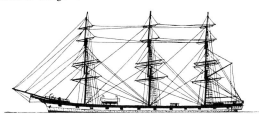

CITY OF PEKIN (I), CITY OF LUCKNOW (I)

188 CITY OF PEKIN (I)
B 1858 Barclay, Curle & Co, Glasgow. **T** 893g.
D 196.9/60 x 31.1/9.48 x 20.8/6.34. **E** Ship rig. **H** Iron. 1 dk.
1858 Delivered; extended the Smith & Sons service beyond Calcutta to the Far East. She was not the first so to do but her name indicated an intention to serve the region consistently.
1873 June 5: Sunk by collision off Cape de Verde, Cape Verde Islands.

189 CITY OF LUCKNOW (I)
As 188 except: **B** 1858 Alex. Stephen & Sons, Kelvinhaugh, Glasgow. **T** 869.
1858 Completed.
1861 Feb 9: Wrecked in Belfast Lough.

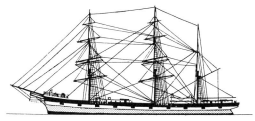

190 CITY OF MADRAS (II)
B 1859 Alex. Stephen & Sons, Kelvinhaugh. **T** 999g, 954n.
D 209/63.7 x 32/9.75 x 21.9/6.67.**E** Ship rig. **H** Iron. 1 dk.
1859 Delivered.
1881 Sold to Montgomerie & Workman, Glasgow. Registered in the name of H. Workman. This is the same family as Workman, Clark the Belfast shipbuilders. Coincidentally the Ellerman group eventually were to become the owners of this firm. Renamed *Duke of Connaught* and sailed under the aegis of Smith & Sons.
1887 Sunk by collision

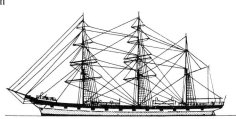

CITY OF NANKIN, CITY OF SHANGHAI (I)

191 CITY OF NANKIN
B 1859 Barclay, Curle & Co, Glasgow. **T** 986g.
D 212.1/64.65 x 32.2/9.81 x 21.4/6.52. **E** Ship rig.
H Iron 1 dk. F 31/9.45. Q 32/9.75.
1859 Oct: Delivered. Her hull was constructed of boiler-iron plates at extra cost.
1881 Sold to Guthrie, McDonald & Hood & Co, Glasgow. Same name.

1883 When T. C. Guthrie formed the Village Line the ship was renamed *Keir*.
1896 Sold to Isaac Zagury, Liverpool.
1897 Condemned and broken up.

192 CITY OF SHANGHAI (I)
As 191. **B** 1860. **T** 989g. **D** 212.5/64.77.
1860 Oct: Delivered.
1881 Sold to Capt. Bramwell. R/n *Nith*. Owned by Bramwell & Gardener, Glasgow.
1893 Sold to John I Jacobs, London. Same name. A company that is still quoted on the London Stock Exchange.
1900 Lost enroute Florida-Sydney N.S.W.

CITY OF CALCUTTA (II), CITY OF BOMBAY (I)
CITY OF CASHMERE, CITY OF NINGPO, CITY OF AMOY

193 CITY OF CALCUTTA (II)
B 1860 Alex. Stephen & Sons, Kelvinhaugh, Glasgow. **T** 984g.
D 212/64.6 x 32/9.75 x 21.7/6.61. **E** Barque rig. **H** Iron 2 dks. Fcsle and quarter decker. Almost the standard type for the Company.
1860 Nov: Completed.
1881 Sold to Capt Charles Barrie. Her name being shortened to *Calcutta*. Barrie had been a Smith captain for some time, having latterly commanded the steamer *City of Venice* (227). He resigned to set up business on his own account based on his native port of Dundee under the title of "The Dundee & Calcutta Line of Clippers' not to be confused with David Bruce & Co's Dundee Clipper Line. *Calcutta* became his seond ship (after *Adelaide Baker*). The firm was eventually to become Charles Barrie & Sons but better known as the 'Den Line'. His most famous sailing ship was *Lawhill* of 1892.
1895 Sept 16: Abandoned off Staten Island, Cape Horn enroute Huanillos-London-Dundee.

194 CITY OF BOMBAY (I)
As 193. **B** 1862. **T** 990 g. **H** F 32/9.75. **Q** 37/11.28.
1862 Completed.
1882 Sold to Capt J. Rhind, Glasgow. Name shortened to *Bombay*.
1884 Owned by N. J. Ward & Son, Fleetwood. Sane name.
1899 Sold to Carl Bech, Tvedestrand, Oslo. R/n *Norden*.
1907 Mar 1: Wrecked on the Seychelles.

195 CITY OF CASHMERE
As 193. **B** 1863. **T** 979g, 945n.
1863 March: Completed.
1882 Jan 15: Lost her anchor at night in a calm sea and drifted ashore onto Ninety Mile Beach, Timaru, New Zealand. Next day she slewed broadside on and in the heavy swell was lost.

196 CITY OF NINGPO
B 1862 Barclay, Curle & Co, Glasgow. **T** 986g, 949n.
D 204/62.18 x 32.4/9.87 x 21.3/6.49. **E** Barque. **H** Iron. F & Q type.
1862 July: Delivered.
1881 Sold to Capt J. Rhind, Glasgow. R/n *Kinloss*.
1888 Became *Gustavo Adolfo* owned by Gustavo Bahr, Hamburg. Nitrate trade Chile-Hamburg. Voyage time usually 105 days; her fastest was 85 days.
1900 Sold to H. Bischoff & Co, Bremen. Same name. Bremen-USA.
1904 Renamed *Valhal* by J. A. Leschbrandt, Norway.
1910 Broken up in the Netherlands.

197 CITY OF AMOY
As 196. **B** 1863. **D** 209.7/63.92 x 32.4/9.87 x 21.4/6.52.
1863 March: Delivered.
1872 Sept 8: Enroute Clyde - 'Frisco her cargo shifted during a gale. Put into the Falklands with a severe list.

1882 Sold to Bramwell & Gardener, Glasgow. R/n *Amoy*. Registered as owned by Robert Bramwell of London.
1889 Oct 8: Wrecked on the Falkland Islands bound for Valparaiso from Paranagua.

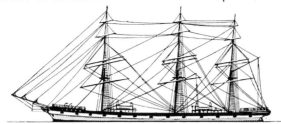

*CITY OF PARIS (I), CITY OF BRUSSELS, CITY OF BERLIN
CITY OF VIENNA (I), CITY OF FLORENCE (I), CITY OF VENICE (I), CITY OF LAHORE (I)*

198 **CITY OF PARIS (I)**
B 1862 Charles Connell & Co, Glasgow. **T** 990g, 95n.
D 210.5/64.16 x 31.8/9.69 x 21.4/6.52. **E** Ship, later Barque.
H Iron. 1 dk. F 30/9.14. Q 38/11.58.
1862 Completed.
1882 Sold to George Traill & Sons, Glasgow. R/n *Kiandra*.
1888 Sold to H. Bischoff & Co, Bremen. Same name. Tramp service.
1895 Rescued the crew of the burning US sailer *Sentinel* in mid-Atlantic.
1902 April: Left Philadelphia and lost with all hands.

199 **CITY OF BRUSSELS**
As 198. **B** 1863. **T** 990g, 953n. **D** 211.3/64.4.
1863 May: Completed.
1881 Sold to Hugh Hogarth, Ardrossan. Name shortened to *Brussels*.
1891 Sold to Shaw, Savill & Co, London. Same name.
1903 Owned by the Niger Company, London.
1904 July: Hulked on the Niger River, West Africa.

200 **CITY OF BERLIN**
As 198. **B** 1864. **T** 1,011g, 980n. **D** 213/64.92. **D** 2 dks.
1864 Oct: Completed. The first vessel in the fleet to exceed 1,000 grt.
1881 Sold to T. C. Guthrie, Glasgow. R/n *Dalswinton*. Barque rig.
1884 March: Lost by a fire in her coal cargo at Trincomalee.

201 **CITY OF VIENNA (I)**
As 198. **B** 1866. **T** 990g. **D** 213/64.92. **H** F 28/8.53. Q 28/8.53.
1866 March: Delivered.
1881 Sold to T. C. Guthrie. R/n *Dunscore*.
1894 Owned by James Currie, Leith. R/n *Carrick*. This vessel was never a member of the Currie Line of Hamburg Steam Packets.
1896 Abandoned off the coast of Australia.

202 **CITY OF FLORENCE (I)**
As 198. **B** 1867. **T** 1,198, 1,162n. **D** 226.9/69.16 x 34.4/10.48 x 22.4/6.83. **H** F 34/10.36. Q 34/10.36.
1867 Jan: Delivered. Sir David Bone, the great commodore of the Anchor Line, served his apprenticeship in this vessel.
1895 Her longest passage was 184 days Vancouver-Cape Horn-Antwerp. The ship was actually given up as lost. On Oct 20, off Cape Horn, the ship was taken aback by a complete change in gale direction and was blown backwards with her stern under water. She had a tarpaulin covered deck cargo which acted as a watershed and the water sluiced overboard otherwise she would have swamped.
1900 Mar 19: Wrecked at Half Moon Bay, California enroute Iquique-'Frisco with nitrate. The master was found to have been over-confident and he 'failed to use the lead line.'

203 **CITY OF VENICE (I)**
As 198. **B** 1867. **T** 1,199g, 1,160n. **D** 230.6/70.29.
1867 April: Entered service to Calcutta.
1871 Oct 6: Wrecked on Rodrigues Island, east of Mauritius, enroute Clyde-Bombay. Nov 7: The ship broke up after £7,000 of cargo had been saved. The ship was valued at £18,000 and the cargo £150,000. The crew were taken to Mauritius.

204 **CITY OF LAHORE (I)**
As 198 except: **B** Alex. Stephen, Kelvinhaugh. **T** 988g and n.
D 202/61.57 x 31.8/9.69. **F** 34/10.36. **Q** 38/11.58.
1864 March: Delivered.
1883 Sold to T. C. Guthrie, Glasgow. R/n *Durisdeer*.
1895 Wrecked on Oyster Bank from Simonstown, South Africa, in ballast.

---

205 **CITY OF FOOCHOW**
B 1864 Barclay, Curle & Co, Glasgow. **T** 1,034g, 1,034n.
D 213.4/65.04 x 32.5/9.9 x 21.4/6.52. **E** Ship rig. **H** Iron. 1 dk.
1864 March: Delivered. Her name also occurs in Lloyd's Register as *City of Foo-Chow*.
1876 Nov 13: Collided with *City of Seringapatam* (207) off La Palma.
1877 Apr 1: Wrecked off Flinder's Isle, Bass Strait, enroute Sydney-California. The ship was valued at £15,000 but her wreck went for £500.

CITY OF BENARES (II), CITY OF SERINGAPATAM
Appearance as *City of Pekin* (1) 188
206 **CITY OF BENARES (II)**
B 1865 Barclay, Curle & Co, Glasgow. **T** 1,182g, 1,150n.
D 224.4/68.4 x 34.2/10.42 x 22.5/6.86.
E Ship. **H** Iron. 2 dks. **Q** 39/11.89.
1865 July: Completed.
1881 Sold to G. Traill & Sons, Glasgow. R/n *Ruthin*. Barque.
1890 Owned by C. H. H. Winters, Elsfleth, Bremen.
1910 Sold to T. H. Poulsson, Stavanger. R/n *Laugen*.
1911 Sunk by ice in the Baltic. Raised but broken up locally.

207 **CITY OF SERINGAPATAM**
As 206. **B** 1866. **T** 1,190g, 1,190n. **D** 225/68.58.
1866 Jan: Completed.
1876 Nov 13: Collided with *City of Foochow* (205) off La Palma Island. Lost seven crew and her mizzen mast. Taken into Puerto Cruz, Teneriffe.
1876 Dec 21: Wrecked on Bona Vista Island, Cape Verde Islands, bound London-Melbourne. All saved.

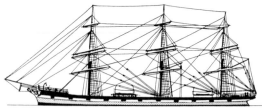

CITY OF ATHENS (1), CITY OF GLASGOW (11), CITY OF DELHI (II), CITY OF EDINBURGH (II), CITY OF DOVER, CITY OF LUCKNOW (II), CITY OF HANKOW (I), CITY OF MADRID (I), CITY OF CORINTH (I), CITY OF SPARTA

208 **CITY OF ATHENS (I)**
B 1867 Robert Steele & Co., Greenock. **T** 1,198g, 1,163n.
D 222.9/67.94 x 34.2/10.42 x 22.8/6.95. **E** Ship rig.
H Iron. 2 dks. **F** 34/10.36. **Q** 35/10.67.
1867 Delivered.
1893 March: Five sailing ships raced 'Frisco-Queenstown (Cobh) with each master taking £50. *City of Athens* won.
1900 Sold to Johan Johanson, Lysaker nr Oslo, all of whose sailing ship's names commenced with the letter 'A'. R/n *Athena*.
1909 Nov 23: Wrecked at Morant Bay, Jamaica.

209 **CITY OF GLASGOW (II)**
As 208 except: **B** Barclay, Curle & Co. **T** 1,168g, 1,131n.
D 228/69.49 x 34/10.36 x 22.2/6.92. **H** **F** 32/9.75. **Q** 33/10.06.
1867 Feb: Delivered. Noted as a very fast sailer.

1874 Chartered to the New Zealand Shipping Co. Jan 3: Left Belfast. Reached Dunedin in 75 days.
1900 Sold to Johan Johanson, Lysaker R/n *Albania*.
1907 May 17: Abandoned enroute New Caledonia-Europe with a cargo of nickel ore.

210 CITY OF DELHI (II)
As 208 except: **B** Barclay, Curle & Co. **T** 1,199g, 1,161n.
D 227.7/69.4 x 34.8/10.61. **H** F 32/9.75. **Q** 42/12.8.
1867 July: Delivered. This ship had an iron hull with wooden bulwarks.
1892 Rounding Cape Horn against gale force head winds the tacking ship logged seeing Cape St. John, Staten Island, on 5 consecutive Sundays.
1900 Sold with her sister to Johan Johanson, Lysaker. R/n *Ailsa*.
1906 Jan 2: Abandoned on fire off Rockall.

211 CITY OF EDINBURGH (II)
As 208 except: **B** 1868 Barclay, Curle & Co. **T** 1,206g.
D 230/70.1 x 35.4/10.79 x 22.4/6.83.
1868 Jan: Completed.
1874 Nov 20: Run down by *French Empire* at Sandheads, Calcutta. Both ships sank.

212 CITY OF DOVER
As 208 except: **B** 1868 Barclay, Curle & Co. **T** 1,199g.
1868 Completed. This ship is not recorded in Lloyds Register during the period of her life. Some records give her as '*Dover*'.
1874 Sold.
1875 Wrecked off the coast of Ireland.

213 CITY OF LUCKNOW (II)
As 208 except: **B** 1869 Barclay, Curle & Co. **T** 1,195g, 1,163n.
D 231.1/70.44 x 35.5/10.82 x 22.2/6.77. **E** Ship rig.
H F 37/11.28. **Q** 35/10.67.
1869 March: Completed. Always a fast sailer and 'handy as a pocket in a shirt.'
1883 Made Adelaide-London in 75 days.
1884 Jan: Collided with J. Howden's *Simla* (ex-P & O) which then sank in tow with the loss of 20 lives. Did London-San Francisco in 109 days.
1889 Sold to Knohr & Burchard, Hamburg. R/n *Reinbek*.
1896 Became *Agostino Terrizano*, owned by E. Terrizano, Genoa.
1907 Sold to Angelo Bertorello, Sampierdarena, Italy.
1909 Broken up at Genoa.

214 CITY OF HANKOW (I)
As 208 except: **B** Alex. Stephen & Sons, Kelvinhaugh. **T** 1,195g, 1,161n.
D 223/67.97 x 35.2/10.73 x 22.3/6.8.
H Composite. F 35/10.67. **Q** 37/11.28.
1869 June: Completed.
1873 Captain G. Napier was washed overboard near to Ascension Island.
1871 The fastest in the fleet; did London-Calcutta-London in 191 days including the stay at Calcutta.
1874 Nov: Did Lizard-Melbourne in 70 days beating *Cutty Sark* by three days. Her next voyage logged London-San Francisco in 96 days.
1900 Sold to G. J. Robertson, Sydney.
1903 Hulked at Thursday Island, Torres Straits. Ended life as a pontoon.

215 CITY OF MADRID (I)
As 208 except: **B** 1869 Chas. Connell & Co, Glasgow. **T** 1,191g, 1,159n.
D 231.6/70.59 x 35.3/10.76 x 22.2/6.77. **H** F 33/10.06. **Q** 41/12.5.
1869 Sept: Delivered.
1888 Sold to S. Goldberg & Sons, Swansea. R/n *Agnes Lilian*.
1898 Became *Lofthus*, J. A. Henschien, Lillesand, Norway.
1915 Broken up in Norway.

216 CITY OF CORINTH (I)
As 208 except: **B** 1870 Barclay, Curle & Co, Whiteinch. **T** 1,219g, 1,190n.
D 235.2/71.69 x 35.5/10.82 x 22.3/6.8. **E** Ship rig.
H F 37/11.28. **Q** 35/10.67.
1870 Feb: Delivered. Her main deck lifeboat was midway between the main and jigger masts.
1889 Mar 8: Sunk by collision with the 4-masted barque *Trafalgar* off the Isle of Wight.

217 CITY OF SPARTA (I)

As 208 except: **B** 1870 Alex. Stephen & Sons, Kelvinhaugh. **T** 1,193g.
D 234.2/71.38 x 35/10.67 x 22.4/6.83. **H** Composite. **F** 37/11.28. **Q** 35/10.67.
1870 March: Completed. The eighth and final ship from the builders. In Nov *Lima*, the 147th and final ship built at Kelvinhaugh was delivered. Stephens then moved to Linthouse. Oddly this was also the final City ship ever to come from Alex. Stephen.
1889 Sold with *City of Madrid* (215) to S. Goldberg & Sons, Swansea. R/n *Florence Stella.*
190? Became *Staut*, J. B. Linaae, Sandefjord.
1912 Sold to A. Gordon-Firing.
1917 Stopped by the German commerce raider *Moewe* then on her second cruise. Sunk by bombs. Not however listed among her successes.

218 CITY OF YORK (II)

B 1869 Randolph, Elder & Co, Glasgow. **T** 1,194g.
D 222.7/67.87 x 35.8/10.91 x 21.7/6.61. **E** Ship rig.
H Iron. 2 dks. **F** 27/8.23. **P** 52/15.84.
1869 Sept: Completed. *City of York* was more correctly a member of the previous *City of Athens* (208) class but with a poop.
1899 July 13: Wrecked at Rottnest Cove, Fremantle, ex-'Frisco. 12 lost. Her cargo was 800,000 linear feet of timber and 5,000 wooden doors. The locals did extremely well out of their beachcombing.

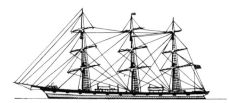

219 CITY OF PERTH (II)

B 1866 Chas Connell & Co, Glasgow. **T** 1,188g.
D 232.5/70.86 x 35.4/10.79 x 22.2/8.29. **E** Ship rig. **H** Iron. **Q** 32/9.75.
1866 May: Delivered. Placed on the Calcutta route. Frozen meat carrier. The builder regarded the ship as his masterpiece. He said she was the most beautiful sailing ship afloat.
1872 Jan 16: Left Calcutta for New York. Did 12,000 miles in 79 days.
1882 May 14: Lying in the Inner Anchorage she was blown ashore at Timaru during the great gale. The adjacent *Benvenue* was wrecked and her crew rowed to *City of Perth*. Then all escaped ashore when she too, grounded. Attempts to secure the ship cost nine lives in swamped lifeboats. June: Sold locally for £800. Refloated and towed to Port Chalmers for repairs.
1883 Acquired by New Zealand Shipping Co. R/n *Turakina*. Made 15 round voyages for them. She became their last sailing vessel when sold.
1895 Feb 14: The ship became famous for her speed when she overtook the NZSCo's steamer *Ruapehu* in the South Atlantic.
1899 Sold to Alexander Bech, Tvedestrand, Norway. R/n *Elida*. Barque rig.
1914 May: Broken up.

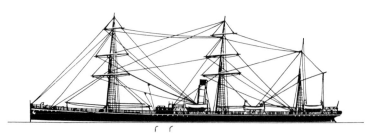

CITY OF OXFORD (I), CITY OF CAMBRIDGE (I), CITY OF POONAH,
CITY OF MECCA

220 CITY OF OXFORD (I)

B 1870 Barclay, Curle & Co, Glasgow. **T** 2,319g, 1,497n.
D 326.1/99.39 x 36.1/11 x 27.7/8.44.
E Sgl scr, 2 cyl comp inv. 200 HP. 60 psi. 12 kts. By builder.

H Iron. 3 dks. Flush. Barque rig. **P** 80.
1870 Oct 10: Launched. George Smith & Son's first steamer. Indian service via the Suez Canal. With the change to steamers the sailing vessels of the fleet were to be progressively released. Dec 13: M/v Clyde-Bombay-Calcutta.
1881 Sold to the Clan Line, Cayzer, Irvine & Co. R/n *Clan Macduff.* Oct 21: Lost in the Irish Sea 40 miles south of Cork en route Liverpool-Bombay. 32 lost.

221 CITY OF CAMBRIDGE (I)
As 220. **T** 2,329g, 1,497n. **D** 326.5/99.52.
1870 Dec 10: Launched. Placed on the Indian service via the Suez Canal.
1876 New boilers fitted.
1881 Sold to the Clan Line. R/n *Clan Maclean.*
1890 March 28: Struck Matamada Rock while entering Galle harbour, Ceylon. Repaired at Colombo.
1893 Triple expansion machinery fitted by Bow, Mclachlan & Co, Paisley.
1903 Aug 13: Wrecked 6 miles north of Cape St Vincent, southern Portugal, en route Clyde-Liverpool-Bombay.

222 CITY OF POONAH
As 220 except: **B** Chas Connell & Co, Glasgow. **T** 2,283g, 1,456n.
D 325.7/99.27. **E** By J. Howden & Co, Glasgow.
1870 Nov 24: Launched.
1871 Jan: Entered service to India.
1878 Sold to the Temperley Line, formerly the British & Colonial SS Co. R/n *Clyde.* Plain black funnel. May 9: First sailing London-Quebec-Montreal. Made four round voyages before the St Lawrence froze. Placed on six months charter to carry troops and stores to Cape Town.
1879 April 7: Wrecked on Dyer's Island, Cape Colony while on charter.

223 CITY OF MECCA
As 220 except: **B** 1871 Chas. Connell & Co. **T** 2,290g, 1,436n.
1871 March 22: Launched. May: Entered service to India.
1881 Sold with her two sisters to Clan Line. R/n *Clan Macleod.*
1883 Became *Procida* of Robert M. Sloman (as drawn).
1990 Dec 20: Sold to the British Admiralty for use as a coal hulk at Simonstown, South Africa.
1901 Renamed *Nubian* and then, more prosaically, *C.370.*
1913 Brought back to the UK and broken up by Thos W. Ward at Morecambe.

Appearance as *CITY OF CANTERBURY* 226
224 CITY OF MANCHESTER (II)
B 1873 Barclay, Curle & Co, Glasgow. **T** 3,126g, 2,046n.
D 374.5/114.15 x 38.5/11.73 x 29.4/8.96.
E Sgl scr, 2 cyl comp inv. 400 NHP. 65psi. 12 kts. By builder.
H Iron. 3 dks.
1873 Completed. The first steamer in the fleet to exceed 3,000grt. Took the Liverpool-Calcutta record with 33 days out and 31 days home.
1885 Lost off Ushant en route Calcutta-London with sugar and cotton. All 57 crew and 4 passengers saved.

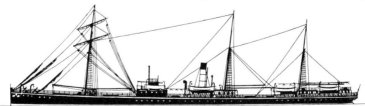

225 CITY OF CARTHAGE (I)
B 1873 Chas Connell & Co, Glasgow. **T** 2,651g, 1,717n.
D 360.3/109.82 x 36.8/11.22 x 26.4/8.05.
E Sgl scr, 2 cyl comp inv. 350 NHP. 70 psi. 12 kts. By J & J Thomson.
H Iron. 2 dks. 3 masts.
1873 Oct: Delivered. Had a very low freeboard. A photograph of her exists with a dark grey hull.
1876 Reduced the Calcutta record to 29 days.
1890 Sold to N. McLean & Sons, Glasgow. R/n *Straits of Magellan.*
1898 Scrapped.

CITY OF CANTERBURY (I), CITY OF VENICE (II), CITY OF KHIOS (I)

226 CITY OF CANTERBURY (I)
B 1875 Barclay, Curle & Co, Glasgow. **T** 3,212g, 2,100n.
D 379.7/115.73 x 38.2/11.64 x 29.2/8.9.
E Sgl scr, 2 cyl comp inv. 440 NHP. 58 psi. 9½ kts. By builder.
H Iron. 3 dks. F 28/8.53. B 132/40.23. **P** 39. Had a flush appearance.
1875 Jan: Completed.
1877 Aug: Loaded a record 17,000 chests of tea at Calcutta.
1897 Wrecked on the James & Mary shoal, Hooghly River, Calcutta. The ship had steam up ready to sail next morning when she grounded and was lost.

227 CITY OF VENICE (II)
As 226. **T** 3,372g, 2,229n. **D** 379.5/115.67.
1875 Completed.
1879 During the Zulu War she first acted as a transport and then HQ's ship for Sir Garnet Wolseley.
1879 July 3: After his defeat, by Lord Chelmsford's troops, at the Battle of Ulundi Chief Cetawayo and his wives were prisoners aboard. The body of the Prince Imperial Bonaparte, speared to death in an ambush at Ulundi, was also taken onto the ship.
1887 Given new boilers of 145 psi and the installation of a quadruple expansion engine by J. Howden, Glasgow.
1899-1900 Used as a Boar War transport at 26 shillings per gross ton per month.
1901 Taken over with the fleet by John Ellerman.
1905 Transferred to Papayanni, Fred Swift manager. Same name.
1908 March: Stranded at San Stephano de Cadore, Italy.
1912 Jan 27: Sold to Italian breakers.

228 CITY OF KHIOS (I)
As 227. **B** 1878. **T** 3,241g, 2,283n. **D** 381.5/116.28 x 38.5/11.73.
E By J. Howden & Co, Glasgow. **H** F 30/9.14. B 130/39.62.
1878 Completed.
1901 Taken over by Ellerman.
1904 Transferred to Papayanni, Fred Swift manager. Same name.
1914 Aug 4: Seized at Smyrna by the Turks.
1915 April: When the Dardenelles campaign started she was sunk as a blockship across the entrance to Smyrna harbour.
1919 Demolished as she lay. By then she was in two halves.

229 CITY OF LONDON (II)
B 1876 Chas. Connell & Co, Glasgow. **T** 3,212g, 2,056n.
D 381.6/116.31 x 38.8/11.83 x 29/8.83.
E Sgl scr, 2 cyl comp inv. 449 NHP. 12 kts. By J. & J. Thomson, Glasgow.
H Iron. 3 dks. F 37/11.28. Fwd B 39/11.89. Aft B 29/8.84.
1876 Jan: Completed.
1885 Reboiled.
1900 Jan: Sold to Wee Bin & Co, Singapore. R/n *Hong Bee*.

1913 Transferred to Ho Hong SS Co, Singapore, formerly Wee Bin, upon its formation by Lim Peng Siang. Same name.
1917 Served as a transport in Indian and East African waters.
1926 Broken up at Singapore.

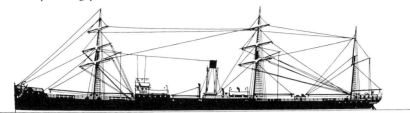

230 CITY OF EDINBURGH (III)
As 229 except: **T** 3,230g, 2,060n.
D 381.5/116.28 x 38.5/11.73.
H Iron. 3 masts. 3 dks. F 28/8.53.
1876 Built.
1886 Tpl expansion installed by J. & J. Thomson.
1889 Transferred to City Line Ltd.
1900 Jan: Sold for £13,000 to Wee Bin & Co, Singapore. R/n *Hong Wan 1*.
1913 Transferred to Ho Hong SS Co upon its formation.
1921 Jan 21: Stranded east of Green Island, Swatow. Beached. Broke in two.

231 CITY OF AGRA (I)
B 1879 Chas. Connell & Co. T 3,274g, 2,133n.
D 385.4/117.5 x 38.7/11.79 x 28.6/8.72.
E Sgl scr, 2 cyl comp inv. 500 NHP. 70 psi. 12 kts. By J. & J. Thomson.
H Iron. 3 dks. F 35/10.67. B 30/9.14.
1879 May: Completed.
1897 Feb 3: Left Liverpool for Calcutta with 75 aboard. Feb 22: the ship was wrecked during a severe north-westerly gale and at night in Aron Bay, 6 miles east of Cape Vilano, Finisterre. Thirty-two crew and two stowaways were saved. Held to be an error of judgement by the master.

CITY OF CALCUTTA (III), CITY OF OXFORD (II) (235)
232 CITY OF CALCUTTA (III)
B 1881 Chas. Connell & Co, Glasgow. T 3,836g, 2,555n.
D 400/121.92 x 42.1/12.83 x 30.1/9.17.
E Sgl scr, 2 cyl comp 583 NHP. 10 kts. By J. & J. Thomson, Glasgow.
H Iron. 3 dks. 3 masts. F 34/10.36.
1881 Completed.
1889 To City Line Ltd.
1901 Aug: Taken over by Ellerman; too old for his needs. Sold to Wee Bin & Co, Singapore. R/n *Hong Moh*.
1913 Transferred to Ho Hong SS Co upon its formation.
1916 Jan 5: Mined off Aden; laid by raider *Wolf*. Made port.

1921 March 3: Wrecked on White Rocks, Lamock Island (Canock Island) off Swatow en route Singapore-Amoy. All saved.

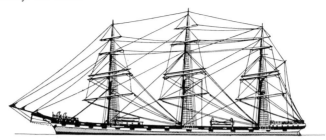

CITY OF BENARES (III), CITY OF MADRAS (III)

233 CITY OF BENARES (III)

B 1882 Barclay, Curle & Co, Glasgow. **T** 1,574g, 1,525n.
D 259/78.94 x 38.2/11.64 x 23/7.01. **E** Ship rig.
H Iron. 2 dks. F 38/11.58. P 28/8.53.
1882 Sept: Delivered. The largest sailing ship yet built for the fleet and the first of the final pair; the company having decided to convert to screw propulsion. Oddly no 4-masted sailing ships were owned.
1891 Sept 17: Put into Port Stanley, Falklands, with weather damage after a mutinous crew turned her back from Cape Horn.
1900 Sold to G. Revell, Nystad, Finland (then Russia), same name. Traded with Baltic timber to Australia.
1911 Oct 1: En route Passage West, Cobh-Sundsvall wrecked in the West Kapelle on her way into Rotterdam.

234 CITY OF MADRAS (III)

As 233. **T** 1,577g, 1,527n. **D** 260/79.25 x 38.4/11.7.
1882 Nov: Delivered; fractionally larger than her sister and the final sailing ship for the company.
1900 Sold to Hatfield, Cameron & Co, Glasgow. R/n *Wemyss Bay*.
1903 Wrecked on the Pacific coast of Mexico at Mazatlan.

Sister of *City of Calcutta* (III) 232

235 CITY OF OXFORD (II)

B 1882 Barclay, Curle & Co. **T** 3,959g, 2,603n.
D 400/121.92 x 43.2/13.17 x 29.8/9.08.
E Sgl scr, 2 cyl comp. 650HP, 80psi, 12 kts. By builder.
H Iron, 3 dks, 2 iron, 1 wood. F 43/13.1. B 62/18.89.
1982 June: Delivered.
1891 Triple expansion and new high pressure blrs installed by builder.
1901 Aug: Acquired by Ellerman.
1903 Transferred to Papayanni's Alexandria service. Fred Swift manager.
1914 Dec: Bought for £25,000 by the Admiralty and rebuilt at Harland & Wolff, Belfast, as the dummy battleship HMS *St Vincent*. R/n *St Vincent A*. Attached with 13 others similarly treated to the Special Services Squadron. Because of confusion with the real battleship R/n *Special Services Ship No. 1*.
1915 Jan: Positioned at Scapa Flow.
1919 Reverted to Ellerman ownership and placed with Bucknall.
1924 Sold for £11,000 to Cantiere Olivo S.A. and broken up in Italy.

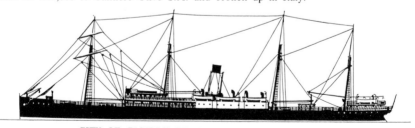

CITY OF CAMBRIDGE (II), CITY OF BOMBAY (II)

236 CITY OF CAMBRIDGE (II)

B 1882 Workman, Clark & Co, Belfast. **T** 3,788g, 2,482n.
D 400/121.92 x 42.1/12.83 x 29.6/9.02.

E Sgl scr, 2 cyl comp. 650 HP. 80 psi. 13½ kts. By J & J Thomson, Glasgow.
H Iron, 3 dks, 2 iron, 1 wood. F 34/10.36. B 156/47.55. 4 masts. **P** 80 saloon, all amidships. Flush decked appearance.
1882 Aug: Completed. The first ship built for the company away from the Clyde. Also believed to be the first ship with the officers berthed forward and the crew aft; a style that was to become almost universal.
1900 Used as a Boer War transport; *Number 15*.
1901 Jan 16: With HMS *Tartar* rescued the crew of the cruiser *Sybille* which had been blown ashore by a gale in Lambert's Bay, South Africa. Aug: Taken over by Ellerman.
1903 Transferred to Papayanni's Mediterranean services. City Line as managers.
1915 March 28: Attacked by submarine gunfire 25 miles northwest by north of Bishop's Rock Light. Escaped by smoke and return of fire. Nov 8: Again attacked. This time in the Mediterranean. Again escaped.
1917 July 3: Torpedoed by *UC-67* 10 miles north of Djidjelli, Algeria.

237 CITY OF BOMBAY (II)
As 236 **T** 4,492g, 2,941n. **D** 404/123.14 x 48/14.6. **H** F 46/14.02 B 150/45.72.
1885 Aug: Delivered; the first ship in the fleet to exceed 4,000 grt.
1901 Aug: Taken over by John Ellerman.
1903 Made three voyages Glasgow-Liverpool-Philadelphia for Allan Line. This was repeated in the summers of 1906 and 1907.
1904 Chartered by Lunn & Co, London, to carry Russian troops Odessa-Vladivostok during the Russo-Japanese war.
1908 May: Sold for £9,250 and broken up in the Netherlands.

238 CITY OF DUBLIN (II)
B 1888 Workman, Clark & Co, Belfast. **T** 3,267g, 2,155n.
D 361.7/110.26 x 42.7/13.01 x 26.4/8.05.
E Sgl scr, tpl exp, 325 NHP, 160 psi. 12 kts. By J & J Thomson, Glasgow.
H Steel 2 dks. F 46/14.02. B 92/28.04.
1888 Jan: Entered service, George Smith & Sons' first steel hull.
1900 Sold to Edmund Haselhurst & Co, London. R/n *Clavering*, operated by the Clavering SS Co. All their ships were single ship owned and had names that commenced with '*Claver*'.
1907 Jan 31: Lost off the mouth of the river Tees.

239 CITY OF DUNDEE (I)
Sister of 238 except: **B** 1890. **T** 3,427g, 2,572n.
E By J. Howden & Co, Glasgow. **H** F 40/12.19. B 88/26.82. P 28/8.53.
1890 Delivered. Differed from her sister by having a poop.
1901 Aug: Became part of the Ellerman group. Papayanni services. City managed.
1908 Oct 4: En route Liverpool-Algiers-Alexandria sank after collision in fog with Elder & Fyffe's *Matina* in St Georges Channel. The captain and two crew were lost.

240 CITY OF PERTH (III)
Details as 238 except: **B** 1890. **T** 3,427g, 2,578n.
H F 40/12.19. B 88/26.82. P 28/8.53.
1890 Delivered.
1901 Aug: Taken over by JRE.
1917 June 11: Torpedoed by *U-70* 195 miles south south west of Fastnet. Eight killed.

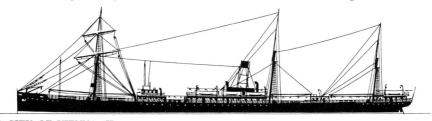

241 CITY OF VIENNA (II)
B 1890 Workman, Clark & Co, Belfast. **T** 4,672g, 2,979.
D 412.3/125.67 x 46.7/14.23 x 29.3/8.93.
E Sgl scr, tpl exp, 653 NHP, 14 kts. By J & J Thomson, Glasgow.

H Steel. 3 dks. F 42/12.8. B 162/49.38. P 40/12.19. 3 masts.
P 100 1st, 250 3rd.
1889 Dec 7: Launched. Flushed deck appearance.
1890 Feb: Delivered. Became a Boer War troopship. Remained on the South African routes. Yards removed.
1899-1902 Boer War transport *No 36*. Chartered at 20 shillings per grt per month.
1901 Aug: Taken over by JRE.
1902 Boer War depot ship for enemy prisoners.
1906 Chartered to Allan Line for three voyages Glasgow-Liverpool-Philadelphia.
1913 Aug: Sold to the National Steam Navigation Co Ltd of Greece, better known as the National Greek Line founded by the Emberics Brothers. R/n *Thessaloniki*. Converted for passengers: **P** 50 1st, 50 2nd, 1,900 emigrant steerage class.
1914 Feb 16: Entered service Piraeus-Kalamata-Patras-Palermo-New York.
1915 Dec 22: When some 500 miles off Sandy Hook, New York her engine failed and assistance was called for. Her passengers were taken off by her consort *Patris* which then took her in tow but the ship was now dead in the water.
1916 Jan 15: With her engine room flooded the ship was scuttled about 350 miles from safety.

242 CITY OF SPARTA (II)
B 1897 Workman, Clark & Co, Belfast. **T** 5,179g, 3,339n.
D 430/131.06 x 50.2/15.3 x 28.5/8.69.
E Sgl scr, tpl exp, 471 NHP, 13 kts. By builder.
H Steel. 3 dks. F 47/14.31. B 130/39.62. P 44/13.41. **P** 80 1st, 16 2nd.
1896 Oct 9: Launched.
1897 With this liner Workman, Clark commenced to build all George Smith & Sons' passenger vessels. Later the Ellerman group continued the practice although with exceptions. Operated to Calcutta.
1901 Aug: Taken over with the fleet.
1913 Taken on charter by Ellerman & Bucknall. South Africa service.
1915 Inaugurated the UK-Fast East service via India and Rangoon.
1920 Oct 25: Placed on Bucknall's American & Indian Line service New York-Suez Canel-Calcutta.
1924 circa: Passenger berths removed. Appearance unaltered.
1931 Broken up by Smith & Houston at Port Glasgow.

243 CITY OF CORINTH (II)
Sister of 242. **B** 1898. **T** 5,443g, 3,491n.
1898 Feb 22: Launched for the Calcutta service.
1901 Aug: Taken over by Ellerman.
1912 Sept: Sold to the newly formed Cie de Nav. Sud-Atlantique who acquired no fewer than six second-hand ships with which to start their service to South America. R/n *Sequana* and classed, with *Samara* (ex-Bibby *Staffordshire*), as intermediate vessels. Nov 23: First sailing Bordeaux-South America.
1916 Chargeurs Réunis became managers of the Company: replacing C.G.T.
1917 June 8: Torpedoed near Ile d'Yeu by *UC-72*.

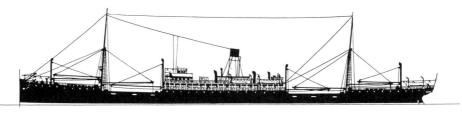

244 CITY OF ATHENS (II)
As 242 except: **B** 1899. **T** 5,159g, 3,571n. **H** F 92/26.04. B 133/40.53. P 88/26.82.
1899 Delivered. Differed from her sisters by having both fcsle and poop extended to their respective masts. This became a feature in many of the subsequent City Line buildings. Some of the space was needed for baggage accessibility for passengers who were unable to stow all their requirements in their cabins.
1901 Acquired by J. R. Ellerman with the purchase of the fleet.
1912-14 On Bucknall S.S. Line service.
1917 Aug 10: Struck a mine at night 20 miles north west of Cape Town laid by the raider *Wolf* II ex *Wachtfels*, D. G. 'Hansa'. 19 lost. The South African Railway's tug *Ludwig Wiener* arrived and in the darkness her searchlight enabled many to be saved. The mines had been laid on the previous Jan 16; an indication of how effective such weapons can be. The master's Certificate was suspended for six months. He passed over a known mined area against Admiralty orders.

245 CITY OF LUCKNOW (II)
B 1896 Barclay Curle & Co, Glasgow. **T** 3,669g, 2,371n.
D 350.5/106.83 x 45.3/13.81 x 17.9/5.46.
E Sgl scr, tpl exp. 220 NHP, 160 psi, 2 sgl blrs. 10 kts. By builder.
H Steel. 1 dk + spar dk. F 39/11.9. B 77/23.46. P 32/9.75.
1896 Nov: Completed as *Guyana* for Caw, Prentice, Clapperton & Co, Glasgow (Later Crown Line).
1898 Acquired by City Line Ltd. R/n *City of Lucknow*.
1900 Ownership changed to George Smith & Sons.
1901 Aug: Taken over by John Ellerman.
1914 Aug: Taken over to carry troops of the British Expeditionary Force to France.
1916 April 30: Torpedoed by *U-21* 60 miles east of Malta.

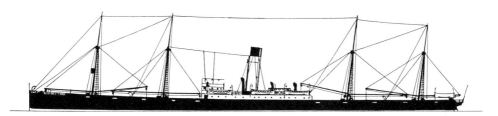

246 MAPLEMORE / CITY OF EDINBURGH (IV)
B 1899 Chas. Connell & Co, Glasgow. **T** 7,803g, 5,842n.
D 459/139.9 x 52.5/16 x 31/9.45.
E Sgl scr, tpl exp, 608 NHP, 2 dbl + 1 sgl blr. 10½ kts. By D. Rowan & Sons, Glasgow.
H Steel. 2 + shelter dk. 4 masts.
1899 Feb: Completed as *Maplemore* owned by Mentmore Ltd, Wm. Johnston & Co, Liverpool as managers. This firm later became Johnston Warren of the Furness Withy group. Cattle carrier; Baltimore-Liverpool service. General cargo outbound. She had cattle pens on the weather deck.
1900 Engaged on trooping and horse carrying to South Africa during the Boer War (with *Pinemore* and *Oakmoor*).
1901 Sept: Acquired by City, initially as *Maplemore* then R/n *City of Edinburgh*.
1914 Aug: The first Ellerman taken over for the carriage of B.E.F. troops Liverpool-France.
1915 July 2: Torpedoed by *U-39* but survived.
1929 May: Broken up by P. & M. McLellan, Bo'ness.

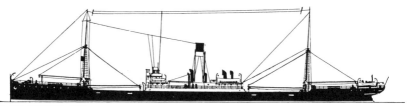

247 **CITY OF DELHI (III)**
B 1901 Barclay, Curle & Co, Glasgow. **T** 4,443g, 2,826n.
D 385.5/117.5 x 48.7/14.84 x 27/8.23.
E Sgl scr, tpl exp, 311 NHP, 80 psi. 10 kts. By builder.
H Steel 2 dks. F 86/26.2. B 106/32.3. P 81/24.69.
1901 Delivered. Aug: Taken over with the fleet.
1923 Aug 27: Sold to N. G. Metaxas, Cephelonia, Greece. R/n *Margarita*.
1925 Oct 10: Lost on the Great Fish Point, South Africa, midway between Durban and Port Elizabeth. All hands lost.

248 **CITY OF MADRID (II)**
B 1901 Workman, Clark & Co, Belfast. **T** 4,901g, 3,135n.
D 406.8/123.99 x 48.8/14.87 x 29.4/8.96.
E Sgl scr, tpl exp, 552 NHP, 180 psi, 2 dbl blrs. 1½ kts. By builder.
H Steel. 2 dks. F 90/27.43. B 121/36.88. P 86/26.21.
1901 July: Built for City Line Ltd. Aug: Taken over by J. R. Ellerman with the fleet of 15 ships.
1927 Sold to Soc, Anon. Commercials Italo-Cilena, Genoa. R/n *Nitro*.
1932 Broken up in Italy.

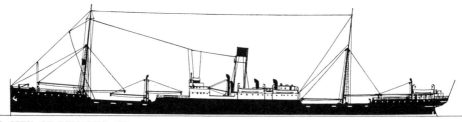

249 **CITY OF BENARES (IV)**
B 1902 Workman, Clark & Co, Belfast. **T** 6,984g, 4,321n.
D 460.5/140.36 x 55.3/16.85 x 31/9.45.
E Sgl scr, tpl exp, 521 NHP. 11½ kts. By builder.
H Steel. 2 dks. F 85/25.9. B 160/48.77. P 84/25.6. P 44 1st, 44 2nd.
1901 Oct 29: Launched.
1902 Feb: Completed for Ellerman Lines Ltd with George Smith & Sons as managers.
1914 Aug 8: Troopship for the British Expeditionary Force.
1919 Jan 16: Took the first post-war sailing of the American & Indian Line. Her second being five weeks later.
1927 On American & Manchurian Line service New York-Far East.
1933 Feb: Broken up by Hughes Bolckow, Blyth.

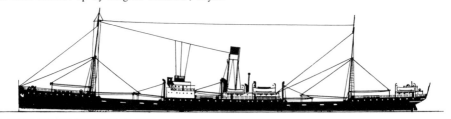

250 **CITY OF MANCHESTER (III)**
B 1903 Barclay, Curle & Co, Glasgow. **T** 5,551g, 3,563n.
D 421/128.32 x 51.5/15.7 x 29.4/8.96.
E Sgl scr, tpl exp, 424 NHP, 10 kts. By builder.

H Steel. 2 dks. F 82/25. B 123/37.49. P 82/25.
1903 Built for Ellerman Lines Ltd with W. S. Workman as manager.
1921 Dec: Inaugurated the Bucknall service Middlesbrough-Continental-Far East.
1933 Broken up by S.A. Cantiere di Portovenere, La Spezia. Realised £4,300.

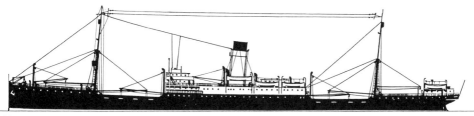

251 CITY OF CALCUTTA (IV)
B 1903 Workman, Clark & Co, Belfast. **T** 7,512g, 4,786n.
D 471.7/143.77 x 56.2/17.13 x 31.9/9.72.
E Sgl scr, tpl exp, 546 NHP. 11½ kts. By builder.
H Steel. 2 dks. F 91/27.73. B 156/47.55. P 86/26.21. **P** 134 1st, 35 2nd.
1903 Mar 17: Launched for Ellerman Lines Ltd, George Smith & Sons managers.
1914-1918 Employed as an Indian Expeditionary Force troopship; mainly Bombay-Marseilles.
1918 Oct 3: 22.50; collided in a three ship convoy, 25 miles south west of Bardsey Island, South Wales, with Elder Dempster's *Burutu* which sank in 9 minutes with the loss of 148 lives including 77 crew. *City of Calcutta* picked up 50 survivors.
1924 Oct 26: On Bucknall's American & Indian Line service New York-India.
1934 Nov: Sold, off lay up, to Japanese breakers. R/n *Calcut* for the voyage to Japan.
1935 Jan 17: Arrived in Japan for scrapping under the 'Scrap and build' scheme, British Shipping (Assistance) Act, 1936.

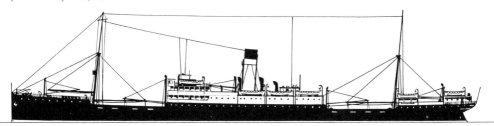

252 CITY OF YORK (III)
B 1904 Workman, Clark & Co, Belfast. **T** 7,844g, 4,935n.
D 485/147.83 x 56.3/17.16 x 32/9.75.
E Sgl scr, tpl exp, 599 NHP 12 kts. By builder.
H Steel. 2 dks. F 89/27.12. B 170/51.82. P 87/26.32. **P** 137 1st, 28 2nd.
1903 Dec 17: Launched.
1904 April: Completed for Ellerman Lines Ltd; managed by G. Smith & Sons.
1921 Aug 17: On American & Indian Line service New York-India.
1936 Sept: Sold to Pedder & Mylchreest, London, as agents for the breakers. R/n *City* and delivered by them to Italy. There she was resold and taken to Japan where she was scrapped.

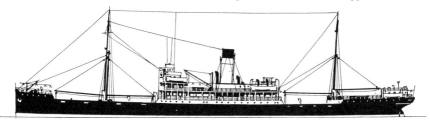

253 CITY OF KARACHI (I)
B 1905 Workman, Clark & Co, Belfast. **T** 5,547g, 3,563n.
D 413.6/126.06 x 51.5/15.7 x 29.2/8.9.
E Sgl scr, 4 cyl quad exp, 402 NHP. 11 kts. By builder.
H Steel. 2 dks. F 41/12.5. B 121/36.88. P 75/22.86.
P 70 1st, 24 2nd.

1905 Completed for Ellerman Lines Ltd; G. Smith & Sons managers. She started the practice whereby almost all City Line passenger liners were built by Workman, Clark which was a concern long related to the Smith family.
1913-14 Operated to South Africa on the Bucknall service but not transferred to their ownership.
1926 Again on the South African route.
1934 Oct 17: Sold for breaking up in Japan. R/n *Karachi* for the voyage.

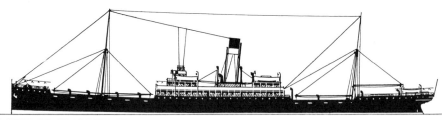

254 **CITY OF GLASGOW (III)**
B 1906 Workman, Clark & Co, Belfast. **T** 6,457g, 4,112n.
D 443/135.03 x 53.6/16.34 x 30.3/9.23.
E Sgl scr, 4 cyl quad exp, 481 NHP, 11 kts. By builder.
H Steel. 2 dks. F 44/13.41. B 144/43.89. P 80/24.38.
P 102 1st, 45 2nd.
1906 Built for Ellerman Lines Ltd, managed by George Smith & Sons.
1914 Aug: Taken over as a British Expeditionary Force troopship.
1918 Sept 1: Torpedoed by *UB-118* 21 miles east by north of Tuskar Rock. 12 lost.

CITY OF LONDON (II), CITY OF PARIS (II)

255 **CITY OF LONDON (II)**
B 1907 Workman, Clark & Co, Belfast. **T** 8,815g, 5,693n, 10,600dwt.
D 506/154.23 oa, 491/149.65 x 57.8/17.62 x 32.5/9.9. Dft 28.4/8.66.
E Sgl scr, 4 cyl quad exp, 660 NHP, 215 psi, 2 dbl, 2 sgl ended blrs. 15 kts. By builder. Fuel 930 tons coal at 80 tons per day.
H Steel. 2 dks. F 83/25.3. B 203/61.87. P 85/25.9. 5 hatches, 5 holds. 16 derricks. **P** 272 1st, amidships. 64 2nd in the poop.
1906 Nov: Launched.
1907 Feb: Trials. Reached 17 knots. Placed on the Bombay service.
1909 Took the Bombay-London record in 18 days 19 hours.
1916 Jan: Taken over and converted into an Armed Merchant Cruiser at Calcutta with 8 x 6 inch guns and 2 x 6 pounders. Served in the Far East.
1919 Refurbished by her builder. T 8,956. P 231 1st, 64 2nd. July 5: Re-entered service to India. The forward lifeboats were resited and placed on a deck abreast of the funnel.
1923 Recorded a voyage time of 23 days Calcutta-Liverpool.
1931-35 Employed on the South African service of Ellerman & Bucknall. Painted in their livery. She then transferred back to the India berth but with the now prevalent grey hull. Now had an upper house aft on the poop.
1939 Nov: Taken over for trooping duties with space for 1,400 troops.
1940 Collided in convoy and in fog with Blue Funnel's *Menelaus* ostensibly trying to avoid the on-rushing PSNC's *Orbita*. Both ships were damaged but neither sank. *Orbita* was later exonerated in the Admiralty Court case.

Dec 25: *City of London* was in a Middle-East bound troop convoy with Shaw Savill's *Tamaroa* as Commodore ship, which was attacked west of Sierra Leone by the German heavy cruiser *Admiral Hipper*. The action of HMS *Berwick*, one of a strong cruiser escort, drove off the attacker which retired to Brest for repairs (the first heavy German unit to use the port). *City of Canterbury* (269) and *City of Derby* (585) were in the same convoy.

1941 April: During the Greek campaign she landed troops at Suda Bay and after the Greeks capitulated on April 20 she evacuated over 3,700 troops from Crete to Alexandria escaping unscathed despite constant air attack. In all some 40,000 men were taken off for the loss of two destroyers and four transports. She remained based at Alexandria.
1946 Jan: Decommissioned. May 13: Arrived at Dalmuir and broken up by W. Arnott, Young & Co.

256 **CITY OF PARIS (II)**

Sister to 255 except: **B** Barclay, Curle & Co, Glasgow. **T** 9,191g, 5,935n.
D 493.2/150.33 bp x 57.7/17.59. **E** By builder. **H** F 84/25.6. **B** 205/62.48. **P** 92/28.04.
1907 Completed for Ellerman Lines Ltd with George Smith & Sons managers. Placed on the Liverpool-Bombay service.
1911 Took the Liverpool-Bombay record with a sailing of 19 days 1 hour.
1915 Employed as a troopship. Then used on Government service including a number of voyages to India with Officials.
1917 April 4: Inbound India-Marseilles with cargo and 13 passengers the ship was torpedoed, shortly after midnight, by *UC-35* 46 miles south by east of Cap d'Antibes; having been warned of U-boats by coded messages she was zig-zagging at the time. The ship was being abandoned when the submarine surfaced and called for the captain who could not be found. *UC-35* then fired on the ship before sinking her with a second torpedo. French patrol boats found four lifeboats with 41 bodies in them. Two further boats were never found. In all 122 lives were lost.

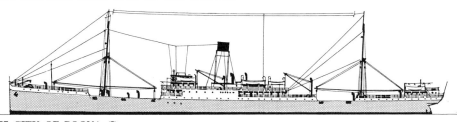

257 **CITY OF POONA (I)**

B 1912 Swan, Hunter & Wigham, Richardson, Newcastle. **T** 7,467g, 4,766n.
D 452/137.77 x 56.6/17.25 x 31.2/9.51.
E Tw scr, 2 x 4 cyl quad exp. 451 nhp. 12 kts. By Wallsend Slipway & Eng. Co, Newcastle.
H Steel. 2 dks. F 87/26.52. B 163/46.69. P 95/28.96. **P** 88 1st, 50 2nd in the poop, as usual. The starboard boat deck was open for its full length.
1912 Jan 21: Launched for Ellerman Lines Ltd; George Smith & Sons managers. The first twin screw vessel for the company.
1929 Sept 9: On American & Indian Line service New York-India.
1934 Nov: Sold for £12,000 and broken up in Japan.

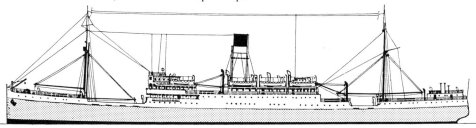

258 **CITY OF EXETER (I)**

B 1914 Workman, Clark & Co, Belfast. **T** 9,447g, 6,023n, 11,170dwt.
D 486.7/148.35 x 58.9/17.95 x 32.6/9.93.
E Tw scr, 2 x 4 cyls quad exp, 584 nhp, 225 psi. 12 kts. By builder. Fuel 1,890 tons coal at 70 pd.
H Steel. 2 dks. F 88/26.82. B 219/66.75. P 98/29.87.
P 180 1st, 62 2nd class.
1914 Apr 1: Launched. June 4: Trials. July: Delivered to Ellerman Lines Ltd, George Smith & Sons as managers. This and the other ships of the fleet operated under the title of the City Line. She was soon transferred to City Line Ltd. Unlike some of the passenger ships she had enclosed bridge deck superstructure port and starboard. The first cruiser stern passenger ship. The funnel top was removable for Manchester Ship Canal transits. India service. Aug: Became an Indian Army troopship.
1915 Returned to Bucknall commercial service.
1917 June 11: Mined 200 miles short of Bombay but safely made port. The mines were laid by *Wolf* (II) ex-*Wachtfels*, D.D-G. 'Hansa'.

1919 Resumed commercial service.

1933 Operated on Ellerman & Bucknall services in their livery. **P** 194 one class.

1939 Sept: Left on commercial service.

1940 May 1: Passed by the German Armed Merchant Cruiser *Atlantis* ex-*Goldenfels*, D.D-G. 'Hansa', Raider C to the British (disguised as *Kashii Maru* of Kokusai S.S. Co), shortly after she had reached her cruising area and before her first victim (Harrison's *Scientist*). Because *Atlantis* could not accommodate *City of Exeter*'s passengers and crew so early in the voyage she decided to allow the ship to proceed unharmed. *City of Exeter* was not fooled and radioed a 'suspicious vessel' warning to Cape Town. The reason was that Kokusai SS Co traded in the Pacific basin; not to the South Atlantic! Her fourth victim was however *City of Bagdad* (261).

1942 Suffered a cargo fire at Bombay.

1946 Carried King Zog of Albania and his entourage back from his wartime domicile in Britain to Port Said.

1950 March 25: Left on her final sailing. Her chief stewardess Miss Katherine Mustarde had served in her for 31 years, out of 38 years afloat. The ship was initially sold for breaking up in Italy but finally, July 11, left the Mersey in tow of Steel & Bennie's *Brigadier* and *Strongbow* for Dalmuir. July 14: Arrived and broken up by W. Arnott Young.

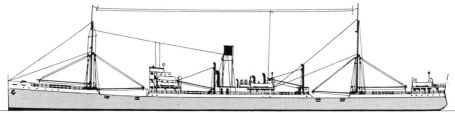

259 **CITY OF ORAN (I)**

B 1915 Wm Gray & Co, West Hartlepool. **T** 7,784g, 5,048n.

D 465.5/141.88 x 58.1/17.71 x 31.7/9.66.

E Sgl scr, tpl exp, 628 NHP, 220 psi, 3 sgl blrs. 11½ kts. By Central Marine Engine Works, West Hartlepool.

H Steel. 2 dks. F 100/30.48. B 171/52.12. P 107/32.6.

1915 Sept: Completed. The first City (but not Hall or Bucknall) vessel to be built on the East Coast. Owned by City of Oran SS Co.

1916 Dec 31: Attacked by U-boat in the English Channel but escaped.

1920 Transferred to Montgomerie & Workman (1920) Ltd., W. S. Workman as manager.

1933 Managed by City Line Ltd. Owned by M. & W.

1936 Transferred to Ellerman Lines Ltd when M. & W. ceased to own ships.

1943 Aug 2: Torpedoed off Mozambique by *U-196*. She was in convoy CB21 (Cape Town-Beira northbound). There were three ships and four escorts so the attack was very daring. Aug 3: *City of Oran* had to be sunk by her escorts.

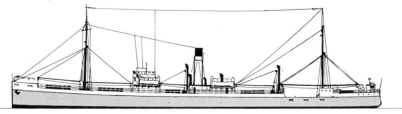

260 **CITY OF BIRMINGHAM (II)**

B 1917 Wm Gray & Co, West Hartlepool. **T** 6,182g, 4,002n.

D 391/119.18 x 54.2/16.52 x 28.9/8.8.

E Sgl scr, tpl exp, 581 NHP, 220 psi, 3 sgl blrs. 11 kts. By Central Marine Engine Works, West Hartlepool.

H Steel. 2 dks. F. & B. 274/83.51. P 48/14.63.

1917 Sept: Delivered to Ellerman Lines Ltd. Registered at Glasgow and employed on Government service.

1922 Transferred to City Line Ltd with George Smith & Sons as managers. As built she had her main mast forward of the poop. Later the poop was extended and she was given side houses abreast the mast (as drawn). Photographs of both profiles exist.

1940 Aug 16: Left Methill, Fife, in a southbound convoy. Parted for Hull and entered the two-cable width swept channel and promptly hit a mine off Spurn Head.

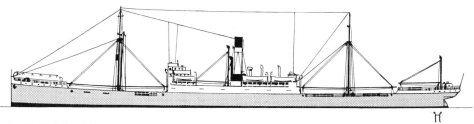

261 CITY OF BAGDAD

B 1919 J. C. Tecklenborg A. G., Geestemunde. **T** 7,506g, 4,710n.
D 469.4/143.07 x 58.4/17.8 x 32.3/9.84.
E Sgl scr, Tpl exp, 710 NHP, 220 psi, 4 sgl blrs. 12 kts. By builder.
H Steel 2 dks. F 59/17.98. B 138/42.06. P 67/20.42. Crew 21 Europeans, 60 Lascars.
1919 Ordered by D. D-G. 'Hansa'. Completed after wartime delays as *Gierfels*. Handed over to the Shipping Controller, G. Thompson & Co, Glasgow as managers.
1920 Acquired by Montgomerie & Workman (1920) Ltd, W. S. Workman as manager. R/n *City of Bagdad,* with no 'H' in the name.
1927 Management was transferred to George Smith & Sons.
1933 Transferred back to W. S. Workman as managers.
1936 Owned by Ellerman Lines Ltd when M. & W. ceased to own ships.
1940 July 11: sunk by explosives from the German Raider C, *Atlantis,* an ex-Hansa vessel herself, 400 miles west of Addu Atol, Indian Ocean. (See 258). Note: Her sister *Rudelsburg* became *City of Westminster* (440).

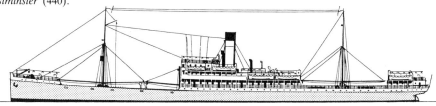

CITY OF LUCKNOW (IV), CITY OF VALENCIA

262 CITY OF LUCKNOW (IV)

B 1908 A. Reiherstieg, Hamburg. **T** 7,248g, 4,520n.
D 441.5/134.56 x 52.7/16.06 x 29.6/9.02.
E Tw scr, 2 x tpl exp, 750 NHP, 213 psi, 4 sgl blrs, 12 kts by builder.
H Steel. 2 dks. F 54/16.45. B & P 264/80.47. **P** 89 1st, 28 2nd.
1908 Nov 19: Launched as *Heluan* for Deutsche D-G 'Kosmos', Hamburg.
1920 Acquired. R/n *City of Lucknow*. Owned by City of Oran SS Co with City Line Ltd, as managers.
1921 Oct 21: On Bucknall's American & Indian Line service New York-India.
1926 Nov 24: Sold to Hamburg America Line; reverted to *Heluan*. Placed on the South American service.
1931 Nov: Broken up at Osaka.

263 CITY OF VALENCIA

Sister of 262. **T** 7,329g, 4,539n. **D** 442.4/134.84. **H** F 66/20.11. F & B 266/81.07.
1908 Jan 14: Launched as *Roda* for 'Kosmos'.
1920 Acquired by City Line Ltd, W. S. Workman as managers. R/n *City of Valencia*. Served on the Karachi direct route.
1921 Nov 18: Placed on American & Indian Line service.
1933 Laid up at Liverpool.
1934 Feb: Broken up by Hughes Bolckow, Blyth.

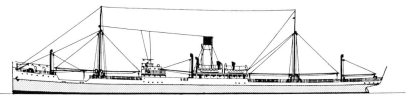

264 CITY OF MILAN (I)

B 1907 Flensburger S. G., Flensburg. **T** 4,222g, 2,558n.

D 387.8/118.2 x 51/15.5 x 25.2/7.68.
E Sgl scr, tpl exp, 473 NHP, 213 psi, 3 sgl blrs. 11 kts. By builder.
H Steel. 2 dks. F 50/15.24. B & P 315/96.01.
1907 March 2: Launched as *Plauen*, Deutsch-Australische D-G, Hamburg. Apr 4: Placed on their Indian service.
1914 Aug: The ship was at Hamburg when World War I started. Laid up.
1917 Taken over by the German Navy (Kriegsmarine) for conversion into an auxiliary cruiser but the work was abandoned.
1918 Dec 17: Released back to her owners.
1919 Apr 13: Handed over to the Shipping controller placed with Watts, Watts & Co, London.
1921 Acquired by Ellerman. R/n *City of Milan*, owned by City Line Ltd with George Smith & Sons as managers.
1930 Sold the Cia Colonial de Nav., Lisbon. R/n *Ganda*.
1941 June 20: Torpedoed by *U-123* in the Atlantic west of Cape St. Vincent.

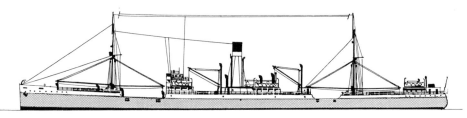

265 CITY OF CAMBRIDGE (III)
B 1920 Workman, Clark & Co, Belfast. **T** 7,058g, 4,557n.
D 454/138.38 x 58.2/17.74 x 34.5/10.52.
E Sgl scr, 4 cyl, quad exp, 647 NHP, 225 psi, 3 sgl blrs. 11 kts. By builder.
H Steel. 2 dks. F 105/32. B 118/35.97. P 112/34.14.
1920 Built for City Line Ltd, W. S. Workman managers.
1934 Oct 10: Wrecked on Pratas Reef in the China Sea.

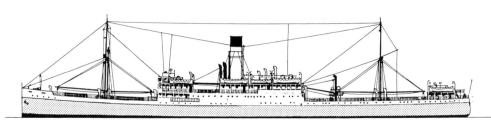

266 CITY OF SIMLA
B 1921 Wm. Gray & Co, West Hartlepool. **T** 9,468g, 5,955n.
D 476.87/145.3 x 58.2/17.74 x 31.3/9.54.
E Tw scr, 4 dbl reduction geared steam turbines, 1,243 NHP, 225 psi, 5 sgl blrs. By Central Marine Engine Works, West Hartlepool.
H Steel. 2 dks. F & B 347/105.76. P 96/29.26. Upper B 78/23.77.
1921 Nov: Delivered to City Line Ltd, George Smith & Sons managers. She had been ordered for Ellerman Lines Ltd. Manchester Ship Canal funnel top. M/v to Yokohama but then went onto the Indian service.
1925 Had a spell on the South African Bucknall route then back to the Bombay service.
1932-33 Laid up River Clyde.
1940 Sept 21: Torpedoed by *U-138* off the Outer Hebrides in convoy OB 216 from the Clyde to North America. Four ships in the convoy were sunk during the attack all by *U-138*.

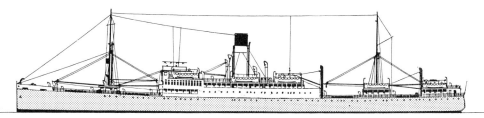

267 CITY OF NAGPUR (II)

B 1922 Workman, Clark & Co, Belfast. **T** 10,146g, 6,280n.
D 489/149 oa, 469.9/143.22 x 59.3/18.07 x 40/12.19.
E Sgl scr, 4 cyl, quad exp, 1,038 NHP, 230 psi, 5 sgl blrs. 14 kts. By builder.
H Steel. 2 + shelter dk. Flush decked (rare for the Company). **P** 350.
1922 May 30: Launched. Sept 12: Delivered. Her main deck was open on the starboard side of the bridge deck; closed port side as drawn. The first City Liner to exceed 10,000grt and odd being single screw. Owned Ellerman Lines Ltd with City Line Ltd as managers. Oct 12: M/v Glasgow-Liverpool-Bombay; then placed on the Japan service.
1933 Laid up in Bombay harbour.
1934 Placed on the South African service.
1936-39 Used on summer cruises to the Norwegian Fjords.
1938 Passenger accommodation modernised during her annual overhaul by Wm Gray at West Hartlepool.
1939 Sept: Her final summer cruise was cancelled.
1941 Apr 24: Torpedoed twice by *U-75* 900 miles west of Fastnet with 300 passengers and 215 crew aboard. All but one passenger were saved but 10 crewmen were lost. The lifeboats kept together and were seen by a patrolling Catalina aircraft, the destroyer HMS *Hurricane* picked up the 504 survivors.

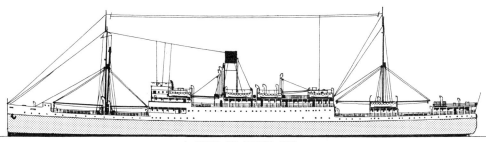

A CITY OF PARIS (III)

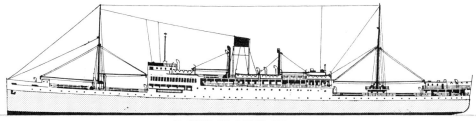

B CITY OF PARIS (III)

268 CITY OF PARIS (III)

B 1922 Swan, Hunter & Wigham, Richardson, Wallsend, Newcastle. **T** 10,840g, 6,855n, 10,100dwt.
D 484.7/149.74 x 59.3/18.07 x 32.6/9.94.
E Sgl scr, 3 dbl reduction geared steam turbines, 1,315 NHP, 225 psi, 5 sgl blrs. 14 kts. By Wallsend Slipway Co, Newcastle.
H Steel 2 + shelter dk. **P** 230 1st, 100 2nd.
1921 Due to a strike her fitting out was completed at Penhoet, St Nazaire. Delivered three months late. She had an open bridge deck on the starboard side. Port plated as drawn.
1922 Feb: Delivered. M/v to Japan then Liverpool — India service. Black Hull.
1924 Sailed in Ellerman's Wilson colours for cruises to the Northern Capitals. Grey hull when she returned to City service. **P** 199 1st.
1932 Laid up in the Greloch.

1936 Placed on the South African route. Terminus: Beira.

1939-1945 Mainly employed on trooping duties. 1,500 men.

1939 Sept 16: Struck the first magnetic mine laid (by air) in the Thames.

1940 June: Carried Senegalese troops to Bordeaux. June 20: France capitulated and the troops were taken back to Dakar.

1942 Feb 7: Took Australian troops Bombay-Singapore but the Japanese took the fortress city on Feb 15 and the ship was diverted to the East Indies and thence, because of the Japanese advance, to Australia.

1942 June: Painted with red, white and blue stripes and with the word 'Diplomatic' on her sides she carried the Japanese legation from Bombay to Lourenco Marques sailing, by agreement with the enemy, with all her lights on. It is reported that she was shadowed by an enemy vessel but this is unlikely so far from the theatre of war.

1944 Returned to the UK for conversion into a Personnel Ship for the Pacific Fleet Train. The work was being completed in Montreal when the war ended.

1945 Sept: Based at Hong Kong as an accommodation ship.

1946 Served as a troopship in the traditional white hulled livery.

1947 Jan: Refitted by her builder and her profile modified (Drawing B). **P** 168 1st. Placed on Ellerman Bucknall service.

1955 Now superseded by the new *City of Port Elizabeth* class her final voyage was Lourenco Marques-Rotterdam-London-Hull-Middlesbrough.

1956 Feb 25: Arrived at Newport for scrapping by John Cashmore & Co.

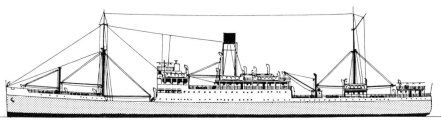

CITY OF CANTERBURY (II)

269 CITY OF CANTERBURY (II)

B 1922 Swan, Hunter & Wigham Richardson, Wallsend. **T** 8,421g, 5,290n, 10,200dwt.
D 448.4/136.67 x 56.4/17.19 x 31.4/9.51.
E Sgl scr, 4 cyl quad, 4,250 ihp at 81 rpm, 230 psi, 4 blrs. 13 kts. By Wallsend Slipway Co, Newcastle.
H Steel. 2 dks. **F** 103/31.39. **B & P** 295/89.92. **P** 120 1st, 48 2nd.

1922 Feb: Entered City Line Ltd's service to India with W. S. Workman as managers. Coal burner; later converted to oil. Black hull. The slowest of the six passenger vessels in the group's fleet.

1924 Inbound she frequently, during the cooler season, routed Bombay-Durban-Cape Town-UK to meet requirements between India and South Africa.

1930 Given a Metropolitan-Vickers impulse electric exhaust turbine, 3,000 rpm sgl reduction geared to 750 rpm driving a disconnectable electric generator connected to an 86 rpm motor attached to the propeller shaft. Power increased by 23%. Her service speed moved up to 14 kts but she now had power in hand whereas previously she was almost flat out. Her time-keeping was thus greatly improved. Placed on E & B service with their funnel (but not white masted).

1940 Taken over for trooping. Capacity 1,500. Dec 25: Acting as Commodore ship of the Glasgow portion she was in the convoy attacked by the German heavy cruiser *Admiral Hipper*. She had 1,500 troops aboard bound for the Middle East. *Hipper* made off when attacked by one of the escorting cruisers HMS *Berwick*. *City of London* (255) and *City of Derby* (585) were also in the convoy.

1941 Feb: Went urgently to Durban to embark anti-aircraft personnel to help man the guns in Crete against mounting German air attack. She also carried 1,500 Marines to the Island. May: She was at Suda Bay, Crete, after the capitulation of Greece to the Nazis and carried the Greek crown jewels to Alexandria together with the survivors of 12 ships that had been sunk. The ship then took 1,000 Italian prisoners of war, with 70 guards, to Durban. *Canterbury* next shuttled up and down the east coast of Africa trooping and moving prisoners.

1942 Jan: Took troops from Durban to Singapore. Feb: At Singapore, her arrival was heralded by 18 attacking Japanese bombers. In all she was attacked 26 times. 2,000 troops and civilians were evacuated to Batavia. From there she carried 500 naval survivors of ships sunk back to Colombo. Next she went to Bombay for overhaul and the repair of war damage.

1943-44 were spent in the Mediterranean theatre.

1944 May: Arrived back in the Clyde. June 9: Embarked troops at North Woolwich for the Normandy beaches, landing them at Arromanches. After more trooping sailings from Southampton to the Omaha

and Utah beaches she returned to the Clyde where she was unexpectedly returned to Ellerman for sailings to India.
1945 Again used for trooping between India and Burma.
1947 Reconditioned by her builder on the Tyne. May: Back in service to India.
1953 June 1: Sold to Bisco for scrap.

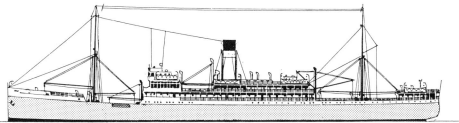

270 CITY OF VENICE (III)
B 1924 Workman, Clark & Co, Belfast. **T** 8,762g, 5,492n.
D 455.2/138.74 x 58.1/17.71 x 31.3/9.54.
E Sgl scr, 4 cyl, quad exp, 230 psi, 4 sgl blrs. 14 kts. By builder.
H Steel. 2 dks. F 86/26.21. B & P 315/96.01. **P** 133 1st, 32 2nd.
1924 Feb 6: Launched. April: Entered service to India for Ellerman Lines Ltd, George Smith & Sons managers. Sept: Placed on American & Indian Line service New York-Calcutta.
1932 Fitted with Bauer-Wach LP exhaust turbine driving a generator-motor geared to the shaft. Laid up at Liverpool.
1936 Carried Princess Mary, the Princess Royal, and Lord Lascelles to Cyprus. (When JRE was alive they were his next door neighbours).
1943 June 24: Left the Clyde. July 4: Torpedoed by *U-375* off Cape Tenez, Mediterranean, and set on fire in convoy KMS 18B (=UK-Med-Slow, 8 knots, B= Bark beach) enroute to Operation Husky, the invasion of Sicily, and destined for the Bark west beach head at Cape Passero. 11 crew and an unspecified but not large number of troops killed. KMS 18B, comprising 17 Motor Transport supply ships and one LSG (Landing Ship Gantry), was carrier for the First Canadian Division whose main infantry force was aboard KMF 18B and KMF 19 (F=Fast, 12 knots). *St. Essylt* (South American Saint Line) and *Devis* (Lamport & Holt) were also lost from the same convoy. With the exception of one vessel from Convoy MWS 36, out of Alexandria, these were the only transports sunk by enemy action during the invasion which put ashore 115,000 British Commonwealth and 66,000 American troops.

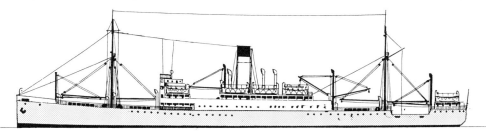

271 CITY OF HONGKONG
B 1924 Earle's S. B. & E. Co, Hull. **T** 9,606g, 6,071n, 11,890 dwt.
D 470.2/143.32 x 61.5/18.74 x 32.2/9.81.
E Sgl scr, 4 cyl, quad exp, 837 NHP, 225 psi, 4 sgl blrs. 12½ kts. By builder.
H Steel. 2 ks. F & P 394/120.09. P 40/12.19. **P** 104 1st.
1923 Laid down as *Colorado* for Ellerman's Wilson Line but converted to passenger, Dec 11: Launched as *City of Hongkong* ostensibly for Wilson but registered as Ellerman Lines Ltd. A sister ship, yard no. 640, was cancelled.
1924 May 15: Trials May: Entered service for the City Line to India.
1926 Managed by Ellerman & Bucknall, South African route.
1930 A Low Pressure exhaust turbine was added driving a reversible electric generator which drove a motor connected to the shaft. Power was increased by one-third, oil consumption dropped from 73 to 66 tons per day and the speed increased to 13½ knots. Other ships had Bauer-Wach; this differed: No reverse and had a hydraulic coupling.
Nov 26: Back in service. New York-Calcutta route of American & Indian Line then back to E & B.
1936 Reverted to City Line. By now the forward set of derrick posts had been removed.
1939-45 War service as a troopship. Took part (May 5-7 1942) in the Madagascar landings.

1946 On the Bombay service. Collided with Furness-Houlder's *Rippingham Grange* at Port Said.
1951 Aug: Sold for £175,000 to Fratelli Grimaldi Armatori, Genoa. R/n *Centauro*, blue funnel, white band. Central America service.
1953 Dec-1954 May: Reconditioned at Genoa.
1955 Feb: Enroute Naples-Hampton Roads called at Bermuda to refuel. In a storm she lost both anchors and went aground. Two tugs refloated her; towed by *Foundation Francis* to Hampton Roads for repairs. March: Left Hampton Roads for Ceuta-Bagnoli-Genoa. Apr 29: Laid up there. June 15: Left in tow for Savona. Broken up.

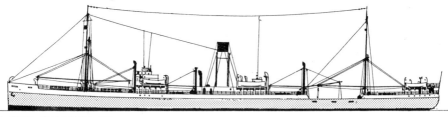

272 CITY OF DELHI (IV)

B 1925 Wm. Gray (1918) Ltd, Wear Shpyd, Sunderland. **T** 7,443g, 4,731n, 11,680 dwt.
D 450.5/137.31 x 58.6/17.86 x 32.1/9.78.
E Sgl scr, 4 cyl, quad exp + Bauer-Wach exhaust turb dbl reduction geared to shaft by hydraulic coupling. 225 psi, 3 sgl blrs, 12½ kts. By builder's Central Marine Engine Works, West Hartlepool.
H Steel 2 dks. B & F 317/96.62. P 74/22.55.
1925 July: Delivered to Ellerman Lines Ltd, W. S. Workman managers.
1956 Sold at Middlesbrough to British Iron & Steel (Salvage) Ltd, London (BISCO) and broken up by P & W McLellan at Bo'ness, Firth of Forth (in 1957).

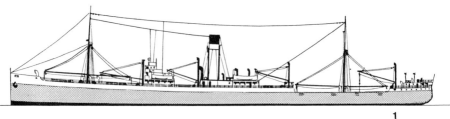

1

273 CITY OF MANDALAY

B Swan, Hunter & Wigham Richardson, Wallsend, Newcastle. **T** 7,049g, 4,511n.
D 443.2/135.09 x 57.9/17.65 x 31.9/9.72.
E Tpl exp, 644 NHP. By Wallsend Slipway, Newcastle.
H F & B 303/92.35. P 43/13.11. C 718,000/20,331.6 cu g.
1925 Jan: Completed for Ellerman Lines Ltd, W. S. Workman managers.
1930s On Ellerman & Bucknall service. Their funnel and a black hull.
1939 Oct 17: Torpedoed at 17.42 by *U-46* off Cape Finisterre in convoy HG3 (Home-Gibraltar) to become Ellerman's first World War II war loss. The attack was carried out by 4 U-boats acting together; the first instance of the Wolf pack tactics. She was standing by Bibby's *Yorshire* which had been hit by *U-46* at 08.35 and by *U-37* (commanded by pack leader Werner Hartmann; *U-45* being the fourth) at 16.40. The survivors of both were picked up by the American ship *Independence Hall*. Another U-boat, *U-48*, was in the attack and she sank *Clan Chisholm*. This, the first instances of a U-boat pack, was at the time experimental but later became standard tactics until the strength of the escorts and aircraft cover made it suicidal.

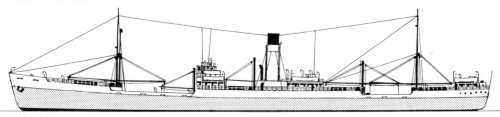

274 CITY OF DIEPPE

B 1929 Wm. Gray, West Hartlepool **T** 7,958g, 4,850n, 10,630 dwt.
D 465.5/141.88 x 58.2/17.74 x 32.2/9.81.

E Sgl scr, 4 cyl quad exp with LP dbl reduction geared turb and hydraulic coupling to shaft. 14 kts. By Central Marine Eng Wks, West Hartlepool.
H Steel. 2 dks. F 83/25.3. B 180/54.86. P 84/25.6.
1929 June: Delivered to Ellerman Lines Ltd, City Line Ltd managers. She was the builder's 1,000th ship and the 774th engine by their adjacent subsidiary Central Marine Engine Works.
1934 Lengthened to 501.8/152.95 F 107/32.61 and fitted with a Maier bow (as drawn). Speed up to 16 kts.
1937 Transferred to Ellerman & Bucknall who already owned her unmodified sister *City of Canberra* (598).
1941 Stationed at Freetown, Sierra Leone, as a storeship for the navy and convoy ships. She relieved *City of Tokio* (446). With no dry dock facilities stationary ships became so weed bound that they had to return to the UK for scraping. This they did whenever the stores were exhausted.
1956 March: Sold for £182,000 to Eastman Shipping Co, Nassau. R/n *Eastman*. British flag.
1959 Broken up in the UK.

CITY OF CHESTER See *City of Chester (I)* Hall 393

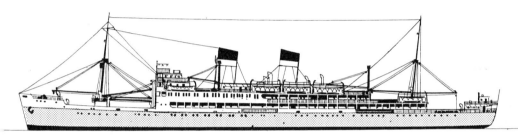

275 **CITY OF BENARES (V)**
B 1936 Barclay, Curle & Co, Glasgow. T 11,081g, 7,758n.
D 509/155.14 x 62.7/19.11 x 34.6/10.54.
E Sgl scr, geared turb, 6,000 SHP, 15 kts, max 17. By Cammell, Laird, Birkenhead. Fuel: 3,500 tons coal.
H Steel. 2 dks. F 41/12.5. P 219 one class. Crew: 180.
1936 Aug 5: Launched. Oct 15: Delivered. Oct 24: M/v Liverpool-Bombay. Ellerman's only two funnelled ship and acknowledged as the most beautiful ship ever owned by them; widely held to be among the loveliest built. Her after funnel was a dummy.
1940 A voyage was fixed, by the Ministry of Shipping, Liverpool-Montreal in ballast and, under the Government's 'Children's Overseas Evacuation Board', to carry 90 children and 10 escorts to the safety of Canada. The voyage being operated by Cunard-White Star.
Sept 12: Embarked her passengers at Prince's floating, landing stage. Then anchored mid-river. Captain Nicholl.
Sept 13: 18.00 sailed with 406 aboard of which 209 were crew, 6 convoy staff and 191 passengers including the children. *City of Benares* was commodore ship of 19 ship 8 knot convoy (half her service speed). The escorts were one destroyer and two sloops. The convoy sailed in three lines with *City of Benares,* as commodore, lead ship of the centre line.
Sept 17: 01.00, the warships left the convoy at the extremity of their steaming range. The convoy thus entered the unescorted gap.
22.05: Torpedoed, one of three sunk by *U-48* that day, in heavy weather and darkness. She was hit in no. 5 hold aft and the ship commenced to settle by the stern listing to port. Abandon ship was ordered. All the lifeboats were launched within 15 minutes but several were swamped by waves. At 22.45 *City of Benares* sank with the loss, in all, of 248 lives, including the captain. Of these 77 were children and 5 escorts.
Sept 18: The destroyer HMS *Hurricane* rescued survivors off a raft and from lifeboats; a total of 105 of whom 5 died aboard ship. These were landed, Sept 20 noon, at Greenock.
Sept 25: A Sunderland aircraft sighted a lifeboat and radioed for assistance. It then returned and dropped food. At 17.00 the destroyer HMS *Anthony* reached them. Sept 26: *Anthony* landed the 45, including six children at Greenock.
The survivors totalled 145,88 crew and 57 passengers of whom only thirteen were children and five were escorts. The evacuation of children by sea ceased.

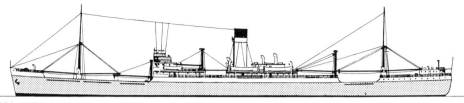

276 CITY OF KARACHI (II)

B 1937 Barclay, Curle & Co, Glasgow. **T** 7,139g.
D 464.3/141.52 x 59.2/18.04 x 31.2/9.51.
E Sgl scr, 3 s.r.g. Parsons Marine turbs, 15 kts. Installed by builder.
H Steel. 2 dks. F 31/9.45. B 195/59.44. P 74/22.55.
1937 Completed for City Line Ltd.
1941 Apr 13: Lost by dive bomber attack at Volo, Crete during the British evacuation of the island. Ellerman Papayanni's *Destro* (94) stood by and added her anti-aircraft fire in a vain attempt to drive off the attackers.

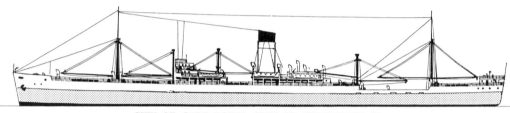

CITY OF CAPE TOWN, CITY OF EDINBURGH (V)
CITY OF CALCUTTA (IV), CITY OF PRETORIA (II)
CITY OF LINCOLN

277 CITY OF EDINBURGH (V)

B 1938 Cammell, Laird & Co, Birkenhead. **T** 8,036g, 3,965n.
D 515.8/157.21 oa, 496.7/151.39 x 62.4/19.02 x 31.3/9.54.
E Tw scr, 2 x 3 sgl reduction geared turbines, 1,867 NHP, 265 psi, 6 sgl blrs. By builder. Bunkers 3,150 tons coal.
H Steel. 2 + part 3rd dk. F & B 351/15.54. P 31.16.
1938 Aug: The first ship built at Birkenhead for City Line. Owned by Ellerman Lines Ltd with City Line Ltd as managers. Employed on the USA-Australia-New Zealand route until 1939.
1941 The ship caught fire when berthed at Takordai. Towed out to sea for fear that she would block the port if she capsized. There the flames were extinguished.
1942 Nov 26: Took part in convoy KMF4 carrying follow up troops for Operation Torch. In heavy weather she fell out of the convoy and, Dec 2, put into Gibraltar.
1943 Sept: Taken over by the Admiralty. Converted at Liverpool into a LSH (Landing Ship Headquarters) for Pacific Operations. Extra radar and wireless installations, 2 x twin 4 inch guns, six sets of oerlikon AA guns and six LCV's (Landing Craft Vehicles), 3 per side on davits. Crew 450.
1944 July: As HMS *Lothian* she was the command ship to Force X, comprising herself as LSH plus six LSI's (Landing Ship Infantry) which was sent to join the US 7th Fleet. Her conversion work was incomplete for example storage hatches were not installed so that goods had to be loaded below decks manually.
Aug 3rd: Force X left the Clyde for the Pacific via New York and Panama. Instead of 450 there were 750 aboard, under the command of Rear Admiral A. G. Tolbot D.S.O., all in very cramped conditions with inadequate ventilation and water that was so insufficient that it had to be rationed.
Sept 1: While docked at Balboa an armed mutiny of 103 men occurred. The only armed mutiny in the Royal Navy since the last century. Armed Royal Marines were used to restore order. There being no relief seamen available and nowhere to imprison the Court Martialled men their sentences were suspended and they continued on duty. Force X proceeded.
Sept 29: HMS *Lothian* joined the US 7th Fleet at Langemack Bay, New Guinea and was allocated to the Philippines Invasion Fleet. However the US navy took no interest in the British force and after fruitlessly sailing around the islands she was sent to Sydney.
1945 Feb 23: Arrived at Sydney where she became flagship to the Rear Admiral Fleet Train (R.A.F.T.), D. B. Fisher CB, CBE, ADC. Her duties were to control the many transports now arriving to supply the British Pacific Fleet. May 29: *Lothian* left to return to Sydney; this time to be prepared as HQ ship for the British invasion forces earmarked for South East Asia. Sept 3: Hostilities having ceased she went into Singapore shortly after the Japanese surrender then to Hong Kong and as far north as Shanghai evacuating British civilians and prisoners of the Japanese.

1946 Feb: Left Trincomalee for the UK and decommissioning. In her 1 year 10 months under the White Ensign she had been the flagship of two admirals (and nearly a third), had an armed mutiny, covered 67,000 miles, and had a baby born on board. Of the 750 men who left the Clyde only 30 completed the full commission. April: Handed back to Ellerman at Port Sunlight, Mersey.
1947 Reconditioning over she was transferred to Ellerman & Bucknall ownership.
1961 Apr 7: Sold to Hong Kong Salvage & Towage Co. R/n *Castle Mount*. Broken up at Hong Kong in the same year.

278 CITY OF CALCUTTA (IV)
Sister to 277 except: **B** 1940. **T** 8,063g, 3,977n. **D** 515.7/157.18 oa.
1940 Aug: Completed, the fifth ship of the *City of Cape Town* class. She differed by having no rake and her derrick posts were slightly staggered.
1941 Feb 28: Prime Minister Winston Churchill wrote: *"City of Calcutta*, due Loch Ewe March 2, is reported to be going to Hull, arriving March 9. This ship must on no account be sent to the East Coast. It contains 1,700 machine guns, 44 aeroplanes engines and no fewer than 14,000,000 cartridges. These cartridges are absolutely vital to the defence of Great Britain which has been so largely confided by the Navy to the Army and the Air Force. That it should be proposed to send such a ship round to the East Coast, with all the additional risk, is abominable. I am sending a copy of this minute to the Minister of Transport."
1952 Mar 17: A hold fire was extinguished.
1961 Dec 16: Sold to the Grosvenor Shipping Co, Hong Kong. R/n *Grosvenor Pilot*.
1962 Broken up at Hong Kong.

CITY OF CAPE TOWN (I) See Hall 473
CITY OF PRETORIA (II) See E & B 590
CITY OF LINCOLN (II) See E & B 591

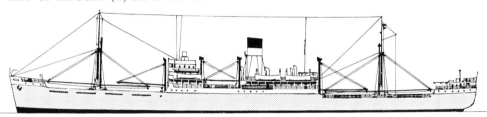

CITY OF BRISTOL (II), CITY OF CHESTER, CITY OF MADRAS
179 CITY OF BRISTOL (II)
B 1943 Swan, Hunter & Wigham Richardson, Wallsend. **T** 8,459g, 4,321n, 10,960dwt.
D 493/150.27 oa, 471.6/143.74 x 64.3/19.6 x 33.9/10.33. Dft 29.9/9.1.
E Tw scr, 2 x 3 turb. By Wallsend Slipway & Eng. Co.
1943 Jan: Delivered. M/v to South Africa.
1952 Nov 15: A fire in her cargo was extinguished.
1961 Sold to the Far Eastern Nav. Corp, r/n *Tung Lee*.
1962 Sept: Her classification at Lloyds ceased.
1963-4 Broken up.

CITY OF CHESTER (II) See Hall 476
CITY OF MADRAS (V) See Hall 477

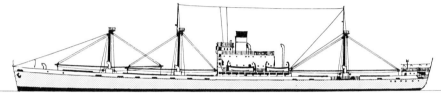

CITY OF ST ALBANS (I), CITY OF CHELMSFORD, CITY OF DONCASTER, CITY OF ELY
CITY OF LICHFIELD, CITY OF NEWPORT, CITY OF PORTSMOUTH
CITY OF ROCHESTER, CITY OF SHREWSBURY, CITY OF COLCHESTER
CITY OF LEEDS (III), CITY OF STAFFORD
280 CITY OF ST ALBANS (I)
B 1943 Bethlehem Fairfield Corp, Baltimore. **T** 7,264g, 4,456n.
D 441.7/134.63 oa, 423.7/129.14 x 57/17.37 x 34.8/10.61.

E Sgl scr, tpl exp, 2,500 bhp at 76 rpm. 240 psi. 11 kts. By General Motors Corp, Hamilton, Ohio.
H Steel. 2 dks.
1943 Dec: Completed as *Frederick Banting* on bare boat charter to M.O.W.T. with City line as managers. Liberty ship.
1946 M.O.W.T. became M.O.T. when the word 'war' was dropped.
1947 Acquired by City. R/n *City of St Albans.*
1959 Nov 19: Sold to Soc. di Nav. Magliveras, Panama. R/n *Marineri.*
1967 R/n *Libertas* by Dolphin Shipping Co, Famagusta.
1969 March: Scrapped at Onomichi, Japan.

CITY OF CHELMSFORD See 593	**CITY OF PORTSMOUTH** See 595
CITY OF DONCASTER See 594	**CITY OF ROCHESTER** See 121
CITY OF ELY See 119	**CITY OF SHREWSBURY** See 122
CITY OF LICHFIELD See 120	**CITY OF COLCHESTER** See 596
CITY OF NEWPORT See 475	**CITY OF LEEDS (III)** See 597

CITY OF STAFFORD See 123

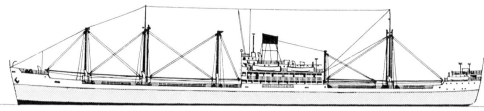

CITY OF DURHAM (IV), CITY OF KHARTOUM (II), CITY OF CARLISLE
CITY OF LUCKNOW (VI), CITY OF POONA (II), CITY OF SWANSEA (I)

281 **CITY OF DURHAM (IV)**
B 1945 Cammell, Laird. Birkenhead. **T** 7,253g, 4,121n.
D 497.5/151.64 oa, 475.5/144.93 x 64.4/19.63 x 28.8/8.78.
E Sgl scr, 2 dbl reduction geared turbs, 2 wt blrs. 15 kts. By Richardsons, Westgarth, West Hartlepool.
H Steel. 1 + shelter + pt 3rd dks. F 40/12.19. P 35/10.67.
1945 March: Delivered to City Line. One of a group of fast standard ships designed towards the end of the war. Their top-mast configurations varied during their careers. *City of Durham* being the only one allocated to City.
1962 Aug 28: Sold to Waywiser Nav Corp, Taiwan. R/n *Yonlee.*
1965 Broken up in Taiwan.

Four ships of this class were managed by Hall Line:
CITY OF KHARTOUM (II) See 478
CITY OF CARLISLE See 598 E & B
CITY OF LUCKNOW (VI) See 479
CITY OF POONA (II) See 481
CITY OF SWANSEA (I) See 480

CITY OF OXFORD (IV), CITY OF BIRMINGHAM (III), CITY OF GLOUCESTER (II)/
CITY OF BROOKLYN, CITY OF COVENTRY, CITY OF LIVERPOOL (I), CITY OF PERTH (V)
CITY OF CARDIFF (III) / CITY OF PHILADELPHIA, CITY OF MANCHESTER (V)
CITY OF BATH (II) / CITY OF CHICAGO, CITY OF GUILDFORD (II)/CITY OF OTTAWA (I)/
CITY OF LEEDS (IV)

282 **CITY OF OXFORD (IV)**
B 1948 John Brown, Clydebank. **T** 7,593g, 4,427n, 10,800dwt.
D 480.3/146.39 oa, 462.6/140.97 x 61.8/18.84 x 30.5/9.3.
E Sgl scr, 3 sgl Parsons reduction geared turbs, 7,200 shp at 115 rpm, 275 psi, 2 Babcock & Wilcox wt

blrs. 15½ kts. By builder. The waste steam pipe ran inside the funnel and vented just below the white band.

H Steel. 2 + shelter dk. **F** 41/12.49. **C** 631,200/17,873.7 cu g.

1948 Dec: Delivered to City; the first of a class of ten ships managed across the fleet by City, Hall and E & B. They supplemented the routes served by the Liberty ships. After the *City of New York* (482) class they were the second set of replacement vessels.

1976 Sold to Union Bros. Marine Corp. S.A., Panama. R/n *Union Arabia.*

1977 She was then operated by Arabian Establishment for Trade, Saudi Arabia.

1978 Jan 4: Arrived Kaohsiung. Feb 20: Demolition commenced by Yu Horng Steel & Iron Co.

283 CITY OF BIRMINGHAM (III)

As 282 except: **B** 1949. **T** 7,599g, 4,430n.

1949 May 3: Trials. These were on the same day as *City of Liverpool* (487).

1971 Laid up at Barry Dock. Oct 9: Arrived at Castellon for breaking up.

CITY OF GLOUCESTER (II)/CITY OF BROOKLYN See 485
CITY OF COVENTRY See 486
CITY OF LIVERPOOL (I) See 487

284 CITY OF PERTH (V)

As 282 except:**B** 1949 Caledon S.B. & E. Co, Dundee. **T** 7,547g, 4,407n.

D 485.1/147.86 oa. **E** By Parsons Marine Steam Turbines, Wallsend. **H** F 43/13.11.

1949 June: Completed for City Line.

1967 Nov 22: Sold to Astro Aspirante Cia. Nav. S.A., Piraeus. R/n *Elenif.*

1968 Jan 3; Struck a wreck at Alexandria. Beached but in heavy seas the ship broke in two and was abandoned. Stripped where she lay.

CITY OF CARDIFF (III)/CITY OF PHILADELPHIA See 488

285 CITY OF MANCHESTER (V)

As 282 except: **B** 1950 J. L. Thompson & Sons, Sunderland. **T** 7,583g, 4,413n.

D 485.3/147.92 oa, 465.8/141.97 x 61.8/18.84. **E** By Wallsend Slipway. **H** F 43/13.11.

1950 March: Delivered to City.

1971 Sold for £90,000 to Kavo Cia. Naviera S.A., Panama. R/n *Kavo Yerakes.*

Nov 11: Arrived at Kaohsiung for demolition by Tung Cheng Steel & Iron Wks.

CITY OF BATH (II)/CITY OF CHICAGO See 489

CITY OF GUILDFORD (II)/CITY OF OTTAWA (I)/CITY OF LEEDS (IV) See 490

Sister of *CITY OF BIRKENHEAD* See Hall 491

286 CITY OF KARACHI (IV)

B 1951 Wm. Denny & Bros, Dumbarton. T 7,320g, 4,192n.

D 484.8/147.77 oa, 465.6/141.91 x 61.8/18.84 x 30/9.14.

E Sgl scr, 2 SRG turbs, 1,210 nhp, 2 wt blrs. 14 kts. By builder.

H Steel. 2 + shelter + pt 4th dk. **F** 45/13.72. Crew 73. **P** 4.

1950 Nov 10: Launched. Made 14.41 knots on trials.

1951 Mar 15: Delivered to City. During her career with Ellerman she had a 'pepper pot' exhaust cone added to her funnel.

1971 Nov: During the East and West Pakistan civil war in which India joined the ship was bombed, unscathed, at Karachi. Her Indian crew members were interned. Officers worked the ship to Bombay.

1972 May 11: Sold at Liverpool for £100,000 to Navieros Progresivos S.A., Panama. R/n *Kavo Kolones.*

1974 Jan 10: Arrived at Kaohsiung and broken up by Chin Ho Fa Steel & Iron Co.

CITY OF ATHENS B 1955. T 8,965. Ex-Jacob's *Beechwood.*

1955 The ship was converted into a dry cargo ship. Owned by Soc de Nav Magliveras, Panama. Served on charter and in Ellerman livery 1955-57.

Sister of *CITY OF NEWCASTLE* (II) See Hall 494
CITY OF RIPON (III), CITY OF COLOMBO (II)

287 CITY OF RIPON (III)

B 1956 Vickers-Armstrong (Eng), Walker-on-Tyne. **T** 7,713g, 4,033n, 10,000dwt.

D 507.2/154.59 oa x 65.9/20.1 x 28.3/8.62.

E Sgl scr, oil; 6 cyl, 2S.SA Doxford, 8,000 bhp, 15 kts. By V-A, Barrow.
H Steel. 1 + shelter + pt 3rd. F 40/12.19.
1956 March: Completed for City Line.
1973 Jan 1: Transferred with all remaining ships of the group to Ellerman City Liners Ltd.
1978 May: Sold to Ben Line Steamers Ltd, Leith. R/n *Benvannoch* (VII).
1979 Apr 20: Arrived at Kaohsiung and broken up by Kao Feng Iron & Steel Co.

288 CITY OF COLOMBO (II)
As 287 except: **B** Barclay, Curle. **T** 7,739g, 4,056n. **E** By builder.
1956 Feb: Completed for City Line.
1973 Jan 1: Passed to Ellerman City Liners Ltd.
1977 Aug: Sold to Ben Line Steamers Ltd, Leith. R/n *Benmohr.*
1979 Feb 7: Arrived at Kaohsiung and scrapped by Gi Yuen Steel Enterprise Co.

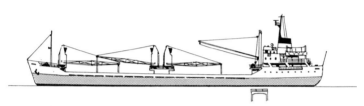

SALMO / CITY OF ATHENS (IV), SALERNO / CITY OF CORINTH (V), SORRENTO / CITY OF SPARTA (III)

289 SALMO / CITY OF ATHENS (IV)
B 1967 Henry Robb Ltd, Leith (later Robb-Caledon). **T** 1,523g, 708n.
D 308/93.88 oa, 280.2/85.35 x 45.67/13.92 x 16.67/5.08.
E Sgl scr, oil; 6 cyl type ALSSDM, 4S.SA, 2,580 nhp at 280 rpm. Direct reversing and turbocharged. 12 kts. By Mirrlees National Ltd, Stockport. Bow thruster.
H Steel. 2 dks. F 36/11. P 69.2/321.1.
1966 Dec 12: Launched. As an economy Mirrlees built 9 identical interchangeable engines for this class and *Spero.*
1967 March: Completed as *Salmo* for Ellerman's Wilson.
1973 Jan 1: Transferred with all ships to Ellerman City Liners. Owned by Ellerman Lines Ltd. Initially as *Salmo.*
1974 All the ECL fleet, excepting those serving Scandinavia, were given 'City' names. R/n *City of Athens.* Remained registered at Hull. Continued on the same services but in Ellerman colours. She later transferred to Papayanni's Mediterranean berths.
1978 This class was replaced by the new *City of Plymouth* (301) Class. Sold to Red Cascade Shipping Co. S.A., Panama. R/n *Aldebaran II.*
1980 Became *Argiro* of Spyrthem Shipping Co., Cyprus.
1988 Sold to Amin Shipping Services Ltd, St Vincent. R/n *Al Ameen.*

290 SALERNO / CITY OF CORINTH (V)
As 289 but **B** 1965. **T** 1,559g, 703n. **D** 307.78/93.81 oa.
1965 Nov: Completed as *Salerno* for Ellerman's Wilson, Hull. First of the 5 'S' class to enter service.
1973 Jan 1: Transferred to Ellerman City Liners as *Salerno.*
1974 R/n *City of Corinth,* Hull.
1978 Sold to Perivale Maritime Inc, r/n *Pyrgos Star.*
1981 Became *Paxi* of Pallada Marine Ltd, Cyprus.
1986 R/n *Lefkas Sun* by Medfleet Kavadas Ltd, San Lorenzo, Honduras.
1988 In service.

291 SORRENTO / CITY OF SPARTA (III)
As 289 except: **B** 1967. **T** 1,523g, 708n.
1967 May 24: Launched as *Sorrento* for Ellerman's Wilson.
1973 Jan 1: Transferred to Ellerman City Liners as *Sorrento.*
1974 R/n *City of Sparta* with the rest of the fleet. Hull.
1978 Became *Gracechurch* of Gracechurch Line Shipping Ltd, London. Runcorn-Mediterranean service.
1983 Became *Weybridge* of Protac Shipping Ltd, Gibraltar. Owners Interlines S.A.
1988 Still in service.

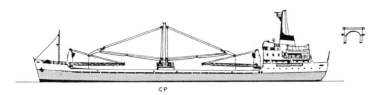

GP

SILVIO / CITY OF PATRAS, SANGRO / CITY OF ANKARA

292 SILVIO / CITY OF PATRAS
As 289 except: **B** 1968. **T** 1,523g, 708n.
1967 Nov 30: Launched.
1968 Jan: Delivered as *Silvio* to Ellerman's Wilson. The position of the goal post masts differed, deck cranes lower.
1973 Jan 1: Managed by Ellerman City Liners.
1974 Became *City of Patras*, Hull.
1978 R/n *City of Tema* by Gulf Maritime Co, Takoradi, Ghana. Her owners were then changed to Meridian Ocean Lines.
1988 R/n *Lemissa* by Teer Shipping Co, Cyprus.

293 SANGRO / CITY OF ANKARA
As 289.
1968 May: Delivered as *Sangro;* the last of the five 'S' class.
1973 Jan 1: Transferred to Ellerman City Liners as *Sangro.*
1974 R/n *City of Ankara.* Hull registry.
1978 Sold to Singapore Enterprises (Pte) Ltd, Panama. R/n *Rezeki.*
1979 Owned by P. T. Abadi Inti Lines, Indonesia. Same name.
1988 Still in service.

SPERO
On Jan 1 1973 Spero of Ellerman's Wilson was also transferred to the Ellerman City Liners Division. On Jan 19 she was withdrawn from the Hull-Zeebrugge service due to lack of support and was sold shortly afterwards to the Maritime Company of Lesvos and renamed **Sappho.** She never became absorbed into the mainstream fleet of the new set up.

CITY OF FAMAGUSTA See *Arcadian* 146

CITY OF VALETTA See *Athenian* 148

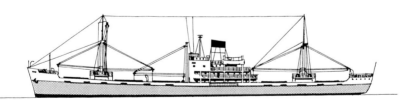

294 RAPALLO / CITY OF LIMASSOL
B 1960 Henry Robb, Leith. **T** 3,402g, 1,453n, 4,644dwt.
D 366.1/111.61 oa, 340/103.64 x 54.5/16.59 x 20.96/6.39.
E Sgl scr, oil; 7 cyl Sulzer, 2S.SA, 3,500 bhp, 13½ kts. By G. Clark & North East Marine (Sunderland) Ltd, Sunderland.
H Steel. 1 + shelter + pt 3rd. F 30/9.14. P 29/8.84.
1960 April: Delivered to Ellerman's Wilson as *Rapallo.*
1968 July 4: Towed T & J Harrison's *Tactician,* disabled by an engine room fire, into Punta Delgada, Azores.
1973 Jan 1: Moved into the Ellerman City Liners Division of Ellerman Lines Ltd.
1975 R/n *City of Limassol.* Hull.
1977 May: Sold to Associated Levant Lines S.A.L., Lebanon. R/n *Beiteddine.*
1986 July 14: Arrived at Aviles for breaking up.

CITY OF CAPE TOWN (II) See 608.

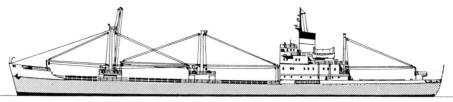

295 CITY OF EXETER (III)
B 1974 Austin & Pickersgill Ltd, Sunderland. **T** 9.014g, 6,383n, 15,088dwt.
D 462.5/141 oa, 440.19/134.17 x 67.19/20.48 x 29/8.85.
E Sgl scr, oil; 5 cyl Sulzer, 2S.SA, 7500 bhp, 15 kts. By Hawthorn Leslie Eng Wks, Newcastle.
H Steel. 1 + pt 2nd dk. **F** 43/13.2 **C** 759,084/21,495cu g. 5 holds/hatches.
1974 July 4: Launched. Oct: Delivered to P & O S N Co as *Strathdare*. One of six type SD 14 replacement standard ships.
1976 R/n *City of Exeter* by City Line to enable them to carry out their share of a joint service with P & O.
1980 Sold to Monodora Shipping Corp, Greece. R/n *Phoevos*.
1982 Became *Safina-e-Barket* of Islamic Investment Shipping Co. One S.A., Panama. On charter to Pan-Islamic SS Co, Karachi.
1986 Off charter. R/n *Nour;* same owner.
1988 Still in service.

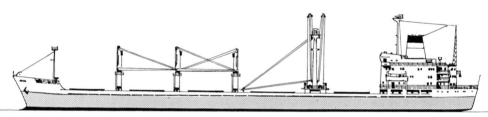

CITY OF WINCHESTER (IV), CITY OF YORK (V), CITY OF CANTERBURY (IV)
296 CITY OF WINCHESTER (IV)
B 1976 Bremer Vulkan, Vegesack. **T** 7,691, 4,494n, 12,550dwt.
D 494.26/150.65 oa, 451.68/139.5 x 69/21.04 x 26.33/8.03.
E Sgl scr, oil; 6 cyl, 2S.SA, MAN K6Z 70/120E type, 8,976 bhp at 145 rpm, 16 kts. By builder. Controlled from the bridge.
H Steel. 2 dks. **F** 48.2/14.7. **P** 46.2/14.1. 5 holds/hatches.
C 829,289/23,483cu g. 322 containers. Has a poop traverse stores loading crane at the rear of the superstructure. Crew 43.
1976 Mar 3: Launched. June: Delivered to Ellerman City Liners. These three ships were of the Bremen Progress type, series B. Europe-East Africa-Persian Gulf service. The speed of technological change was to give them remarkably short lives with Ellerman.
1981 Became *Arc Odysseus* of Solco Inc, Piraeus. The Architug Corp. owners.
1988 Still in service.

297 CITY OF YORK (V)
As 296.
1976 Apr 29: Launched. July: Owned by Lloyds Leasings Ltd on bare boat demise lease to Ellerman City Liners. Aug: Maiden voyage to Persian Gulf.
1986 R/n *Vicman* by Bend Shipping Co, Cyprus. Owned by Starco Shipping Co, Limassol.
1988 Still in service.

298 CITY OF CANTERBURY (IV)
As 296.
B 1976 Sept: Delivered to Ellerman City Liners. Owned by Barclays Export Finances Co, London.
1981 July 11: Arrived at Immingham. Aug: Sold R/n *Arc Aeolos*, Drilco Inc, Piraeus. Owned by Architug Corp.
1988 Still in service.

TRIO CONTAINER SERVICE
Ben Line Containers Ltd, Hapag-Lloyd AG, Mitsui-OSK Lines, NYK Line, Overseas Containers Ltd

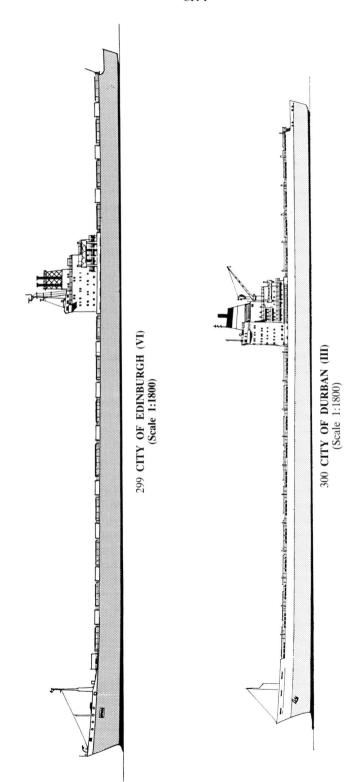

299 CITY OF EDINBURGH (VI)
(Scale 1:1800)

300 CITY OF DURBAN (III)
(Scale 1:1800)

299 CITY OF EDINBURGH (VI)

B 1973 Howaldswerke-Deutsche Werft, Hamburg. **T** 58,284g, 34,387n, 48,810dwt.
D 950/289.57 obb x 106.1/32.34 x 42.73/13.02.
E Tw scr, 2 x 2 steam turbs, 88,000 shp, 26½ kts. By G. E. C. Turbine Generators Ltd, Manchester.
H Steel. 2+ pt 3rd dk. F & B 879.2/268. 2,804 TEU's. 9 cellular holds with fixed guides. 15 hatches.
1973 Mar 5: Launched for Ben Line Steamers Ltd, Leith. Nov: Completed; owned by Bernard Street Holdings, London. Operated by William Thomson & Co (Ben Line) Ltd, Leith, for Ben Line Containers Ltd in which Ellerman have a share. Wears Ellerman livery; her two sisters, *Benalder* and *Benavon* are in Ben Line colours. Represents Ellerman's Far East interests in the Trio consortium.

ELLERMAN HARRISON CONTAINER LINE
EHCL

CITY OF PRETORIA

1976 Nov: When EHCL started at Tilbury they chartered, for one year, Common Bros' *Ria Jean McMurtry* which was renamed *City of Pretoria;* Ellerman funnel over a black hull.
1977 Reverted to *Simonburn* off charter.

300 CITY OF DURBAN (III)

B 1978 A. G. Weser, Bremen. **T** 53,790g, 34,895n, 47,209dwt.
D 848.26/258.5 obb x 106/32.31 x 42.73/13.03.
E Tw scr, oil; 2 x 8 cyl MAN, 51,360 bhp, 21½ kts at 122 rpm. By Masch. Augsburg-Nurnberg, Augsburg. 2 x controllable pitch bow thrusters.
H Steel. 1 dk. F & B 808/246.3. 2,436 TEU's (886 cooled). 656 on deck, 1,735 stowed. 7 cellular holds with fixed guides. 1,740,297/49,280 cu ref. 13 central hatches, 26 wing hatches.
1977 Sept 16: Launched for Ellerman Harrison Container Line Ltd. (EHCL).
1978 Container ship. Feb 6: Delivered to Ellerman Lines & Charente S.S.Co. Owned 2/3 and 1/3 respectively. Operates within the SAECS consortium (Southern Africa Europe Container Services).
1983 Chartered to Overseas Container Line (P & O); r/n *Portland Bay.*
1984 Reverted to *City of Durban.*
1986 Transferred to Associated Container Lines (Australia) as *ACT 8;* registered at Douglas, Isle of Man.
Present fleet.

ELLERMAN CITY LINERS

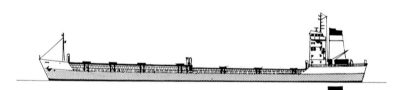

CITY OF PLYMOUTH, CITY OF PERTH (VI) / CITY OF LISBON (II),
CITY OF HARTLEPOOL / CITY OF MANCHESTER (VI), CITY OF IPSWICH, CITY OF OXFORD (V)
301 CITY OF PLYMOUTH

B 1978 Appledore Shipbuilders Ltd, Appledore, Devon. **T** 1,559g, 1,084n, 4,184dwt.
D 341.76/104.17 obb, 55.02/16.77 x 18.24/5.56.
E Sgl scr, oil; 3 cyl, 2S.SA, 6000 bhp, 14½ kts. By Doxford Engines Ltd, Sunderland. Bow thruster fitted.
H Steel. 2 dks. 2 holds/hatches. 296 TEU's with 50 refrig. F 34.1/10.4. P 61/18.6.
1978 Nov: Delivered to Ellerman City Liners; owned by Finance for Ships Ltd. Cost £4 million. Replacing the eight 'Hustler' (and others) the class of five provided, with their consorts, sailings to the Mediterranean every ten days. Ellerman-Strath from Hull and Ellerman-Prince from Ellesmere Port. The partner vessels were *Manchester Clipper, Manchester Faith, Manchester Fulmer, Crown Prince* and *Royal Prince.*
1987 The owners became Cunard-Ellerman Ltd when Cunard purchased the group.
1989 Present fleet.

302 CITY OF PERTH / CITY OF LISBON (II)

As 301.
1978 June 23: Floated out; the ships were built under cover.
1979 Feb: Completed for Ellerman City Liners; owned by Investors in Industry plc.

1983 Laid up at Chatham.
1986 R/n *City of Lisbon*. This name fitted her trading more appropriately.
1987 Owned by Cunard-Ellerman.
1989 Present fleet.

303 CITY OF HARTLEPOOL / CITY OF MANCHESTER (VI)
As 301
1979 Feb 3: Floated out. Mar 29: Named; although Hartlepool is not a city. May: Completed for Container Rentals Ltd; operated by Ellerman City Liners.
1984 Became *Laxfoss,* on charter, to H/f Eimskipafalag Islands, (the Iceland S.S. Co.) Bahamas registry; same owners.
1986 Off charter. R/n *City of Manchester* (because Manchester is a city); Owners now Bahamas based.
1987 Owned by Cunard-Ellerman. Present fleet.

304 CITY OF IPSWICH
As 301
1979 May 9: Floated out. July: Completed for Lloyd's Leasings Ltd on long term charter to Ellerman City Liners.
1981 R/n *Manchester Fulmar* on charter to Manchester Liners.
1983 Reverted to *City of Ipswich.*
1984 Became *Liverpool Star;* Ellerman livery and the same owners.
1987 Owned by Cunard-Ellerman.

305 CITY OF OXFORD (V)
As 301. **D** 341.7/104.15 obb.
1981 Mar 6: Launched for Ellerman Lines plc. May: Delivered with Ellerman City Liners as operators.
1983 R/n *Bakkafoss* on charter to Iceland S.S.Co. Registered at Nassau, Bahamas.
1987 Owned by Cunard-Ellerman. Present fleet out on charter.
1988 R/n *Oxford* by Cunard-Ellerman.

ROBERT ALEXANDER & CO. SUN SHIPPING CO. HALL LINE
Chronological History

Robert Alexander senior was a Belfast merchant who had a financial interest in a number of sailing ships.

1835 His son Robert Alexander was born.

1849 James Alexander, Robert senior's brother, established a ship broking business in Liverpool and was appointed agent for Robert Alexander's ships.

1853 Robert Alexander, junior, came from Belfast to join James in Liverpool.

1855 The Crimean War led to the Government need of many ships. James Alexander & Partners purchased *Echunga* and chartered her to the Crimea. They next purchased the new Belfast built steamer *Khersonese* for the same purpose.

1857 In commercial service *Khersonese* proved to be unprofitable; too little cargo needed too much coal. She was sold to the North Atlantic Steam Navigation Co, Weir, Cochrane & Co managers.

1860 By now the Liverpool firm operated a substantial fleet of sailing ships all owned on the prevalent 64ths system by several business associates. The firm of Liston Young & Co was formed in which Robert Alexander (II) was a partner. Their principal interest was cotton from the United States but the civil war there caused them to diversify to India. There they found not only cotton but jute, rice and other commodities.

1861 Liston Young & Co became Alexander & Young.

1862 Robert Alexander's first ship was *Bavelaw* (323) in which he was the controlling shareholder.

1864 *Bayard* was built for Alexander & Young.

1868 Robert founded the Sun Shipping Co, Liverpool with his new firm of Robert Alexander & Co as managers. His policy, he decided, was to build large volume cargo ships of moderate speed; not the racers that the tea trade demanded. With the advent of his new venture his partnership in Alexander & Young ceased but it continued to be operated as such by James Alexander and Liston Young. Furthermore the ships in which Robert had shares remained with them.

Thus ships in which he had an interest still appeared under the names of either of the two concerns.

Robert Alexander, aged 33, now moved into separate premises in Water St, Liverpool.

In September *Haddon Hall* (337), quite a large ship compared with most in the India trade, became the first ship owned by Sun Shipping and managed by Robert Alexander & Co. In her Liston Young had a share. His second ship was *Elizabeth Fry* (321), which he bought while awaiting the delivery of *Haddon Hall's* sister *Locksley Hall* (338). When orders were placed for further ships they were referred to as 'for the Hall Line' and it is by this name that the company became known.

1869 The Royal Liverpool Seaman's Orphan Institution was formed to care for the children of seafarers who had perished at sea. It was founded at the instigation of James Beazley, managing Director of British Shipowners Co, and Robert Alexander was treasurer. He was to take a lifelong interest in such philanthropy.

Nov 17: The opening of the Suez Canal drastically curtailed the journey to India. Initially it had no effect on the policy of large capacity moderate speed carriers for which the modern sailing ship was well suited.

1871 *Rydal Hall* (344) became the first steamer built for the firm. In service she was nowhere near as profitable as anticipated because her cargo capacity was still out of phase with the coal required for the voyage.

1873 saw the inclusion of Karachi as a main port of call.

1874 The steamer *Rydal Hall* was sold out of the fleet and, uniquely for times when steam was burgeoning into its dominant position, replaced by a sailing ship which, to rub salt into the wound, was given the same name. RA knew that the future lay in steam; the evidence was to be seen in the Mersey every day. He decided to replace the sold steamer with a ship that had a transatlantic steaming range. Inman's famous *City of Baltimore* (348) was available and with her passenger accommodation proved ideal. Voyage profits were such that conversion to steam was to follow.

To prepare for the future the Sun Shipping Company Ltd was formed with an authorised capital of £500,000, in shares of £10, of which £250,000 was issued. The principal shareholders were: RA £40,000, Lloyd and Roderick Rayner £55,000, Radcliffe family £41,300 and Liston Young £6,470. The private firm of Robert Alexander & Co remained managers.

1875 The Calcutta Lines conference agreement was signed whereby the members were bound by fixed tariffs from Liverpool to Calcutta plus regular sailings irrespective of load. In November a similar agreement was signed in respect of Bombay. The signatories were Anchor Line, British India SN Co, City Line, Clan Line, Hall Line and P & O SN Co.

This was also the year in which Benjamin Disraeli purchased for the British Government the majority shareholding of Ismail, the Khedive of Egypt, in the Suez Canal.

1877 Percy Radcliffe became a junior partner in Robert Alexander & Co. The family had strong broking and trading ties with cotton as well as holding £41,300 in Sun Shipping. In deference to this the firm's title was changed to Alexander, Radcliffe & Co. A new partner was Robert Elly Graves.

1880 On January 1st Bombay's Princes Dock was opened so that steamers could now berth alongside; not everyone was pleased. Ships in the roadstead had unloaded port and starboard; now it was starboard only but two sided unloading soon recommenced. W & A Graham were appointed Bombay agents; they also represented Anchor, an act which RA disliked. At this time the Hall Line owned six steamers.

At Karachi Sir Charles Forbes & Co (later Forbes, Forbes, Campbell & Co) became the agents and obtained the contract to carry 2,000 tons of coal a month for the North Western Railway Co whose terminus was at that port. As coal was not a full load NWR agreed to ship via Hall its general needs. In return Hall was to make regular sailings to the port.

1882 Edward Bates & Co, who were also prominent Liverpool shipowners, replaced W & A Graham, with whom they had been running in tandem for Hall, as Bombay agents.

1883 After a little over five years Percy Radcliffe returned to his family's cotton business. Robert Graves replaced him and the managers of the Sun Shipping Co Ltd again became Robert Alexander & Co.

1884 Seven British directors were appointed to the board of Compagnie Universalle du Canal de Suez, Paris, of which RA was one.

1885 An All India Conference agreement was signed which embodied all the prior ports plus Madras and Karachi. It also consolidated inland tariffs and those for fine goods etc. To the signatories of 1875 were added: Thos & Jas Harrison, McDiarmid, Greenshields (The Ducal Line), Rathbone Brothers (The Star Line) and Seater, White & Co. (The Bird Line). An immediate challenge was mounted when Charles (brother in law to Charles Graves) and Henry McIver formed the City of Liverpool SN Co to trade to the East (which is India, China is the Far East) and quoted lower through rates. His incursions lasted almost a decade during which, in some years, Sun Shipping paid no dividend. At one stage the £10 shares could be had for £2.50.

1887 Arthur Alexander, RA's son joined the firm principally to cushion his father's increasing poor health.

The Karachi coal contract was renewed by a personal visit from RA.

1888 Three ships with accommodation for 60 passengers were built for the Karachi service. They were *Locksley Hall, Branksome Hall* and *Rufford Hall* (368-70). They were better and faster than the non-Conference opposition.

1891 Due to family difficulties with his father, with whom he was no longer on speaking terms, Arthur Alexander left the company with Robert Graves taking his place. It was thus that the real line of succession was severed and the family interest weakened. In an attempt to strengthen the hierarchy James H. Beazley and George J. C. Gill became partners in Robert Alexander & Co. By now Robert — still only 56 — was wintering in Madeira.

1894 The McIvers withdrew from the India trade and employed their ships to Africa in conjunction with Elder, Dempster & Co.

The Karachi coal contract was put up for public tender coupled with the suggestion that the rate be the same as that to Bombay; namely ten shillings per ton. RA refused to come below twelve shillings and sixpence. His position was strong because profits were good and, with City Line out of Glasgow, he was the foremost trader to Karachi from the west coast of Great Britain with the east coast and London lagging well behind. He achieved the coal contract once again: mainly because Hall Line guaranteed the regularity of the sailings which were in turn dependant upon a good supply of make up cargo outbound and full inward loads — it was securing the latter all year round which alarmed the Competition.

1895 Robert Graves retired from the day to day business and went to reside in Rome until his death in 1906.

1898 The North Western Railway contract ended. By now coal for the industries of the Sind was being carried economically in colliers to depot ports.

P & O purchased the three 1888 built Karachi passenger ships; the proceeds were distributed to the shareholders as a bonus.

1899 Another son, Frederick Alexander, joined the partners but he was without the deep experience that was needed. The question of the future arose starkly. Re-organisation took place. Sun Shipping Co Ltd went into liquidation and was replaced by a tidied up Hall Line Ltd. The Sun Shipping shareholders receiving new shares fully paid pro-rata to their holding with Robert Alexander & Co continuing as managers but now on a commission basis; it was formerly management fee plus profit share. The original founding shareholders were given debenture stock. With its £10 shares at par Hall Line Ltd was a marketable proposition.

1901 Sept: John Ellerman paid off the debenture holders and purchased Hall Line Ltd and Robert Alexander & Co for £434,000. Included in the deal were 11 steamships: *Aston Hall* (357), *Crewe Hall* (371), *Eden Hall* (358), *Haddon Hall* (363), *Hardwick Hall* (364), *Methley Hall* (367), *Rydal Hall* (359), *Stanley Hall* (362), *Trentham Hall* (365), *Wistow Hall* (361) and *Worsley Hall* (366).

He appointed George J. C. Gill as manager.

Robert Alexander had created and masterminded the company all the way through its existence. His skill and dedication was irreplaceable from within but a worthy successor was to be found in the guise of the new owner. RA went to live in milder Wimbledon where he died in 1911, aged 76.

Livery

Sailing ships		Two varieties are depicted in early paintings: ie *Bavelaw:* Black bulwarks and top strake, grey band with black 'gun-ports', white base to hull with red waterline
		ie *Echunga:* Black hulls, red water line. But *Haddington,* at least, had white strake with gun-ports. Masts: Varnished wood. Lifeboats: White.
Steamers		
Funnel	1871-1901	Yellow. Light rather than deep; not cream.
	1901-1973	Ellerman livery.
Hull	1871-1934ish	Black. Red waterline then grey.

Uppers	1871-1914	Bright russet-brown heavily varnished. Many fittings were white ie davits, stanchions and deck rails (with mahogany top rails).
	1921-1973	White
Masts	1871-1914	Buff-brown
	1921-1973	Ellerman colours
Ventilators	193?-39	Black or funnel yellow then to Ellerman style. Undated: Some ships had the top 1½ metres of the sampson posts and ventilators white painted. Known examples are indicated in the text.
Lifeboats		White. Interiors white and then ochre; change not identified.

EARLY ALEXANDER VESSELS
Robert Alexander (I), James Alexander, Robert Alexander (II) and
Liston Young

306 STEWARTS
This was Robert Alexander senior's first schooner; it was captained by one of his relatives.

___

307 SYLPH
B 1850 Dumbarton. **T** 298. **H** Wood. Barque rig.
1850 Built for Robert Alexander (I). M/v Glasgow-Belfast-Valparaiso.
1861 Wrecked.

___

308 NEW MARGARET
B 1844 Whitehaven. **T** 370.
D 109.2/33.28 x 26.8/8.17 x 18.5/5.64. **H** Wood. Barque rig.
1850 Acquired by James Alexander, traded to China.
1874 Condemned and broken up.

___

309 HELENA
B 1841 Nova Scotia. **T** 265. **H** Wood. Ship rig.
1841 Completed.
184? Owned by Edmunds & Son, Dublin.
1851 Acquired by James Alexander, brother of Robert Alexander (I). Liverpool was her home port. No further trace.

___

310 GREAT BRITAIN
B 1843 Poole. **T** 467. **H** Wood.
1843 Completed.
1853 Acquired by Robert Alexander (I). Managed by brother James Alexander with Robert Alexander (II) as a junior partner.
1861 Managed by Alexander & Young and then R. Alexander & Co.
1867 Wrecked.

___

311 ANNIE HALL
B 1853 Prince Edward Island. **T** 280. **H** Wood.
1853 Completed.
1856 Acquired by Robert Alexander (I). Registered at Belfast. Served on Dublin-New York and Glasgow-New York. Carried 24 passengers.
1858 Liverpool based. James and Robert (II) managers.
1861 Managed by Alexander & Young and then by R. Alexander & Co.
1867 Wrecked.

ECHUNGA

STAR OF THE SOUTH

312 ECHUNGA
B 1853 M. Cochran, Moncton, New Brunswick. **T** 1,118.
D 163.9/49.96 x 31.9/9.72 x 21.6/6.58. **E** Ship rig. **H** Wood.
1853 Built for William Johnston (not Wm Johnston, later Johnston & Warren of Furness Withy which dates from 1872).
1855 Acquired by James Alexander for use as a Crimean War transport and supply ship.
1857 With the war over re-sold Wm Johnston who sold her to Taylor & Co., Liverpool.
1862 Owned by Potter & Co., Glasgow. Lengthened: **D** 172/52.42 x 36/10.97.
1874 Broken up.

---

313 COURIER
B 1836 Sunderland. **T** 369. **H** Wood. Barque rig.
1849 Lengthened to 110.2/33.59 x 26.6/8.11 x 17.8/5.42.
1955 Acquired by Liston Young & Co., London. Robert Alexander (II) being agent at Liverpool and part owner. Ship based at Liverpool.
1858 Sold to Williams & Co., Liverpool. Trace lost.

---

314 PANOLA
B 1851 Quebec. **T** 893. **H** Wood. Ship rig.
1851 Completed.
1855 Acquired by Robert Alexander (II) and his partners at Liverpool. India service.
1859 Abandoned at sea enroute Liverpool.

315 STAR OF THE SOUTH
B 1853 James Nevins, St John, New Brunswick. **T** 1,252g.
D 174.6/53.22 x 33.9/10.33 x 23.1/7.04. **H** Ship rig.
1853 Built for M de Mill, St John.
1855 Bought by James Alexander for £17,000. R. Alexander & Co managers.
1857 Sold to Ramsey & Co, Liverpool. Australian service.
1863 Out of Register.

---

316 MORNING STAR
B 1854 F & J Ruddick, St John, N.B. **T** 1,327g.
D 204/62.3 x 35.5/10.82 x 22.6/6.89.
H Irons. 2 dks. Ship rig.
1854 Completed for Alexander & Co. Cost £17,200.
1859 Sold to Fernie Bros., Liverpool.
1880 May 7: Foundered enroute Quebec-Liverpool. Crew picked up.

---

317 MAGOOLA
B 1854 New Jersey. **T** 549.
1954 Completed.
1855 Acquired by James Alexander.
1883 Sold and broken up.

---

318 STARLIGHT
B 1854 USA. **T** 366.
1854 Ordered by Robert Alexander (I). Owned by Robert (I) and James.
1855 Jan: Completed. USA-India service then via Liverpool according to season. This ship led the Alexanders to become involved in *Khersonese* because steam was beginning to take precedence on the North Atlantic particularly where passengers were concerned.
1859 Owned by H. Churchill, Liverpool.
1866 Scrapped.

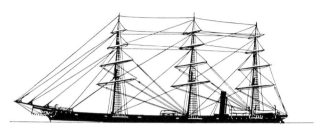

319 KHERSONESE
B 1855 Robert Hickson & Co, Belfast. **T** 1,409g.
D 246.1/75.01 x 38.9/11.86 x 24.7/7.53.
E Sgl scr, 2 cyl beam geared. 9 kts. By Randolph, Elder & Co, Glasgow.
H Iron. 2 dks. P 1st and 3rd. Troops and their mounts in 'tween decks.
1855 Oct 4: Launched for the Liverpool, Newfoundland & Halifax S.N.Co of which James and Robert Alexander (I) were major shareholders.
1856 Apr: Taken up for Crimean troop repatriation work. Aug 23: M/v Liverpool - Canada - Portland, Maine. Lost her propeller inbound and completed the voyage under sail.
1857 Acquired by the North Atlantic S.N.Co. Same service but with *Circassian* as running mate. Then became an Indian Mutiny transport with Robert Alexander (II) as manager.
1859 Ownership passed to Weir, Cochrane & Co, Liverpool, managers of the North Atlantic S.N.Co. James Alexander recorded that she sailed for him over four years 'at little profit'.
1863 Sold to Robert Duncan & Co. Jan 23: Liverpool-New York.
1866 Reduced to barque rig. Engines removed.
1889 Dutch owned. Same name.
1891 July 22: Destroyed by fire at Montevideo.

EGERIA, ELIZABETH FRY

320 EGERIA
B 1859 Fisher, New Brunswick. **T** 1,066. **H** Wood. Barque.
D 176.5/53.8 x 36.3/11.06 x 22.9/6.98.
1859 Completed.
1861 Purchased by Alexander & Young. Traded to India, Australia and South America on a triangular routage.
1877 Laid up.
1879 Condemned.

321 ELIZABETH FRY
B 1861 Fisher, New Brunswick. **T** 1,094.
D 180/54.85 x 35.6/10.85 x 22.5/6.86. **H** Wood.
1861 July: Completed. A sister to *Egeria*.
1862 Managed by Alexander & Young for various shareholders.
1868 Acquired by Sun Shipping Co.
1871 Sold to Bickell & Co, Liverpool. India service.
1872 Owned by P. Dale & Co, North Shields. New Orleans trade.
1885 Broken up.

Appearance of *Haddon Hall* 337

322 CORNWALLIS
B 1862 Thos. Vernon & Sons, Liverpool. **T** 1,214.
D 214.6/65.41 x 34.9/10.64 x 23.1/7.04. **H** Iron. 1 dk.
1862 June: Owned by Liston Young & Co, Robert Alexander part owner.
1872 Sold to Balfour, Williamson of Liverpool.
1877 Trace lost.

BAVELAW, BAYARD (327)

323 BAVELAW
B 1862 Thos Vernon & Sons, Liverpool. **T** 1,027.
D 123/37.49 x 26.7/8.14 x 12.6/3.84. **H** Wood. F & P. Ship rig.
1862 July: Completed with Robert Alexander as the sole shareholder, Alexander & Young managers.
1868 Sold to S. Vaughan, Glasgow.
1879 Owned by W. Dixon, Newcastle-upon-Tyne.
1881 Feb 23: Went missing enroute New York-London with canned petrol.

324 BOLINGBROKE
B 1863 Morton, Leith. **T** 1,255g.
H Wood. Ship rig.
1863 Owned by Liston Young & Co. Robert Alexander partner.
1869 Wrecked.

325 ROBERT LEES
B 1863 Thos Vernon & Sons, Liverpool. **T** 1,239g, 1,200n.
D 210.4/65.16 x 34.8/10.61 x 22.8/6.95. **E** Ship rig.
H Iron. 2 dks. F 37/11.28. P 57/17.37.
1863 April: Completed for Liston Young & Co, London. Liverpool berthed with R. Alexander & Co as managers.
1880 Sold to J. H. Worthington.
1881 R/n *Roscrana;* same owner.
1886 Abandoned at sea.

326 DRAGON
B 1864 M. Pearse & Co, Stockton. **T** 696.
D 182.7/55.69 x 28.9/8.81 x 18.5/5.64. **E** Ship rig.
H Iron. 2 dks.
1864 Sept: Owned by T. Haviside. Liston Young & Co., managers. India run.
1879 Sold to S. D. Grant.
1882 Sold to Major Pratt, his only ship.
1888 Owned by Ship Dragon Co, London, F. M. Tucker manager.
1889 Scrapped.

Appearance as *Bavelaw* 323

327 BAYARD
B 1864 Thos. Vernon & Sons, Liverpool. **T** 1,028.
D 180/54.86 x 34.4/10.48 x 22/6.7. **H** Wood. 1 dk. Ship rig.
1864 April: Completed for Alexander & Young. Glasgow-Calcutta-Burma (rice)-Glasgow.
1868 Transferred to Sun Shipping Company upon its formation; she thus lays claim to being the Company's first ship.
1881 Sold to Foley & Co.
1893 Norwegian owned.
1911 Hulked at Calcutta.

328 MALLENEY
B 1868 Thos Royden & Sons, Liverpool. **T** 1,026.
D 204.7/62.39 x 34.8/10.61 x 20.9/6.37.
H Iron 2 dks. Ship rig.
1868 June: Built for James Alexander. R. Alexander & Co managers.
1872 Sold to Horatio N. Hughes, Liverpool. India service.
1888 Wrecked.

329 RUNNYMEDE
B 1868 W. Pile & Co, Sunderland. **T** 700g. **H** Barque rig.
D 200/60.96 x 30.2/9.2 x 18/5.49.
1868 March: Completed for Redfern, Alexander & Co., London.
1884 Sold to H. Joyau, Nantes. Same name.
1889 Owned by Madam Vivienne Cazer, Port Aven, Finisterre. Registered still at Nantes.
1902 Broken up still as *Runneymede*.

330 HADDINGTON
B 1946 Thos Vernon & Sons, Liverpool. **T** 1,271g, 1,206n.
D 217.3/66.22 x 33/10.06 x 29.5/8.99. **E** See below.
H Iron. 2 dks.
1846 Built, with *Pottinger*, for P & O S.N. Co. Suez-Calcutta service. Paddle, 2 x 1 cyl oscillating. 10 psi. By Bury, Curtis & Kennedy. Dec 5: M/v Southampton-Cape-Calcutta.
1854 Converted to ship rig at Blackwall. Aug 12: Returned to service; stores supply ship and cadet training ship.
1871 Mar 26: Sold for £8,696 to T. Haviside, London. Liston Young & Co, managers. Later Robert Alexander (II) acted as managing agent (for all Liston Young ships). London-China service.
1882 Owned by E. B. Hatfield & Co, London-Calcutta service.
1885 Sold to E. A. Kinnear, London. Cardiff-tramping with coal.
1888 Burned off Iquique.

331 LORD PALMERSTON
B 1862 New Brunswick. **T** 1,057.
1862 Completed.
1865 Acquired by Alexander & Young.
1869 Lost.

332 THERMUTIS
B 1864 Quayle & Co, USA. **T** 310.
D 139/42.36 x 25.9/7.89 x 12.1/3.68.
1864 March: Delivered to Cunningham & Co, Liverpool. Galveston service.
1870 Acquired by Alexander & Co.
1881 Out of Register.

333 VERNON
B 1864 Thos. Vernon & Sons, Liverpool. **T** 1,319.
D 210.64 x 36/10.97 x 23.2/7.07. **H** Wood. 1 dk. Ship rig.
1864 Oct: M/v Glasgow-Australia-San Francisco (wheat)-Cape Horn-Glasgow.
1880 Sold to Thompson, Anderson & Co., Liverpool.
1882 Out of Register.

334 ESTEPONA
B 1872 A & J Inglis & Co, Glasgow. **T** 1,049g, 676n.
D 202.5/61.72 x 30.6/9.32 x 23/7.01.
E Sgl scr, 2 cyl comp inv. 120 nhp, 60 psi 9½ kts. By builder.
H Iron 2 dks. Flush. Topsail schooner rig.
1872 Sept: Built for Liston Young & Co, London. Clyde-Spain service.
1879 Sold to Ramsey & Sawyer, Hull.
1881 Her owners were re-styled Massey & Sawyer.
1882 Broken up.

---

335 MARLBOROUGH
B 1862 Pile, Spence & Co, West Hartlepool. **T** 879.
D 193.5/58.98 x 31.3/9.54 x 20/6.09.
H Iron. Ship rig.
1862 Aug: Built for Mills & Bros., Stockton.
1873 Bought by Liston Young & Co, London, Barque rig.
1883 Out of Register.

---

336 SCOTIA
B 1856 Quebec. **T** 921.
D 172/52.42 x 35.5/10.82 x 21.6/6.58.
H Wood. 1 dk. F 18/5.48. Q 29/8.84. Barque rig.
1856 Built.
1865 Owned by Hamilton, Greenock.
1868 Owned by A. F. Mackay, Liverpool.
1873 Purchased by J. Alexander & Co.
1878 Owned by R. W. Muir with W. Harrison, manager.
1882 Still as *Scotia* owned by T. Howatt, Liverpool.
1884 Scrapped.

SUN SHIPPING CO

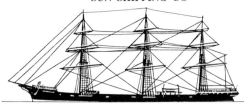

HADDON HALL (I), LOCKSLEY HALL (I), ROKEBY HALL, CORNWALLIS (322)

337 HADDON HALL (I)
B 1868 Thos. Royden & Sons, Liverpool. **T** 1,491g, 1,416n.
D 225.4/68.7 x 37.9/11.55 x 23.6/7.19. **E** Ship rig. **H** Iron. 2 dks. F 28/8.53. P 28/8.53.
1868 Sept: Completed for Sun Shipping Co, Glasgow. Alexander & Young managers. The first 'Hall'.
Except for purchases all were to carry Hall names until Ellerman introduced 'City of'.
1878 Sold to Liston Young & Co, Liverpool.
1880 Owned by J. J. de Wolff & Co, Liverpool. Same name.
1913 Feb 1: Enroute Liverpool-Cape Town went ashore and was lost at Port Morison, Cape Colony.

338 LOCKSLEY HALL (I)
As 337 except: **B** 1869. **T** 1,356. **D** 227/69.18. **H** F 36/10.97.
1869 Delivered to Sun Shipping Co, India service.
1881 As the last sailing ship in the fleet sold to Lowden, Edgar & Co, Liverpool.
1887 Aug 27: Inbound from San Francisco the ship was being towed up the Mersey by tug when she was in collision with ss *Regulus* (Red 'R' SS Co.) and sank across the top of the Mersey underground railway tunnel but also across the channel. She could not, therefore, be dynamited and had, with great difficulty in the tide race, to be lifted by Bullivent & Co, who beached her at Tranmere where she was repaired. Sold to R. Singlehurst & Co, Liverpool, owners of the Red Cross Line. R/n *Carvoeira*. Brazil trade. She then became one of their hulks on the Amazon.
1901 Passed to Booth Line with the amalgamation of the Singlehurst ships into the Booth Steamship Co, (1901) Ltd.
1922 Broken up.

339 **ROKEBY HALL**
B 1863 Thos. Vernon & Sons, Liverpool. **T** 1,004.
D 202.6/61.75 x 33/10.06 x 22.5/6.86.
E Ship rig. **H** Iron. 2 dks. Fcsle and poop.
1863 Aug: Delivered.
1868 Transferred to Liston Young & Co.
1875 Owned by Balfour, Williamson & Co, Liverpool.
1913 Scrapped.

CORNWALLIS See 322

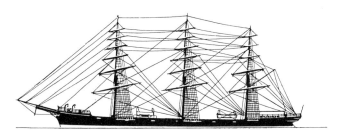

EATON HALL, KNOWSLEY HALL (I), MISTLEY HALL, RYDAL HALL (II)

340 **EATON HALL**
B 1870 Thos. Royden & Sons, Liverpool. **T** 1,860g, 1,779n.
D 257/78.33 x 42/12.8 x 23.9/7.28.
E Ship rig. **H** Iron. 2 dks. F 42/12.8. P 63/19.2.
1870 March: Delivered to Sun Shipping Co.
1874 Apr 20: Left Liverpool. Made Melbourne in 72 days then San Francisco in 63 days. Oct 30: Back in Liverpool after 10 months 20 days. A very fast passage for her style of heavy capacity vessel.
1875 Sold to Balfour, Williamson & Co, Liverpool.
1908 Aug: Enroute New South Wales-Valparaiso she was demasted in a cyclone. Became a hulk at the Society Islands.

341 **KNOWSLEY HALL (I)**
As 340 except: **B** 1873 R & J Evans & Co, Liverpool. **T** 1,860g, 1,774n.
D 260/79.25 x 42.3/12.89. **H** F 40/12.19. B 56/17.07.
1873 Sept: Delivered. Australian trade.
1879 June 14: Left; bound London-Lyttleton, N.Z. June 17: Reported as passed Start Point. Disappeared with 53 passengers and 35 crew. It was presumed that she was lost in the Bay of Biscay which was hit by a storm in late June but she ought to have weathered it without difficulty.

342 **MISTLEY HALL**
As 340 except: **B** 1874 R & J Evans & Co, Liverpool. **T** 1,867g, 1,772n.
D and **H:** as 337.
1874 May: Completed for Sun Shipping Co.
1878 Sold to Wm Herron, same name. His first iron ship.
1882 Transferred to Herron, Dunn & Co, when Captain C. G. Dunn came into partnership.
1887 The name of the company became Globe Shipping Co. Later changed again to C. G. Dunn & Co.
1900 Sold to Enrico Beraldo, Recco, Genoa. R/n *Ascensione*.
1905 Broken up.

343 **RYDAL HALL (II)**
As 340 except: **B** 1874 R & J Evans & Co, Liverpool. **T** 1,771g, 1,682n.
D 260/79.25. **E** & **H** As 337.
1874 Feb: Completed for Sun Shipping. She was under construction when *Rydal Hall* (I), 344, was taken out of service and put up for sale. Thus this new ship took her name.
1876 Oct 17: Ashore on Cape Pillar, near Punta Arenas. 9 lost. The ship was salvaged, repaired and sold to Brazil. Trace lost.

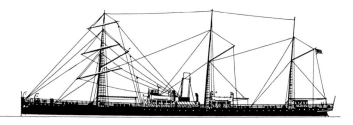

RYDAL HALL (I), BRANKSOME HALL (I), TRENTHAM HALL (I), CHILDWALL HALL
344 RYDAL HALL (I)
B 1871 London & Glasgow Co, Glasgow. **T** 2,114g.
D 330.5/100.74 x 34.4/10.48 x 24.3/7.41.
E Sgl scr, 2 cyl simple. 250 nhp, 60 psi, 2 sgl blrs. 9 kts. By builder.
H Iron. 2 dks. flush. 3 masts.
1871 July: Delivered to Sun Shipping Co. Their first steamer. The vessel was a disappointment in service; the principal reason being that she had a single expansion engine. Her sisters emerged with compound. She was built just at that point in time when compounding was ready to take off. Holts had had three lone pioneer ships in 1865 and Cunard's *Batavia* had just become the first compound Atlantic liner. *Rydal Hall* (I) was replaced by the sailing ship *Rydal Hall* (II). Four years later the class was continued with the construction of the final trio.
1874 Sold to the West Indian & Pacific S.N.Co, r/n *Chilean*.
1885 Taken by Harland & Wolff in part payment. Converted to tpl exp. 160 psi.
1888 Sold to Carlisle & Co (London) Ltd, as *Chilian*.
1890 Owned by MacBeth & Gray, Belfast. Same name.
1894 Jan: Abandoned at sea.

345 BRANKSOME HALL (I)
As 344 except: **B** 1875. **T** 2,086g, 1,347n. **D** 331.4/101 x 34.2/10.42.
E 2 cyl comp inv, 1,600 ihp, 80 psi. 10 kts. By builder.
1875 Nov: Completed for Sun Shipping Co.
1881 Sold to Cia. Trasatlantica Espanola. R/n *Panama*, registered at Havana. Service New York-Havana.
1898 Captured by USS *Mangrove* during the American-Spanish war. After initial use as a transport. Dec 10: By the Treaty of Paris the Philippines were ceded to the USA.
1899 Following the ceding it was decided to lay US Army communication cables between the islands. Renamed *Hooker*. She was converted by Morse Shipyard, Brooklyn, into a cable layer for the US Army Corps of Signals. A fcsle, three cable tanks and a single bow shear were fitted. Her task was to lay cables between the Philippine Islands. After leaving New York for Manila via the Suez Canal she had to put into Gibraltar for boiler repairs. Wrecked during her maiden operation on Corregidor, Manila Bay, while laying part of her 240 miles of cable.

346 TRENTHAM HALL (I)
As 344 except: **B** 1876. **T** 2,101g, 1,359n. **D** 331.5/101.04. **E** Comp.
1876 Jan: Delivered.
1881 Sold to Cia Trasatlantica, Spain. R/n *Mexico*. New York-Havana service.
1901 Sunk.

347 CHILDWALL HALL
As 344 except: **B** 1876.**T** 2,017g, 1,361n. **D** 331.8/101.13. **E** Comp. **H** B 30/9.14.
1876 March: Completed.
1877 Sold to James Wood jr, James Wood & Sons, Liverpool.
1878 April: Wrecked.

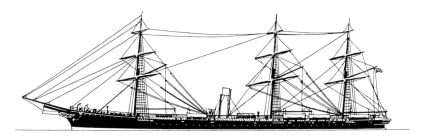

348 CITY OF BALTIMORE
B 1855 Tod & Mcgregor. **T** 2,292g, 1,444n.
D 330.7/100.8 x 39/11.89 x 26/7.92.
E Sgl scr, 2 cyl comp inv, 300 nhp, 70 psi. 11 kts. By J. Jack Rollo & Co, Liverpool. **H** Iron 2 dks.
1855 Jan 20: Launched for the Inman Line. As completed she had a 2 cyl twin beam geared simple expansion engine of 10 psi. The Crimean War (started July 1854) required more transports and the ship was chartered by the French. Mar 20: M/v Liverpool/Marseilles (as drawn).
1856 Apr 23: Entered North Atlantic service to Philadelphia.
1866 Compounded and new boilers fitted. Nov: Resumed service. Square rigged foremast only.
1874 Acquired by Robert Alexander for Sun Shipping Co, in order to restart his steamer service to India while the three new ships, *Branksome Hall*, *Trentham Hall* and *Childwall Hall* (345-47) were under construction. She inaugurated the Liverpool-Bombay service and was profitable.
1882 Sold to Spain. R/n *Fivaller* and then *Benicarlo*, J. Ripolles, Valencia.
1892 Broken up.

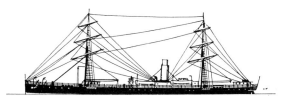

349 MARINA
B 1870 Barclay, Curle & Co, Glasgow. **T** 1,358g, 861n.
D 240.8/73.39 x 32.6/9.94 x 23.8/7.25.
E Sgl scr, 2 cyl comp inv. 135 hp. 10 kts. By builder.
H Iron. 3 dks. **P** 20 1st, 240 3rd. Crew 40.
1870 Oct 25: Launched for Donaldson Bros. Dec 10: M/v Glasgow-River Plate.
1873 Sold to the Brazil S.S. Co, Alexander, Radcliffe & Co. Same service.
1878 Owned by the Hall Line with Alexander, Radcliffe & Co, as managers.
1881 Became *Maria*, Rocco Piaggio & Sons, Genoa.
1885 R/n *Paraguay*, Navigazione Generale Italiana (NGI).
1910 Sold to S. A. Nazionale di Servizi Marittimi.
1921 Owned by G. Randazzo, Palermo. R/n *Torrero*. Palermo-South America route.
1928 Sold to Angelo Bertorello, Genoa. Same name.
1929 Broken up at Genoa aged 59.

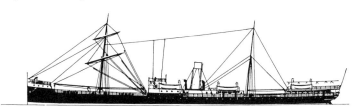

RYDAL HALL (III), SPEKE HALL, WISTOW HALL (I)
350 RYDAL HALL (III)
B 1878 London & Glasgow Co, Glasgow. **T** 2,708g.
D 362.1/110.39 x 37/11.28 x 26.4/8.05.
E Sgl scr, 2 cyl comp. By builder.

H Iron. 2 dks. F 28/8.53. B 36/10.97. Crew 59.
1878 Feb: Completed for Sun Shipping Co.
1888 Sold to Navigazione Generale Italiana. R/n *Nilo*.
1911 Sold to Soc. Nazionale di Servizi Marittimi, Palermo. Same name.
1916 Broken up in Italy.

351 **SPEKE HALL**
As 350 except: **B** Chas. Connell & Co, Glasgow. **T** 2,672g.
D 361.4/110.15. **E** By J & J Thompson, Glasgow. **H** F 30/9.14. B 35/10.67.
1878 March: Delivered to Sun Shipping Co.
1885 June 3: Enroute Cardiff-Bombay with a cargo of coal the ship foundered in a cyclone 180 miles from Aden. 58 drowned out of 59.

352 **WISTOW HALL (I)**
As 350 except: **B** Chas. Connell & Co, Glasgow. **T** 2,674g.
D 360.5/109.88. **E** By J & J Thompson, Glasgow.
1878 Entered service. Recorded by Lloyds as having three masts; no proof.
1886 Sold to Nav. Gen. Italiana, Genoa. R/n *Bosforo*.
1910 NGI decided (in 1908) to concentrate on the Americas; they therefore gave up all other routes and transferred them, June, together with 65 ships, to the new Soc. Anon. Nazionale di Servizi Marittimi, Palermo. Same name. Indian service.
1920 Broken up.

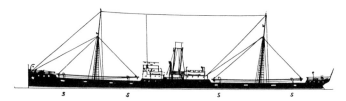

353 **BRETTON HALL**
B 1881 Chas. Connell & Co, Glasgow. **T** 2,421g, 1,918n.
D 320/9.75 x 36.2/11.03 x 25.5/7.77.
E Sgl scr, 2 cyl, comp, 300 nhp, 75 psi. 10 kts. By J & J Thompson, Glasgow.
H Iron. 2 dks. F 38/11.58. B 75/22.86. P 28/8.53.
1881 Delivered.
1883 On charter to Bucknalls, their funnel.
1885 Dec 6: Wrecked on Starkham Point, Devon. All saved.

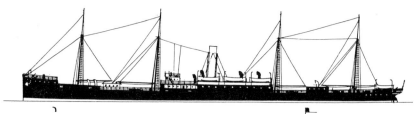

MERTON HALL, WERNETH HALL

354 **MERTON HALL**
B 1881 Gourlay Bros., Dundee. **T** 4,053g, 2,647n.
D 400.5/122.07 x 42.2/12.86 x 29.7/9.05.
E Sgl scr, 2 cyl comp, 500 nhp, 80 psi, 10 kts. By builder.
H Steel. 3 dks. F 22/6.7. B 74/22.56.
1881 Dec 28: Launched for Sun Shipping with Alexander & Radcliffe as managers. Both had square sails on fore mast.
1889 Sold for £38,158 to Donaldson Bros., Glasgow. R/n *Amarynthia*.
May 7: First sailing Glasgow-Canada. Pole masts (as drawn).
1894 Grounded close to Montreal due to pilot error.
1902 Jan 4: Last sailing to St John, New Brunswick. March: At Genoa for breaking up.

355 WERNETH HALL

As 354 except: **B** 1882 Chas. Connell & Co, Glasgow. **T** 4,100g, 2,690n.
D 401/122.22 x 42/12.8. **E** By J & J Thompson. **H** F 42/12.8.
1882 Entered service.
1899 Transferred to Hall Line Ltd. Same managers.
1901 June: Now an oldish ship and also large with passenger accommodation. She was therefore excluded from the sale to J. R. Ellerman and put up for disposal. Laid up at Liverpool.
1902 March: Sold to Macbeth & Co, Glasgow. Same name.
1906 March: Sold to G. E. Olsen, Arendal. R/n *Coronel*.
1907 Scrapped.

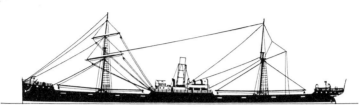

356 KIRBY HALL

B 1882 London & Glasgow Co, Glasgow. **T** 2,691g, 1,759n.
D 329.9/100.55 x 40/12.19 x 25.9/7.89.
E Sgl scr, 2 cyl comp, 300 nhp, 80 psi. 10 kts. By builder.
H Iron. 2 dks. F 38/11.58. B 66/20.01. P 28/8.53.
1882 Nov: Completed for Kirby Hall S.S. Co, with R. Alexander & Co, as managers. The poop boat was starboard side only.
1896 Sold to Chas. Burrell & Son. R/n *Aquileja* for the Austro-Americana S.S. Co, Trieste for the service in its title.
1900 When the Trieste licence was not renewed for the British the ship and the service was taken over by Cosulich & Co, Trieste.
1903 Cerutti Brothers became managers.
1904 Broken up.

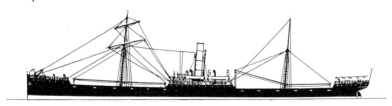

ASTON HALL, EDEN HALL, RYDAL HALL (IV), NETHERBY HALL (I),
WISTOW HALL (II), STANLEY HALL, HADDON HALL (II), HARDWICK HALL,
TRENTHAM HALL (II)

357 ASTON HALL

B 1882 Gourlay Bros. & Co, Dundee. **T** 3,568g, 2,323n.
D 360/109.72 x 42.6/12.98 x 28/8.53.
E Sgl scr, 2 cyl comp, 400 nhp, 85 psi. 10 kts. By builder. Coal 363 tons.
H Steel. 2 dks. F 50/15.24. B 76/23.16. P 40/12.19.
1882 Sept: Delivered to Sun Shipping Co, Liverpool. Square sails as drawn.
1899 Transferred to Hall Line Ltd. No square sails by now.
1901 June: Sold to J. R. Ellerman. Hall Line Ltd with the fleet of 11 ships. R. Alexander & Co remained managers.
1909 Broken up in Turkey after a collision in the Bosphorous.

358 EDEN HALL

As 357 except: **B** 1883. **T** 3,610g, 2,332n.
1883 April: Completed for Sun Shipping Co. Square sails as drawn.
1899 Ownership passed to Hall Line Ltd.
1901 June: Sold to J. R. Ellerman with the remainder of the Hall fleet.
1911 Transferred to Westcott & Laurence, London. J. R. Westcott manager.
1928 Jan: Broken up.

359 RYDAL HALL (IV)
As 357 except: **B** 1889 Caird & Co, Greenock. **T** 3,315g, 2,139n.
D 349.5/106.53 x 42.1/12.83. **E** Tpl exp. By builder.
H Steel. 2 dks. **F** 47/14.33. **P** 37/11.28.
1889 Dec: Delivered to Sun Shipping Co. No sails on the triple expansion engined ships.
1899 Owners became Hall Line Ltd.
1901 June: Transferred to J. R. Ellerman. Same owners and managers.
1917 Dec 1: Torpedoed by UC-75 near Eastbourne, off the Royal Sovereign Lightship. 23 killed.
Euphorbia, Stag Line, was sunk in the same attack.

360 NETHERBY HALL (I)
As 357 except: **B** 1890 Caird & Co, Greenock. **T** 3,316g, 2,139n.
D 349.5/106.53 x 42.1/12.83. **E** Tpl exp by builder.
H **F** 47/14.32. **P** 37/11.28.
1890 March: Delivered to Sun Shipping Co.
1898 Sold to L. Dixon & Sons, Belfast. R/n *Belfast*.
1915 R/n *Tharros* by Aristides Milonas, Corfu.
1922 Sold to the Oriental Shipping Co, Corfu. A. A. Caparis manager.
1928 Owned by Artistide Mylonas & Co, Piraeus.
1930 Broken up.

361 WISTOW HALL (II)
As 357 except: **B** 1890 Caird & Co, Greenock. **T** 3,314g, 2,139n.
D 349.5/106.53 x 42.1/12.83. **E** tpl exp by builder.
1890 Jan: Completed for Sun Shipping Co.
1899 Owned by Hall Line Ltd.
1901 June: Company bought by J. R. Ellerman. Same managers.
1903 Inaugurated the South American service; the first for Ellerman but Robert Alexander had operated Brazil S.S. Co.
1912 Jan 18: Wrecked on Buchan Rocks, Aberdeenshire. 54 lost (45 Lascars, 8 Europeans and 1 pilot). Her captain was the only European taken from the sea and he had a broken leg. There is a memorial stone at North Cruden and a plaque in St. James's Episcopal church, Aberdeen.

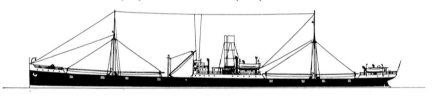

STANLEY HALL, HADDON HALL (II), HARDWICK HALL, TRENTHAM HALL (II)
362 STANLEY HALL
As 357 except: **B** 1894 Palmers' Co, Jarrow. **T** 4,104g, 2,660n.
D 378/115.21 x 45.3/13.81. **E** Tpl exp. 365 nhp, 180 psi. By builder.
H **F** 36/10.97. **P** 34/10.36.
1894 March: Entered service for Sun Shipping Co.
1899 Ownership changed to Hall Line Ltd.
1901 June: Hall Line purchased by J. R. Ellerman.
1920 In E & B colours but her masts were not white. It is possible to spot ships on voyage charter to Bucknall by this; Bucknall always repainted the funnel, even for one voyage — a more common practice than realised (British India is another example).
1928 Apr 22: Sold to Alloa Metal Industries and broken up at Alloa.

363 HADDON HALL (II)
As 357 except: **B** 1895 Palmers' Co, Jarrow. **T** 4,177g, 2,677n.
D 380/115.82 x 45.3/13.81 x 29.1/8.87. **E** Tpl scr, 365 nhp, 180 psi; by builder.
H **F** 37/11.28. **B** 74/22.56. **P** 34/10.36.
1895 Dec: Completed for Sun Shipping Co.
1899 Owned by Hall Line.
1901 June: Hall Line taken over by Ellerman.
1913 Feb 1: Wrecked five miles north of Saldanha Bay, South Africa, enroute Liverpool-Durban with a general cargo. At the time she was taking an Ellerman & Bucknall sailing to South Africa with onwards passage to India thence to the UK. It is an example of the interchangeability between Hall, City and Ellerman & Bucknall on the South African berths. Interestingly few E & B served to India.

364 **HARDWICK HALL**
As 357 except: **B** 1896 Palmers' Co, Jarrow. **T** 4,175g, 2,676n.
D, E & H as *Haddon Hall.*
1896 Jan: Completed for Sun Shipping Co.
1899 Owned by Hall Line.
1901 Hall Line Ltd taken over by John Ellerman.
1903 Oct 18: Wrecked on Farquhar Island north of Madagascar enroute Delagoa Bay-Calcutta.

365 **TRENTHAM HALL (II)**
As 357 except: **B** 1897 Palmers' Co, Jarrow. **T** 4,173g, 2,662n.
D 380/115.82 x 45.3/13.81 x 29.1/8.87 **E** as *Haddon Hall.*
H r 36/10.97. B 78/23.77. P 33/10.06.
1897 Oct: Entered service for Sun Shipping.
1899 Title changed to Hall Line Ltd.
1901 The whole fleet bought by J. R. Ellerman.
1917 May 21: Wrecked on Pluckington Bank by the Albert Dock, Liverpool.

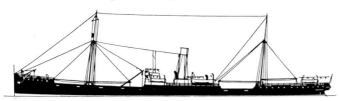

WORSLEY HALL, METHLEY HALL

366 **WORSLEY HALL**
B 1886 Palmers' Co, Jarrow T 3,489g, 2,238n.
D 330/100.5 x 43.5/13.26 x 29.1/8.87.
E Sgl scr, tpl exp, 400 nhp, 150 psi. 10 kts. By builder.
H Steel. 2 dks. F 47/14.33. P 92/28.04, mainmast to stern.
1886 Aug: Delivered to Sun Shipping Co. 40 passengers in the poop.
1899 Owned by Hall Line Ltd, Liverpool.
1901 Acquired by John Ellerman.
1920 Jan 6: Sold to Hydra S.S.Co., George M. Chruassachi, London, for trade to the Black Sea. Same name.
1922 Sept: During the Greco-Turkish fighting she evacuated Greeks from their enclave in Smyrna (Izmir). In all 800,000 Greeks fled from Asia Minor. In due course most of the Moslems (ie excepting those in Western Thrace) were expelled from Greece.
1924 Broken up in Germany.

367 **METHLEY HALL**
As 366 except: **T** 3,492g, 2,242n, **H** P 37/11.27.
1886 Oct: Built for Sun Shipping Co. No passengers.
1899 To Hall Line Ltd.
1901 Went to John Ellerman with the rest of the fleet.
1908 Apr 13: Arrived at Briton Ferry, South Wales, for scrap.

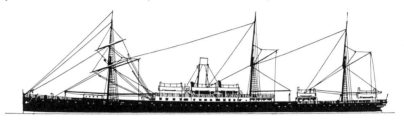

LOCKSLEY HALL (II), BRANKSOME HALL (II), RUFFORD HALL (I)

368 **LOCKSLEY HALL (II)**
B 1888 Palmers' Co, Jarrow. **T** 3,957g, 2,579n.
D 380/115.82 x 45.3/13.82 x 27.4/8.35.
E Sgl scr, tpl exp, 550 nhp, 150 psi. 10 kts. By builder.
H Steel. 2 dks. F 47/14.33. B 130/39.62. P 43/13.11. P 60.
1888 Jan: Delivered to Sun Shipping Co.

1899 Jan: Sold to P & O S.N.Co. for £33,531 to enable them to step up their Far East sailings to one every two weeks. But at once taken up for use as a Boer War transport. R/n *Pekin*.
1901 In P & O service while new larger ships were constructed.
1906 Sold for £7,446 to Esafji Tajbhoy Borah, Bombay (who also took her sister ship). R/n *Shah Nawaz*.
1909 Became *Najmi,* Hajaz S.N.Co., Bombay for pilgrim work to Jeddah.
1911 Broken up at Bombay.

369 BRANKSOME HALL (II)
As 368 except: **T** 3,839g, 2,555n.
1888 Feb: Delivered.
1898 Dec: Followed her sister to P & O. Realised £32,802. R/n *Tientsin*.
1906 July: Sold to the same owner for £7,435. R/n *Shah Mazir*.
1909 Became *Fakhri* of Hajaz S.N.Co. Also for pilgrimage work Bombay-Jeddah. The Hadj, which every Moslem, unless sick or too poor, has to make to Mecca once in a lifetime only occurs in the twelfth month of the Moslem year with a lesser pilgrimage in the seventh month. Thus the 'Pilgrim Ships' to Jeddah undertook other duties for about seven months of the year (many pilgrims arrived early or departed later). The ceremony involves a first circumambulating of the Kaaba (a square building inside the Great Mosque with the Black Stone set in one wall), kissing the Black Stone, visiting on foot Arafat, a hill six hours distant where prayers are said, running between Mawra and Safa and finally repeating the Kaaba walk. Once the visit is achieved the word 'Hadjee' takes the place of 'Mr'. Nowadays the journey is made mainly by air although vast numbers walk both ways; it can take a year.
1911 Wrecked on Perim Island, Gulf of Aden. All saved.

370 RUFFORD HALL (I)
As 368 except: **T** 3,840g, 2,580n.
1888 March: Delivered.
1898 Dec 9: Sold for £33,523 to P & O. R/n *Nankin*.
1899 Used as a Boer War transport.
1904 Sold for £20,956 to M. Y. Kawasaki, Kobe. R/n *Kotohera Maru No 2*.
1907 Wrecked in the Soya Strait, the extreme northern tip of Hokkaido. Broken up as she lay.

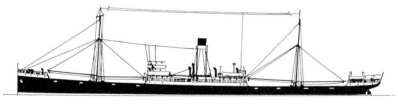

371 CREWE HALL
B 1898 Palmers' Co, Newcastle. **T** 4,218g, 2,691n.
D 380/115.82 x 47.3/14.42 x 29.2/8.9.
E Sgl scr, tpl exp, 404 nhp, 200 psi. 10½ kts. By builder.
H Steel. 2 dks. F 34/10.36. B 108/32.92. P 37/11.28.
1898 Nov: Completed for Sun Shipping, R. Alexander manager.
1899 Owned by Hall Line Ltd.
1901 Went with the fleet into Ellerman ownership.
1929 Oct 2: At Blaine Wharf, Newport for breaking up by J. Cashmore.

ADALIA see *Adalia* Papayanni 19

ANATOLIA see *Anatolia* Papayanni 18

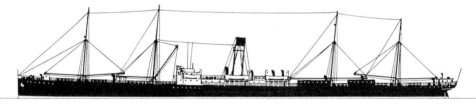

372 PINEMORE

B 1898 Chas. Connell & Co, Glasgow. **T** 6,306g, 4,072n.
D 459/139.9 x 52.6/16.02 x 31/9.45.
E Sgl scr, tpl exp, 608 nhp, 200 psi. 12 kts. By D. Rowan & Co, Glasgow.
H Steel. 2 dks. **P** 12
1898 Built as *Pinemore* for Wm Johnston; Eastbound North Atlantic live cattle trade with general cargo westwards. Had cattle pens on the weather deck.
1901 Acquired by J. R. Ellerman for the Antwerp-Canada service but he sold the rights back to Leyland together with the three ships involved.
1902 R/n *Oxonian*, Frederick Leyland (1900) Ltd.
1928 Broken up.

MAPLEMORE see *City of Edinburgh* (IV) 246

373 **PROME / LOCKSLEY HALL (III)**

B 1893 Wm. Denny & Bros, Dumbarton. **T** 3,580g, 2,299n, 5,385dwt.
D 345/105.15 x 44.1/13.44 x 27.3/8.32.
E Sgl scr, 329 nhp, 200 psi, 2 sgl blrs. 10½ kts. By builder.
H Steel. 2 dks. F 43/13.11. B 80/24.38. P 30/9.14. C 233,680/6,617.1 cu g.
1893 Oct 30: Launched. Dec 9: Delivered to Burmah S.S.Co., P. Henderson & Co, managers. Cost £46,010. Dec 20: M/v to Rangoon.
1901 Acquired by Hall Line Ltd. Initially as *Prome*. Then r/n *Locksley Hall*. Served South Africa-India repatriating Indian troops from the Boer War.
1917 May 12: Torpedoed by U-32 30 miles east south east of Malta. 6 dead. May 13: The crew were picked up by a launch and landed at Marsa Scirocco.

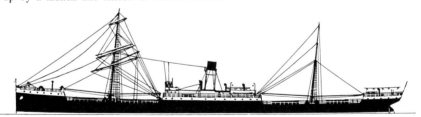

374 **MERTON HALL (II)**

B 1889 Palmers' Co, Jarrow. **T** 4,327g, 2,773n.
D 400.5/122.07 x 47.2/14.39x 27.9/8.5.
E Sgl scr, tpl exp, 435 nhp, 150 psi, 2 dbl blrs. 11 kts. By builder.
H Steel. 3 dks, F 47/14.32. B 105/32. P 41/12.4.
1889 May 16: Launched as *Knight Templar* for Greenshields, Cowie & Co, Liverpool. One of four sisters by Palmers. July 11: On trials she reached over 13 kts. Owned by the Knight Companion S.S.Co. with *Knight Companion* (the ship drawn).
1891 Both ships transferred to Knight S.S.Co., which owned the remainder of the fleet.
1903 Sold for £21,500 to Ellerman. R/n *Merton Hall*.
1918 Feb 11: Torpedoed by *U-53* 30 miles off Ushant on passage New York-La Pallice with a cargo of steel. The ship sank instantly with the loss of 57 lives.

KNOWSLEY HALL (II), CROSBY HALL, BRANKSOME HALL (III), NEWBY HALL (II)
LANGTON HALL (I), NETHERBY HALL (II), SUTTON HALL, SANDON HALL

375 KNOWSLEY HALL (II)
B 1903 Swan, Hunter & Wigham Richardson, Newcastle. **T** 4,190g, 2,705n.
D 373/113.69 x 46.7/14.23 x 27.7/8.44.
E Sgl scr, tpl exp, 320 nhp, 180 psi, 2 sgl blrs. 10 kts. By Wallsend Slipway Co, Newcastle.
H Steel. 2 dks. **F** 42/12.8. **B** 93/28.35. **P** 35/10.67.
1903 Built for Hall Line. Like so many Hall, ie Liverpool, ships she had telescopic masts and a removable funnel top for the Manchester Ship Canal. The funnel top was taken off by a pair of sheer legs at the entry lock; it was done in the time it took to adjust the water level.
1928 Oct 1: Sold to T. N. Epiphaniades, Piraeus. R/n *Wanda*.
1934 Oct: Broken up in Italy.

376 CROSBY HALL
As 375. **T** 4,052g. 2,597n. **D** 365/111.25. **H** **F** 38/11.58. **B** 94/28.65. **P** 31/9.45.
1903 Completed for the Hall Line.
1927 Jan 7: Sold to D. G. Coucoubanis, Salonika. R/n *Georgios P.*
1944 June: Sank as a block ship at Arromanches, the artificial Mulberry harbour in the British sector of the Normandy beach-head.

377 BRANKSOME HALL (III)
As 375 except: **B** 1904. **T** 4,662g, 2,728n. **D** 374.7/114.21 x 46.6/8.44.
H **B** 96/29.26. **P** 41/12.5.
1904 Built for the Hall Line.
1906 Transferred to the Glen Line, McGregor, Gow & Co, Liverpool. R/n *Glenavon*.
1910 Reverted to Hall Line and *Branksome Hall*.
1917 June 17: Missed by torpedo in the English Channel. Nov 2: Hit by a torpedo from *UC-65* in the English Channel and beached. Safely repaired.
1918 July 14: Torpedoed by *UB-105* 68 miles off Marsa Susa, North Africa.

378 NEWBY HALL (II)
As 375 except: **B** 1905 Barclay, Curle & Co, Glasgow. **T** 4,391g, 2,841n.
D 375/114.3 x 47.2/14.39. **E** 330 nhp; by builder.
1905 Completed for the Hall Line.
1930 July 10: Sold to G. Andreou, Andros. R/n *Yiannis*.
1936 Became *Amiral Pierre*, French.
1942 Sept 30: Scuttled off Madagascar when intercepted by the British destroyers *Hotspur* and *Nizam*.

379 LANGTON HALL (I)
As 375 except: **B** 1905. **T** 4,437g, 2,882n. **D** 377.5/115.06 x 47.5/14.48.
H **B** 96/29.26. **P** 41/8.65.
1905 Delivered to Hall Line.
1906 May: Took the first Hamburg-UK-Marmagao sailing.
1915 Nov. 30: Captured and sunk by gunfire from *U-33* 112 miles east of Malta. Hall's first World War I loss.

380 NETHERBY HALL (II)
As 375 except: **B** 1905. **T** 4,461g, 2,855n. **D** 381.6/116.31 x 47.5/14.48.
H **B** 96/29.26. **P** 41/12.5.
1905 Laid down as *Netherby Hall* but completed as *Glenearn* for McGregor Gow as part of the deal whereby Hall supplied ships to share their under-manned Far East service (see history).
1910 Because the results of the joint Glen venture were un-profitable the ship was returned to Hall Line and r/n *Netherby Hall*.
1917 Jan 10: Captured by the German commerce raider *Moewe* 300 miles east by north of Pernambuco. After the removal of some needed cargo the ship was sunk by bombs. *Moewe* now had 250 prisoners aboard and these were put aboard the *Hudson Maru*, Tatsuuma Kisen K.K., taken as a prize a week earlier, and sent into Pernambuco.

381 SUTTON HALL
As 375 except: **B** 1905. **T** 4,460g, 2,870n. **D** 375.4/114.42 x 47.4/14.45.
H **B** 96/29.26. **P** 41/12.5.
1905 Delivered to the Hall Line.
1915 March 3: While on Belgian relief work and carrying the internationally agreed bright paintwork she was missed by a torpedo in the English Channel enroute Plymouth (the relief transit port) — Antwerp.
1916-17 On loan to France.

1920's: Served with E & B funnel but not with white masts.
1930 Dec 18: Sold for breaking up.

382 SANDON HALL (I)
As 375 except: **B** 1906. **T** 5,134g, 3,293n. **D** 401.4/122.35 x 50.2/15.3.
H F 46/14.02. B 97/29.56. P 40/12.19.
1906 Entered service with the Hall Line.
1918 Jan 1: Torpedoed by the Austro-Hungarian *U-40* 22 miles north north east of Linosa, midway between Malta and Tunisia. The ship was carrying stores and ammunition but all the crew got away safely.

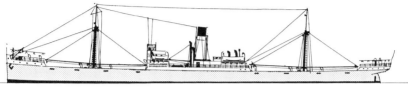

LOCKSLEY HALL (IV) / CITY OF AGRA (II),
RUFFORD HALL (II) / CITY OF MADRAS (IV)
CITY OF KARACHI (III)

383 LOCKSLEY HALL (IV) / CITY OF AGRA (II)
B 1903 Workman, Clark & Co, Belfast. **T** 4,808g, 3,096n.
D 400/121.92 x 50.2/15.3 x 28.9/8.81.
E Sgl scr, tpl exp, 379 nhp. 180 psi, 2 blrs. 10 kts. By builder.
H Steel. 2 dks. F 41/12.5. B 110/33.53. P 31/9.45.
1903 Ordered as *Locksley Hall*. Completed as *City of Agra*, Hall Line.
1932 April 12: Sold for £2,850 for scrapping in Italy.

384 RUFFORD HALL (II) / CITY OF MADRAS (IV)
As 383 except: **B** Palmers' Co, Jarrow. **T** 4,684g, 3,048n. **D** 395.4/120.52 x 49.6/15.12. **E** By builder.
H F 37/11.28. B 108/32.92. P 34/10.36.
1903 Laid down as *Rufford Hall* but delivered as *City of Madras*.
1931 Sept 9: Sold for breaking up in Italy.

385 CITY OF KARACHI (III)
As 383 except: **B** 1905. **T** 5,547g, 3,563n. **D** 413.6/126.08 x 51.5/15.7 x 29.2/8.9.
H F 41/12.5. B 121/36.88. P 75/22.86.
1905 Mar 8: Launched. June: Completed for Hall Line. Differed by having a long poop from mainmast to stern. **P** 69 1st, 19 2nd.
1908 She was transferred to the management of George Smith & Sons and placed on City Line services but her owners remained Ellerman Lines Ltd. This was a particular aspect of City; few vessels were owned by the firm of City Line Ltd.
1921 Dec 16: New York-India for American & Indian Line.
1934 Oct 17: Sold and scrapped in Japan.

386 TRAFFORD HALL
B 1905 Barclay, Curle & Co, Glasgow. **T** 5,321g, 3,437n.
D 397.2/121.07 x 50/15.24 x 29/8.84.
E Sgl scr, tpl exp, 369 nhp, 180 psi, 2 blrs. 11 kts. By builder.
H Steel. 2 dks. F 48/14.63. B 124/37.79. P 49/14.93.
P 70 1st, 24 2nd. Crew 70.
1905 Oct 28: Launched. The first passenger ship built for the Hall Line after its acquisition and the only one with a 'Hall' name and which was never changed.
1912 Served on the Bucknall Steamship Lines service owned by Ellerman since 1908. Bucknall funnel.
1914-18 Enjoyed a peaceful commercial career even though under government orders. Her bridge

lifeboats were now slung not decked.
1919 Feb 24: Placed on American & Indian Line service.
1929 Enroute Hamburg-South Africa and 2,000 miles short of Cape Town her cargo took fire. It was damped down with hoses for eight days before she reached safety.
1934 Sept 4: Sold for £7,000 and broken up in Italy.

DENBIGH HALL, THORNTON HALL / CITY OF CARTHAGE (II)
WALTON HALL, CITY OF NAPLES (I), CITY OF COLOMBO (I)

387 DENBIGH HALL
B 1906 Barclay, Curle & Co, Glasgow. **T** 4,943g, 3,211n.
D 401/122.22 x 50.2/15.3 x 29.5/9.
E Sgl scr, tpl exp, 353 nhp, 225 psi, 2 sgl blrs. 11 kts. By builder.
H Steel. 2 dks. F 40/12.19. B 115/35.05. P 40/12.19.
1906 Completed.
1914-18 Indian Govt. transport and supply ship then British Govt. Collier out, grain home for food rations.
1918 May 18: Torpedoed by *U-55* 90 miles south west of Bishops Rock Light.

388 THORNTON HALL / CITY OF CARTHAGE (II)
As 387 except: **T** 5,524g. **D** 411.2/25.33 x 52.7/16.06.
1906 Laid down as *Thornton Hall* but delivered as *City of Carthage* for the Far East service which was carried out by 'City boats'.
1907 Aug 10: Wrecked at Kamodasaki, Japan enroute Philadelphia-Hiogo with case oil.

389 WALTON HALL
As 387 except: **B** 1907. **T** 4,932g, 3,203n.
1907 Delivered. The derrick post abaft the bridge deck was 15 ft clear of the superstructure.
1931 Oct 10: Sold for breaking up. Nov: At Port Glasgow for scrap.

390 CITY OF NAPLES (I)
As 387 except: **B** 1908 Swan, Hunter & Wigham Richardson. **T** 5,739g, 3,714n.
D 418.3/127.5 x 53.3/16.24 x 30.4/9.26.
E 369 nhp. By Wallsend Slipway, Newcastle. **H** F 57/17.37. B 110/33.53. P 41/12.5.
1908 Entered service.
1926 June 15: Wrecked on Zenisu Reef, Miyaki Island, Japan enroute Dunkirk-Yokohama with a general cargo.

391 CITY OF COLOMBO (I)
As 387 except: **B** 1909 Swan, Hunter & Wigham Richardson, Newcastle. **T** 5,598g, 3,901n. **D** 425/129.54 x 54.1/16.49 x 30.9/9.42. **E** 402 nhp. By Wallsend Slipway. **H** F 57/17.37. B 115/35.05. P 48/14.63.
1909 Completed.
1917 Aug 1: Beat off an attack by *U-155* while going to the assistance of the sailing vessel involved. She caught the submarine broadside on and her shots hit the conning tower. Aug 4: The ship was again attacked, probably by the same U-boat. Escaped into the dusk.
1918 Oct: Under City Line management.
1921 March: Wrecked on the coast of Nova Scotia.

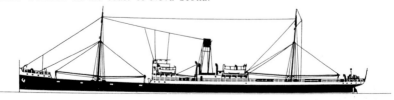

392 CROXTETH HALL (I)
B 1905 Craig, Taylor & Co, Stockton. **T** 3,991g, 2,435n.

D 358/109.12 x 49.3/15.03 x 18.2/5.55.
E Sgl scr, tpl exp, 391 nhp, 180 psi, 3 sgl blrs. 10 kts. By North East Marine, Sunderland.
H Steel. 1 + spar dk. F 32/9.75. B & P 228/69.49.
1905 Sept: Completed as *Claverhill*, Claverhill S.S. Co, London, with E Haselhurst as managers. Her sister was *Claverburn* (as drawn).
1909 Acquired. R/n *Croxteth Hall*. The ship was pre-grey hulls.
1913 Sold to W. Crosby & Co, Melbourne. R/n *Ooma*. Australia-Pacific islands.
1920 The ship was Suva registered.
1926 Feb 8: Wrecked on Sydney Point, Ocean Island (Banaba). She was enroute Sydney-Ocean Island-Nauru with with coal and general cargo.

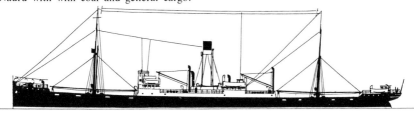

CITY OF CHESTER (I), CITY OF BOMBAY (III), CITY OF BARODA (I) CITY OF DURHAM (I)

393 CITY OF CHESTER (I)
B 1910 Barclay, Curle, Glasgow. **T** 5,413g, 3,521n.
D 410.5/125.12 x 52/15.85 x 30.4/9.26.
E Sgl scr, tpl exp, 362 nhp. 11 kts. By builder.
H Steel. 2 dks. F 40/12.19. B 148/45.11. P 47/13.41.
1910 Completed for Hall Line Ltd. This series of ships with a bridge deck hatch aft with serving vented sampson-posts set an Ellerman style that, with variations, followed for 30 years across the fleet. Bucknall were to adopt it in 1913 (*Kathlamba*) but City were last with their post-WW I ships.
1924 Transferred to City services; managed by Graham Smith but not otherwise changed. Her owners were Ellerman Lines Ltd.
1932 Managed by City Line Ltd.
1933 Dec: Sold for scrap.
1934 Jan: The first ship to be broken up at Arnott & Young's new yard.

394 CITY OF BOMBAY (III)
As 393 except: **B** Palmers', Jarrow, Newcastle. **T** 5,186g, 3,355n.
D 401.2/122.28 x 50.8/15.48 x 29.7/9.05. **E** 509 nhp. By builder.
H B 142/43.28. P 43/13.11.
1910 Sept: Delivered to Hall Line Ltd.
1932 May: Broken up at Glasgow by Douglas & Ramsey.

395 CITY OF BARODA (I)
As 393 except: **B** 1911. **T** 5,032g, 3,279n. **D** 401.7/122.44 x 50.8/15.48.
H B 140/42.67. P 39/11.88.
1911 May: Entered services for Hall Line Ltd, as managers for all were owned by Ellerman Lines Ltd.
1917 June 4: Torpedoed by *UC-53* 90 miles north west of Tory Island. 6 dead.

396 CITY OF DURHAM (I)
As 393 except: **B** 1911 Palmers' Co. **T** 5,356g, 3,460n.
D 407/124.05 x 51.4/15.67. **E** 521 nhp by builder.
H F 42/12.8. B 147/44.8. P 44/13.41.
1911 Feb: Delivered.
1933 Jan 26: Sold for £3,850 and broken up in Italy.

397 **CITY OF BIRMINGHAM (I)**

B 1911 Palmers S.B.Co, Newcastle. **T** 7,498g, 4,839n.
D 452/137.77 x 55.7/16.98 x 31.5/9.6.
E Sgl scr, quad exp, 756 nhp, 225 psi, 4 sgl blrs. 12 kts. By builder.
H Steel. 2 dks. F 48/14.63. B 183/55.78. P 92/28.04. **P** 130 1st, 40 2nd.
1911 Nov: Completed for Hall Line passenger service to India.
1914-1916 Used as an Indian Expeditionary Force troopship.
1916 Nov 27: Torpedoed aft by U-32 in the Atlantic. She carried 170 passengers and a crew of 145, of whom some 70 were children. The ship was abandoned within ten minutes and only four crew were lost. The captain, W. J. Haughton, went down with the ship but shot to the surface and was picked up. All were rescued three hours later by Donaldson's *Letitia* in her hospital ship livery.

---

398 CITY OF LINCOLN (I)
B 1911 Palmers S.B.Co, Jarrow-on-Tyne. **T** 5,867g, 3,784n.
D 422/128.62 x 53.4/16.28 x 30.9/9.42
E Sgl scr, tpl exp, 581 nhp, 220 psi. 11 kts. By builder.
H Steel. 2 dks. F 42/12.8. B 160/48.77. P 44/13.41.
1911 Delivered.
1917 Sept 18: Torpedoed by *UB-32* off the Scilly Isles. 9 killed. Towed into port and repaired.
1934 Jan 25: Sold for £6,250 and scrapped in Italy.

399 CITY OF LAHORE (II)
B 1911 Swan, Hunter & Wigham Richardson, Wallsend. **T** 6,948g, 4,471n, 10,000dwt.
D 438.5/133.65 x 54.1/16.49 x 31.2/9.51.
E Sgl scr, 4 cyl, quad exp, 434 nhp, 180 psi. 12 kts. By Wallsend Slipway.
H Steel. 2 dks. F 57/17.37. B 153/46.63. **P** 89/27.13. **P** 73 1st, 40 2nd.
1911 Mar 14: Launched. Passenger vessel.
1919 Nov 7: On American & Indian Line service. Bucknall funnel, black hull.
1922 Dec 1: Went ashore in fog on the coast of Antrim. Came off next day; nevertheless repairs cost £30,130.
1926 En route Rotterdam-River Plate she collided in the English Channel with the Greek *Agia Marina*.
1927 Oct: On American & Manchurian Line service. E & B funnel.
1932 Laid up in the Gareloch.
1933 Aug: Sold for £6,500 and broken up at Troon.

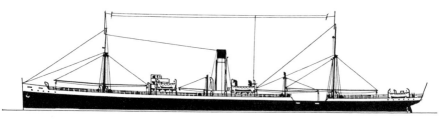

400 MELFORD HALL (I)
B 1911 Barclay, Curle & Co, Glasgow. **T** 5,514g, 3,506n.
D 411.2/125.33 x 54.8/16.7 x 29/8.84.
E Sgl scr, tpl exp, 369 nhp. 12 kts. By builder.
H Steel 2 dks. F & B 287/87.48. P 107/32.61.
1911 Completed.
1915 Nov: Inaugurated the Manchester-New York service.
1917 June 22: Torpedoed by *U-100* 95 miles north by west of Tory Island.

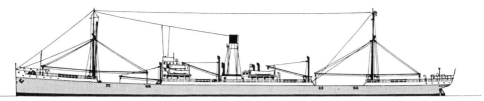

401 CITY OF BRISTOL (I)

B 1912 Swan, Hunter & Wigham Richardson, Wallsend. **T** 6,741g, 4,345n.
D 452/127.77 x 56.6/17.25 x 31.6/9.63.
E Sgl scr, tpl exp, F 86/26.21. B 165/50.29. P 92/28.04.
1912 Delivered to Hall Line.
1936 Dec 1: Sold to Barry Shipping Co with B & S Shipping Co as managers.
R/n *St. Woolos* Antwerp-River Plate service; members of the 'Outward Continental, Brazil and River Plate Conference'.
1937 Disposed of, with *Syrie,* under the 'Scrap and build scheme'. She was replaced by *St Rosario.*
1938 Broken up by A. Kitagawa at Osaka.

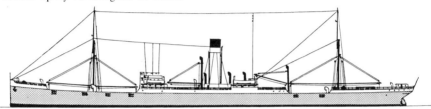

402 CITY OF DUNKIRK

B 1912 Barclay, Curle & Co, Glasgow. **T** 5,861g, 3,759n, 9,850dwt.
D 420.7/128.23 x 54.2/16.52 x 30.3/9.23.
E Sgl scr, tpl exp, 379 nhp. 11 kts. By builder.
H Steel. 2 dks. F 41/12.5. B 150/45.72. P 82/25.
1912 Oct: Completed.
1914-18 Commercial service but under Government control.
1950 Jan 9: Sold to Luigi Monta fu Carlo (fu = for the late), Genoa. R/n *Marilen.*
1953 May: *Minerva,* 'Minerva' Imprese Marittimi s.r.l., Genoa.
1959 Broken up at La Spezia.

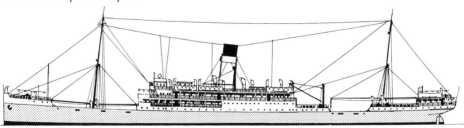

403 CITY OF MARSEILLES

B 1913 Palmers S.B.Co, Newcastle. **T** 8,250g, 5,284n.
D 469.3/143.04 x 57/17.37 x 32.1/9.78.
E Tw scr, 2 x 4 cyl quad exp, 851 nhp, 225 psi, 4 sgl blrs. 14 kts. By builder.
H Steel. 2 dks. F 53/16.15. B 200/60.96. P 92/28.04.
1912 Oct 26: Launched for the Hall Line.
1913 Jan 26: M/v Liverpool-New York-Port Said-Bombay. Then Liverpool-Bombay.
1915 Nov 23: Attacked by submarine en route Liverpool-Bombay. Hit it with her gunfire.
1916 Nov: Picked up, 95 out of 721 survivors from P & O's *Arabia* torpedoed 112 miles southwest of Cape Matapan.
1921 On the American & Indian Line's service New York-Port Said-Bombay. Later via Marseilles and Naples.
1923 Regular seasonal trooping to India with Bibby and British India.
1930 Replaced as a troopship by Bibby's *Lancashire.*
1940 Jan 6: Damaged by a mine 1½ miles from the No.1 Black Buoy, River Tay.

1943 Jan 22: Stranded en route Liverpool-Madras-Calcutta near Batticaloa, Ceylon but safely refloated.
1947 Scrapped.

CITY OF NORWICH, CITY OF CORINTH (III), CITY OF MYSORE, CITY OF FLORENCE (II)

404 CITY OF NORWICH
B 1913 Wm. Gray & Co, West Hartlepool. **T** 6,382g, 4,346n.
D 434.4/132.4 x 54.7/16.67 x 31.2/9.51.
E Sgl scr, tpl exp, 606 nhp, 220 psi, 3 sgl blrs. 12 kts. By Central Marine Eng Wks, West Hartlepool.
H Steel. 2 dks. F 81/24.69. B 165/50.29. P 77/23.47. 13 winches, 14 derricks. **P** 3.
1913 July: Completed. Introduced cruiser sterns into the Hall fleet.
1955 Feb 22: Sold to T. Maglivers, Panama. R/n *Marinucci*. Her bow was rebuilt with a sharp rake to it. She was also given a thicker funnel.
1959 Broken up at Yokohama.

405 CITY OF CORINTH (III)
B 1913 Barclays, Curle & Co, Glasgow. **T** 5,870g 3,773n.
D 420/128.06 x 55.3/16.85 x 29.8/9.08.
E Sgl scr, tpl exp, 391 nhp. 12 kts. By builder.
H Steel. 2 dks. F 38/11.58. B 153/46.63. P 79/24.08.
1913 Completed.
1917 May 21: Torpedoed by *UB-31* 12 miles south west of the Lizard, Cornwall.

406 CITY OF MYSORE
B 1914 Palmers S.B. Co, Jarrow. **T** 5,294g, 3,416n.
D 401.1/122.25 x 51.3/15.63 x 16.7/5.09.
E Sgl scr tpl exp. 534 nhp, 2 sgls blrs. 12½ kts. By builder.
H Steel. 2 dks. F 45/13.72. B 150/45.72. P 76/23.16.
1914 Delivered.
1915 Feb 23: Wrecked after only six months service om Komuriya Reef, Ceylon en route Calcutta-London-Dunkirk with a cargo of jute and tea.

407 CITY OF FLORENCE (II)
B 1914 Palmers S.B. Co, Jarrow. **T** 5,399g, 3,490n.
D 407.2/124.11 x 51.3/15.63 x 29.7/9.05.
E Sgl scr, tpl exp, 547 nhp, 220 psi 2 sgl blrs. 12 kts. By builder.
H Steel. 2 dks. F 45/13.72. B 156/47.55. P 77/23.47.
1914 Entered service. Single pair of lifeboats on funnel deck.
1917 July 20: Torpedoed by *UC-17* 188 miles off Ushant.

408 RUFFORD HALL (III)
B 1914 Swan, Hunter & Wigham Richardson, Jarrow. **T** 5,506g, 3,553n.
D 409.5/124.81 x 53.1/16.18 x 30/9.14.
E Sgl scr, tpl exp, 390 nhp, 220 psi, 2 sgl blrs. 12 kts. By Wallsend Slipway.
H Steel. 2 dks. F 89/27.13. B 153/46.63. P 82/25.
1914 Completed.
1915 Oct 6: Wrecked in the Tsugaru Strait near Omazaki en route New York-Honolulu-Vladivostok with a general cargo.

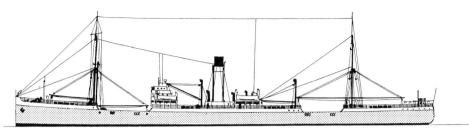

**CITY OF RANGOON, CITY OF VIENNA (III), CITY OF WINCHESTER (I),
CITY OF NEWCASTLE (I), CITY OF HANKOW (II), CITY OF CANTON (II)**

409 CITY OF RANGOON

B 1914 Wm Gray & Co, West Hartlepool. **T** 6,633g, 4,272n.
D 443/135.02 x 55.3/16.85 x 31.2/9.51.
E Sgl scr, tpl exp, 617 nhp, 220 psi, 3 sgl blrs. 12 kts. By Central Marine Eng. Wks, West Hartlepool.
H Steel. 2 dkrs. F 83/25.3. B 165/50.29. P 104/31.7. C 579,900/16,421 cu g. 13 winches, 16 derricks.
1914 June: Completed. There were eight look-alike ships between 1914-18 which are depicted by this drawing.
1944 Sustained bottom damage but was repaired.
1945 Oct 25: Bought by the Ministry of War Transport and r/n *Oscar III;* managed by Hall Line and operated by Oscar Ltd. Loaded with coal and sent to the Far East.
1946 Used as a coal store and then hulk at Singapore.
1950 Dec 10: Arrived at Bombay for scrapping.

410 CITY OF VIENNA (III)

As 409 except: **B** Workman, Clark, Belfast. **T** 6,111g, 3,917n.
D 420.3/128.11 x 55.7/16.98 x 30.9/9.42.
E 424 nhp. By builder. **H** F 86/26.21. B 153/46.63. P 102/31.09.
1914 Delivered.
1918 July 2: Wrecked at Ketch Harbour, Sambro, Nova Scotia en route Montreal-Halifax in ballast.

411 CITY OF WINCHESTER (I)

As 409 except: **B** Earles S.B.Co, Hull.**T** 6,800g.
D 449.2/136.92 x 56.8/17.31 x 33.3/10.15. **E** 641 nhp. By builder.
H F 82/25. B 180/54.86. P 74/22.55.
1914 Delivered. Her sister *Keelung* (575) went to Ellerman & Bucknall.
1914 Aug 6: The brand new ship, inbound on her maiden voyage, was captured by the German light cruiser *Konigsberg* 280 miles east of Aden en route Colombo-UK with a cargo of tea, value £250,000. *Konigsberg* was based at Dar-es-Salaam and left there on July 31 prepared for a long time at sea. She took her prize into Makalla, on the Arabian coast, where the crew were transferred to the German steamer *Zeiten,* Norddeutcher Lloyd (herself torpedoed Nov. 17, 1917), for transfer to POW camp. After the coal and stores had been shared between her captors *City of Winchester* was taken out to sea and scuttled, Dec 6, off Soda Isle in the Kuria Muria Islands. Ellerman's first World War I loss — but see *City of Khios* (452).

412 CITY OF NEWCASTLE (I)

As 409 except: **B** 1915 Wm Gray & Co, West Hartlepool. **T** 6,291g, 4,462n.
D 456.5/139.14 x 56.4/17.19 x 31/9.45. **E** 616 nhp. By Central Marine Eng Wks, West Hartlepool.
H F 91/27.74. B 171/52.12 P 104/31.7.
1914 Dec 16: German battlecruisers bombarded the Hartlepools, Scarborough and Whitby during which *City of Newcastle* was damaged while fitting out.
1915 Jan 19: Completed. **T** 7,280g. Taken over as a transport for the Indian Expeditionary Force; one of several involved.
1917 April: Came under the Liner Requisition Scheme.
1922 Tonnage as above.
1926 Because the cook was a Buddist twenty nine Moslem crew refused to sail and were left at Philadelphia.
1940 Suffered heavy weather damage which had to be repaired at Cape Town.
1943 July: Acted as a supply ship to the invasion of Sicily. While discharging at Augusta she was damaged by aerial bomb attack.
1951 May: Sold to Soc. Nav. Magliveras, Panama. R/n *Marinucci.*
1952 Aug 11: Arrived for breaking up at La Spezia.

413 CITY OF HANKOW (II)

As 409 except: **T** 8,420g, 5,869n.
D 465.4/141.85 x 58.2/17.74 x 31.8/9.69. **E** Quad exp, 738 nhp. By Central Marine; owned by Wm Gray & Co. **H** F 100/30.48. **B** 171/52.12. **P** 107/32.61.
1915 Completed.
1922 **T** 7,368g, 4,765n. Owned by Oran S. S. Co, Hall Line as managers.
1924 Operated for City Line. Owned by Montgomerie & Workman (1920) Ltd. Managed by Hall Line.
1936 M & W ceased to own ships. Proprietors Ellerman Lines Ltd. with Hall as managers.
1942 Dec 18: Wrecked at Saldhana Bay.

414 CITY OF CANTON (II)

As 409 except; **B** 1916 Swan, Hunter & Wigham Richardson, Newcastle.
T 6,982g, 4,471n. **D** 466.4/142.16 oa, 56.9/17.34 x 31.1/9.48.
E 2 turbs sgl reduction geared, 751 nhp. By Wallsend Slipway, Newcastle.
H F 89/27.13. **B** 192/58.52. **P** 89/27.13.
1916 Sept: Completed for Hall Line. Had deck house between aft derrick posts and tall white vents at bridge front.
1943 July 16: Torpedoed by *U-178* off Beira. The survivors were adrift on rafts for seven days without food or water before being rescued.

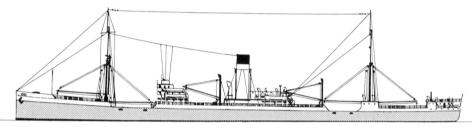

CITY OF MANILA, LANGTON HALL (II) / CITY OF CARDIFF (I)

415 CITY OF MANILA

As 409 except: **B** 1916 Wm Gray & Co, West Hartlepool. **T** 8,340g, 4,834n.
D 475/144.78 x 58.2/17.74 x 31.8/9.69. **E** Quad exp + Dbl reduction geared low pressure turb connected by hydraulic coupling. 859 nhp. By Central Marine Eng Wks. **H** F 101/30.78. **B** 180/54.86. **P** 107/32.61.
1916 June: Completed.
1923 **T** 7,463g, 4,823n. Still Hall Line.
1942 Aug 18: Torpedoed by *U-406* off the Azores. She was in convoy SL 118, Sierra Leone (Freetown)-UK.

416 LANGTON HALL (II) / CITY OF CARDIFF (I)

As 409 except: **B** 1918 Craig, Taylor & Co, Stockton. **T** 5,661g, 4,211n.
D 419.5/127.86 x 54.4/16.58 x 29.8/9.08. **E** 552 nhp. By North East Marine, Newcastle.
H F 85/25.91. **B** 153/46.63. **P** 88/26.82
1918 Jan: Delivered. Had Manchester Ship Canal funnel top with the usual heavy flange and walkway.
1926 R/n *City of Cardiff*. Hall Line.
1932-33 Laid up with eight other Ellerman ships in the Gareloch. The others were: Cities of *Carlisle* (573), *Chester* (393), *Eastbourne* (449), *Harvard* (582), *Lahore* (399), *Mobile* (569), *Nagpur* (417) and *Paris* (268).
1942 Aug 28: Torpedoed off Cape Finisterre by *U-566* in convoy SL 119, Sierre Leone inbound. Remained afloat but she was taking in water faster than could be pumped out. She was abandoned and sank next day. *Zuiderkerk*, Vereenigde, was hit in the same attack and had to be scuttled by the escorts.

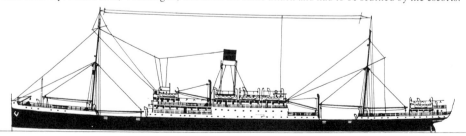

417 CITY OF NAGPUR (I)

B 1914 Workman, Clark & Co, Belfast. **T** 8,331g.
D 465.3/141.82 x 58.3/17.76 x 31.6/9.63.
E Sgl scr, 4 cyl, quad exp, 492 nhp, 14½ kts. By builder.
H Steel. 2 dks. F 94/28.65. B 180/54.86 P 104/31.7. **P** 222 1st, 92 2nd.
1914 Entered service Liverpool-India.
1917 Aug 23: Wrecked enroute Durban-Bombay on Danea Shoal, Delagoa Bay, South Africa. There were 195 aboard and all were saved.

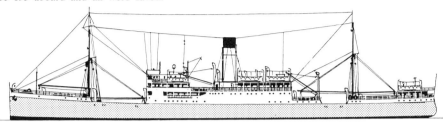

418 CITY OF CAIRO
B 1915 Earles S.B. Co, Hull. **T** 7,882g, 5,024n.
D 449.9/137.13 x 55.7/16.98 x 31.3/9.54. Dft 27.7/8.44.
E Sgl scr, 4 cyl quad exp, 774 nhp, 3,900 ihp, 225 psi, 3 sgl blrs. 12 kts on 70 tons coal pd. By builder.
P 133 1st, 43 2nd.
1914 Oct 2: Launched.
1915 Jan: Completed.
1927 Mar 6: On E & B's American & Indian Line service. Their funnel; black hull. She added Rangoon to the ports of call but still with Calcutta as the terminus.
1942 Nov 6: At 20.30 hrs and 500 miles south of St Helena *City of Cairo* was torpedoed by *U-68* five days out from Cape Town. Three passengers and 18 crew were killed by this first hit. A second torpedo smashed all but two lifeboats leaving many people in the water. Captain Rogerson, in the lesser crowded and undamaged No 1 lifeboat went ahead for help and was never heard of again. No 2 boat contained 54 people, 23 Europeans, including 2 women and the 12 year old Diana Jarman plus 31 Lascars. Dec 12: After almost five weeks only three survivors, quartermaster MacDonald, steward Edmead and Diana Jarman were picked up by, of all ships, the German blockade runner *Rhakotis*, Hamburg America Line. Despite an immediate operation to clear her blocked septic throat Miss Jarman died. Jan 1: *Rhakotis* was scuttled off Cape Finisterre to avoid capture by the British cruiser *Scylla*. The boat carrying Edmead reached Spain and he was repatriated only to be lost in his next ship. MacDonald and 33 Germans were picked up by a U-boat which was sighted by a Coastal Command aircraft, depth charged but survived. Next Bordeaux was under blockade and course was set for St Nazaire; enroute she was detected by a British destroyer and depth charged. Jan 4: St Nazaire was reached and Angus MacDonald went to Milag Nord, Wilhelmshaven.

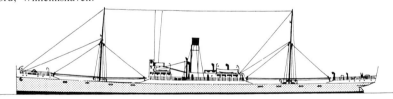

HERMISTON, BORDERER

419 HERMISTON
B 1901 R. Duncan & Co, Port Glasgow. **T** 4,389g, 2,831n.
D 374.6/114.18 x 48.1/14.66 x 27.9/8.5.
E Sgl scr, tpl exp, 360 nhp, 180 psi, 3 sgl blrs. 10 kts. By D. Rowan, Glasgow.
H Steel. 1 + spar dk. F 38/11.58. B 90/27.43. P 31/9.45.
1901 Built as *Hermiston* for Borderdale Shipping Co, Glasgow with J. Little & Co as managers.
1917 Acquired as a war loss replacement by Ellerman Lines for the City of Oran S.S. Co. Same name.
1919 R/n *Athena* by E. Engelis, Piraeus.
1922 Became *Charalambos* of Alex. G. Yannoulato, initially Argostoli registered but then Piraeus.
1938 Broken up.

420 BORDERER
As 419 except: **B** 1904 Russell & Co, Port Glasgow. **T** 4,372g, 2,835n.
D 374.5/114.1 x 48.9/14.9. **E** 418 nhp. By Clyde S.B. & E Co, Port Glasgow.

H B 102/31.09. P 33/10.06.
1904 Dec: Entered service as *Borderer* for Border Union S.S.Co, Glasgow with J. Little as managers.
1917 Acquired with her sister. Initially operated by Papayanni and owned by Joshua Nicholson S.S.Co Liverpool, with H. H. McAllester as manager.
1921 Transferred to Hall Line Ltd.
1929 Sold to Reederei Eugen Friederich, Bremen. R/n *Emmy Friederich*.
1939 Nov 1: Scuttled to avoid capture by a British warship.

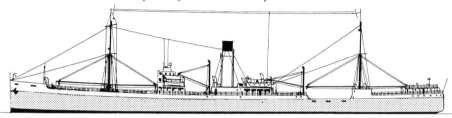

CITY OF WINCHESTER (II), CITY OF ADELAIDE (I), CITY OF CORINTH (IV)
CITY OF BRISBANE (I), MELFORD HALL (II) / CITY OF JOHANNESBURG (I)
CITY OF PEKIN (II), CITY OF ADELAIDE (II), CITY OF BRISBANE (II)

421 CITY OF WINCHESTER (II)
B 1917 Palmers S.B.Co, Newcastle. **T** 7,891n, 5,164n, 12,000dwt.
D 456.1/139.02 x 57.9/17.65 x 31.3/9.54.
E Sgl scr, 2 turbs, 736 nhp, 200 psi, 2,900 ihp, 3 sgl blrs. 12½ kts. By builder.
H Steel. 2 dks. B & P 318/96.93. P 99/30.27.
1917 Oct: Completed.
1918 Apr 15: Torpedoed by *UC-77* but made port.
1941 May 9: Torpedoed west of Dakar by *U-103*.

422 CITY OF ADELAIDE (I)
As 421 except: **B** Wm Gray & Co, West Hartlepool. **T** 8,389g, 4,179n.
D 433/131.98 x 57.4/17.49 x 30.2/9.2. **E** By Central Marine En. Wks.**H** F & B 308/93.88. P 89/27.13.
1917 April: Delivered.
1918 Aug 11: Due to influenza among the crew the ship had to leave her convoy and she set course for Malta. Torpedoed by *U-63* 60 miles east-north-east of Malta. 4 killed. HMS *Asphodel* picked up the crew.

423 CITY OF CORINTH (IV)
As 421 except: **B** 1918 Wm Gray, West Hartlepool. **T** 5,318g, 3,424n.
D 391/119.18 x 54.2/16.52 x 28.9/8.81. **E** Tpl exp, 581 nhp; by Central Marine Eng Wks.
H F & B 274/83.51. P 84/25.6.
1918 Jan: Entered service.
1940 Dec 21: Hit by bombs and incendiaries during an air raid on Liverpool.
1942 Nov 17: Torpedoed off Trinidad by *U-508*.

424 CITY OF BRISBANE (I)
As 421 except: **B** 1918 Swan, Hunter & Wigham Richardson, Wallsend. **T** 7,138g, 4,527n. **D** 463.6/141.3 x 58.8/17.92 x 30.9/9.42. **E** 885 nhp. By Walsend Slipway. **H** F & B 332/101.9. P 98/29.87.
1918 Delivered.
1918 Aug 15: Torpedoed by *UB-57* in the English Channel 1½ miles off Newhaven. The ship sank in 7 minutes. All saved.

425 MELFORD HALL (II) / CITY OF JOHANNESBURG (I)
As 421 except: **B** 1920 Barclay, Curle & Co, Glasgow. **T** 5,669g, 3,583n.
D 417.2/127.16 x 54.8/16.7 x 29/8.84. **E** By builder
H F & B 287/87.48. P 107/32.61.
1920 Completed as *Melford Hall*.
1926 Oct 15: R/n *City of Johannesburg*.
1942 Oct 23: Torpedoed by *U-504* off East London.

426 CITY OF PEKIN (II)
As 421 except: **B** 1920. **T** 6,960g, 4,426n, 11,800dwt.
D 442.8/134.96 x 58.7/17.89.
E 3 stm turbs. **H** F & B 309/94.18. P 97/29.56.

1920 Dec: Completed. She had twin white vents to bridge top level immediately abaft her bridge. Painted, at one stage, with white tops to her ventilators and sampson posts. See *City of Salisbury* (461).
1930 Apr 10: Struck a rock and sank at Brook Island, between Korea and Japan enroute Vladivostok-Dairen.

427 CITY OF ADELAIDE (II)
As 421 except: **B** 1920 Wm Gray, Wear Shipyard, Sunderland. **T** 6,589g, 4,178n.
D 450.7/137.37 oa, x 57.4/17.49 x 30.2/9.2. **E** 767 nhp. By Central Marine, West Hartlepool.
H F & B 308/93.87. **P** 89/27.13.
1920 Nov: Delivered. Had lifeboats on poop house.
1944 Mar 30: Nine days out of Karachi for the UK the ship was attacked by torpedo and gunfire by the Japanese *I-8* to become the final World War II Ellerman loss. They were thus 'loss free' for over a year.

428 CITY OF BRISBANE (II)
As 421 except: **B** 1920 Swan, Hunter & Wigham Richardson, Newcastle. **T** 7,138g, 4,527n.
D 463.6/141.3 x 58.8/17.92 x 30.9/9.42. **E** By Wallsend Slipway. **H** F & B 332/101.19. **P** 98/29.87.
1920 June: Completed.
1940 Aug 2: Bombed and set on fire by German aircraft off Long Sands in the Thames Estuary. In flames the ship settled and broke in two. 8 dead.

Sister of City of Manila (415)
429 CITY OF LUCKNOW (V)
B 1917 Wm Gray, West Hartlepool. **T** 8,293g, 4,973n.
D 475/144.78 x 58.2/17.74 x 31.7/9.66.
E Sgl scr, 4 cyl, quad exp, 758 nhp, 225 psi, 3 sgl blrs. 12 kts. By Central Marine, West Hartlepool.
H Steel. 2 dks. F 101/30.78. B 180/54.82. P 106/32.31.
1917 June: Completed for the Oran S.S.Co with Hall Line as managers.
1917 Dec 21: Torpedoed by *UB-50* 50 miles north east of Cani Rocks, Tunisia.

430 CITY OF SHANGHAI (II)
B 1917 Earles S.B.Co, Hull. **T** 5,528g, 3,748n.
D 418.5/127.56 x 55/16.76 x 29.4/8.96.
E Sgl scr, tpl exp, 565 nhp, 220 psi, 2 sgl blsrs. 12 kts. By builder.
H Steel. 2 dks. F 48/14.63. B 212/64.62. P 86/26.21.
1917 Aug: Entered service. Her long bridge deck forward of the bridge was unique to Ellermans.
1941 May 11: Torpedoed by *U-103* off St Paul's Rocks, 980 miles from Pernambuco while enroute Rosyth-Cape-Suez Canal-Turkey. The first boat load of survivors was rescued after two days by Union Castle's *Rochester Castle* and the second boat by an Argentine steamer after 5 days. Both were landed at Pernambuco.

Appearance as City of Florence (11) (433)
431 CROXTETH HALL (II)
B 1917 Palmers S.B.Co, Newcastle. **T** 5,872g, 3,741n.
D 414.1/126.22 x 52.5/16 x 29.5/8.99.
E Sgl scr, tpl, exp, 556 nhp, 220 psi, 2 sgl blrs. 11 kts. By builder.
H Steel. F 95/28.95. B 153/46.63. P 90/27.53.
1917 July, Built for the Barcelona S.S.Co, Hall Line Ltd managers.
1917 Nov 17: Sunk off Bombay by one of 465 EMC (Electric Mine Type C) mines laid by the raider *Wolf* (II) ex *Wachtfels*, 'Hansa'. In all 13 cargo vessels were sunk by them.

MISTLEY HALL built 1917, a wartime standard 'A' type was not Hall but owned by Charles G. Dunn who purchased *Mistley Hall* (342) back in 1887.

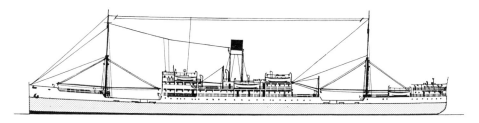

432 CITY OF BARODA (II)

B 1918 Barclay, Curle & Co, Glasgow. **T** 7,129g, 4,500n.
D 433.4/132.1 x 57.2/17.43 x 30.6/9.33.
E Sgl scr, tpl exp, 447 nhp, 220 psi. 12½ kts. By builder.
H Steel. 2 dks. F 85/25.9. B 171/52.12. P 90/27.43. **P** 113 1st.
1918 June 26: Launched. The final Hall Line passenger ship for the Calcutta service. Intended as a cargo ship she was altered during fitting out. Her intended outline was always visible to the eye but she was, nevertheless, a most handsome ship.
1927 Feb 3: Placed on E & B's American & Indian Line service out of New York.
1943 Apr 2: Torpedoed by *U-509* off Luderitz Bay, South Africa. One crewman and 13 passengers lost.

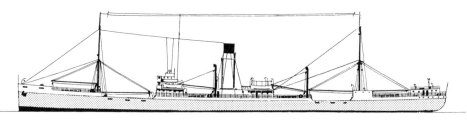

433 CITY OF FLORENCE (III)

B 1918 Wm. Gray, West Hartlepool. **T** 6,862g, 4,391n.
D 448.8/136.79 x 56.2/17.13 x 31.4/9.57.
E Sgl, scr, tpl exp, 621 nhp, 220 psi, 3 sgl blrs. 12 kts. By Central Marine Eng Wks.
H Steel. 2 dks. F 93/28.35. B 171/52.12. P 104/31.7.
1918 Feb: Completed.
1956 Made her final voyage to Liverpool; the oldest vessel in the fleet. It was the end of an astonishing saga. Several years earlier there had been a Ceylonese stowaway aboard who was a stateless person with no documents and no-one would allow him to land. At Liverpool the disposal of the ship caused a problem which was solved by giving the stowaway a resident's permit for six months.
Sold for £285,000 via Rallis Shipping Co to F. Theodorides, London. R/n *Mount Olympus*.
1959 Broken up in Japan.

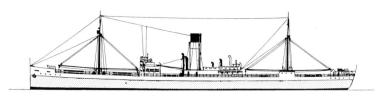

434 KIOTO (II)

B 1918 Wm. Gray, West Hartlepool. **T** 4,397g, 2,777n.
D 347.5/105.92 oa, 333.8/101.74 x 46.6/14.2 x 24.4/7.44.
E Sgl scr, tpl exp. 384 nhp, 220 psi, 2 sgl blrs.
H Steel. 2 + shelter dk. Flush.
1918 April: Purchased. The ship was a war time simple ship which was taken up to replace losses. She fitted no class but in service was satisfactory and served out her career with Hall.
1942 Sept 15: Torpedoed by *U-514* in the North Atlantic.

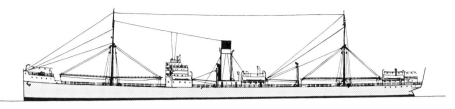

435 CITY OF MELBOURNE (I)
B 1919 J. L. Thompson, Sunderland. **T** 6,630g, 4,125n.
D 412.5/125.73 x 55.5/16.92 x 34.4/10.48. Dft 28.5/8.69.
E Sgl scr, tpl exp, 597 nhp, 180 psi. 12 kts. By J. Dickinson & Sons, Sunderland.
H Steel. 1 + shelter dk. F 36/10.97. C 567,508/16,070cu g. 9 winches, 14 derricks.
1919 June: Completed for Hall.
1942 May 13: Torpedoed off the Leeward Islands by *U-156*.

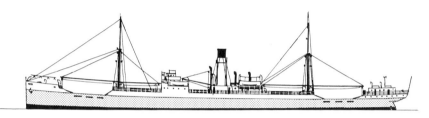

436 ROMEO / CITY OF GUILDFORD (I)
B 1919 Wm. Gray (1918) Ltd, West Hartlepool. **T** 5,157g, 3,236n.
D 400/121.92 x 52.3/15.94 x 28.5/8.69.
E Sgl scr, tpl exp, 517 nhp, 180 psi, 3 sgl blrs. 11 kts. By Central Marine, West Hartlepool.
H Steel. 2 dks. F 39/11.89. B 219/66.75. P 49/14.93.
1919 Mar 17: Launched as *War Midge*, a standard B type hull. June: Completed with a long bridge deck as *Romeo* for Hall Line. The chosen name indicates an intention to use her on Ellerman's Wilson routes.
1928 R/n *City of Guildford*.
1943 Mar 27: Torpedoed by *U-593* off Madeira. A spread of 4 torpedoes was fired followed by three detonations. *U-593* concluded that two ships had been sunk but in reality only *City of Guildford* fell victim.

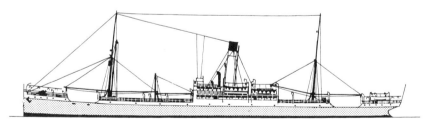

437 MERTON HALL (III) / CITY OF SALFORD
B 1905 Swan, Hunter & Wigham Richardson, Newcastle. **T** 4,988g, 3,134n.
D 392.7/119.69 x 47.9/14.6 x 28.3/8.62.
E Sgl scr, tpl exp, 380 nhp, 10 kts. By Wallsend Slipway.
H Steel. 2 dks. F 50/15.24. B 239/72.85. P 38/11.58. **P** 850 emigrants. 47 crew.
1905 June 17: Launched as *Santa Cruz* for the Hamburg Sud-Amerika Linie.
Sept 14: M/v Hamburg-La Plata-Rosario.
1914 Aug: Became *Sperrbrecher 7* German navy. Oddly she later bore the names *Sperrbrecher 6* and then *Sperrbrecher 5* (Sperr= blockade, brecher= breaker).
1918 Reverted to Hamburg Sud-Amerika.
1919 Mar 26: Ceded to Great Britain, the Shipping Controller. Managed by MacVicar, Marshall & Co.
1921 Acquired. R/n *Merton Hall*.
1926 R/n *City of Salford*.
1933 Nov: Broken up by Douglas & Ramsey, Glasgow.

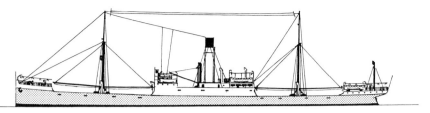

438 BRANKSOME HALL (IV)

B 1905 Swan, Hunter & Wigham Richardson. **T** 4,467g, 2,808n.
D 386.9/117.93 x 51.8/15.79 x 24.9/7.59.
E Sgl scr, 4 cyl quad exp, 440 nhp, 213 psi, 2 sgl blrs. 11 kts. By builder.
H Steel. 1 + spar dk. F 42/12.8. B 116/35.36. P 48/14.63.
1905 Sept: Completed as *Arensburg* for Deutsches Dampschiffahrts Gesellschaft 'Hansa', Bremen.
1919 March: Ceded to Great Britain, the Shipping Controller. Manager G. Heyn & Sons, Belfast.
1920 Acquired by Ellerman, Hall. R/n *Branksome Hall.*
1933 Collided with Southend Pier. Found not to be worth repairing. July 31: Arrived in Italy for scrapping.

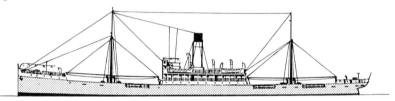

439 CROXTETH HALL (III)

B 1909 Rickmers A. G., Bremerhaven. **T** 4,243g, 2,621n.
D 367/111.86 x 47.7/14.54 x 27.3/8.32.
E Sgl scr, tpl exp, 327 nhp, 185 psi. 11 kts. By Bremer Vulkan, Vegesack.
H Steel. 2 dks. F 55/16.76. B 95/28.96.
1909 Aug 14: Launched. Sept 11: Completed as *Etha Rickmers* one of twelve very similar sisters built for the company between 1905 and 1911.
1914 July 31: At Sevastopol when World War I started. Taken as a war prize. R/n *Kaca*. Used as a floating workshop to the Black Sea fleet.
1918 Used to repatriate German troops Turkey-Wilhelmshaven.
1920 Ceded to Great Britain. Acquired by Hall. R/n *Croxteth Hall.*
1929 Feb 28. Wrecked in dense fog close to the Wandelaar Lightship near Blankenberghe, Belgian Coast.

Sister of City of Bagdad 261

440 CITY OF WESTMINSTER

B 1916 Flensburger S. G., Flensburg. **T** 6,094g, 3,771n.
D 470.4/143.41 x 62.1/18.93 x 25.3/7.71.
E Sgl scr, tpl exp, 701 nhp, 200 psi, 5 blrs. 12 kts. By builder.
H Steel. 1 + part 2nd dk. Upper F 58/17.68. F & B 336/102.41. P 67/20.42.
1916 Built as *Rudelsburg* for Deutsches D-G 'Hansa', Bremen.
1919 Passed to the Shipping Controller; Andrew Weir & Co, Managers.
1920 Acquired by Oran S.S. Co, Hall Line as managers. R/n *City of Westminster.*
1923 Oct 10: Wrecked on the Runnelstone, Cornwall enroute Port Natal-Belfast-Rotterdam.

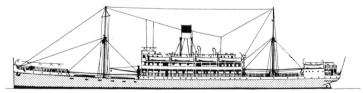

441 CITY OF GENOA (I)

B 1906 Blohm & Voss, Hamburg. **T** 6,365g, 4,008n.
D 411.6/125.45 x 50.7/15.45 x 28.6/8.72.
E Tw scr, 2 x tpl exp, 625 nhp, 220 psi, 4 sgl blrs. 12 kts. By builder. Fuel: 1,120 tons coal.

H Steel 2 + pt 3rd dk. F 60/18.29. B & P 260/79.25. C 293,000/89,306cu g.
P 96 1st, 62 2nd, 80 3rd. Crew 125.
1905 Nov 8: Launched as *Gertrud Woermann,* Woermann Linie.
1906 Jan 25: M/v Hamburg-West Africa service.
1907 Apr 25: Sold to Hamburg America Line. R/n *Windhuk;* joint service with Woermann to West Africa.
1914 Aug 4: At Hamburg. Used as a depot ship.
1919 Apr 1: Transferred to the Shipping Controller; Elder Dempster as managers.
1921 Acquired by Ellerman Lines Ltd, H. H. MacAllester manager. Hall Line service to Africa. R/n *City of Genoa.*
1928 Sold to Cia Colonial, Loanda. R/n *Joao Belo.* Africa service.
1950 July 5: Sold to BISCO for scrap. Broken up at Thornaby.

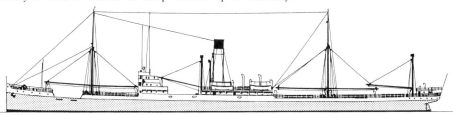

442 CITY OF SYDNEY (I)
B 1914 J. C. Tecklenborg A. G., Geestemunde. **T** 5,775g, 3,486n.
D 451.1/137.49 x 51.3/15.63 x 25.4/7.74.
E Sgl scr, tpl exp + LP turb DRG by hydraulic coupling .872 nhp, 223 psi, 4 sgl blrs. 12½ kts. By builder.
H Steel. 2 + pt 3rd dk. F 51/15.54. B & P 381/116.13.
1914 Mar 12: Launched as *Freiburg* For Deutsche Australienische D-G, Hamburg. Aug 4: Interned at Soerabaja. The Netherlands remained neutral.
1919 July 22: To the Shipping Controller with British India as managers.
1921 Acquired by Montgomerie and Workman, H. H. MacAllester as manager. Placed in Hall Line service as *City of Sydney.*
1923 Bought back by Deutsche Australienische, now owned by Deutsche D-G 'Kosmos', Hamburg. R/n *Luneburg* (they now had a *Freiburg).*
1926 Passed with the Kosmos fleet to Hamburg America line. **T** 5,828g, 3,668n.
1939 Sept 30: Became *Sperrbrecher IX.*
1940 July 30: R/n *Sperrbrecher 9.*
1944 July 1: Scuttled at La Pallice as a blockship across the harbour mouth.
1946 Raised and beached pending survey.
1948 Beyond repair; broken up.

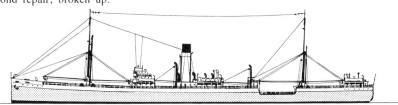

CITY OF GLASGOW (IV), CITY OF CHRISTIANIA, CITY OF PITTSBURG (I)
CITY OF TOKIO, CITY OF EVANSVILLE, CITY OF ATHENS (III)
CITY OF EASTBOURNE (I), CITY OF SINGAPORE (I), CITY OF OSAKA

443 CITY OF GLASGOW (IV)
B 1920 Wm. Gray, West Hartlepool. **T** 5,321g, 3,401n, 12,100dwt.
D 391.3/119.27 x 54.2/16.52 x 28.9/8.81.
E Sgl scr, 2 dbl reduction steam turbs, 632 nhp, 225 psi, 3 sgl blrs. 12 kts. By Central Marine.
H Steel. 2 dks. F & B 274/83.51. P 84/25.6. C 569,000/16,112cu g. of which 74,200/2,101.1 ref in the 'tween decks. 6 hatches, 12 winches, 17 derricks.
1920 Dec: Completed. One of a considerable group of ships spread across the Ellerman group with a combined fcsle and bridge and with a long poop. They were almost indistinguishable from each other even though the details varied and few were true sisters. Many later had side houses added abreast the main mast.
1956 July: Sold to Westport Shipping, London. R/n *Marianne B.*
1958 Broken up.

444 CITY OF CHRISTIANIA
As 443 except: **B** 1921 Earles, Hull. **T** 4,940g, 3,031n.
D 380.1/115.85 x 53/16.15 x 28.5/8.69. **E** Tpl exp, 550 nhp. By builder.
H F & B 266/81.08. **P** 85/25.91. 1 x 25 ton derrick to no. 2 hatch.
1921 Aug: Completed. Had well deck bulwarked.
1957 Oct: Broken up.

445 CITY OF PITTSBURG (I)
As 443 except: **B** 1921 Palmers, Jarrow. **T** 7,377g, 4,719n.
D 465.7/141.94 x 58.6/17.86 x 31.8/9.69. **E** 3 dbl reduction geared turbs. 759 nhp. By builder.
H F & B 329/100.28. **P** 98/29.87.
1921 Jan: Entered service.
1930s E & B service with their funnel.
1942 Jan: Stranded at the entrance to Alexandra harbour. Cargo salved but the vessel broke her back and became a total loss.

446 CITY OF TOKIO
As 443 except: **B** 1921 Craig, Taylor & Co, Stockton. **T** 6,993g, 4,426n.
D 442.5/134.87 x 59/17.98 x 31.6/9.63. **E** 3 sgl reduction turbs. 746 nhp. By Palmers, Newcastle.
H F & B 309/94.18. **P** 97/29.56.
1921 Sept: Completed. Funnel deck had two lifeboats each side.
1940 Based at Freetown, Sierra Leone, as a stores ship for the navy.
1941 Replaced at Freetown by *City of Dieppe* (274). The ships remained on station until their supplies were exhausted although they were in part replenished by others. The determining factor in their replacement was marine growth below the water line.
1951 June 7: Arrived for scrap at Dalmuir.

447 CITY OF EVANSVILLE
As 443 except: **B** 1922. **T** 6,528g, 4,141n. **D** 450.8/137. 4 oa, 433.2/132.04 x 57.3/17.46 x 30.1/9.17.
E Tpl exp; 617 nhp. **H** F & B 307/93.52. **P** 88/26.82.
1922 Oct: Delivered. Later houses abreast the mainmast were added.
1926 All the triple expansion powered ships in this group had a Low Pressure turbine added with either a hydraulic or electric coupling to the propeller shaft. This ship had a hydraulic coupling. 729 nhp.
1932 March: After the official opening of Sydney Harbour Bridge she was the first British merchantman to pass under it.
1940 After the fall of France French troops were given the choice of returning home or serving in the Free French Forces under the technically traiterous General de Gaulle. July: Repatriated 1,500 troops to Morocco from where 1,400 British refugees were brought home.
1951 A fire in her cargo of jute was put out before it managed to take hold.
1957 Oct 31: Sold to Pan Norse S.S.Co., r/n *Dorca*.
1950 Broken up at Keelung.

448 CITY OF ATHENS (III)
As 443 except: **B** 1923. **T** 6,558g, 4,187n. **D** 450.7/137.37 oa, 435/131.98 x 57.4/17.49 x 30.2/9.2.
E Tpl exp; 665 nhp. **H** B & F 308/93.88. **P** 85/25.91.
1923 July: Completed.
1927 Engine augmented as 447. 728 nhp.
1942 Oct 8: Torpedoed by *U-179* off Cape Town en route Takoradi-Cape Town.

449 CITY OF EASTBOURNE (I)
As 443 except: **B** 1923. **T** 5,563g, 3,509n. **D** 421.9/128.59 oa, 406.2/123.81 x 54.2/16.52 x 28.8/8.78.
E Tpl exp. **H** F & B 287/87.48. **P** 87/26.52.
1923 May: Completed for Ellerman Lines with H. H. MacAllester manager; he was followed by W. T. Murray.
1928 Mar 22: Picked up a faint radio message from *Asiatic Prince*, Prince Line, then 1,890 miles from Los Angeles. This was the last ever heard of her.
1930 Given an LP turb with electric drive to a motor attached to the shaft.
1932 Laid up during the depression in the Gareloch, Clyde. Wisely the Ellerman ships rotated in lay up so that there would be the least amount of deterioration. At any given moment there were eight there.
1939-45 Commercial service. Deckhouses added abreast the mainmast, boat to starboard.
1952 Grounded on the Indian Coast but came off unscathed.
1953 Nov 21: Sold to Francesco Pittaluga, Genoa. R/n *Ninin Pittaluga*.
1959 Broken up at La Spezia.

450 CITY OF SINGAPORE (I)
As 443 except: **B** 1923. **T** 6,55g, 4,161n. **D** 450.7/137.37 oa, 433/131.98 x 57.3/17.46 x 30.2/9.2.
E Tpl exp, 617 NHP. **H** F & B 307/93.57. **P** 88/26.82.
1923 March: Completed. H.H. McAllester manager.
1924 March: Severely damaged by an explosion followed by fire. The ship was initially declared lost but
she survived and was rebuilt.
1929 Refitted as 447.
1943 May 1: Torpedoed off Freetown by *U-515* in convoy TS 37 en route Takoradi-Freetown.

451 CITY OF OSAKA
As 443 except: **B** 1923 at Gray's Wear Shipyard. **T** 6,614g, 4,223n.
D 433/131.98 x 57.4/17.49 x 30.2/9.2. **E** Tpl exp; 617 nhp. **H** F & B 308/93.88. **P** 89/27.13.
1923 Jan: Completed as *Colorado (III)* for Ellerman's Wilson Line. Their livery.
1924 Transferred to Ellerman Lines Ltd ownership with Hall Line as managers.
1930 Sept 22: Wrecked near Buchaness, Aberdeenshire.

452 RYDAL HALL (V) / CITY OF KHIOS (II)
As 443 except: **B** 1925 Barclay, Curle, Glasgow. **T** 5,574g, 3,537n.
D 417.5/127.25 oa, 400/121.92 x 55/16.76 x 29.7/8.84. **E** Tpl exp; 474 nhp. By builder.
H F & P 289/82. **P** 68/20.73.
1925 Jan: Completed as *Rydal Hall*. R/n *City of Khios* during the year.
1955 June 6: Sold to Securities Shipping Co., r/n *Empire Merchant*. Operated by Pacific Export Lines,
Hong Kong.
1956 Her owners were Stanley Shipping Co, Hong Kong. Same name.
1962 R/n *Rantau Panjang*, same owners. Feb: Classification withdrawn and placed on the disposal list
for scrapping.
1963 Broken up.

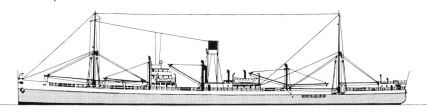

453 CITY OF WELLINGTON
As 452 except: **B** 1925 Barclay, Curle, Glasgow. **T** 5,733g, 3,642n. **D** 427.5/130.3 oa, 411.5/125.42 x
55/16.76 x 29.7/9.05. **E** tpl exp; 551 nhp. **H** F & B 276/84.12. **P** 68/20.73.
1925 Nov: Delivered.
1932 Low pressure turb with electric drive fitted. 647 nhp.
1942 Aug 21: Torpedoed by *U-506* off Freetown.

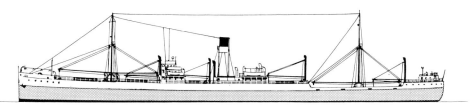

CITY OF LYONS, CITY OF ROUBAIX
454 CITY OF LYONS
B 1926 Swan, Hunter & Wigham Richardson, Newcastle. **T** 7,063g, 4,461n.
D 455.5/138.84 x 58.1/17.71 x 31.8/9.69.
E Sgl scr, 3 sgl reduction geared turbs, 709 nhp, 240 psi, 3 sgl blrs. 12½ kts. By Wallsend Slipway & Eng.
Co. Coal 58 tons p d.
H Steel. 2 dks. F & B 309/94.18. **P** 44/13.41.
1926 Feb: Completed, oil burner. Oddly: Two ships with unduplicated names.
1960 Final voyage Chalna-Dublin. Dec 5: Sold for scrap to BISCO and broken up by P & W MacLellan,
Bo'ness. The last of the 1920s type.
Dec 10: Arrived after 34 years of service.

455 CITY OF ROUBAIX

As 454 except: **B** 1928. **T** 7,108g, 4,555n. **D** 456.1/139.02 x 58.4/17.8.
E 1,029 nhp. **H** F & P 310/94.49. **P** 50/15.24.
1928 Feb: Delivered. Thicker funnel than her sister.
1941 Apr 6: Sunk at Piraeus. During a German air raid *Clan Fraser*, Clan Line, loaded with explosives, was hit and blew to smithereens taking with her *City of Roubaix*, Prince Line's *Cyprian Prince* and the Greek *Patris*. An ammunition train alongside also detonated. The harbour was devastated and the number killed never known.

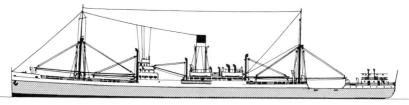

456 CITY OF BATH (I)

B 1926 Wm Gray, West Hartlepool. **T** 5,079g, 3,154n.
D 408/124.36 oa, 393.2/119.85 x 52.2/15.91 x 28.2/8.59.
E Sgl scr, quad exp, 532 nhp, 265 psi, 3 sgl blrs. By Central Marine, West Hartlepool.
H Steel. 2 dks. F & B 310/94.49. **P** 38/11.58.
1926 June: Entered service.
1942 Dec 12: Torpedoed by *U-508* off Trinidad.

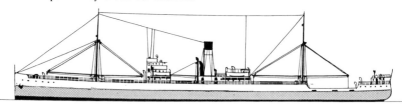

457 CITY OF WORCESTER (I)

As 456 except: **B** 1927 Earles, Hull. **T** 5,469g, 3,430n. **D** 397.2/121.1 x 53.4/16.28.
E Tpl exp. 523 nhp, 225 psi. By builder. **H** F & B 313/95.4. **P** 32/9.75.
1927 Oct: Delivered.
1952 Jan 25: A fire in her cargo took 24 hours to extinguish.
1955 May 19: Became *Scillin II*, Navagazione Peloritana S.p.A.; Messina.
1959 Broken up at Genoa.

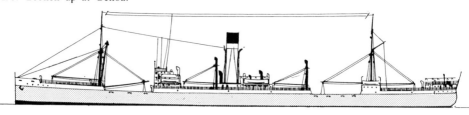

SANDON HALL (II) / CITY OF DUNDEE (II), CITY OF YOKOHAMA

458 SANDON HALL (II) / CITY OF DUNDEE (II)

B 1921 Palmers, Jarrow. **T** 5,273g, 3,309n.
D 423.3/129.02 oa, 406/123.75 x 52.1/15.88 x 29.2/8.9.
E Sgl scr, 3 dbl reduction geared turbs, 609 nhp, 220 psi, 2 sgl blrs. By builder.
H Steel. 2 dkgs. F 78/23.77. B 147/44.8. **P** 80/24.38.
1921 March: Delivered as *Sandon Hall*. The final vessel to bear a 'Hall' name.
1926 R/n *City of Dundee*. Same operators.
1957 Jan: Her final voyage ended at Manchester. Put up for disposal there.
Aug 20: Arrived at Port Glasgow and scrapped by Smith & Houston.

459 CITY OF YOKOHAMA

As 458 except: **B** 1922 Wm Gray, West Hartlepool. **T** 7,341g, 4,721n.
D 465.1/141.76 x 58.1/17.71 x 31.8/9.69. **E** 2 turbs, 917 nhp. By builder (rare).
H F 97/29.56. B 171/52.12. **P** 107/32.61.

1922 March: Entered service.
1958 Jan: Sold. R/n *Trinity Pioneer* by Transatlantic Nav. Corp, Monrovia.
1959 Became *Transpioneer* and broken up at Hong Kong.

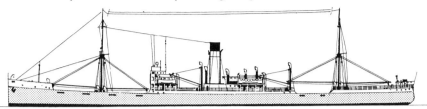

CITY OF BEDFORD, CITY OF SALISBURY

460 CITY OF BEDFORD
As 458 except: **B** 1924 Wm Gray, West Hartlepool. **T** 6,407g, 4,107n.
D 430/131.06 x 55.1/16.79 x 31.1/9.48. **E** Quad exp, 728 nhp, 2,280 ihp, 250 psi. By Central Marine.
H F 42/12.8. B 162/49.38. P 89/27.13.
1924 Oct: Completed.
1940 Dec 30: Lost 280 miles off Iceland in collision with Elder Dempster's *Bodnant* when two convoys
came too close to each other. No lives were lost but 7½ million rifle cartridges went down; the largest
munitions loss in the war to that date. Winston Churchill was 'greatly distressed' and demanded to know
why all the ammunition was in one ship. He laid down that, in future, the loads be spread over sufficient
vessels to ensure the safe arrival of 'sufficient of the weapons without which we cannot wage war'.

461 CITY OF SALISBURY
As 458 except: **B** 1924 Wm Gray. **T** 5,946g, 3,794. **D** 415/126.49 x 54/16.46 x 30.3/9.23.
E Tpl exp, 574 nhp. By Central Marine. **H** F 42/12.8. B 150/45.72. P 89/27.13.
1924 June: Delivered. A few ships were painted with white tops to vents and king posts, as drawn. *City
of Pekin* (426) was another example.
1938 Apr 23: Grounded in fog near Graves Lighthouse, Boston, Mass. Broke in two at forefront of the
funnel. Much cargo salvaged.

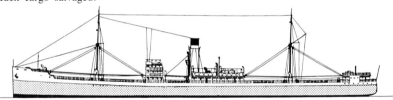

462 CITY OF DURBAN (I) / CITY OF GLOUCESTER (I)
B 1921 Earles, Hull. **T** 5,850g, 3,672.
D 379.7/115.73 x 52.1/15.88 x 20.6/8.11.
E Sgl scr, 3 dbl reduction geared turbs, 607 nhp, 225 psi, 3 sgl blrs. By builder.
H Steel. 2 + shelter dk. F 40/12.19.
1921 March: Completed. Purchased as a war loss replacement while the ship was building having been
laid down by Earle's 'for sale subject to contract'.
1945 The lifeboats abreast the funnel were added.
1952 April: R/n *City of Gloucester* in order to free the name for the ship building for Ellerman &
Bucknall.
1957 Aug 7: Arrived at Giants Grave, Briton Ferry for breaking up by Thos W. Ward.

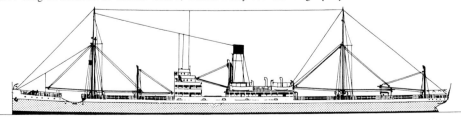

463 CITY OF BOSTON
B 1912 J. C. Tecklenborg A.G., Geestemunde. **T** 5,885g, 3,681n, 9,500dwt.
D 450.9/137.43 x 57.2/17.43 x 27/8.23. Dft 25.2/7.68.

E Sgl scr, tpl exp, 697 nhp, 223 psi, 4 sgl blrs. By builder.
H Steel. 2 + pt 3rd. F 45/13.72. B & P 392/119.48.
1912 Feb 4: Launched as *Dusseldorf* for Deutsche D-G Australische. Mar 26: Delivered.
1914 Aug: At Barcelona when World War I started; interned.
1919 Aug: Initially allocated to the French Government for transport work.
1921 Feb 14: Ceded to Great Britain. Allocated to Ellerman. R/n *City of Boston*.
1927 Became *Grandon*, Norddeutscher Lloyd. South American service.
1934 Transferred to Hamburg America Line. Same name.
1937 R/n *Patagonia;* same owner.
1942 Dec 15: Commissioned as a Naval transport.
1944 May 14: Damaged by Russian bombs at Kirkenes.
1945 May 15: Found at Brunsbuttel Koog at the end of the war. Oct 4: Scuttled in the Skaggerak loaded with surplus ammunition.

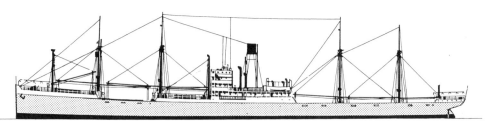

464 **CITY OF DUNEDIN**
B 1917 Bremer Vulkan, Vegesack. **T** 7,857g, 4,870n.
D 475.3/144.87 x 60.7/18.5 x 32.9/10.03.
E Sgl scr, tpl exp, 817 nhp, contra-rotating. 12 kts. By builder.
H Steel. 2 dks. F 86/26.21. B 143/43.59. P 28/8.53.
1917 Completed as *Porta* for Norddeutscher Lloyd.
1919 Transferred at Leith to the Shipping Controller. Lamport & Holt managers. Used to ferry to Antwerp the German crews of the warships surrendered in the Forth, then laid up at Cowes.
1921 April: Acquired by Ellerman. R/n *City of Dunedin*. Hall Line.
1927 Aug: Grounded without damage on Pluckington Bank, Mersey. She hit almost at low water and came off within the hour. Ships unlucky enough to ground on the falling tide race were usually doomed.
1928 Sold back to Norddeutscher Lloyd for £90,000. R/n *Lippe;* they already had a *Porta*, built 1922.
1940 Apr 13: Sunk in Narvik Fjord during the Second Battle of Narvik when the battleship *Warspite* and 9 destroyers sank the 8 trapped German destroyers and *U-64*.

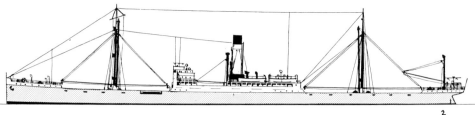

465 **CITY OF AUCKLAND (I)**
B 1915 A. G. 'Weser', Bremen. **T** 8,336g, 5,288n.
D 500.2/152.46 oa, 478.6/145.88 x 62.2/18.96 x 33/10.06.
E Sgl scr, quad exp, 845 nhp, 213 psi, 4 sgl blrs. 12 kts. By builder.
H Steel. 2 dks. F 59/17.98. B 140/42.67. P 45/13.72.
1914 Completed as *Weissenfels* for Deutsche D-G 'Hansa', Bremen.
1919 War prize. Owned by the Shipping Controller. Andrew Weir's Bank Line as managers.
1921 Acquired by Montgomerie & Workman (1920) Ltd. H. H. McAllester manager. Operated on the Hall Line berth. R/n *City of Auckland*.
1936 M & W ceased to own ships. Transferred to Ellerman Lines Ltd with Hall Line, Liverpool, as managers.
1940 Feb-June: Carried military supplies to France.
1941 July 7: Avoided four torpedoes from *U-109* and then drove her off by gunfire.
1947 Oct 17: Sold to the Christopher S.S.Co., r/n *Karteria*.
1950 July: Became *Steva* of I.N.S.A., Genoa. Oct: Scrapped at La Spezia.

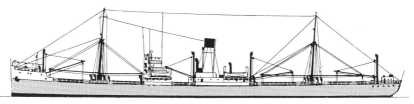

466 CITY OF STOCKHOLM
B 1915 Barclay, Curle, Glasgow. **T** 5,075g, 3,155n.
D 411.8/125.52 x 55.4/16.88 x 26.3/8.02.
E Sgl scr, oil; 3 cyl 2S. DA by North British Diesel Eng. Wks., Glasgow.
H Steel. 1 + shelter dk. F 40/12.19.
1925 Aug: Laid down as *Frederick Gilbert*. Purchased on the stocks. R/n *City of Stockholm*.
1927 Sold to Hopemount Shipping Co, Stamp, Mann & Co, Newcastle. Sold before a change of name for £85,000 to Venatus Shipping Co, Howard Tenens Ltd, London. Became *Prunus*. Converted to tpl exp, 504 nhp by Swan, Hunter & Wigham Richardson, Wallsend. 12 kts.
1932 Dec: Re-sold to Hopemount Shipping Co; r/n *Hopetor*. Stott, Mann & Co, managers.
1936 Jan: Went ashore in Australia but survived.
1937 Sold for £25,000 to Barry Shipping Co; r/n *St Merriel*.
1939 Her owners were re-styled South American Saint Line.
1943 Jan 2: Bombed and sunk by Axis aircraft at Bone.
1950 Salved. Aug 4: Broke in two and foundered off Capo Noli while in tow to Savona for scrapping.

CITY OF KOBE See *Malvernian* 106

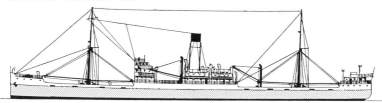

467 CITY OF HEREFORD (I)
B 1927 Barclay, Curle, Glasgow. **T** 5,101g, 3,215n.
D 385.4/117.47 x 51.7/15.76 x 30.3/9.23.
E Sgl scr, tpl exp, 523 nhp, 225 psi, 2 sgl blrs. 12 kts. By builder.
H Steel. 2 dks. F 37/11.28. B 111/33.83. P 31/9.45.
1927 May: Entered Hall's New York-Philadelphia-Far East service.
1940 Transferred to Ellerman & Bucknall.
1945 Managed by Westcott & Laurence Ltd.
1955 Sold to Williamson & Co, Hong Kong, for £78,000. R/n *Inchona*.
1956 Became *Golden Alpha,* World Wide S.S.Co., London with World Wide Shipping Co. (Managers), Hong Kong, as managers.
1959 Broken up at Osaka.

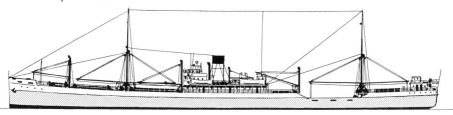

468 CITY OF LILLE
B 1928 Barclay, Curle, Glasgow. **T** 6,588g, 4,052n, 10,359dwt.
D 465.7/141.94 oa, 447.7/139.46 x 57.9/17.65 x 33.9/10.33.
E Sgl scr, oil; 4 cyl opposed Doxford 5,000 bhp. 12 3/4 kts. By builder.
H Steel. 2 dks. F & B 312/95.1. P 70/21.34.
1928 July: Entered service for a career virtually free from trouble. The first newly built motorship for the fleet.
1955 Dec: While anchoring in the Bristol Channel she lost an anchor and five cables of chain.

1956 Sept: En route Newport, Mon-Beira suffered her only machinery breakdown. Some bolts sheered. Repaired at Cape Town.
1957 May 27: Sold at Glasgow for £300,000 to International Union Lines, Monrovia. R/n *Union Capitol*.
1963 Broken up at Taiwan.

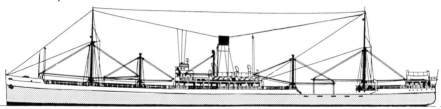

469 CITY OF SYDNEY (II)
B 1930 Workman, Clark. Belfast. **T** 6,986g, 4,326n.
D 454.2/138.44 x 58.4/17.8 x 31.7/9.66.
E Sgl scr, tpl exp, 4 cyl + 2 LP turbs dbl reduction geared by hydraulic coupling. 905 nhp, 265 psi, 4 sgl blrs. 13 kts. By builder.
H Steel. 2 dks. F & B 313/95.4. P 58/17.68.
1930 May: Delivered. Her fuel consumption was 20 tons oil per day, half that of a steamer. She also had eight fewer crew. Even so she was an experimental vessel and it was to be 22 more years before Ellerman finally switched to oil burners in all their new ships.
1956 Feb 19: With a pilot aboard and in a snow storm she ran down and cut in two Cory's *Corchester* off the Haisboro' Light. 8 killed.
1958 Mar 31: In the Indian Ocean she rescued 1,300 passengers from the burning *Skaubryn*, I. M. Skaugen. There was insufficient food, water or room as *City of Sydney* set off towards Aden but in response to her radio signal the Italian liner *Roma*, Achille Lauro, raced in at 18 knots and took off the stranded people. The hulk was taken in tow by Wijsmuller's *Cycloop* but foundered on April 6.
May 28: Sold to Tsavliris (Shipping) Ltd, London. R/n *Nicholaos Tsavliris*.
1959 Sold and broken up.

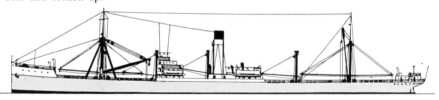

470 CITY OF BARCELONA
B 1930 Barclay, Curle, Glasgow. **T** 5,787g, 3,524n.
D 444/135.33 oa, 428/130.45 x 58.2/17.74 x 27.3/8.32.
E Sgl scr, tpl exp, 4 cyl (2 x LP) + LP turb with electric drive. 638 nhp, 265 psi, 2 sgl blrs. 12½ kts. By builder.
H Steel. 2 + shelter dk. F 34/10.36.
1930 May: Her fore mast was strutted, as drawn, to carry a 30 ton derrick. She was the first 'heavy lift' in the fleet and at the time the heaviest in the British Mercantile Marine.
1958 May 20: Sold and broken up at Antwerp.

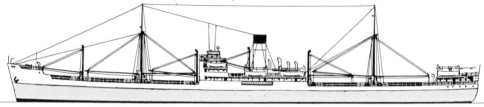

471 CITY OF MANCHESTER (IV)
B 1935 Cammell, Laird. Birkenhead. **T** 8,917g, 5,572n.
D 498.5/151.94 x 64.3/19.6 x 29.9/9.11.
E Tw scr, 2 x 3 turbs. 1,625 nhp, 275 psi, 5 sgl blrs. 13 kts. By builder.
H Steel. 2 + shelter dk. F 38/11.58.
1935 July: Delivered.
1942 Feb 27: Left Tjilatjap, Java. Feb 28: Torpedoed by the Japanese submarine *I-153* off Java.

472 CITY OF AGRA (III)
B 1936 Wm. Denny & Bros, Dumbarton. **T** 6,361g, 3,866n, 9,500dwt.
D 459.9/140.18 oa, 445.9/135.91 x 56.2/17.13 x 30.6/9.33.
E Sgl scr, 3 sgl reduction Parsons geared turbs, 450 nhp each, 275 psi, 3 sgl blrs. 13½ kts. By builders.
Fuel: 186 tons coal/oil.
H Steel. 2 dks. F 42/12.8. B 197/60.04. P 80/24.38. Crew: 94.
1935 Aug 20: Ordered. Nov 25: Keel laid.
1936 Oct 2: Launched. Dec 18: Delivered as a coal burner which required 10 stokers. Made 14.81 knots
on trials. Cost £149,943. Her holds were clear of stanchions for the carriage of bulky cargoes.
1965 May 10: Sold at Glasgow to Dutch interests, the oldest in the fleet, but then re-sold and broken up
at Bilbao.

Appearance as City of Edinburgh (V) 277

473 CITY OF CAPE TOWN (I)
B 1937 Cammell, Laird. Birkenhead. **T** 8,046g, 3,935n.
D 515.5/157.12 oa, 496.7/151.39 x 62.4/19.02 x 31.3/9.54.
E Tw scr, 2 x 3 sgl reduction geared turbs. 1,867 nhp, 265 psi, 6 sgl blrs. 13½ kts. By builder.
H Steel. 2 + pt 3rd dk. F & B 351/106.98 P 76/23.16.
1937 Oct: Completed for Hall Line but served frequently on E. & B. services.
1939-45 Commercial service.
1942 March: Carried a full cargo of munitions to India.
1962 Sold to Harbour Line Ltd, Bermuda. R/n *Mangrove Harbour.*
1951 May: In thick fog went ashore in the River St Lawrence but came off the same day with only
propeller damage; towed to Halifax where the spare was fitted.
1964 Broken up in Hong Kong.

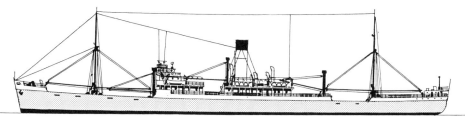

474 CITY OF BOMBAY (IV)
B 1937 Barclay, Curle, Glasgow. **T** 7,140g, 4,270n.
D 464.3/141.52 x 59.2/18.04 x 31.2/9.51.
E Sgl scr, 3 sgl reduction geared turbs, 750 nhp, 13½ kts. By Parsons Marine Steam Turbines,
Newcastle.
H Steel. 2 dks. F 30/9.14. B 195/59.43 P 3/22.25.
1937 Completed.
1942 Dec 13; Torpedoed in the South Atlantic off St Pauls Rocks by *U-159.*

Liberty ship. Appearance see City of St Albans 280
475 CITY OF NEWPORT
B 1943 Bethlehem Fairfield S.B, Baltimore. **T** 7,270g, 4,452n, 10,414 dwt.
D 441.7/134.63 oa, 423.7/129.14 x 57/17.37 x 34.8/10.61.
E Sgl scr, tpl exp, 240 psi, 2 wt blrs, 2,500 ihp at 76 rpm. By General Machinery Corp., Hamilton.
H Steel. 2 dks.
1943 Launched as *William R. Cox.* Completed as *Samtweed*, bare boat charter to M.O.W.T. with Hall
Line as managers. Their only Liberty ship.
1947 Oct; Acquired. R/n *City of Newport;* Hall Line.
1961 R/n *Istros II*, Veritas Shipping Corp, Greece.
1967 April: Broken up at Trieste.

CITY OF CHESTER (II), CITY OF MADRAS (V)
Appearance as *City of Bristol* 279

476 CITY OF CHESTER (II)
B 1944 Barclay, Curle, Clydeholm Yd, Linthouse. **T** 8,380g, 4,954n.
D 493/150.27 oa, 465.7/141.94 x 64.3/19.6 x 29.9/9.11.
E Tw scr, quad exp, 2 x 4 cyl, 9,000 bhp. 14 kts. By builder.
H Steel. F 37/11.28. B 166/50.6. P 44/13.41.
1944 March: Delivered to Hall Line.
1971 June 8: Sold to Embajada Cia Nav. S.A., Panama for one loaded delivery voyage to the breakers.
R/n *Chester*. Broken up in China.

477 CITY OF MADRAS (V)
As 476 except: **B** 1945 Swan, Hunter & Wigham Richardson. **T** 8,520g, 4,270n.
D 471.6/143.74. **E** By Wallsend Slipway. **H** F 39/11.58. B 176/52.73. P 48/14.32.
1945 Feb: Delivered.
1961 Sept 29: Sold to Far Eastern Nav. Corp., r/n *Wei Lee*.
1963 Broken up at Taiwan.

CITY OF KHARTOUM (II), CITY OF LUCKNOW (VI), CITY OF SWANSEA (II), CITY OF POONA (II)
Appearance see *City of Durham* (IV) 281

478 CITY OF KHARTOUM (II)
B 1946 Barclay, Curle. Whiteinch, Glasgow. **T** 9,955g, 6,128n.
D 475.7/145 x 64.2/19.57 x 40/12.19.
E Sgl scr, oil. 6 cyl Doxford 2S.SA, 6,600 bhp, 14½ kts. By builder.
H Steel. 3 dks. F 33/10.06. P 38/11.58. P 12 C 699,685/19,813 cu g.
1946 Jan: Completed. Hall Line as managers.
1968 Feb 15: Sold to Wm. Thomson's Ben Line, Leith. R/n *Benalligin*.
1972 Sept 27: Arrived at Kaohsiung for scrapping by Nan Feng Steel Enterprise Co.

479 CITY OF LUCKNOW (VI)
As 478 except: **B** Wm. Denny Bros., Dumbarton. **T** 9,961g, 5,954n.
E 3 dbl reduction geared Parsons turbs, 880 nhp, 430 psi, 2 Babcock & Wilcox wt blrs. By builder.
Crew: Europeans: 16 officers, 11 ratings, 3 stewards. Lascars 64 = 94.
1945 Nov 21: Launched. Funnel squatter and slightly thicker.
1946 May 7 and 14: Trials; 17.615 kts at 102 rpm. May 14: Delivered to Hall.
1963 Dec 12: Sold to Alexandra Nav. Corp, Liberia. R/n *Lisboa*.
1970 Owned by Outerocean Nav. Corp., Taiwan. Same name.
1971 Mar 3: Left Esperance Bay for breaking up in Taiwan.

480 CITY OF SWANSEA (II)
As 478 except: **B** 1946 Barclay, Curle, Glasgow. **T** 9,959g, 7,053n. **E** By builder.
1946 April: Delivered to Hall.
1968 Mar 23: Sold to Ben Line, Leith. R/n *Benkitlan*.
1972 Sept 3: Arrived at Kaohsiung and scrapped by Chin Tai Steel Enterprise Co.

481 CITY OF POONA (II)
As 478 except: **B** 1946 Swan, Hunter & Wigham Richardson. **T** 9,962g, 7,051n.
E By builder. **H** F 40/12.1 P 39/11.89.
1946 July: Delivered to Hall. Had four tall thin pole topmasts.
1968 Sold to Ben Line, Leith. R/n *Benarkle*. Masts as drawn.
1974 June 16: Arrived at Kaohsiung. Scrapped by Li Chong Steel & Iron Wks.

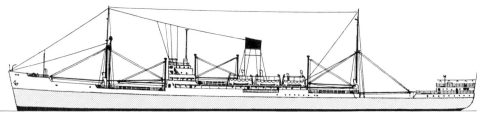

CITY OF NEW YORK, CITY OF HULL (I), CITY OF LONDON (IV)
CITY OF PRETORIA (III)

482 CITY OF NEW YORK
B 1947 Vickers, Armstrong, Walker, Newcastle. **T** 8,420g, 4,201n.
D 500/152.4 oa, 478.9/145.97 x 64.3/19.6 x 32/9.75.
E Tw scr, 2 x 3 turb, HP was DRG, IP and LP SRG; 430 psi, 3 wt blrs. 14 kts. By builder, Barrow.
H Steel. 2 + pt 3rd dk. F & B 372/113.38. Upper F 43/13.11 P 47/14.32.
1947 Jan: Completed for Hall. The first pair were Hall the second pair E & B. They were designed to reach the Cape in 15 days (The first steamer, East India's *Enterprize, (sic)*, took 58 days).
1967 May 23: Sold to Mardevoto Cia. Nav. S. A., Greece. R/n *Kavo Matapas*.
1969 July 31: Left Keelung for the breakers yard at Kaohsiung.

483 CITY OF HULL (I)
As 482. **T** 8,458g, 4,250n.
1947 Oct: Delivered to Hall Line.
1950 Transferred to Ellerman & Bucknall management.
1967 Apr 10: Sold to Embajada Cia. Nav., Panama for a single loaded voyage to the Far East followed by demolition. R/n *Essex*. June 22: Arrived at Aioi, Japan, and broken up.

CITY OF LONDON (IV) See E & B 599
CITY OF PRETORIA (III) See E & B 600

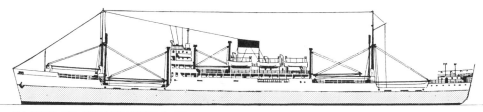

484 CITY OF JOHANNESBURG (II)
B 1947 Barclay, Curle. Glasgow. **T** 8,207g, 4,831n.
D 497.5/151.64 oa, 476.1/145.11 x 64.2/19.57 x 32.3/9.84.
E Tw scr, 2 x 4 cyl, 2S.SA, 4,000 BHP, 15 kts. By builder.
H Steel. 2 dks. F 85/25.91 B 223/67.97. P 47/14.32.
1947 Nov: Delivered to Hall Line. Initially intended as the fifth of the *City of New York* class but completed as a motorship for comparison with steam. But this does not explain her very different profile. E & P were, at the time, introducing their motor driven *Crosbian* class.
1953 Dec 24: Collided with and sank Everard's *Alf Everard* in Sea Reach, Thames Estuary.
1970 Jan 26: Sold to Fairy Cia. Naviera S.A., Greece. R/n *Filothei*.
1972 R/n *Lykavitos* by Rodini Cia. Nav. S.A., Greece.
1973 Feb 7: Arrived at Kaohsiung for demolition.

CITY OF GLOUCESTER (II) / CITY OF BROOKLYN, CITY OF COVENTRY,
CITY OF LIVERPOOL (I), CITY OF CARDIFF (III) / CITY OF PHILADELPHIA,
CITY OF BATH (III) / CITY OF CHICAGO (III)
CITY OF GUILDFORD (II) / CITY OF OTTAWA (I) / CITY OF LEEDS (V)
Appearance see *City of Oxford* (IV) 282

485 CITY OF GLOUCESTER (II) / CITY OF BROOKLYN
B 1949 Swan, Hunter & Wigham Richardson, Wallsend. **T** 7,557g, 4,411n.
D 485.3/147.92 oa, 465.7/141.94 x 61.8/18.84 x 30.6/9.33.
E Sgl scr, 3 SRG turbs, 300 psi, 2 wt blrs. 14 kts. By Wallsend Slipway.
H Steel. 2 + shelter dk. F 43/13.11.
1949 May: Delivered to Hall Line. Laid down as *City of Gloucester*.
1963 April: In collision at Avonmouth with Bristol S.N.Co's *Cato*.
1967 Sold for £165,000 to Astro Dinamicos Cia. Nav. S. A., Panama. R/n *Lefkadios*.
1970 Sept 27: Abandoned on fire 600 miles south of Colombo enroute Bordeaux-Shanghai. Next day, with her decks awash, she was still burning and sank soon afterwards.

486 CITY OF COVENTRY
As 485 **T** 7,568g, 4,400n.
1949 May: Completed for Hall Line.
1967 Sold to Austin Nav. Corp., Liberia. R/n *Ingrid*.
1969 R/n *Annie* by Outerocean Nav. Corp, Keelung.
1970 Apr 27: Left Yokohama and broken up at Kaohsiung, Taiwan.

487 CITY OF LIVERPOOL (I)

As 485 except: **B** 1949 Cammell, Laird. Birkenhead. **T** 7,612g, 4,435n.
E Parsons SRG impulse turb, 7,200 bhp, 115 rpm, 650 psi, 2 Babcock & Wilcox wt blrs. By builder.
H F 44/13.41. 1 x 150 ton derrick.
1948 Nov 4: Launched by the Mayoress of Liverpool.
1949 May 3: Trials. May 4: Accepted. May 6: M/v Liverpool-Canada-USA-Far East. There had been no previous vessel of this name in the fleet because until now there had always been a *City of Liverpool* on the British register.
1967 July: Sold for £107,000 to Astro Tridente Cia. Nav S. A., Panama. R/n *Kavo Grossos*.
1973 Jan 16: Left Singapore for Shanghai to be broken up.

488 CITY OF CARDIFF (III) / CITY OF PHILADELPHIA

As 485 except: **B** 1949 Furness S. B. Co, Haverton Hill-on-Tees. **T** 7,591g, 4,464n. **E** By Parsons Marine Steam Turbine Co, Wallsend. **H** F 42/12.8.
1949 Dec: Completed for Hall Line. Laid down as *City of Cardiff*.
1967 Sept 1: Sold to Marbrava Cia. Nav S. A., Piraeus. R/n *Kaptaspyro*.
1970 R/n *Spyro* by Spyros Shipping Co, Famagusta.
1971 Mar 4: Left Singapore Roads for breaking up at Whampoa.

489 CITY OF BATH (II)/CITY OF CHICAGO (III)

As 485 except: **B** 1950 Vickers-Armstrong. Walker. **T** 7,622g, 4,427g.
E By builders at Barrow.
1950 June: Completed for Hall Line. Laid down as *City of Bath*.
1967 July 7: Sold for £150,000 to Marepico Cia. Nav S. A., Piraeus. R/n *Kaptamarco*. Panamanian flag.
1970 R/n *Marco* by Marcos Shipping Co, Famagusta.
1971 Nov 29: Arrived at Shanghai for breaking up.

490 CITY OF GUILDFORD (II) / CITY OF OTTAWA (I) / CITY OF LEEDS (V)

As 485 except: **B** 1950 Vickers-Armstrong. **T** 7,622g, 4,427n.
E By builder at Barrow.
1950 Aug: Completed as *City of Ottawa* for Hall Line. Laid down as *City of Guildford*.
1971 R/n *City of Leeds*. Same managers.
1976 Sold to Gulf (Shipowners) Ltd, London. R/n *Gulf Venture*.
1977 Aug 12: Arrived Karachi and, Nov, Broken up at Gadani Beach.

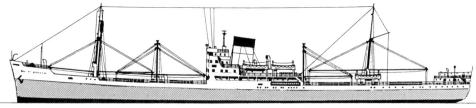

CITY OF PITTSBURG (II) / CITY OF BIRKENHEAD, CITY OF BEDFORD (II),
CITY OF KARACHI (IV), CITY OF SINGAPORE (II)

491 CITY OF PITTSBURG (II) / CITY OF BIRKENHEAD

B 1950 Cammell, Laird. Birkenhead. **T** 7,942g, 4,282n.
D 484.8/147.77 oa, 465.6/141.91 x 61.8/18.84 x 30/9.14.
E Sgl scr, 3 SRG turbs, 300 psi, 2 wt blrs. 15½ kts. By builder.
H Steel. 2 + shelter + pt 4th dk. F 43/13.11.
1948 Joint discussions on the design commenced between the three builders involved. An indication of the lead time for modern vessels.
1950 March: Delivered to Hall Line. Laid down as *City of Pittsburg*. Entered service as *City of Birkenhead* (which is not a city). This ship entered service without the gravity lifeboats abreast the main mast. They were the final class of steamers built for Ellerman.
1954 Transferred to Ellerman & Bucknall management.
1971 Dec 16: Sold to China Marine Investment Co, Hong Kong. R/n *Liberty Trader*. Dec 21: Left Hong Kong for Kaohsiung.
1972 Aug 5: Demolition began at Kaohsiung by Yi-Ho Steel Iron Works.

492 CITY OF BEDFORD (II)

As 491 except: **B** 1950 Alex Stephen & Sons, Glasgow. **T** 7,341g, 4,203n.
E By Cammell, Laird.

1950 Nov: Delivered to the Hall Line.
1972 June 5: Sold to Aguikar y Peris S. L. Valencia and broken up there.

CITY OF KARACHI (IV) See City Line 286

493 CITY OF SINGAPORE (II)
As 491 except: **B** 1951. Alex Stephen & Sons. **T** 7,738g, 4,204n.
1951 March: Delivered to Hall Line.
1973 Jan 1: Transferred to Ellerman City Liners management. Nov. 10: Grounded Southern Africa en route Tees-Lobitos. Nov 26: Refloated with only marginal damage.
1975 Sold to Gulf Shipping Lines Ltd, r/n *United Mariner.*
1976 R/n *Gulf Mariner;* same owner.
1977 May 1: Arrived at Gadani Beach for demolition.

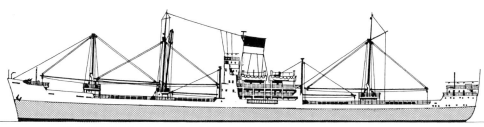

CITY OF NEWCASTLE (II), CITY OF WINNIPEG (II) / CITY OF DELHI (V),
CITY OF RIPON (IV), CITY OF WELLINGTON (II), CITY OF COLOMBO (II),
CITY OF AUCKLAND (II)

494 CITY OF NEWCASTLE (II)
B 1956 Alex Stephen & Sons, Glasgow. **T** 7,727g, 4,047n, 10,000wt.
D 507.2/154.59 oa, 470/143.25 x 65.8/20.05 x 28.3/8.62.
E Sgl scr, oil; 6 cyl, 2S.SA Doxford, 8,000 bhp, 15 kts. By builder.
H Steel. 1 + shelter + pt 3rd dk. **F** 38/11.58. **P** 33/10.06.
1956 April: Delivered to Hall Line. Apr 9: M/v Liverpool-Beira. This class introduced oil engines into the cargo vessels of the fleet (E & B had the four motor driven 1952 passenger ships). Steam ceased from now on.
1968 May 25: Bare boat to Wm Thomson's Ben Line Steamers Ltd. R/n *Benratha.* Registered in their name.
1970 Dec 29: Reverted to *City of Newcastle,* Ellerman & Bucknall as managers.
1973 Jan 1: Her managers were Ellerman City Liners.
1978 Sold to Gulf East Ship Management Ltd, Singapore. R/n *Eastern Envoy.*
1978 Sold to Venture Bay Shipping Co, Singapore. Liberian flag. Same name. The same holding company also purchased *City of Wellington* (496).
1980 Oct 23: Arrived at Chittagong for breaking up.

495 CITY OF WINNIPEG (II) / CITY OF DELHI (V)
As 494 except: **B** Caledon S. B. & E, Co, Dundee. **T** 7,716g, 4,020n.
E By Wallsend Slipway.
1955 Sept 29: Launched.
1956 March: Completed for Hall Line.
1968 Jan 18: On bare boat charter to Ben Line Steamers Ltd. R/n *Benedin* and registered as owned by them.
1970 Nov 23: Reverted to *City of Delhi.* E & B as managers.
1973 Jan 1: Transferred into the Ellerman City Liners division.
1976 Sold to Beaumaris Shipping Inc, Monrovia. R/n *Fexl Glory.*
1980 Sept 14: Arrived at Chittagong for breaking up.

CITY OF RIPON (IV) see City 287
CITY OF COLOMBO (II) see City 288
CITY OF AUCKLAND (II) see E & B 609

496 CITY OF WELLINGTON (II)
As 494 except: **B** 1956 Cammell Laird, Birkenhead. **T** 7,702g, 4,041n.
D 507.3/155 oa. **E** By Wallsend Slipway, Wallsend-on-Tyne. **H** F 40/12.19.
1956 Oct: The final one of three delivered to Hall.

1973 Jan 1: Transferred to the Ellerman City Liners division.
1978 June: Sold to Mulroy Bay Shipping Co, Liberia. Singapore flag. R/n *Eastern Enterprise.*
1979 Feb 13: Arrived at Kaohsiung and scrapped by Tung Ho Steel Enterprise Corp.

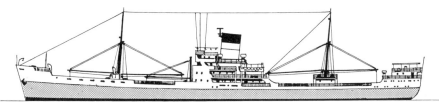

CITY OF GUILDFORD (III), CITY OF LANCASTER (II),
CITY OF HEREFORD (II) / CITY OF GLASGOW (V)

497 CITY OF GUILDFORD (III)

B 1957 Swan, Hunter & Wigham Richardson, Newcastle. **T** 4,945g, 2,517n, 7,760dwt.
D 434/132.28 oa, 405/123.44 x 59.2/18.04 x 24.7/7.53.
E Sgl scr, oil; 8 cyl Sulzer, 2S.SA, 5600 bhp, 14½ kts. By G. Clark & N. E. Marine (Sunderland) Ltd.
H Steel. 1 + shelter dk. F 39/11.89. P 38/11.58.
1957 Jan: Delivered to Hall.
1969 Nov: At Tilbury ex-Bombay a fire in no. 1 hold took three hours to bring under control.
1973 Jan 1: Moved to the Ellerman City Liners fleet.
1979 Sold to Eurydice Maritime Co, Greece. R/n *Eurydice.*
1981 R/n *Mighty Spirit* by Chimadea Shipping Maritime Co, Owned by Mighty Management S. A.
Panama.
1984 Sold to Wonder Shipping & Maritime Co Malta. R/n *Nirav.* Resold to Tricommerce Ltd, Malta for
delivery to Bagladesh breakers. Sept 17: Arrived at Chittagong for demolition.

498 CITY OF LANCASTER (II)

As 497 except: **T** 4,949g, 2,524n, 7,720dwt. **E** By Sulzer Bros, Winterthur.
1958 Aug: Completed for Hall Line.
1973 Jan 1: Transferred to Ellerman City Liners.
1979 Sold to Lancaster Shipping Co, Greece. r/n *Lancaster.* Sept 25: Collided en route Calcutta-
Glasgow with the tanker *Thistle Venture.* Arrived at Dublin the same day and abandoned there. Mar 16:
Towed to Glasgow to discharge her cargo then to be scrapped.
1980 The abandoned ship was taken over by the Clyde Port Authority and put up for sale.
1981 Nov 25: Left the Clyde in tow for San Esteban de Pavia, Spain. Her owners were now Andover
Shipping Co, Greece.
1982 Jan 10: Arrived from Aviles and scrapped.

499 CITY OF HEREFORD (II) / CITY OF GLASGOW (V)

As 497 except: **B** 1958 Robb Caledon Ltd, Dundee. **T** 4,954g, 2,529n, 7,610dwt. **E** By G. Clark & N. E.
Marine (Sunderland) Ltd.
1958 Nov: Delivered to Hall Line.
1971 R/n *City of Glasgow.* Same managers.
1973 Jan 1: Her owners were Ellerman Lines Ltd and managed by Ellerman City Liners.
1978 Sold to Porter Shipping Co, Greece. R/n *Myrna.*
1980 Apr 23: Left Manila for breaking up at Kaohsiung.

Appearance see *City of St Albans (II)* 611

500 CITY OF WORCESTER (II)

B 1960 Robb Caledon Ltd, Dundee. **T** 4,790g, 2,517n, 7,833dwt.
D 434/132.28 oa, 405.4/123.56 x 59.2/18.04 x 24.8/7.56.
E Sgl scr, oil; 8 cyl, Sulzer 2S.SA, 5,600 bhp. 14¾ kts. By G. Clark & N. E. Marine (Sunderland) Ltd.
H Steel. 2 dks. F 39/11.89. P 39/11.89.
1968 Sept: Delivered to Hall Line. Second of a class of five. She was the final vessel built for the Hall
Line. Within three years the Group was restructed into Divisions and all ships, except Scandinavian
servers, went into the Ellerman City Liners division.
1973 Jan 1: Into the new set up.
1979 Sold to Vermont Steamship Co, the Diamantides Maritime Co, Greece. R/n *Maria Diamanto.*
1982 R/n *Cape Greco* by Seadust Navigation Co, Cyprus. Nov 26: Enroute Turkey-Djibouti suffered a
machinery failure. Dec 19: Arrived at Djibouti in tow; discharged cargo. Laid up there.
1983 Sold to Ashraf Bros for breaking up. Aug 1: Arrived, laden, in tow at Chittagong. Aug 20: After
unloading she was run onto Fouzderhat Beach ready for scrapping.

ELLERMAN & BUCKNALL

1742 Henry Bucknall & Son was formed in London to act as cork merchants for the forests owned in Portugal and handled by an office in Lisbon. In New York the family introduced and developed cork within the USA. From their earliest days the company used chartered sailing vessels to carry out their business; a normal pattern in the era before fleets were owned by one name.

1880 Th old established business was now Henry Bucknall & Company and was in the hands of three Bucknalls: Henry Corfield, John Lloyd and Richard Corfield. The growth of trade within the, then, British Empire led them into shipowning and trading beyond that of their traditional Iberian field.

1888 Edward Lloyd joined the Company from the Cardiff shipbrokers Edwards, Robertson & Co. His task was to manage and build up the shipowning side of their affairs.

1890 Bucknall Bros was formed to act as ship brokers and charterers with Alan, Sidney and Percy Bucknall, three sons of the 1880 partners, operating it. At the same time the vessels owned were transferred to a new concern: Bucknall Nephews run by a further three sons, each, of course a nephew of the other two sons: Ernest, Leslie and Harry Bucknall. But the main-spring of the shipping side was Edward Lloyd.

1891 Encouraged by G. H. Payne & Co, South African specialists who were at odds with the existing Conference system, the British & Colonial Steam Navigation Company was formed. All the shares being held by Bucknalls. Paynes were appointed agents in South Africa and, against fierce competition from Donald Currie's Castle Line and Sir Francis Evans' Union Line, they obtained the three year contract to carry stores for the Netherlands South African Railway Co which was being constructed between Delagoa Bay and Pretoria. The ships were to pick up at Amsterdam at the rate of £21.25 per ton then to proceed to London's West India Dock to complete loading cargo. At Delagoa Bay the railway goods were unloaded into lighters.

For this contract nine ships were built to give a sailing every seventeen days: *Afrikander, Basuto, Bloemfontein, Kaffir, Manica, Mashona, Pondo, Transvaal* and *Zulu* (521-529). Despite this large order chartered ships were still necessary and these were taken from Charles Burrell's Strath Line and Andrew Weir's Bank Line.

1892 Mar 14: *Afrikander* took the first sailing Amsterdam-London-Cape Town-Port Elizabeth-East London-Durban-Delagoa Bay (Lourenco Marques). The homeward voyage lacked sufficient cargo and so most steamers crossed to Burma to load rice.

British & Colonial were then admitted to the South African conference (Outward Trade) but with the proviso that B & C would not load for Durban direct and that every third ship would carry no cargo London-Durban. As compensation for these restrictions both the Castle and Union Lines each agreed to pay £1,500 per annum.

1893 With the Castle Line Edward Lloyd of Bucknall Bros formed the American & African Line with Norton & Co as New York agents. The route was New York-Cape Town-Calcutta. One of the main cargoes to the Cape was mules for the Cape Town tramways.

1894 Bucknalls built three passenger vessels, *Bulawayo, Fort Salisbury* and *Johannesburg*(530-2) for the contract service. The fare was £24-£28 according to cabin position.

The American & African Line was extended to Calcutta-New York.

1895 Bucentaur Steamship Company was formed to cater for those routes not served by the contract ships of British & Colonial. The new routes included Canada, the USA and both New Zealand and Australia.

1898 Bucknalls had evidence that the Mail Companies were in breach of the Conference conditions. An Arbitrator found that they were charging 'cargo rates' instead of 'mail rates' and that Clan Line was undercutting both.

1899 The October outbreak of the (second) Boer War quickly led to congestion at South African ports. Ships frequently lay for several weeks awaiting a berth. To counter this B & C purchased three small servicing coasters: *Balgay, Balgowan* and *Ready* (544-46).

1900 Bucknall Steamship Lines was formed with a capital of £1,250,000. The issued script was 8,500 £10 shares, all to the Bucknall family members, 40,000 £10 preference shares, £600,000 in 4½ debenture bonds. The Fleet of the company stood at 12 but chartered ships were still much in evidence. To reduce this need five ships were purchased; three from Burrell: *Strathness* (534) *Strathairly* (537) and *Strathtay* (538) plus *Oolong* (535) and *Monmouth* (533).

1901 The expansion of the Company was swift, too swift as it was to turn out, and 8 ships joined the fleet.

Dec 1: All the ships of the fleet were transferred to Bucknall Steamship Lines.

The South African services showed a trading loss of £250,000 largely due to the port congestion coupled with priority given to Government war supply ships. The Bucknalls tried to claim against the Government but the case failed because of the 'exigencies of war' clause.

1902 Six ships joined the fleet. At the Annual General Meeting, where the loss was reported, the debentures, which are stocks that have preference over all else, were met by the Directors foregoing their fees and the Bucknall family making up the shortfall.

May: By the Treaty of Vereeniging the Boer War ended. This produced an immediate surplus of tonnage on the route. Worse; there were thousands of troops to be repatriated with no outward cargo to be had. A slump set in that took almost five years to work out of the system.

1903 Bucknall's South African cargo only ships had no inbound freight and opened up a service to the Persian Gulf in conjunction with Frank Strick and the West Hartlepool S. N. Co. A six year agreement provided for 66 sailings per annum in the ratio Bucknalls 26, Strick 26 and West Hartlepool 14. Conference type agreements allow for all eventualities; in this case the maximum size of the ships was laid down.

The South African trade remained poor and losses were recorded.

1907 J. T. Lilly, the manager of Norton & Co became a partner in the firm and the name became Norton, Lilly & Co. The vessels operating for them wore the Norton Lilly funnel: black, white band, red arrow with a white 'N' in its centre. Norton Lilly operated, themselves to South America.

1908 The finances of Bucknall Steamship Lines were under severe pressure which was put down to the early century overbuilding coupled with the post Boer War slump. Survival in the face of bankruptcy seemed bleak and the only way out of the growing indebtedness appeared to be the sale of the fleet or by its piecemeal break up. The sad thing was that the ships were good, the organisation sound, if dull, and only a shortage of liquidity beset them. The ships were all in use to secure the loans while the overdraft facility was at its upper limit. This was not a 'Trade' but a 'City' problem. The independent advice of John Reeves Ellerman was sought.

Ellerman's view was simple and accepted: inject cash and line up the capital with the financial position. He injected £180,000 to meets current needs and restored solvency for this 1000 £1 management shares were created and all of these he took. Each of the 85,000 £10 shares were reduced to 5 shillings (25p) and then each 8 of these was converted into one £2 second preference share. The original prefence shares were reduced from £10 in value to £2 and the un-issued ones written off. The end result was that the capital of Bucknall Steamship Lines stood at 1000 Management shares, all held by JRE, plus 51,615 first and second Prefence shares. The Debentures remained at £782,570. The security for the structure was John Ellerman and a fleet which had been valued by H. G. Kellock at £690,000. Above all John Ellerman was in control.

1909 Aug 31: The Company's year end yet again revealed a loss but it was significantly less and the forecast was for improving freight rates. With John Ellerman as chairman the directors at the time were Percy Bushnall, Edward Lloyd, James Westcott, G. G. Burt and W. B. Gladstone.

1912 The intergration of the fleets had so far not been much in evidence; there were several cases of inter-company wet charters but now Bucknall Steamship Lines withdrew (temporarily in the event) from passenger services and these were taken over by the City and Hall Lines.

1914 Jan 1: The Company was renamed Ellerman & Bucknall Steamship Company Ltd. Integration within the Ellerman group now commenced and was to be accelerated by the outbreak, in August, of World War I. The history of the company continues under the Ellerman history.

1973 Ellerman & Bucknall was amalgamated into Ellerman City Liners.

Livery

Funnel	1880-1935	Black with six white diamonds (see cover) Three were visible from any viewing angle.
	1935-1973	Ellerman livery.
Hull	1880-1935	Black, red waterline. Then Ellerman grey although some ships retained E & B funnels over grey hulls.
Uppers		Sailing ships: Varnish brown. Steamus: White.
Masts		Sailing ships: Varnish brown. Steamus: White. Even under Ellerman livery several continued white until 1939 when grey took over.
Ventilators	1880-1935 1935-1973	Black around funnel. White elsewhere. Ellerman pattern.
Lifeboats		White

It was possible, by their buff masts, to see ships transferred to Bucknall from within the fleet. This actually applied prior to the Ellerman take over in 1908. Bucknalls even repainted funnels for single voyage charters — this was to aid South African port identification for those who could not read English. Everyone recognised 'diamonds'.

Illustrated Fleet List

501 CAMBRIA
B 1825 at Sunderland. **T** 124. **D** 76/23.16. **E** Schooner. **H** Wood 1 dk.
1825 Built for Cardiff & London Shipping Co. Then sold to E. Bartlett, Exeter. Later owned by Captain G. Treatt of Exeter.
1851 Acquired by Henry Corfield Bucknall. The first ship wholly owned.
1854 Sold.

502 BRITISH ENSIGN
B 1857 at Dumbarton. **T** 196. **D** 101/30.78 x 22.1/6.74 x 13.1/3.99.
E Brig rig. **H** Wood. 1 dk. Crew 8.
1857 The first ship built for Henry Bucknall; traded to South America.
1862 Sold to King & Co., same name. Bristol-Mediterranean.
1876 Owned by William Kemp, junior, Whitstable.
1880 Wrecked.

503 ALECTO
B 1866 Jenkins, Prince Edward Island. **T** 199.
D 106.5/32.46 x 23.8/7.25 x 12.8/3.9. **E** Brigantine. **H** Wood. 1 dk.
1866 Aug: Completed for Henry Bucknall. Employed on the Mediterranean trade.
1878 Sold when her A1 classification expired. No new owners listed. The ship remained thus for several years before deletion.

504 LUSITANIA
B 1867 W. Salisbury, London. **T** 219g, 203n.
D 110.1/32.56 x 25.8/7.86 x 12.8/3.9. **E** Barque. **H** Wood. 1 dk.
1867 Aug: Completed for the Lisbon trade.
1880 Sold. Trace lost. Presumed condemned.

505 LISBON (I)
B 1852 Rostock, Germany. **T** 221.
D 105.1/32.03 x 25.1/7.65 x 14.1/4.3. **E** Brig rig. **H** Wood. 1 dk.
1852 Built as *Alexander Brandt* for A. Brandt, Rostock.
1866 Sold to J. Mitchell, Glasgow.
1868 Acquired at Glasgow for the Lisbon trade. R/n *Lisbon*. In this service for the remainder of her life.

506 OCEAN SPRAY
B 1863 by Laroche, Quebec. **T** 274. **D** 115.5/35.2 x 27.2/8.29 x 12.6/3.84.
E Sgl scr, 1 cyl simple exp, **H** Iron. 3 masted barquentine. 1 dk.
1863 Oct: Completed as *Ocean Spray* for R. Beauvais, London.
1869 Acquired by Henry Bucknall.
1873 Trace lost.

507 RUBY
B 1868 W. Salisbury, London. **T** 266. **D** 125.4/38.22 x 26.9/8.2 x 12.9/3.93.
E Barque rig. **H** Wood. 2 dks.
1868 Built as *Ruby*.
1869 Acquired by Henry Bucknall.
1889 Sold to East Downshire Sailing Ship Co., Belfast. The final sailing ship owned by Bucknalls.
1900 Owned by John T. Williams, Fowey.
1914 Sold to A. Anderson, Whitstable; same name.
1915 Nov 13: Wrecked six miles north of Hartlepool en route London-Tyne.

---

508 VANGUARD
B 1872 Cole Brothers, Newcastle. **T** 905g, 567n.
D 222.7/67.88 x 30/9.14 x 16.1/4.9.
E Sgl scr, 2 cyl comp inv. 75 NHP, 65 psi, 9 kts. By D. & W. Dudgeon, London.
H Iron. 1 dk.. **F** 26/7.92. **P** 34/10.36. 3 masts.
1872 Feb: Built for Henry Bucknall & Sons. Newcastle-Spanish trade.
1883 Feb 26: Went missing with a cargo of cork and minerals en route Lisbon-London. All 23 lost including one passenger.

509 TAGUS (I)
Sister to 508 except: **T** 1,250g, 953n.
D 229/69.8 x 30.4/9.26 x 16.6/5.06.
E Sgl scr, 2 cyl comp inverted.95 RHP, 75 psi, 9 kts. By J. & W. Dudgeon, London.
H Iron. 1 + spar dk. 3 masts. No mention of fcsle or poop; probably had both.
1872 Sept: Completed for Henry Bucknall & Sons. Spar deck gave extra gross tonnage.
1890 Transferred to Bucknall Nephews.
1896 Sold to A. Gardella y Cia, Buenos Aires. Same name. **T** 1366g, 1069n.
1900 Owned by S. N. Savas, Buenos Aires.
1901 Jan 6: Destroyed by fire at Antonia loading coffee and yerba tea for Buenos Aires.

510 SYDENHAM
Sister to 508 except: **B** 1873. **T** 1,279, 996n.
D 231.6/70.59 x 29.8/9.08. **E** By Ouseburn Engine Works Co., Newcastle.
H 2 dks + par dk. **F** 27/8.23. **P** 121/36.88.
1873 July: Completed. Distinguished from her sisters by the long poop.
1886 Aug 8: Sunk in collision off Portugal with the steamer *Lovaine*, M. S. Carr, North Shields, en route Cartegena-Hartlepool with iron ore. 1 dead. *Lovaine* took the survivors to Lisbon.

511 SAN DOMINGO
B 1874 M. Pearse & Co, Stockton-on-Tees. **T** 1,087g, 563n.
D 230/70.01 x 31.1/9.48 x 16/4.88.
E Sgl scr, 2 cyl comp inv. 142 NHP, 75 psi, 2 sgl blrs. 9 kts By Blair & Co. Stockton.
H Iron. 1 dk. F 23/7.01. B 54/16.46. Q 87/26.52.
1874 May: Completed for Henry Bucknall & Sons, Newcastle.
1889 Sold to Hine Bros, Maryport, Cumberland. Same name.
1899 Sold to Angf. Aktiebolaget Smaland of Oskarshamn, Sweden. R/n *Blenda* with T. Linnell as manager.
1920 Nov 21: Mined and sunk off Hango en route Viborg-Hull.

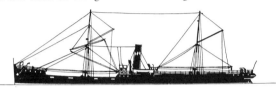

JOHN DIXON, JOSEPH DODDS, EGYPT

512 JOHN DIXON
B 1872 Schlesinger Davies & Co, Newcastle. **T** 1,522g.
D 250.1/76.23 x 32.2/9.81 x 19.4/5.91.
E Sgl scr, 2 cyl comp, 130 NHP, 9 kts. By C. D. Holmes & Co, Hull.
H Iron, 1 dk. Schooner rig. Fcsle and long poop.
1872 Aug: Built for E. W. King, Newcastle. The three were the same to look at although not built as sisters.
1876 Acquired by Henry Bucknall & Sons.
1889 Sold to North of England Shipping Co. (G. Nelson & Sons), Liverpool.
1894 Owned by Hagerup, Doughty & Co, Grimsby.
1895 Became *Bengal* of Act. Damps Bengal, Drammen, Norway.
1905 New boilers fitted.
1910 Oct 13: Foundered off Finmark, north Norway en route Kirkenes-Blyth. All 17 lost.

513 JOSEPH DODDS
B 1871 Richardson, Duck & Co, Newcastle. **T** 1,058g, 839n.
D 219.3/66.84 x 30.1/9.17 x 17.5/5.33.
E Sgl scr, 2 cyl comp inv, 99 HP, 9 kts. By Blair & Co, Stockton.
H Iron. 1dk. Fcsle and long poop.
1871 Built for W. T. Henley, Cardiff. Joseph Dodds was one of the partners.
1876 Acquired by Henry Bucknall & Sons.
1883 June: Struck a rock 40 miles north west of Dog Rock Lighthouse, Tunisia. Only the captain was lost; he went to his cabin to secure the ship's papers.

514 EGYPT
B 1878 Wigham Richardson & Co, Newcastle. **T** 1,556g, 1,001n.
D 250/76.2 x 33.4/10.18 x 19.4/5.91.
E Sgl scr, 2 cyl comp inv, 140 HP, 65 psi, 9 kts. By Tyne Engine Works, Newcastle.
H Iron. 1 dk. F 32/9.75. P 136/41.45.
1878 Nov: Completed for Henry Bucknall & Sons, Newcastle. Ident: no yard or gaff on fore mast. Long poop.
1887 Feb 23: Left New York with a cargo of wheat for Lisbon. March 3: In heavy seas her engine room flooded to 14 ft and the fires were put out and the ship foundered. All 23 saved by the barque *Hannah Blanchard*.

515 MADRID
B 1879 Wigham Richardson & Co, Newcastle. **T** 1,961g, 1,270n.
D 280/85.34 x 35.2/10.73 x 24.6/7.5.

E Sgl scr, 2 cyl comp inv, 200 NHP, 75 psi, 9 kts (11 on trials). By Wallsend Slipway Co, Newcastle.
H Iron. 2 dks. F 36/10.97. B 21/6.4.
1879 June 5: Launched. July 26: Trials and handover to Henry Bucknall & Sons, Newcastle for their Atlantic and India routes.
1887 June 16: Went missing with a cargo of phosphates en route Norfolk, Va-Dublin. 22 lost.

MANITOBA, MERIDA

516 MANITOBA
B 1887 Edward Withy & Co, West Hatlepool. **T** 2,127g, 1,386n.
D 275/83.82 x 37.2/11.34 x 19.2/5.85.
E Sgl scr, 3 cyls, tpl exp, 203 NHP, 160 psi, 2 sgl blrs, 10 kts. By Blair & Co, Stockton.
H Siemens-Martin steel. 1 dk. F 30/9.14. B 110/33.52. Q 78/23.77. P 29/8.83. **P** 12.
1887 March: Completed for Henry Bucknall & Sons, Newcastle. The ship marked a big step forward; she was their first steel hull and the first triple expansion in the fleet. Placed on the Indian rice ports service with tramping out of season. All officers and passenger accommodation aft.
1890 Owned by Bucknall Nephews.
1899 Sold to Orbe y Gobeo, Bilbao. R/n *Valle*, her owners were later restyled Cia. Cantabrica de Nav. She was replaced by *Manica* (529).
1900 Jan 28: Lost off Bilbao en route to Rotterdam with iron ore. 13 lost, 12 survivors were rescued by the Spanish steamer *Servando*.

517 MERIDA
Sister of 516 except: **B** 1888. **T** 2,365g, 1,383n. **D** 290/88.39 x 38.1/11.61.
E 212 NHP. **H** The quarter deck was 10ft/3.05 longer.
1888 Feb 10: Launched for Henry Bucknall & Sons.
1888 March: Completed; same service.
1890 Transferred to Bucknall Nephews.
1900 March: Acquired by Orbe y Gobeo to replace their lost ship (516) R/n *Valle*. Owners then became Cia Cantabrica de Nav. Replaced by *Mashona* (528).
1917 Jan 17: Torpedoed by *UC-18* in the Bay of Biscay.

DELCOMYN

518 DELCOMYN
B 1880 Wigham Richardson & Co., Newcastle. **T** 1,827g, 1,221n.
D 280/85.34 x 35.3/10.76 x 22.6/6.89.
E Sgl scr, 2 cyl comp inv, 260 NHP, 90 psi, 9 kts. By builder.
H Iron. 2 dks. F 30/9.14. B 16/4.88. P 26/7.92.
1880 Oct 6: Launched. Nov 20: Trials, made 11 knots. Nov 27: Delivered for Lund's Blue Anchor Line. London-Australia via South African ports.
1889 Acquired by Henry Bucknall & Sons.
1890 Transferred to Bucknall Nephews.
1897 Sold to J. B. Lussich, Buenos Aires. R/n *Felipe Lussich*.
1904 Became *Corcega*. Owned by F. Francione, Buenos Aires.
Sold in the same year to Cia Argentina de Nav (Nicholas Mihanovich) Ltda. Buenos Aires. R/n *Patagonia*.
1914 Sold to A. Gardella who bought *Tagus* (509); same name and port.
1916 Scrapped.

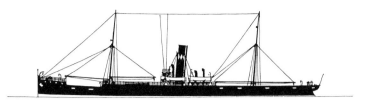

519 **ELBA**
B 1889 Raylton Dixon & Co, Middlesbrough. **T** 2,293g, 1,498n.
D 295.2/89.98 x 38.2/11.64 x 20.2/6.16.
E Sgl scr, tpl exp, 300 NHP, 160 psi. 10 kts. By T. Richardson, Middlesbrough.
H Steel. 1 dk. F 30/9.14. B 122/37.18. Q 116/35.36.
1889 June: Launched for Henry Bucknall & Sons but completed for Bucknall Nephews.
1893 July 4: Collided in fog enroute Bombay-Hull, with wheat, with *William Balls*, W. D. C. Balls & Son, 30 miles north of the Humber. Both sank; all saved.

520 **ETONA**
B 1890 Richardson, Duck & Co, Stockton. **T** 2,513g, 1,613n.
D 297/90.52 x 40/12.19 x 19/5.79.
E Sgl scr, tpl exp, 245 NHP, 160 psi, 2 sgl blrs. 10 kts. By Blair & Co, Stockton.
H Steel 1 + part awning dk 176/53.64. Q 92/28.04. P 29/8.94.
1890 Laid down for Henry Bucknall & Sons, completed for Bucknall Nephews. July 31: Trials 11 kts. Aug 2: Delivered.
1908 Sold to Nisbet, Calder & Co's Clydesdale Nav Co.
1913 Her owners became George Nisbet & Co.
1914 Sold to Moji Kisen K.K.; r/n *Buzen Maru*.
1919 Owned by Kuribayashi Shosen K.K. Same name.
1934 Broken up in Japan.

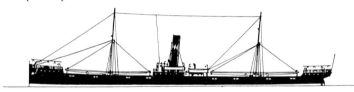

AFRIKANDER, KAFFIR, ZULU, TRANSVAAL, BASUTO, BLOEMFONTEIN (I), PONDO MASHONA (I) / PARANA, MANICA (I) / CORONDA

521 **AFRIKANDER**
B 1892 Raylton Dixon & Co, Middlesbrough. **T** 2,755g, 1,793n, 4,500dwt.
D 329/100.27 oa, 309.5/94.18 x 40.6/12.37 x 17.5/5.3.
E Sgl scr, tpl exp, 500 nhp, 160 psi, 2 sgl blrs. 10 kts. By T. Richardson & Sons, Hartlepool.
H Steel. + spar dk. F 36/10.97. B 34/10.36. P 31/9.45.
1891 Dec 28: Launched for the British & Colonial Steam Nav Co (B & C) with Bucknall Brothers as managers.
1892 Mar 5: Trials 12½ kts. April 14: M/v inaugurated the London-South Africa service. She was the first of a class of nine ships all built with a shallow draft to cross the bar at Durban and East London.
1906 Sold to Adolphe (later Armament) Deppe, Antwerp, one of three purchased by him. *Euphrates* and *Tigris* (547-8) being the others. R/n *Uruguay*. South American route.
1907 Renamed *Bulgare*, same owners. Black Sea route.
1910 Jan 8: Went missing enroute Kustindje-Antwerp. Wreckage found on the Belgian coast.

522 **KAFFIR / PERSIAN (II)**
As 521. **T** 2,374g, 1,724n.
1891 Dec 29: Launched for B&C, the day after her sister.
June 16: Trials. Same service.
1906 Transferred to Ellerman Papayanni. R/n *Persian*. Fred Swift manager. Mediterranean service.
1916 July 4: Collided with Royal Mail Steam Packet Co's *Monmouthshire* off Cape Malea, Greece, and sank.

523 **ZULU**
As 521. **T** 2,746g, 1,760n. **D** 309.8/94.43.
1892 Feb 29 (Leap year): Launched for B&C.

1906 Sold to Royal Mail Steam Packet Co. R/n *Marima*.
1911 Became *Marika*, G. Coulouras, Andros.
1916 Sold to Hannevig Bros, Christiania (Oslo). Same name.
Apr 4: Foundered.

524 TRANSVAAL

As 521 **T** 2,746g, 1,781n. **D** 309.6/94.37.
1892 March 14: Launched for B&C.
1906 Sold with her sister to Royal Mail. R/n *Manau*. March: While in dry dock she was accidentally flooded and submerged. Pumped out; but the smell that remained caused crew problems. May 22: Wrecked 7 miles north of Bahia, Brazil, enroute Southampton-Bahia. Broke in two. Stripped where she lay.

525 BASUTO

As 521 except: **B.** James Laing & Co, Sunderland. **T** 2,742g, 1,784n.
D 310/94.49. **E** By G. Clark & Co, Sunderland.
1892 May: Delivered to B & C.
1902 Went missing enroute London-Bussorah, Persian Gulf with a general cargo. 57 lost.

526 BLOEMFONTEIN (I) / ARABIAN (II)

As 521 except: **B** James Laing & Co. **T** 2,745g, 1,718n. **D** 310/94.49.
E G. Clark.
1892 March 29: Launched for B&C.
1906 Transferred to Ellerman's Papayanni Line. R/n *Arabian*. Fred Swift as manager. Black Sea service.
1914 Serviced for a spell on the London-East Africa route.
1915 Oct 2: Back on the Mediterranean run she was captured by *U-33* off Cerigo Island (Kithera) Greece, and sunk by gunfire after the crew were safely away.

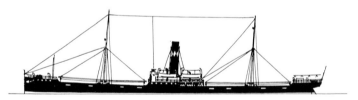

527 PONDO

As 521 except: **B** James Laing. **T** 2,741g, 1,723n. **D** 310/94.49.
E By G. Clark.
1892 Oct: Delivered to B&C.
1912 Sold, the last in the fleet of the nine sisters, to G. Katsuda of Kobe. R/n *Taisho Maru*.
1914 Owned by Uchida Kaisha K.K., Nishonomiya. Same name.
1924 Oct 1: Wrecked on Kanabuse Rock, Shimonoseki Strait.

528 MASHONA (I) / PARANA

As 521 except: **B** Wm. Gray & Co, West Hartlepool. **T** 2,735g, 1,781n.
D 310/94.49. **E** By Central Marine Eng. Wks, West Hartlepool.
1892 Feb 16: Launched for B & C. Apr 12: Trials, made 13½ kts.
1899 Transferred to Bucknall Nephews as a replacement for *Manitoba* (516). R/n *Parana*.
1900 Oct 28: Wrecked on Lobos Island, Uruguay, enroute New York-Buenos Aires. Broke in two. To replace her *Arabistan* (550) was purchased.

529 MANICA (I)/CORONDA

As 521 except: **B** Wm Gray. **T** 2,733g, 1,779. **D** 310.3/94.58. **E** By Central Marine Eng. Wks.
1892 May: Delivered to B & C.
1900 Renamed *Coronda* and transferred to Bucknall Nephews to replace *Merida* (517).
1908 Sept: Sold to Christian Salvesen. Same name. Nov 7: Left Tonsberg to set up a new whaling station at New Island, Falklands.
1909 Oct: Arrived from Norway to establish a whaling station at Leith Island, South Georgia. Continued as supply ship for the remainder of her annual whaling voyages.
1917 Mar 13: Torpedoed by *U-18* 180 miles north west of Tory Island, N. Ireland.

JOHANNESBURG, FORT SALISBURY, BULAWAYO

530 JOHANNESBURG
B 1895 Armstrong, Mitchell & Co, Newcastle. **T** 4,495g, 2,862n.
D 360/109.73 x 47/14.32 x 27.7/8.44.
E Sgl scr, tpl exp, 578 nhp, 180 psi, 3 sgl blrs. 14 kts. By Hawthorn, Leslie & Co, Newcastle.
H Steel, 3 dks. F 39/11.88. B 98/29.87. P 38/11.58.
1895 January: Completed for B&C with, as usual, Bucknall Brothers as managers. Inaugurated the South African passenger service. The fare to Cape Town was £24.
1900 Her owners became Bucknall Steamship Lines; same managers.
1913 Sold with her sister *Bulawayo* to Andrew Weir & Co, for £35,000. Placed on their India-Africa passenger service. R/n *Surat.*
1926 April: Broken up by Sui Dah at Shanghai.

531 FORT SALISBURY
As 530. **T** 4,456g, 2,824n. Had a visibly shorter funnel.
1895 March: Completed for B&C South African passenger service.
1900 Transferred to Bucknall SS Lines.
1913 Sold to Booth Steamship Co, Liverpool. R/n *Vincent.* Entered service in their colours but re-sold to Andrew Weir in order to make up his India-Africa trio. R/n *Gujarat.* Cost £35,000.
1919 Sold to Hajee M. H. Nemazee, Hong Kong. Same name.
1921 R/n *Gorjistan;* same owner. Employed on pilgrim work.
1923 Transferred to Oriental Nav. Co., same name.
1926 Reverted to Nemazee ownership.
1928 Owned by Borg & Co., same name.
1928 Oct 5: Arrived at Kobe and scrapped.

532 BULAWAYO
As 530. **T** 4,456g, 2,824n.
1895 May: Entered the South African service for B & C. Her arrival gave a monthly sailing.
1900 Transferred to Bucknall SS Lines.
1913 Sold to Andrew Weir for £35,000. R/n *Kathiawar.*
1921 Sept 5: Left Alexandria for Rotterdam and laid up for sale.
1922 Broken up in Belgium.

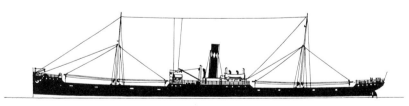

BUCRANIA, BUCEROS, BUCENTAUR, KAREMA (566)

533 BUCRANIA
B 1896 Tyne Iron SB Co., Newcastle. **T** 4,069g, 2,593n.
D 365/111.25 x 47.1/14.36 x 27/8.23.
E Sgl scr, tpl exp, 368 NHP, 170 psi, 2 sgl blrs. 10 kts. By North East Marine Eng. Co., Newcastle.
H Steel. 2 dks. F 35/10.67 B 86/26.21 P 30/9.14.
1896 March: Completed as *Fitzpatrick* for Charles Burrell & Sons, Glasgow.
1898 Oct: Sold to Elder, Dempster & Co. R/n *Monmouth.* Glasgow registered.
1899 Acquired by Bucentaur S.S. Co., London. Bucknall Brothers managers. R/n *Bucrania.*
1900 Transferred to Bucknall SS Lines.
1911 Sold to B. G. Ashdown who then sold her to Kishimoto Kisen K. K. R/n *Shinsei Maru.*
1915 Owned by M. Naruse, Kobe. R/n *Seiko Maru.*
1916 Mar 15: Left Seattle. Mar 23: Sailed from Port Townsend for Yokohama and disappeared.

534 BUCEROS

As 533 except: **B** 1894 Wm. Gray & Co., West Hartlepool. **T** 4,038g, 2,595n.
E By Central Marine Eng. Wks, West Hartlepool. **H** F 36/10.91. B 87/26.52. P 31/9.45.
1894 Built as *Strathness*, Charles Burrell & Sons, Glasgow.
1902 Acquired by Bucknall SS Lines, London. R/n *Buceros*.
1911 Sold to J. Bryde, Sandefjord. R/n *Oestkysten* then *John Bryde*.
1913 Became *Svend Foyn I*, P. Bogen. Used as an Antarctic whaling factory ship of the old type whereby the whale flensing was carried out alongside the ship which was anchored in a sheltered bay (The stern ramp and flensing deck dates from 1923).
1923 Purchased by Johann Rasmussen. Owned by Hvalfanger A/S Sydhavet, Sandefjord. Antarctic supply and whale oil carriage. Made annual voyages to South Shetland, Grahamland and the Palmer Peninsula. Out of season, viz our summer, laid up at Sandefjord.
1931 World slump. Out of commission and laid up at Sandefjord.
1934 Broken up.

535 BUCENTAUR

Not a sister of *Bucrania* but with the same appearance.
B 1893 London & Glasgow SB Co., Glasgow. **T** 3,593g, 2,223n.
D 360/109.73 x 44.2/13.47 x 26.9/8.2.
E Sgl scr, tpl exp, 297 nhp, 2 sgl blrs. 10 kts. By builder.
H Steel. 2 dks. F 44/13.41. B 72/21.94 P 17/5.18.
1893 Aug: Completed as *Oolong*, China Mutual S.N. Co., Liverpool. Far east service. This was pre-Alfred Holt ownership of China Mutual.
1898 Acquired by Bucentaur S.S. Co., Bucknall Brothers managers. R/n *Bucentaur*.
1911 Sold to Meiji Kaiun K.K., r/n *Saikai Maru*.
1915 Owned by M. Naruse, Kobe.
1918 Her owners were G. Katsuda later Katsuda Kisen K. K., Kobe.
1931 Renamed *Shoehi Maru*, Nippon Kosan K.K., Kobe.
1935 Feb: Scrapped at Kobe.

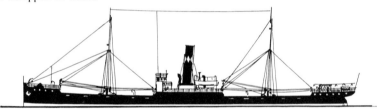

536 BEIRA

B 1894 Alex. Stephen & Sons, Linthouse, **T** 4,120g, 3,025n.
D 345/105.16 x 47/14.33 x 26.7/8.14.
E Sgl scr, tpl exp, 379 nhp, 160 psi, 3 sgl blrs. 10 kts. By builder.
H Steel. 2 dks. F 40/12.19. B 74/22.56. P 46/14.02.
1894 Aug: Built as *Turkistan* for Frank C. Strick & Co.
1897 Acquired by B & C. R/n *Beira*.
1900 To Bucknall SS Lines.
1910 Sold to Kishimoto Kisen K.K. R/n *Shinkai Maru*.
1915 Became *Yubari Maru*, Mitsui Bussan Kaisha, Kobe.
1922 Sold to Hokkaido Tanko Kisen K.K., Kobe.
1930 Sold to Sugaya K.K. R/n *Miharu Maru*.
1935 Broken up in Japan.

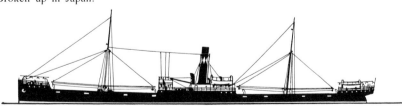

MASHONA (II), BECHUANA

537 MASHONA (II)

B 1894 Russell & Co., Greenock. **T** 4,142g, 2,665n.
D 368.7/112.38 x 47.5/14.48 x 26.9/8.2.

E Sgl scr, tpl exp, 399 nhp, 170 psi, 3 sgl blrs. 10 kts. By Blackwood & Gordon, Port Glasgow.
H Steel. 2 dks. F 38/11.58. B 82/25. P 52/15.85.
1894 Built as *Strathairly*, Charles Burrell & Sons, Glasgow.
1899 Acquired by B & C. R/n *Mashona*.
1900 To Bucknall SS Lines.
1915 July 18: While on commercial service the ship was wrecked 30 miles west of Zavora Point, Lourenco Marques, en route London-Beira.

538 BECHUANA
AS 537. **T** 4,148g, 2,659.
1894 Built as *Strathtay*, Charles Burrell & Son, Glasgow.
1899 Acquired by B & C. R/n *Bechuana*.
1900 Transferred to Bucknall SS Lines.
1914 Sept: Transport duties.
1915 Employed as a naval collier.
1919 Sold to Julio Benito del Valle, later Cia Naviera Valle. R/n *Eusebia de Valle*.
1932 March: Sunk by collision in the Bay of Biscay.

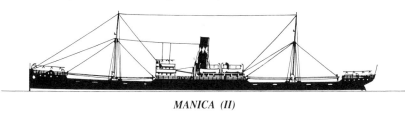

MANICA (II)

BAROTSE, BARALONG / MANICA (III), BANTU

539 MANICA (II)
B 1900 James Laing & Sons, Sunderland. **T** 4,117g, 2,626n.
D 360.5/109.99 x 47/14.33 x 28/8.53.
E Sgl scr, tpl exp, 530 NHP, 180 psi, 3 sgl blrs. 10 kts. By T. Richardson, Hartlepool.
H Steel. 2 dks. F 40/12.19. B 96/29.26 P 36/10.97.
1900 Dec: Delivered to Bucknall Steamship Lines, Bucknall Brothers managers. Had stump masts for the first year.
1914 Aug: Sold to the Admiralty and, 1915, converted into a balloon observation ship for the Dardenelles campaign. Her fore mast was removed and replaced by a pole mast out of the bridge. Her baloons carried men to observe the fall of shot.
1915 April: Attached to the 2nd Squadron at the Dardanelles.
1916 Oct: Renamed *Huntball* so that her name could be given to *Baralong* (541). Fitted with cylindrical tanks and converted into a bulk oil carrier for the Navy.
1918 Sold to Anglo-Saxon Petroleum Co. R/n *Phorus*.
1930 Aug 12: Arrived Hong Kong and laid up.
1931 July 3: Arrived at Osaka for scrapping.

540 BAROTSE
As 539 except: **B** 1901. **T** 4,119g, 2,723.
1901 March: Completed for Bucknall SS Lines.
1922 Sold to Goshi Kaisha K.K. R/n *Kyokutu Maru No 2*.
1926 Renamed *Sanyo Maru*, Sanyo Sha Goshi Kaisha, Darien.
1932 Nov 30: Went aground at Niigata. Salvaged.
1934 Broken up.

541 BARALONG / MANICA (III)
As 539 except: **B** 1901 Armstrong, Whitworth & Co., Newcastle. **T** 4, 192g.
1901 May: Delivered to Bucknall SS Lines. A ship destined to have an extraordinary career.

1902 Sept 8: Left her builders yard towing a 30,000 dwt floating dock bound for Durban. The dock had a false bow fitted and carried a crew of 15, known as 'runners'. Twin cables, 'bridles', attached the two. A speed of 5 knots was all that could be achieved. In a storm off Mossel Bay the bridle snapped and the dock, despite efforts by tugs, drifted ashore and was lost. (A replacement was at once ordered against the insurance).

1905 Aug 22: Ran down at night and sank the Japanese Inland Sea ferry *Kinjo Maru* off Shimishima. 160 lives were lost. Hundreds more were saved by *Barotse*. The Inquiry found the ferry was steaming without the correct lights.

1914 Sept: Taken up as a naval supply ship.

1915 Converted into a 'Q' ship. These were vessels disguised as merchant ships but armed with concealed guns with which to attack any submarine that could be induced to surface. Even the officers adopted false names. *Baralong* was commanded by 'Captain MacBride' whose real name was Godfrey Herbert. For these duties she was renamed HMS *Wyandra*. Aug 19: White Star's *Arabic* signalled that she was under submarine attack but at the position givien there was no sign of her (she was 10 miles in error) and it was angrily assumed that she had sunk with all souls. However at the spot *U-27* was caught in the act of sinking Leyland's *Nicosian*. An armed German boarding party was in possession and the crew had abandoned ship. *Baralong* placed *Nicosian* between herself and *U-27* and when cover was broken the submarine was sunk by gunfire. It is alleged that some survivors reached *Nicosian* which carried rifles on the bridge.

The barbarous 'Baralong Incident' followed, The crew of *Nicosian* were picked up and they confirmed that there were German sailors aboard *Nicosian*. A strong party was sent across from *Baralong* and they combed the ship from stem to stern shooting all the enemy that they met, including those who were hiding. The event reached the papers and a furore followed. Berlin demanded that the crew be charged with murder. Sept 24: *Wyandra/Baralong* sank *U-41* and the German outcry against her was redoubled. As a precaution *Wyandra* was transferred to the Mediterranean. Other measures were taken to conceal the ships against any later German action against their crews. *Nicosian* was renamed *Nevision* while the name *Baralong* was totally deleted from Lloyd's Register. The ship was given the name *Manica* and the original *Manica* (539) became the oil tanker *Huntball* so that when *Wyandra* was decommisioned in 1917 she emerged as the ex-balloon ship *Manica*. To further confuse things for the enemy both ships were decommisioned at the same time.

1923 Sold to Goshi Kaisha K.K. Dairen. R/n *Kyokuto Maru*.

1925 Renamed *Shinsei Maru No 1*, Shinsei Kisen Goshi K.K., Dairen.

1934 Broken up in Japan.

542 **BANTU**

As 539 except: **B** 1901 Armstrong, Whitworth & Co., Newcastle. **T** 4,230g, 2,655n. **D** 360/109.72. **E** By Wallsend Slipway & Engineering Co. **H** F 42/12.8.

1901 Oct: Delivered to Bucknall SS Lines.

1910 Sold to United Steel's subsidiary the Isthmian S.S. Co for £23,000. Owned by the Isthmian Line. R/n *Orpheus*. British flag.

1930 Sold to M. Kulukundis, Piraeus. Same name. Sold again in the same year to P. Hadjilias.

1931 Broken up by Hughes Bolchkow, Blyth.

543 **LOTUS**

B 1863 Earle's SB & E Co., Hull. **T** 621g, 363n. **D** 207.8/63.34 x 24.2/7.38 x 15.7/4.78. **E** Sgl scr, 2 cyl comp. 8 kts. By builder. **H** Iron. 2 dks.

1863 March: Delivered to Moss S.S. Co., Liverpool. Her sister was *Cecile*.

1873 New compound engines installed by T. Brassey, Liverpool.

1890 Owned by Walsh Brothers, Liverpool.

1891 Reboilered.

1897 Sold to F. Alexander, Antwerp.

1900 Acquired by Bucknall SS Lines and stationed at Busoorah in the Persian Gulf for feeder work.

1914 Jan: Transferred to Ellerman & Bucknall with the change of name.

1921 Scrapped.

544 **BALGAY**

BALGAY, BALGOWAN

B 1897 Dundee S.B. Co., Dundee. **T** 303g 131n. **D** 130.2/39.68 x 22.8/6.95 x 9.7/2.96. **E** Sgl scr, 2 cyl comp. 60 NHP, 1 sgl blr. 8 kts. By Cooper & Greig, Dundee. Machinery aft. **H** Steel. 1 dk. F 16/4.87. B 12/3.66, Q 41/12.49.

1897 Oct: Built for W. Kinnear & Co., Dundee.

1901 Due to the Boer War congestion at South African ports ships were having to swing at anchor for long periods awaiting a berth. *Balgay* and *Balgowan* were purchased and sent south in order to unload waiting Bucknall vessels. Once the emergency was over the ships were sold.

1904 May 2: Took to Madagascar J. B. Turnbull and his staff with the first gold dredging plant to be taken to the island.

1905 Sold to Hadjee Ahmed Nassam, Bombay, same name.

1907 Owned by the Bombay Steam Navigation Co.; same name.

1924 Sold to the Nawanagar State Tramways Department.

1931 Broken up in India.

545 **BALGOWAN**

As 544. **T** 286g. **D** 125.3/38.19. **E** By A. Hall & Co., Dundee. **H** F 15/4.57.

1897 March: Completed for W. Kinnear & Co., Dundee.

1901 Purchased with her sister.

1904 Aug 9: Sailing in ballast, wrecked in fog on Eastern Cliff, Spence Bay en route Swakopmund-Cape Town. Bucknall's *Ready* (546) rescued the crew of nine.

546 **READY**

B 1896 R. Craggs & Sons, Middlesbrough. **T** 251g, 137n.

D 119.6/36.45 x 25.1/7.65 x 8.2/2.5.

E Sgl scr, 2 cyl comp, 65 RHP. 8 kts. By J. Stewart & Sons, Middlesbrough.

H Steel. 1 dk F 14/4.27. Q 37/11.28.

1896 Built as *Ready* for Hawthorn Bros., Middlesbrough.

1901 Acquired for the same use as *Balgay* (544).

1907 Sold to George Wills, London, registered in Port Adelaide and on arrival sold to Charles F Rischbeith.

1916 Sold to Howard Smith's Australian Steamships Proprietary, Sydney.

1931 Became a salvage ship owned by Penguin Ltd, H. P. Stacey & J. Williams. Still as *Ready*.

1938 Sold to E. Moller, Shanghai, R/n *Ready Moller*.

1941 Dec 8: Taken off Amoy by the Japanese. R/n *Amoy Maru II*.

1946 Reverted to E. Moller ownership and name.

1949 Owned by the Anglo-Chinese Shipping Co, Shanghai: Mollers managers.

1951 Broken up locally.

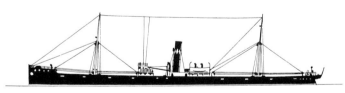

EUPHRATES, TIGRIS

547 **EUPHRATES**

B 1901 Armstrong, Whitworth & Co, Walker-on-Tyne. **T** 2,809g, 1,794n.

D 300/91.44 x 43.7/13.32 x 16.8/5.12.

E Sgl scr, tpl exp, 280 nhp, 160 psi, 3 sgl blrs. 10 kts. By North East Marine, Newcastle.

H Steel. 1 + spar dk. F 29/8.84.

1901 Oct 24: Launched for Bucknall SS Lines.

1902 Jan 25: Trials; averaged 11 knots. Persian Gulf service.

1906: Sold with her sister to Adolf Deppe's Cie. Nationale Belge de Transportes Maritimes, Antwerp. Same name.

1917 Jan 22: Torpedoed by *U-57* off Ushant.

548 **TIGRIS**

As 547. **T** 2,805g, 1,792n.

1901 Dec 11: Launched.

1902 Feb: Delivered. Persian Gulf trade.

1906 Sold to Adolf Deppe; same name and owner as 547.

1930 Left Antwerp for Alexandria and last seen off the Isle of Wight. She then disappeared.

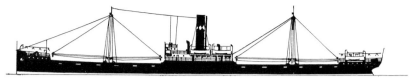

SWAZI

549 SWAZI

B 1901 Armstrong, Whitworth & Co, Walker-on-Tyne. **T** 4,941g, 3,174n.
D 380/115.82 x 50/15.24 x 29.1/8.87.
E Sgl scr, tpl exp, 443 nhp, 180 psi, 3 sgl blrs. 10 kts. By Wallsend Slipway & Eng Co, Newcastle.
H Steel. 2 dks. F 36/10.97. B 76/23.16. P 42/12.8.
1901 Aug: Delivered to BSSL.
1926 Sold to Z. M. Scheldestroom, Ghent. R/n *Scheldrestrand.*
1933 Nov: Scrapped in Italy.

550 ARABISTAN

B 1893 Alex. Stephen & Sons, Linthouse, Glasgow. **T** 3,194g, 1,928n.
D 325/99.06 x 42/12.8 x 18.9/5.76.
E Sgl scr, tpl exp, 306 nhp, 160 psi, 3 sgl blrs. 10 kts. By builder.
H Steel. 1 + spar dk. B 42/12.8. Q 36/120.97.
1893 Built as *Arabistan* for Frank C. Strick & Co; their first ship.
1902 Jan: Acquired by Bucknall Nephews, Bucknall Brothers as managers, to replace the lost *Parana* (528). Same name.
1910 Sold to F. Chiama & Danova, Genoa. R/n *Giano.* This was the end of Bucknall Nephews.
1911 Dec 24: Wrecked on the coast of Cyrenaica. All saved.

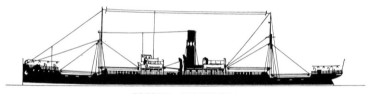

GRIQUA, AMATONGA

551 GRIQUA

B 1902 Armstrong, Whitworth & Co, Walker-on-Tyne. **T** 3,344g, 2,099n, 5,200 dwt.
D 330/100.58 x 45.2/13.78 x 17.3/5.27.
E sgl scr, tpl exp, 387 nhp, 180 psi, 3 sgl blrs. 12 kts. By North East Marine & Eng. Co., Newcastle.
H Steel. 1 + spar dk. F 39/11.89. B 180/54.86. P 33/10.05
1902 Dec: Delivered to BSSL. M/v Newcastle-Hamburg-Antwerp-South Africa.
1914 Jan 1: Transferred to Ellerman & Bucknall ownership.
1916 Dec 20: Attacked by submarine in the Mediterranean.
1917 May 7: Again attacked by submarine gunfire and again escaped.
1927 Sold with her sister to Adria S.A., Fiume. R/n *Aleardi.*
1934 June: Broken up in Italy.

552 AMATONGA

As 551 except: **T** 3,331g, 2,093n.
1903 Jan 10: Launched. Feb 10: Trials. BSSL ownership.
1914 Transferred to Ellerman & Bucknall.
1927 Sold to Adria S.A., Fiume. R/n *Foscolo.* Each of the pair cost £16,000.
1933 Apr 13: Arrived at Fiume then sold and broken up.

Appearance as *Bucrania* 533

553 CASILDA

B 1902 Sir James Laing & Co., Sunderland. **T** 3,928g, 2,463n.
D 365.8/111.49 x 47.1/14.36 x 24.8/7.56.
E Sgl scr, tpl exp, 362 nhp, 180 psi, 3 sgl blrs. 11 kts. By G. Clark, Sunderland.
H Steel. F 40/12.19. B 96/29.26. P 37/11.28.
1902 Completed for Bucknall Nephews, Bucknall Bros managers.
1908 Sold to Soc. Les Affreteurs Réunis, Rouen. R/n *Ceres.*

1913 Oct 27: Sold to Deutsche Levante Linie; r/n *Lipsos*.
1914 Aug 1: With the outbreak of war the ship was seized at Antwerp. This was three days before Great Britain declared war on the Central Powers. Oct 9: The ship was still at Antwerp when the Germans took the port.
1919 June 28: Allocated to the Shipping Controller with Lyle Shipping Co, Glasgow as managers.
1920 Became *Ovid*, Shakespeare Shipping Co, Glover Brothers managers.
1933 Broken up at Genoa by Alberto Trivero.

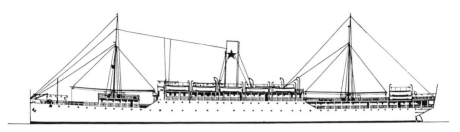

554 MARITZBURG

B 1904 Armstrong, Whitworth & Co, Walker-on-Tyne. **T** 6,847g, 4,175n.
D 420/128 x 51.6/15.73 x 27.7/8.44.
E Tw scr, 2 x tpl exp, 851 nhp, 180 psi, 5 sgl blrs. 12½ kts. By Wallsend Slipway & Eng Co, Newcastle.
H Steel. 2 + Shelter dk. **B** 165/50.29.
1904 May 16: Launched, for BSSL. The advent of the ship was hit by the severe slump in South Africa which followed the Boer War and her fitting out was slowed while the ship was put up for sale. She was never to wear Bucknall livery. She was sold for £180,000 before completion and given accommodation for 130 1st and 1,500 3rd class passengers. R/n *Endova*. Her eventual purchaser was Erasmo Piaggio for Soc. di Nav. Lloyd Italiano, Genoa which was formed on Nov 7, 1904. R/n *Mendoza*; yellow funnel and thinnish black band one width below a black top.
1905 Oct 10: M/v Genoa-Buenos Aires.
1910 Navigazione Generale Italiana (N.G.I.) took a controlling interest in Lloyd Italiano; they already owned La Veloce and Italia. This led to the switches that followed during the career of the ship.
1912 Placed, with *Taormina*, on the Genoa-New York service.
1914 Renamed *Caserta*; same owners and service.
1918 June 1: NGI absorbed Lloyd Italiano. *Caserta* appeared in NGI colours.
1923 Transferred to La Veloce; r/n *Venezuela* and reverted to the South American service but to Valparaiso via the Panama Canal. **T** 7,028g. (As drawn; yellow funnel, red star.)
1924 Sept 21: La Veloce was dissolved and the ships transferred back to NGI.
1928 Replaced by a new ship and broken up.

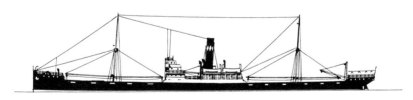

555 MATOPPO (I)

B 1904 Armstrong, Whitworth & Co, Walker-on-Tyne. **T** 3,942g, 2,526n.
D 360/109.73 x 47.5/14.39 x 26.7/8.14.
E Sgl scr, tpl exp, 403 psi, 3 sgl blrs, 10 kts. By Wallsend Slipway & Eng. Co, Newcastle.
H Steel. 2 dks. F 35/10.67. B 84/25.5 P 29/8.84.
1904 May 11: Launched as *Lady Strathcona* for W. Peterson Ltd, Newcastle.
1905 May: Acquired for £44,000 by BSSL. R/n *Matoppo*. On her first voyage she shed two of her three propeller blades. One spare was fitted by trimming her bows down until the screw was out of the water. At 5 knots she made Walvis Bay where the second was affixed. En route to Cape Town she shed a further blade. Two new screws were forged at Cape Town. Oct: Sold for £45,000 to Union SS Co of New Zealand. R/n *Wairuna*.
1917 June 2: Captured en route Auckland-San Francisco by the German raider *Wolf (II)* off Kermadoc Island, north of New Zealand. The ship was sighted by *Wolf's* scouting aircraft. Taken to Sunday Island where 1,500 tons of coal was transferred. June 17: Towed out and sunk by bombs.

556 MATOPPO (II)

B 1905 Wm. Hamilton & Co., Port Glasgow. **T** 5,280g, 4,320n.
D 400.5/122.07 x 52/15.85 x 28.2/8.59.
E Sgl scr, tpl exp, 487 nhp, 200 psi, 3 sgl blrs. 10 kts. By D. Rowan, Glasgow.
H Steel. 2 dks. F 39/11.89. B 121/36.88. P 34/10.36.
1905 Nov: Purchased on the stocks as a replacement for *Matoppo (I)* and given the same name. Owned by BSSL.
1908 Aug: When John Ellerman took control of Bucknall's *Matoppo* was the first ship to be transferred to Ellerman duties and was placed on the East Indies and Pacific routes.
1914 Jan 1: Transferred to Ellerman & Bucknall.
1916 A German plot was discovered to blow her up with a bomb while berthed in the USA. A man named Schiller received a life imprisonment sentence.
1930 Dec: Sold at Liverpool to Thos. W. Ward for £5,500 and broken up at Preston.

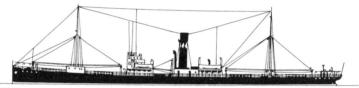

557 KORANNA

B 1905 Armstrong, Whitworth & Co, Walker-on-Tyne. **T** 3,585g, 2,267n.
D 350/106.68 x 52/15.85 x 23.4/7.13.
E Sgl scr, tpl exp, 337 nhp, 180 psi, 3 sgl blrs. 10 kts. By North East Marine Eng. Wks, Newcastle.
H Steel. 1+ shelter dk.
1905 Feb: Delivered to BSSL.
1914 Transferred to Ellerman & Bucknall.
1916 Apr: Became an Indian Army transport.
1929 Sold for £13,000 to Z. A. Valmos of Andros. R/n *Apikia*.
1936 Sold to Ding Yao Dung, Chefoo, for £12,000. R/n *Chang Kwang*.
1937 Her name was changed to *Shoko*. Same owner; Japan trade.
1938 Became *Niitoku Maru;* Akai Shoten K. K., Osaka.
1944 Feb 14: Sunk in the Pacific by U.S.S. *Snook*.

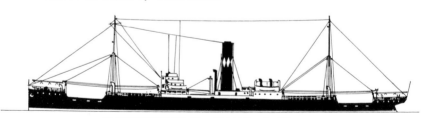

BLOEMFONTEIN (II), KASAMA, KAZEMBE

558 BLOEMFONTEIN (II)

B 1906 A. McMillan & Son, Dumbarton. **T** 4,654g, 2,958n.
D 401.1/122.25 x 50/15.24 x 18.1/5.52.
E Sgl scr, tpl exp, 478 nhp, 180 psi, 2 sgl blrs. 10 kts. By Dunsmuir & Jackson, Glasgow.
H Steel. 1 + spar dk. F 41/12.5. B 229/69.8. P 38/11.58.
1905 Sept 18: Launched.
1906 Oct: Delivered; at that time the largest vessel in the BSSL fleet.
1914 Jan 1: Transferred to Ellerman & Bucknall.
1932 July: Sold for £1,900 in slump conditions for breaking up with hand over 'as is' on the Tyne. July 31: Left for Italy.

559 KASAMA
As 558 except: **B** 1908. **T** 4,635g, 2,945n.
1907 June: Delivered.
1914 Jan 1: Transferred to Ellerman & Bucknall.
1932 Oct: Sold for £2,750 to G. Ricardi, Genoa for scrap.

560 KAZEMBE
As 558 except: **B** 1907 Alex. Stephen & Sons, Linthouse, Glasgow. **T** 4,658g, 2,938n. **D** 400.3/122.01.
E By builder.
1907 May: Completed.
1914 Jan 1: Transferred to Ellerman & Bucknall.
1915-18 Government service for the Navy.
1932 July: Sold to Smith & Houston for £1,875 and scrapped at Port Glasgow.

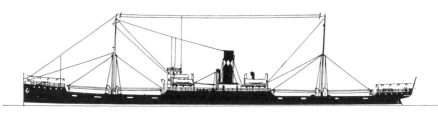

KALOMO/CITY OF HALIFAX

561 KALOMO / CITY OF HALIFAX
B 1907 Robert Duncan & Co, Port Glasgow. **T** 5,019g, 3,209n.
D 400/121.32 x 52.3/15.94 x 20.1/6.13.
E Sgl scr, tpl exp, 401 nhp, 180 psi, 3 sgl blrs. 10 kts. By Rankin & Gilmore, Greenock.
H Steel. 1 + spar dk. F 46/14.02. B 112/34.14. P 41/12.5.
1907 Feb: Completed for BSSL.
1914 Jan 1: Transferred to Ellerman & Bucknall.
1926 Renamed *City of Halifax*; same owners. Registered at South Shields.
1931 Nov: Sold for £3,500 to Thos. W. Ward and scrapped at Inverkeithing.

KARONGA (I), KATUNA/CITY OF SWANSEA (I), KABINGA, KASENGA (I)

562 KARONGA (I)
B 1907 Armstrong, Whitworth & Co., Walker-on-Tyne. **T** 4,665g, 2,932n.
D 400/121.92 x 52.1/15.88 x 27/8.23.
E Sgl scr, tple exp, 477 nhp, 180 psi, 3 sgl blrs. 10 kts. By North East Marine Eng Wks, Newcastle.
H Steel. 2 dks.
1907 June: Entered BSSL service.
1914 Jan 1: Transferred to Ellerman & Bucknall.
1917 Apr 29: Torpedoed by *U-63* in the Strait of Messina. Chief Steward Furneaux received the Albert Medal. A Lascar fireman was trapped by the legs one of which Furneaux freed. As the ship began to sink rapidly he amputated the other leg with a jack-knife and carried the man to the boats. He survived the ordeal. 18 killed. Captain taken prisoner.

563 KATUNA / CITY OF SWANSEA (I)
As 562 **T** 4,641g, 2,927n. **E** Wallsend Slipway & Eng. Co, Newcastle.
1907 April: Trials. May: Delivered; waited over a month before entering service due to crew shortages.
1914 Jan 1: Transferred to Ellerman & Bucknall.
1929 Renamed *City of Swansea*; same owners.
1937 Sold for £25,500 to Barry Shipping Co. (B&S Shipping), Cardiff. R/n *St Glen*.
1939 The owners were renamed South American Saint Line.
1940 Sept 6: Bombed and sunk by German aircraft off the east coast of Scotland.

564 **KABINGA**

As 562. **T** 4,657g, 2,925n.
1907 July: Completed for BSSL.
1914 Jan 1: Transferred to Ellerman & Bucknall ownership.
Sept 11: Left Sandheads, River Hooghly for the UK. By what was to be great good fortune the captain had his wife and child aboard. The German light cruiser *Emden*, with her collier *Markomannia* (Hamburg America) and wearing a dummy fourth funnel to look 'British', came from Tsingtau into the Indian Ocean for commerce raiding. Sept 12: *Kabinga* was captured by *Emden* at dusk in a heavy swell. Because of the woman and child the transfer and subsequent sinking were postponed until daylight. Next day at dawn *Killin*, outbound and loaded, was taken stripped of her stores and fuel and sunk; her crew being put aboard *Kabinga* which was thus reprieved. This continued as other ships were captured until *Kabinga* was released with those aboard and sent back to Calcutta.
1938 Oct 20: Sold to African & Continental S S Co, r/n *Lulca*.
1939 Aug: Became *San Leonardo*, Cia. Ligure di Nav., Genoa.
1940 June 10: In port in the USA when Italy entered the war and interned.
1941 Dec: Taken over by the United States Maritime Commission. R/n *Reigh Court*. Panama flag.
1943 June 5: Sunk by collision in position 44 N, 63 W, the east coast of America.

565 **KASENGA (I)**

As 562. **T** 4,652g, 2,923n. **E** By Wallsend Slipway & Eng. Co, Wallsend.
1907 Aug: Delivered to BSSL.
1914 Jan 1: Transferred to Ellerman & Bucknall.
1915 Used as a supply ship by the French Government, mainly to colonies cut off from normal trade by war.
1917 Apr 1: Torpedoed by U-boat off Cape Palos, near Cartagena, Spain.

In appearance a sister to 533 *Bucrania*

566 **KAREMA**

B 1894 Palmers' S. B. Co, Newcastle. **T** 5,263g, 3,362n.
D 410/124.97 x 49.4/15.1x 32.1/9.78.
E Sgl scr, tpl exp, 445 nhp, 180 psi, 3 sgl blrs. 10 kts. By builder.
H Steel. 2 dks. **F** 14/4.27. **B** 89/27.13. **P** 38/11.58.
1894 Built for Caledonia Steamship Co, Liverpool as *Ranza*.
1909 Acquired by BSSL. R/n *Karema*.
1914 Jan 1: Transferred to Ellerman & Bucknall.
1917 Nov 25: Torpedoed by *U-39* off Cabo de Gata, Almeria, Spain.

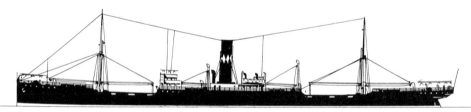

KANSAS / CITY OF WINNIPEG (I), KIOTO (I), KENTUCKY / CITY OF MOBILE

567 **KANSAS / CITY OF WINNIPEG (I)**

B 1910 Workman, Clark, Belfast. **T** 6,074g, 3,931.
D 431.7/131.58 x 54.9/16.73 x 30.9/9.42.
E Sgl scr, tpl exp, 403 nhp, 180 psi, 3 blrs. 11½ kts. By builder.
H Steel. 2 dks. **F** 90/27.43. **B** 139/42.37. **P** 78/23.77.
1910 Built for BSSL. USA services. The curious thing about this class was that the bridge deck of each succeeding ship was longer than that of the previous one.
1914 Jan 1: Transferred to Ellerman & Bucknall.
1926 Renamed *City of Winnipeg*.
1932 March: Put into Plymouth with a leak forward. Cargo trimmed to expose the hole which was repaired without having to drydock her.
1934 Dec 28: Sold for scrap. R/n *Winny*. Left Houston with cargo for Kobe.
1935 Broken up in Japan.

568 **KIOTO (I)**

As 567 except: **B** Swan, Hunter & Wigham Richardson, Newcastle. **T** 6,182g, 4,020n. **D** 432/131.67 x 54.1/16.5. **E** By Wallsend Slip. & Eng. Co, Newcastle. **H** F 88/26.82. **B** 145/44.2. **P** 87/26.52.

1910 Delivered.
1914 Jan 1: Owned by Ellerman & Bucknall.
1917 July 11: Torpedoed by *U-87* 20 miles west of Fastnet.

569 KENTUCKY / CITY OF MOBILE
As 567 except **B** 1912. **T** 6,588g, 4,250n. **E** 4 cyl quad exp. **H** F 92/28.04. B 153/46.6. P 99/30.1.
1912 Oct 29: Launched. Dec 10: Trials; made 14 kts. M/v Cardiff-New York.
1914 Jan 1: Owned by Ellerman & Bucknall.
1926 Renamed *City of Mobile.*
1932-33 Laid up in the Gareloch.
1940 Sept 16: Bombed and sunk by air attack in the Irish Channel.

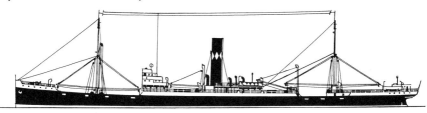

KAFUE, KARROO / CITY OF KHARTOUM (I)

570 KAFUE
As 567 except: **B** 1913 Palmers' SB Co, Jarrow. **T** 6,064g, 3,889n.
D 423.7/129.14 x 54.4/16.61. **E** 589 nhp. By builder. **H** F 45/13.72. B 160/48.77. P 73/22.25.
1913 Apr 5: Trials; 13 kts. Apr: M/v for BSSL.
1914 Jan 1: Owned by Ellerman & Bucknall.
1915 On charter to the Italian Govt. as a collier.
1918 Apr 30: Torpedoed by *U-86* 11 miles south west of the Mull of Galloway.

571 KARROO / CITY OF KHARTOUM (I)
As 567 except: **B** 1913 Palmers' SB Co, Jarrow. **T** 6,127g, 3,941n.
E 601 NHP, by builder. **H** F 42/12.8. B 171/52.12. P 71/21.64.
1913 May 6: Trials. Entered service for BSSL. Their final ship with a counter stern.
1914 Jan 1: Transferred to Ellerman & Bucknall. Aug 4: At Brisbane when war was declared. Taken over as an Australian Govt transport to convoy troops to Port Suez. Nov 9: En route, in radio silence, she picked up the signal 'strange warship at entrance' from the cable station at Cocos Keeling Island. The stranger was clearly the German cruiser *Emden*. In order to protect its whereabouts *Karroo* hand signalled her intention to leave the convoy. When well clear she radioed H.M.A.S. *Melbourne* (which had already had the message but this does not detract from *Karroo's* alertness) and H.M.A.S. *Sydney*, which was nearer, was on her way to destroy *Emden* which she did that day.
1917 Apr 22: En route Halifax-Devonport missed by 2 torpedoes. May 21: Fought off *U-6* in the English Channel.
1918 July 6: *Karroo* was again in escaping action in the English Channel against U-boat gunfire.
1927 Renamed *City of Khartoum;* same owners.
1936 Sept: Sold for £11,500 to Stephens, Sutton Ltd under the 'Scrap and build' scheme and broken up by Luigi Pittaluga in Italy.

572 SALDANHA
B 1912 Swan Hunter & Wigham Richardson, Wallsend. **T** 4,594g, 2,950n.
D 385.9/117.62 x 48.8/14.87 x 29.8/9.08.
E Sgl scr, tpl exp, 339 nhp, 180 psi, 10 kts. By Wallsend Slipway & Eng. Co, Newcastle.
H Steel. 2 dks. F 48/14.63. B 112/34.14. P 45/13.72.
1912 Completed for BSSL.
1914 Jan 1: Owned by Ellerman & Bucknall.
1918 March 18: Torpedoed by *UB-52* 95 miles north of Algiers. Six killed.

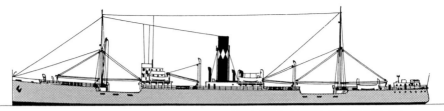

KATHLAMBA / CITY OF CARLISLE (I), KANDAHAR / CITY OF PERTH (IV)

573 KATHLAMBA / CITY OF CARLISLE (I)
B 1913 Wm. Gray & Co, West Hartlepool. **T** 6,382g, 4,104n.
D 434/132.28 x 54.7/16.67 x 31.2/9.51.
E Sgl scr, tpl scr, 586 nhp, 220 psi, 3 sgl blrs. 12 kts. By Central Marine Eng Wks, West Hartlepool.
H Steel. 2 dks. F 81/24.69. B 165/50.29. P 77/23.47.
1913 Aug 2: Trials, 14 ¾ knots, for BSSL. The first cruiser stern for the Company.
1914 Jan 1: Owned by Ellerman & Bucknall.
1917 June 18: Hit by a torpedo in the English Channel. Made port.
1920 She had a rare accident in the Thames when at anchor. The ship next to her, British India's *Nerbudda*, caught by the wind, did not swing with the tide and when she did her propeller holed the bow of *Kathlamba*.
1926 R/n *City of Carlisle*.
1932-34 Laid up in the Gareloch. May: Sold off lay-up for £8,100. June: At Dalmuir for breaking up.

574 KANDAHAR / CITY OF PERTH (IV)
As 573 except: **B** Swan, Hunter & Wigham Richardson, Wallsend. **T** 6,415g, 4,153n. **D** 434.6/132.47.
E By Wallsend Slipway Eng Wks, Newcastle.
H F 87/26.52. B 174/53.03. P 90/27.43.
1913 Sept: Delivered, the final ship for Bucknall Steamship Lines.
1914 Jan 1: Transferred to Ellerman & Bucknall when the name was changed.
1926 Renamed *City of Perth*.
1943 March 26: Torpedoed by *U-431* off Oran.

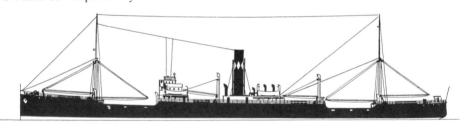

575 KEELUNG (I)
B 1914 Earle's SB & E Co, Hull. **T** 6,672g, 4,279n.
D 449.2/136.92 x 56.8/17.31 x 30.8/9.39.
E Sgl scr, tpl exp, 641 nhp, 220 psi, 3 sgl blrs. 12 kts. By builder.
H Steel. 2 dks. F 82/25. P 180/54.86. P 74/22.55.
1914 The first ship to enter service for Ellerman Lines Ltd with Ellerman & Bucknall Steamship Lines as managers.
1918 June 27: Torpedoed by *U-53* 110 miles west by south of Ushant six killed.

576 KEELUNG (II) / CITY OF KEELUNG
B 1919 Earle's SB Co, Hull. **T** 5,186g, 3,199n.
D 412/125.58 oa, 400.4/122.04 x 52.2/15.91 x 28.5/8.69.
E Sgl scr, tpl exp, 368 nhp, 220 psi, 3 sgl blrs. 12 Kts. By builder.
H Steel. 2 dks. F 39/13.41. B 22/35.36. P 47/14.32.

1919 Oct: Building as *War Walrus*, a standard Type B hull, when taken over by E & B and finished to their specifications. Lloyd's Register gives incorrectly F 44/13.4. P 116/35.36 and these remained printed until well after the war.
1936 Renamed *City of Keelung*.
1947 June: Sold to China Hellenic Lines. R/n *Hellenic Trader*.
1951 Became *Nichian Maru*, Nissan Kisen K.K.
1960 April: Scrapped at Shimizu, Japan.

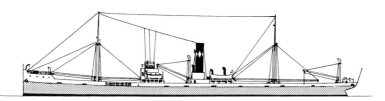

577 **RIALTO**

B 1911 A. G. 'Neptun', Rostock. **T** 2,948g, 1,773n.
D 339/103.33 x 48.1/14.66 x 20.9/6.37.
E Sgl scr, tpl exp, 309 nhp, 190 psi, 2 sgl blrs. 10 kts. By builder.
H Steel. 1 + shelter dk. F 33/10.06.
1911 Mar 11: Launched. May 10: Delivered as *Olympos* for Deutsche Levante Linie (as drawn); one of a class of seven.
1914 Aug 1: In port in Germany. Used in the Baltic.
1919 Ceded to Britain; Shipping Contoller with Thos. Law & Co, London, as managers.
1921 Acquired by Ellerman & Bucknall, r/n *Rialto* — although the name indicates an Ellerman's Wilson vessel.
1928 Sold to Les Cargoes Algeriens S. A., Algiers. R/n *Madali*.
1940 June: Fled from Rouen to Bordeaux. Aug 8: Taken by the Germans.
1941 Earmarked for Seeloewe, the invasion of Britain. R/n *H.*7 After the invasion was cancelled the ship was decommissioned and chartered to Johs. Fritzen & Sohns and used as a supply ship to the occupied Channel Islands.
1943 Sept 27: Under strong escort attacked by British and Dutch MTB's and MGB's. Torpedoed and sunk off Etaples. The method used by the Germans was to bring through the Channel one (or two) merchant ships hugging the French coast in the dark on moonless nights and along the mineswept channel. Each sortie was protected by every available escort and E-boat and the English side was illuminated by star shells so as to reveal the attackers as well as blinding them. The English side was also surface mined, each having a streamer which could be caught in MTB's propellers. The MTB's, based at Dover, regularly attacked every convoy but not actually with the degree of success deserved by their bravery.

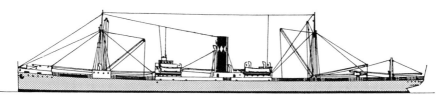

578 **KOSMO**

B 1913 Wm. Doxford & Sons, Sunderland. **T** 5,170g, 3,106n.
D 419.9/127.18 x 54.1/16.5 x 26.4/8.05.
E Sgl scr, tpl exp, 577 nhp, 180 psi, 3 sgl blrs. 10 kts. By builder.
H Steel. 2 + shelter dk.
1913 Built as *Nordmark* for Hamburg America Line; sister *Sudmark*.
1919 Mar 23: Ceded to Britain, Shipping Controller.
1920 Acquired by E & B. R/n *Kosmo*.
1928 Sold to Norddeutscher Lloyd, Bremen. R/n *Nurnburg*.
1932 Became *Wellen*, USSR. Registered at Vladivostok. The open deck below the funnel boats was plated in at some stage.
1959 Deleted from the Register.

579 KASENGA (II)
B 1899 Wigham, Richardson & Co, Newcastle. **T** 7,160g, 4,634n.
D 456/139 x 58.1/17.71 x 22.5/6.86.
E Sgl scr, 4 cyl, quad exp, 588 nhp, 210 psi, 3 sgl blrs. 10 kts. By builder.
H Steel. 1 + spar dk. F 51.15.54. B 110/33.53. P 62/18.9.
1899 Dec: Completed as *Drachenfels*, D. D-G 'Hansa', Bremen.
1919 Ceded to Britain, the Shipping Contoller. Managed by British India S.N. Co.
1920 Acquired by E. & B. R/n *Kasenga*.
1928 Sold to I.N.S.A. (Industrie Navali S.A.), Genoa. R/n *Adelia*.
1933 Broken up in Italy.

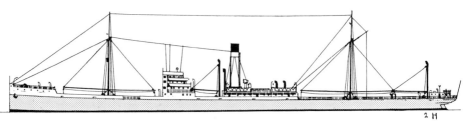

580 LORENZO / CITY OF CHRISTCHURCH
B 1915 J. C. Tecklenborg, Geestemunde. **T** 6,009g, 3,749n.
D 491/149.65 oa, 470.5/143.51 x 62.1/18.93 x 25.3/7.71.
E Sgl scr, 4 cyl, quad exp, 725 nhp, 4 sgl blrs, By builder.
H Steel. 1 dl + part 2nd. Upper F 52/15.84. F & B 394/120.1. P 62/18.9
1915 July: Completed as *Aschenburg* for D. D-G 'Hansa'.
1919 Transferred to the Shipping Controller; managed by Rankin, Gilmour & Co, Liverpool; British & Foreign S.S. C, better known as the Saint Line.
1920 Acquired by E & B. R/n *Lorenzo*.
1929 R/n *City of Christchurch*.
1943 Mar 21: Sunk off Lisbon by Bordeaux based German bombers.

581 CITY OF BATAVIA
B 1907 Swan, Hunter & Wigham Richardson, Wallsend. **T** 5,597g, 3,457n.
D 437.3/133.29 oa, 424.7/129.45 x 53.1/16.18 x 29.1/8.87.
E Sgl scr, tpl exp, 556 nhp, 180 psi, 3 sgl blrs. 10 kts. By Wallsend Slipway & Eng. Wks, Newcastle.
H Steel. 2 dks. F 44/13.41. B 181/55.17. P 37/11.28. **P** 12.
1907 July: Completed as *Ganelon*, Roland Line A. G., Bremen.
1920 Ceded to Britain. Acquired by E & B. R/n *City of Batavia*.
1938 Nov: Sold for £150,000 to Soc. Anon. Industria Armamento, Genoa. R/n *Voluntas*.
1940 June: Interned at Buenos Aires when Italy came into the war. Taken over by the Argentine Govt. R/n *Rio Teuco*, Flota Mercante del Estado.
1946 Reverted to her owners and *Voluntas*.
1949 Her name became *Volonta*, 'Trasmarina' S.p.A., Genoa.
1955 Apr 12: Wrecked at Ushant.

582 CITY OF HARVARD
B 1907 Bremer Vulkan A. G., Bremen. **T** 7,091g, 4,410n.
D 428.6/130.64 x 54.5/16.61 x 27.9/8.5.
E Sgl scr, 4 cyl quad exp, 606 nhp, 180 psi, 3 sgl blrs. 12 kts. By builder.
H Steel. 2 dks. **F** 75/22.85. **B** & **P** 285/86.87. **P** 83 1st, 46 2nd.
1907 Dec 4: Launched as *Giessen*, Norddeutscher Lloyd, Bremen. African and Far East intermediate service.
1913 May: Bremen-New York service.
1919 March: Ceded to Britain.
1920 Acquired by E & B. R/n *City of Harvard*.
1921 April: Placed on the New York-Port Said-Bombay-Karachi-Abadan route of E & B's American & Indian Line. Later New York-India-Rangoon.
1933 Laid up in the Gareloch; never sailed again commercially.
1934 Broken up in Italy.

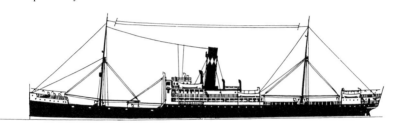

CITY OF ALEXANDRIA, CITY OF PALERMO

583 CITY OF ALEXANDRIA
B 1905 J. C. Tecklenborg, Geestemunde. **T** 4,697g, 2,866n.
D 362.1/110.37 x 46.7/14.23 x 26.2/7.98.
E Sgl scr, tpl exp, 415 nhp, 205 psi, 3 sgl blrs. 11 kts. By builder.
H Steel. 2 dks. **F** 40/12.19. **B** & **P** 226/68.88.
1905 May 20: Launched as *Dalmatia* for Hamburg America Line. Sept 1: M/v Hamburg-Rio Grande.
1907 June 21: Sold to Hamburg Sud-Americanische. R/n *Pio Pardo*.
1914 Aug: At Hamburg. taken over by the Kreigsmarine. R/n *Sperrbrecher 11*, later *Sperrbrecher 4*. Sperrbrecher — Blockade breaker.
1919 Mar 25: Transferred to Britain, the Shipping Controllor, as a war prize. Orient Line as managers.
1920 Ellerman & Papayanni managers.
1921 Jan 29: Acquired by E & B. R/n *City of Alexandria*, South African passenger service.
1933 July: Sold to Petersen & Albeck, Hamburg. Laid up.
1936 Broken up in Scotland at Haulbowline.

584 CITY OF PALERMO
As 583 except: **T** 4,699g, 2,866n. **D** 362.3/110.43.
1905 Feb 20: Launched as *Rio Negro* for Hamburg Sud-Americanische. Apr 29: M/v Hamburg-Rio Grande.
1914 Aug 4: At Para, Brazil. Became a supply ship to the German cruiser *Karlsruhe* which was destroyed on Nov 4 by an internal explosion, old gun-cotton, killing 263 men. *Rio Negro* then returned to Kiel.
1917 Became *Sperrbrecher 1*.
1918 Nov: Returned to Hamburg Sud-Americanische.
1919 Mar 29: Ceded to Britain. Managed by Orient Line for the shipping controller as *Rio Negro*.
1920 Oct: Passed to Ellerman & Papayanni as managers. Same name. Used to transport refugees to Istanbul and Piraeus from Yalta and the Black Sea ports of Russia.
1921 Jan 29: Acquired by E & B. R/n *City of Palermo*.
1933 Sold to Italiana Generale Navagazione but broken up in the July.

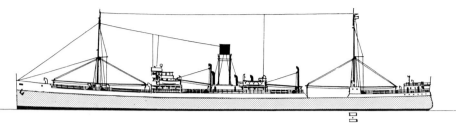

585 KAROONGA (II) / CITY OF DERBY

B 1921 Wm Gray & Co (1918), Wear yard, Sunderland. **T** 6,616g, 4,190n.
D 433/131.98 x 57.4/17.5 x 30.2/9.20.
E Sgl scr, 2 dbl reduction steam turbines, 767 nhp, 225 psi, 3 sgl blrs. 12 kts. By Central Marine Eng. Wks, Newcastle.
H Steel. 2 dks. F & B 308/93.88. P 89/27.13.
1921 Nov: Completed as *Karoonga* for E & B. One of several of similar profile built during the 20s and 30s for the Ellerman group.
1927 R/n *City of Derby*.
1934 Jan: Took the Company's last Manchester-New York sailing.
1940 Dec 24: The ship was in the convoy attacked by the German heavy cruiser *Admiral Hipper*. See *City of London* (255).
1957 Feb: Sold to Fairtrade Steamship Co, Monrovia. R/n *Fairtrade*.
1959 Feb: Broken up.

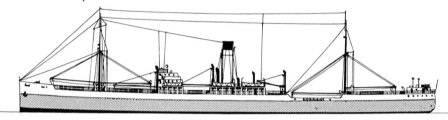

586 CITY OF KIMBERLEY

As 585 except: **B** 1925. **T** 6,169g, 3,954n. **D** 436.5/133.04 oa x 56.3/17.16.
E Tpl exp with LP turbine to electric drive. 6,832 nhp.
H F & B 288/87.78. P 68/20.73.
1925 April: Delivered.
1960 Sold at Birkenhead to Argonaut Shipping & Trading Co, R/n *Fairhurst*. In effect she replaced *Fairtrade* (585). River Plate trade.
1964 Sold to the People's Republic of China. Sept 5: While on tow Hong Kong to Shanghai she broke adrift in a gale and was driven ashore and lost.

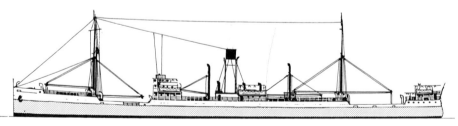

587 KNARESBORO' / CITY OF WINDSOR

B 1923 Wm Gray & Co, Wear yard, Sunderland. **T** 7,247g, 4,616n, 11,550dwt.
D 447.5/136.4 x 57.8/17.62 x 32.1/9.78.
E Sgl scr, tpl exp with LP turn dbl reduction geared, hydraulic coupling to shaft. 12 kts. By Central Marine Eng. Wks, Newcastle.
H Steel. F 92/28.04. B 210/64. P 38/11.58.
1928 Delivered. USA/Canada-Africa-India service. Had a profile that was unique to the whole group.
1928 July: Renamed *City of Windsor*.
1939 Sept 3: Unloading in the Clyde. To Southampton and carried munitions to France.

1940 June: Sent to Cherbourg to evacuate men and their guns. Brought away over 1,000 under air attack. She next took 1,070 Vichy French sailors to Casablanca. Brought away to Gibraltar a load of British civilians and other refugees. From Gibraltar she went to Alexandria and remained in those waters.

1941 Took part in the Greek campaign and the June evacuation. At one point on her third voyage back to Alexandria with troops she was simultaneously attacked by three bombers, three torpedo planes and a submarine. After Greece she reinforced the Persian Gulf forces through Basra.

1943 In the Mediterranean and carried munitions north from South Africa. Sept 9: *City of Windsor* was present at the Salerno landing.

1944 Released for overhaul at Liverpool and a return to commercial use.

1945 Back in E & B service.

1953 July 14: Arrived at Briton Ferry and broken up by BISCO.

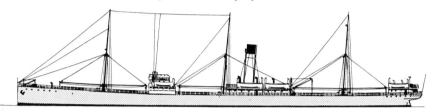

588 **CITY OF PRETORIA (I)**
B 1899 Wm. Denny & Bros., Dumbarton. **T** 6,237g, 4,025n, 8,080dwt.
D 425.7/129.75 x 54.1/16.48 x 29.8/9.08.
E Sgl scr, tpl exp, 628 nhp, 180 psi, 5 sgl blrs. 12 kts. By builder.
H Steel. 2 + shelter dk. F & B 309/94.19. P 97/29.56. C 440,800/12,482cu g. of which 240,660/6,815 refrigerated in holds 1 and 5 **P** 4 1st, 209 emigrant. Crew 84.
1898 Dec 15: Launched. Cost £85,120.
1899 Feb 26: Delivered to Shaw, Savill & Albion as *Waiwera*. Nov: Boer War transport.
1917 Missed by a torpedo off the Lizard, Cornwall. Taken up under the Liner Requisition Scheme.
1926 Sept 30: Acquired by E & B. R/n *City of Pretoria*. **T** 5,904g.
1928 March 5: Sold for £11,000 and arrived at Morecambe for breaking up by Thos W. Ward.

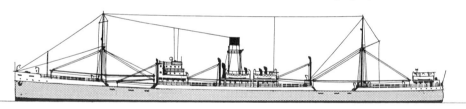

589 **CITY OF CANBERRA (I)**
B 1927 Wm. Gray & Co., West Hartlepool. **T** 7,485g, 4,681n.
D 453.2/138.13 x 57.8/17.62 x 31.9/9.72.
E Sgl scr, 4 cyl. quad exp + LP turb electric drive, 984 nhp, 265 psi, 4 sgl blrs. 12 kts. By Central Marine Eng. Wks., West Hartlepool.
H Steel. 2 dks. F 89/27.13. B 162/49.38. P 83/25.3.
1927 Dec: Completed. Lifeboats were added to the bridge during her career and 1 x 50 ton derrick to foremast.
1957 July 31: Sold to Thos. W. Ward, Inverkeithing for scrap after a sale to the Yugoslavs broke down due to a shortage of convertible currency.

Sisters of *City of Edinburgh* (V) 277
CITY OF PRETORIA (II), CITY OF LINCOLN (II)
590 **CITY OF PRETORIA (II)**
B 1937 Cammell Laird & Co (SB & E) Ltd., Birkenhead. **T** 8,046g, 3,977n.
D 516/157.27 oa, 496.7/151.39 x 62.4/19.02 x 31.3/9.54.
E Tw scr, 2 x 3 sgl reduction geared turbs, 1,867 nhp, 265 psi, 6 sgl blrs. By builder.
H Steel. 2 + part 3rd dk. F & B 351/106.98 P 76/23 16.
1937 Dec: Delivered. One of the five *City of Cape Town* class (473).
1942 Nov 26: Left the Clyde in the 30 ship convoy KMF4 carrying reinforcements for Operation Torch, the North African landings. Her destination was Gibraltar.
1943 Feb 27: Left New York for Liverpool with general cargo and munitions. Mar 3: Torpedoed twice by *U-172* well off Cape Race, Newfoundland. The ship blew up immediately and all were lost.

591 CITY OF LINCOLN (II)

As 590 except: **B** 1938 **T** 8,039g, 3,963n.

1938 Dec: Completed.

1939-45 Government service.

1946 Nov 9: Enroute Baltimore-Beira wrecked at Quion Point near Cape Agulhas, South Africa.

1947 Mar 9: Salved and towed by two tugs to Cape Town. After unloading she was stripped, using her own gear, at the Eastern Mole, Duncan Dock.

1950 May 8: The remainder of the hull was towed out to sea and sunk by bombs and rockets of the South African Airforce.

CITY OF HEREFORD See 467

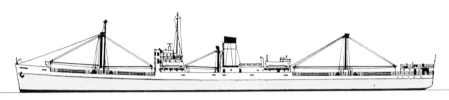

592 CITY OF CARDIFF (II)

B 1942 Wm Lithgow, Port Glasgow. **T** 6,987g, 4,193n, 10,043dwt.

D 446/135.94 oa, 431/131.37 x 56.2/17.13 x 34.2/10.42. Dft: 26.5/8.08.

E Sgl scr, tpl exp, 520 nhp, 220 psi, 2 sgl blrs. 12½ kts. By Fullerton, Hodgart & Barclay, Paisley. **H** Steel. 2 dks. Flush. **C** 546,884/15,486cu g.

1942 Apr: Built as *Empire Spartan*, M.O.W.T. initially with Clark & Service, Glasgow and then E & B as managers. Thin stove pipe funnel.

1946 Her owners became Ministry of Transport. Same managers.

1951 June: Owned by E & B, R/n *City of Cardiff*. Given funnel as drawn.

1959 Sold to Kam Kee Nav. Co, Hong Kong. R/n *Shun Wing*.

1971 Sold to Chan Moo Chu with Kam Kee as managers. Then Jebshun Shipping became managers. Flag of the Somali Republic.

1972 Sept 29: Arrived at Kaohsiung for demolition.

Liberty ships; appearance see 119

CITY OF CHELMSFORD, CITY OF DONCASTER, CITY OF PORTSMOUTH
CITY OF COLCHESTER, CITY OF LEEDS (III)

593 CITY OF CHELMSFORD

B 1943 Bethlehem Fairfield, Baltimore. **T** 7,271g, 4,457n.

D 423.7/129.14 x 57/17.37 x 34.8/10.61.

E Sgl scr, tpl exp, 2,500 bhp at 76 rpm, 240 psi, 2 wt blrs, 11 kts. By General Machy Corp, Hamilton, Ohio. **H** Steel. 2 dks.

1943 Launched as *Lionel Copley*. Aug: Completed as *Sambrake*, like all the Liberties, on bare-boat charter to M.O.W.T., E & B managers.

1946 Charterers became M.O.T.

1947 July: R/n *City of Chelmsford*.

1958 Became the first ship to tie up at Princess Margaret Quay, Dar-es-Salaam.

1959 June 24: Sold to Cia Naviera Vaptistis, Panama. R/n *San George*.

1960 Converted to diesel at Newport, Mon, by Mirrlees, Bickerton.

1968 Became *Suerte*, Suerte Shipping Co, Cyprus.

1971 Oct 6: Arrived at Split for breaking up by Brodospas.

594 CITY OF DONCASTER

As 593. T 7,257g, 4,452n.

1943 Launched as *Emma Lazarus*. Sept: Completed *Samara* but delivered to M.O.W.T. as *Samshire*, E & B managers.

1946 Charterers became M.O.T. when the word 'War' was dropped.

1947 Sept: Acquired. R/n *City of Doncaster*.

1961 Jan 13: Sold to Trader Line Ltd, London. R/n *Pembroke Trader*.

1966 R/n *Galletta* by Doreen S.S. Corp, Liberia.

1970 Apr 10: En route Chittagong-Chalna with rice went aground 60 miles from Chalna. May 12: Some cargo removed and attempts to refloat failed. Abandoned but then, May 21, salved and towed first to Chalna and then to Singapore. July 1: Sold to Fuji, Marden & Co, and arrived at Hong Kong for scrap. Aug: Demolition commenced there.

595 CITY OF PORTSMOUTH
As 593. **T** 7,216g, 4,440n.
1943 Launched as *Henry van Dyke*. Aug: Completed as *Samhain*, M.O.W.T. E & B. managers.
1946 To M.O.T. This ship had a taller funnel than her sisters.
1947 Oct: Acquired. R/n *City of Portsmouth*.
1959 Became *Efcharis*, Demetrios P. Margaronis, Piraeus.
1970 Dec 13: Laid up at Piraeus.
1971 July: Broken up at Kynosoura, Greece.

CITY OF ELY See 119

CITY OF LICHFIELD (I) See 120

CITY OF ROCHESTER See 121

CITY OF SHREWSBURY See 122

596 CITY OF COLCHESTER
As 593 except: **B** 1944. **T** 7,238g, 4,408n. **E** By Ellicott Mchy. Corp, Baltimore.
1944 March: Completed as *Samlea*, M.O.W.T., E & B as managers.
1946 M.O.T. charterers.
1947 Aug: Acquired. R/n *City of Colchester*.
1953 Mar 25: Sold to Alberta S.S. Ltd, Monrovia. R/n *Sunset*.
1966 Became *Maria Eleni*. M & A Shipping Co, Liberia.
1967 R/n *Blue Wave*, Island Maritime Associates S.A., Monrovia. Dec 23: Left Osaka for scrapping at Matsuyama.

597 CITY OF LEEDS (III)
As 593 except: **B** 1944, **T** 7,250g, 4,473n.
1944 May: Completed as *Samcrest*, M.O.W.T., E & B as managers.
1946 Charterers name changed to M.O.T.
1947 May: Acquired. R/n *City of Leeds*.
1960 June 3: Sold to Grosvenor Shipping Co, London. R/n *Grosvenor Explorer*.
1965 March: Broken up at Hong Kong.

CITY OF STAFFORD See 123

Appearance see *City of Durham* (IV) 281
598 CITY OF CARLISLE (II)
B 1946 Cammell, Laird, Birkenhead. **T** 9,913g, 5,900n.
D 497.3/151.57 oa, 475.8/145.02 x 64.4/19.63 x 40/12.19.
E Sgl scr, 3 dbl reduction geared turbs, 2 wt blrs. 14½ kts. By builder.
H Steel 2 + pt 3rd dk. F 40/12.19. P 35/10.67.
1946 Feb: Delivered to E & B, Funnel: flat top with pepper pot exhaust.
1963 Final voyage Yokohama-London. Aug 27: Almost one year to the day after the purchase of *City of Durham* (281) sold to Waywiser Nav Corp, Keelung, Taiwan. R/n *Jeannie*.
1970 Broken up at Kaohsiung.

Appearance as *City of New York* 482
599 CITY OF LONDON (IV)
B 1947 Swan, Hunter & Wigham Richardson, Wallsend. **T** 8,434g, 4,220n.
D 500/152.4 oa, 478.9/145.97 x 64.3/19.6 x 32.9/10.03.
E Tw scr, 2 x 3 turb, HP dbl rg with IP and LP srg. 3 wt blrs. 15 kts. By Wallsend Slipway.
H Steel. 2 + pt 3rd dk. F & B 372/113.38. Upper F 43/13.11. P 47/14.32. **P** 12.
1947 May: Delivered to E & B.
1953 June 15: Represented the Ellerman at the Coronation Spithead Review.
1967 Jan 11: Sold to Somia Cia Mar, Greece. Owned by Union Commercial S.S.Co. R/n *Sandra N.*
1968 Dec 30: Arrived at Kaohsiung for demolition.

600 CITY OF PRETORIA (III)
As 599 except: **B** 1947 Cammell, Laird. Birkenhead. **T** 8,450g, 4,152n.
E By builder.
1947 Nov: Delivered to E & B.
1967 Feb 2: Sold to Embajada Cia Nav, Panama. R/n *Proxeneion* for loaded delivery voyage to the Far East and the breakers at Osaka.

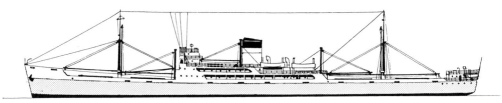

601 CITY OF BATH (II)

B 1947 Blythswood S.B.Co, Glasgow. **T** 7,030g, 3,699n.
D 483.6/147.4 oa, 464/141.43 x 62.5/19.05 x 28/8.5. Dft 27.6/8.41.
E Sgl scr, oil; 6 cyl, 2S. SA, 6,800 bhp at 116 rpm, 15½ kts. By Barclay, Curle.
H Steel. 1 + shelter dk. F 43/13.11. **P** 12.
1947 Trials 16.96 knots. June: Built as *Langleescot* for Medomsley Steam Shipping Co, the British subsidiary of the Dutch Van Ommeren group. Her sister was *Langleeclyde*. H. G. Mann manager. The catering staff were entirely female.
1952 July: Acquired by Ellerman Lines Ltd with E & B as managers. R/n *City of Bath*.
1969 Sold to Constantinos Shipping Co, Famagusta. R/n *Lena*.
1972 March 22: Arrived at Castellon in tow from St John, N.B. for breaking up by I. M. Varela Davalillo.

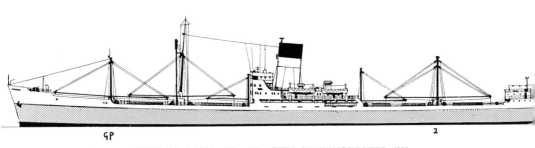

GP   2

CITY OF BRISBANE (III), CITY OF WINCHESTER (III)

602 CITY OF RIPON (II) / CITY OF BRISBANE (III)

B 1951 Cammell, Laird. Birkenhead. **T** 10,595g, 6,087n, 13,249dwt.
D 567.9/142.61 oa, 543/165.51 x 71.3/21.73 x 31.4/9.57.
E Sgl scr, 3 DRG turbs, 14,300 shp, 490 psi, 2 wt blrs. 17½ kts. By builder.
H Steel. 2 + shelter dk. F 47/14.32. **P** 30/9.14. **C** 598,469/16,946.8cu g. Crew 97.
1951 Ordered as *City of Ripon*. Nov: Delivered as *City of Brisbane* to E & B.
1970 Oct 27: Sold to Ben Line Steamers Ltd, Leith. R/n *Bencairn*.
1975 Mar 21: Arrived at Kaohsiung and broken up by Sing Cheng Yung Iron & Steel Co.

603 CITY OF WINCHESTER (III)

As 602 except: **B** 1952 Wm Denny & Bros, Dumbarton. **T** 10,594g, 6,079n.
D 568.1/173.16 oa. **E** By builder. **H** F 46/14.02.
1949 Design discussions commenced. This is instanced to show the lead time involved in ordering a modern ship. In times of radical change in design this may result in a vessel becoming obsolescent at the time of delivery. A life of only 13 years for so fine a ship perhaps demonstrates this.
1952 Mar 27: Launched. Oct 16: Delivered to E & B. Her lifeboats had a green circle at the bow on the starboard pair and a red diamond on those to port.
1970 Sept: Sold to Ben Line of Steamers Ltd, Leith. R/n *Benvannoch*.
1975 July 2: Arrived at Kaohsiung and scrapped by Li Chong Steel Co.

CITY OF NEWCASTLE (II) See Hall 494

CITY OF DELHI (V) See Hall 495

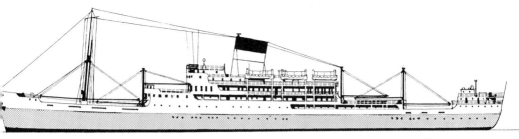

**CITY OF PORT ELIZABETH, CITY OF EXETER (II), CITY OF YORK (IV)
CITY OF DURBAN (II)**

MEDITERRANEAN SEA, MEDITERRANEAN SKY

604 CITY OF PORT ELIZABETH
B 1952 Vickers-Armstrong, Newcastle. **T** 13,363g, 7,573n, 10,700dwt, 19,645disp.
D 541/164.9 oa, 516.2/157.34 x 71.2/21.7 x 36/10.97.
E Tw scr, oil; 2 x 6 cyl Doxford, 2S, SA, 12,650 bhp at 115 rpm. 16½ kts. By Hawthorn, Leslie & Co.,
Newcastle. Fuel 1,340 tons oil.
H Steel. 3 dks. F 46/14.02. B 150/45.72. P 36/10.97. C 616,000/17,443.3cu g. 5 holds. 14 derricks.
P 107 1st.
1952 Mar 12: Launched. Dec 10: Delivered to E & B; the first post-war passenger ships for Ellerman
and the first class of motorships.
1953 Jan: M/v London-Las Palmas-Cape Town-Port Elizabeth-East London-Durban-Lourenco Mar-
ques-Beira.
1967 All four sisters had their passenger accommodation renewed.
1969 All her berths were taken over by the City of London Livery Club for a cruise. Her Captain was
then made a Freeman.
1971 July: All four were in lay up pending a sale. Sept 10: Sold for $700,000 each to Michail. A.
Karageorgis Lines Corp. R/n *Mediterranean Island*. Owned by his Occidental Ultramar SA, Piraeus.
The intention was to rebuild her at Perama into a passenger (850) and vehicle ferry (400) for service
between Patras-Ancona. Initially two were laid up at Perama, Piraeus while work proceeded on the
other pair.
1975 Conversion commenced but suspended due to the plan to complete her for cruising only. R/n
Mediterranean Sun. Laid up once more.
1980 Mar 12: Left Piraeus in tow of tug *Amsterdam* for Kaohsiung. June 3: Breaking up by Long Jong
Industry Co began.

605 CITY OF EXETER (II)
As 604 except: **E** By Vickers-Armstrong, Barrow.
1952 July 7: Launched for E & B.
1953 April 29: Delivered. May: Maiden voyage.
1971 Sept: Sold to M.A. Karageorgis. R/n *Mediterranean Sea*. Owned by Benigno Nav. S.A., Piraeus.
Same intentions as her sisters. Rebuilt as drawn. **T** 15,212g. 246 cabins for 850 passengers.
1972 Dec: Entered service. Patras-Brindisi-Ancona.
1974 Registered at Famagusta. **T** 16,384g.
1975 Owned by Mikar Ltd, Limassol. Same name.
1988 Still in being.

606 CITY OF YORK (IV)
As 604 except: **B** 1953.
1953 Mar 30: Launched for E & B. Oct 26: Delivered. Nov: M/v London-Beira.
1971 June 4: Left Cape Town on the final Ellerman passenger sailing which dated from 1892. Sept: Sold

to M.A. Karageorgis, Pandiestra Oceanica Nav S.A., Piraeus. R/n *Mediterranean Sky*. Rebuilt at Perama as was *City of Exeter*. T 14,941g.
1974 June: Entered Ancona-Rhodes service.
1988 Still in being.

607 **CITY OF DURBAN (II)**
As 604 except: **B** 1954.
1953 May 28: Launched for E & B.
1954 May: Delivered. London-Beira service.
1971 Sept: Sold to M. A. Karageorgis, Mundial Armadora S.A., Panama. R/n *Mediterranean Dolphin*. Intended for similar passenger ferry conversion but laid up at Perama.
1974 Mar 30: Arrived at Kaohsiung for scrap.

ALMERIAN (II)/CITY OF LEEDS (I) See Papayanni 141

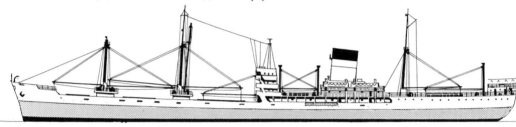

608 **CITY OF MELBOURNE (II) / CITY OF CAPE TOWN (II)**
B 1957 Alex. Stephen & Sons, Linthouse. **T** 9,914g, 5,312n, 12,300dwt.
D 545.2/166.18 oa, 510/155.5 x 71.2/21.7 x 28.9/8.81.
E Sgl scr, oil; 12 cyl sulzer, 2S. SA, 14,700 bhp, 18 kts. By builder.
H Steel. 1 + shelter + pt 3rd dk. F 45/13.72. P 95/28.96. C 612,450/17,343cu g + 168,185/4,712cu ref.
1957 Completed for E & B.
1968 When the refrigerated container ships entered the Australian service she was transferred to the South African routes. R/n *City of Cape Town;* same managers.
1973 Jan 1: Transferred to Ellerman City Liners.
1978 R/n *Ota Gold*, Atlantic Gold Shipping Pte, Singapore.
1979 May 19: Delivered to Goldwils (Hong Kong) Ltd. Resold to Taiwan breakers. May 22: Arrived at Kaohsiung.

Appearance as *City of Newcastle* (II) see Hall 494
609 **CITY OF AUCKLAND (II)**
B 1958 Vickers-Armstrong, Newcastle. **T** 8,181g, 4,359n, 10,345dwt.
D 507.2/154.59 oa, 470/143.26 x 67/20.42 x 28/8.53.
E Sgl scr, oil; 6 cyl, 2S. SA, 8000 bhp, 15 kts. By Vickers-Armstrong at Barrow.
H Steel. 1 + shelter + pt 3rd dk. F 38/11.58. P 34/10.36. C 570,100/16,143.5cu g + 86,830/2,458.7cu ref.
1958 Feb: Delivered to E & B, one of a class of six spread over City (2), Hall (3) and E & B.
1971 Laid up at Barry Docks due to a surplus of tonnage.
1973 Jan 1: Became a part of the Ellerman City Liners division.
1978 Sold to Gulf Shipping Lines Ltd, London. R/n *Gulf Falcon*.
1982 Aug 24: Laid up at Jebel Ali, U.A.E.
1983 July 27: Arrived at Bombay for breaking up.

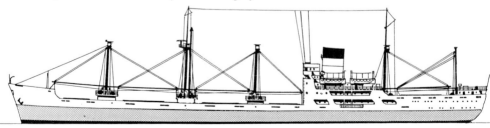

610 **CITY OF SYDNEY (III) / CITY OF MONTREAL**
B 1960 Barclay, Curle, Glasgow. **T** 10,155g, 5,888n, 11,570dwt.
D 511.7/155.97 oa, 470.9/143.53 x 67.3/20.51 x 30.5/9.3.
E Sgl scr, oil; 9 cyl Sulzer, 2S.SA, 11,535 bhp, 17½ kts. By builder.

H Steel. 3 dks. F 44/13.41. P 70/21.34. C 543,280/15,384cu g + 106,230/3,008.1cu ref. **P** 12.
1960 Oct: Delivered to E & B.
1971 Jan 1: Transferred to Ellerman City Liners. R/n *City of Montreal* when she was transferred to the St. Lawrence service of the 'Canadian City Line.'
1977 Sold to Hooton Shipping Co Inc, Panama. Owned by Yatco Enterprises Ltd. R/n *Yat Fei*.
1979 May 25: Arrived at Kaohsiung. June 19: Demolition commenced by Han Tai Iron & Steel Co.

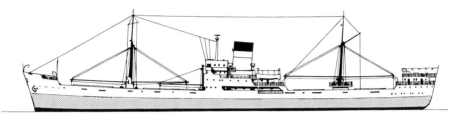

CITY OF ST. ALBANS (II), CITY OF WORCESTER (II), CITY OF LICHFIELD (II), CITY OF DUNDEE (III), CITY OF GLOUCESTER (III)

611 CITY OF ST. ALBANS (II)
B 1960 Wm Denny & Bros, Dumbarton. **T** 6,980g, 3,911n, 8,832dwt.
D 433.7/132.19 oa, 405.4/123.56 x 59.2/18.04 x 26.9/8.2.
E Sgl scr, oil; 8 cyl Sulzer, 2S.SA, 5,600 bhp, 14 ¾ kts. By builder.
H Steel. 2 dks. F 39/11.89. P 37/11.28.
1960 Dec: Delivered to E & B.
1971 Nov: En route Calcutta-Chalna during the East-West Pakistan civil war the ship was fired on at night, by an unidentified gunboat and hit 49 times by 40mm shells; no casualties. Repaired at Calcutta.
1973 Jan: Her owners remained Ellerman Lines Ltd but she became a member of the new Ellerman City Liners Division.
1977 June: Took part in the Queen's Silver Jubilee review in the Mersey.
1979 Sold to Venture Investment Trust Inc, Piraeus. R/n *Island of Marmora*. On her first voyage for them she collided with Everard's *Conformity* in St. George's Channel. Towed into Swansea for repairs.
1983 Sept 29: Left Dubai for breaking up. Oct 8: Demolition began at Jamnagar by Mastan Taherbhai.

CITY OF WORCESTER (II) See Hall 500

612 CITY OF LICHFIELD (II)
As 611 except: **B** 1961. **T** 4,795g, 2,530n, 7,821dwt.
1961 March: Delivered to E & B.
1973 Jan 1: Transferred to Ellerman City Liners.
1978 R/n *Leeds*, Serenity Maritime Co., Cyprus.
1980 Sold to Ross Navigation Co, Cyprus. R/n *City of Leeds*. Nov 11: Damaged by stranding at Antalya while leaving the anchorage in heavy weather.
1981 Jan 12: Reported refloated and docked. Abandoned by owners.
1982 Sept 20: Sold by public auction to Onur Marine Ltd.
1983 Dec 29: Left Antalya under her own power for Aliaga, Izmir.
1984 Jan 30: Sold for breaking up to Bektasoglu Makina Sanayii ve Ticaret Ltd of Sirketi. Beached at Aliaga for demolition.

613 CITY OF DUNDEE (III)
As 611 except: **B** 1961 Robb Caledon, Dundee. **T** 4,798g, 2,524n, 7,863dwt.
D 434/132.28 oa. **E** By G. Clark (Sunderland) Ltd.
1961 May: Completed for E & B. June 20: M/v to Bombay-Karachi.
1973 Jan 1: Became a unit of Ellerman City Liners fleet.
1978 R/n *Dundee* by Dundee Maritime Co, Cyprus.
1980 Became *City of Dundee* of Kilkis Navigation Co, Cyprus. Owned by Lifedream Cia Naviera, Limassol.
1984 Jan 17: Arrived at Gadani Beach and scrapped there by Panama Shipbreaking Co.

614 CITY OF GLOUCESTER (III)
As 611 except: **B** 1963. **T** 4,803g, 2,521n, 7,761dwt.
1963 March: Delivered to E & B.
1973 Jan 1: Her owners were Ellerman Lines Ltd. Ellerman City liners managers.
1979 Sold to Lionheart Maritime Inc, Piraeus. R/n *Suerte*. Owners: Ilios Shipping S.A.
1985 Apr 1: Arrived at Dalian, China, for demolition.

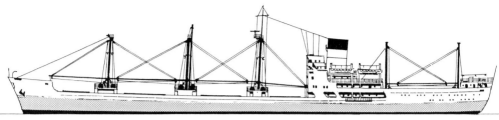

615 **CITY OF CANBERRA (II)**

B 1961 Barclay Curle, Glasgow. **T** 10,306g, 5,318n, 11,130dwt.
D 510.8/155.69 oa, 470.9/143.53 x 67.3/20.51 x 30/9.14.
E Sgl scr, oil; 9 cyl Sulzer, 2S.SA, 11,700 bhp. 18 kts. By builder.
H Steel. 3 dks. F 44/13.41. P 76/23.16. C 338,750/9,592cu g + 239,930/6,794cu ref.
1961 Dec: Delivered to E & B.
1973 Jan 1: Transferred to Ellerman City Liners.
1978 R/n *Tasgold*, Tasman Gold Shipping Pty Ltd, Singapore.
1980 Oct 18: Sold to Wiltopps (Asia) Ltd, Hong Kong. Oct 20: Left Hong Kong for Taiwan.
Oct 21: Resold to Kaohsiung breakers. Nineteen years is not a bad life for a ship but not a good one. The main problem with the faster ship was that on Conference services for Ellerman speed was the seller. As a tramp 14 knots was sufficient but the saving in oil was not comparable.

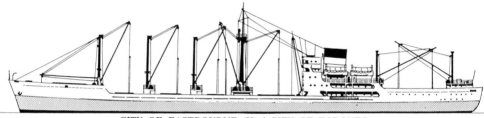

CITY OF EASTBOURNE (II) / CITY OF TORONTO,
CITY OF GLASGOW (VI) / CITY OF OTTAWA (II)

616 **CITY OF EASTBOURNE (II) / CITY OF TORONTO**

B 1962 Vickers-Armstrong, Newcastle. **T** 10.006g, 5,500n, 10,723dwt.
D 508/154.84 oa, 465.5/141.88 x 66.8/20.36 x 29.6/9.02.
E Sgl scr, oil; 8 cyl Sulzer, 2S.SA, 10,300 bhp. 18 Kts. By V-A, Barrow.
H Steel. 3 dks. F 96/29.26. P 65/19.81. C 674,131/19,089.4cu g. 6 hatches, 5 holds.
1962 March: Completed for E & B.
1971 Placed on the Canadian City Line service to the St. Lawrence. R/n *City of Toronto* by E & B.
1973 Jan 1: Owned by Ellerman Lines Ltd with Ellerman City Liners as managers.
1978 Sold to Y.C. Cheng's Pacific International Lines (Pte), Singapore. (P.I.L.). R/n *Kota Cantik*.
1984 Oct 16: Arrived at Kaohsiung for scrapping.

617 **CITY OF GLASGOW (VI) / CITY OF OTTAWA (II)**

As 616 except: **B** 1963. **T** 10,017g, 5,576n, 10,628dwt.
1963 April: Delivered to E & B although she spent some time on the Hall Line berths.
1971 R/n *City of Ottawa* by E & B for the Canadian service.
1973 Jan 1: Became a unit of the new Ellerman City Liners division.
1978 Sold to Y.C. Cheng's Pacific International Lines (Pte), Singapore. R/n *Kota Cahaya*.
Singapore-Persian Gulf service with her sister.
1985 July 31: Arrived at Nantong, China, for demolition.

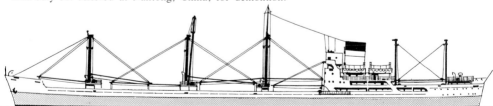

618 **CITY OF ADELAIDE (III) / CITY OF CANTERBURY (III)**

B 1964 Barclay, Curle, Glasgow. **T** 10,511g, 5,934n, 11,230dwt.
D 510.7/155.66 oa, 471.1/143.59 x 67.4/20.54 x 30.5/9.3.

E Sgl scr, oil; 9 cyl Sulzer, 2S.SA, 14,200 bhp, 18 1/4 kts. By builder.
H Steel. 3 dks. F 44/13.41. P 42/12.8. C 341,120/1,164.4cu g + 236,060/6,684.5cu ref.
1964 Jan: Delivered to E & B.
1972 R/n *Cap Cleveland* by Ellerman Lines for her charter to Hamburg Sud-Americanische.
1973 Reverted to Ellerman and r/n *City of Canterbury*. Now a unit of Ellerman City Liners.
1976 Sold to Cie Maritime Belge S.A., Antwerp. R/n *Rubens*.
1983 Became *A. L. Pioneer* of Crisela Ltd, Gibraltar. Aug 28: Arrived at Chittagong for breaking up.

CITY OF LEEDS (II) See *Venetian* (II) Papayanni 133

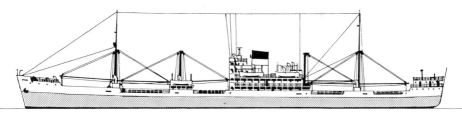

619 **CITY OF BRISTOL (III)**
B 1945 Cammell Laird, Birkenhead. **T** 7,096g, 4,019n, 9,250dwt.
D 451/137.46 oa, 426.5/130 x 58.8/17.92 x 28.3/8.63.
E Tw scr, oil; 2 x 3 cyl, 2S.SA, 5,200 bhp. 14 kts. By Wm Doxford & Sons, Sunderland.
H Steel. 2 dks. F 44/13.41. P 34/10.36. C 460,836/13,049cu g. 5 holds/hatches.
1945 Aug: Completed as *Sacramento* for Ellerman's Wilson Line, Hull.
1964 Transferred to E & B. R/n *City of Bristol*.
1969 R/n *Felicie* by Anna Shipping Co, Famagusta. No lifeboats abreast the fore derrick mast. Her funnel was also heightened by about 10ft/3.05m.
1970 Sold to the Republic of Cuba. R/n *30 de Noviembre*. Operated by Lineas Mambisa (Empresa Consolidada de Nav. Mambisa), Havana.
1977 July 27: Arrived at Faslane, Scotland for scrapping by Shipbreaking Industries Ltd.

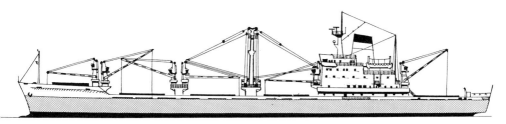

CITY OF LIVERPOOL (II), CITY OF LONDON (V), CITY OF HULL (II)

620 **CITY OF LIVERPOOL (II)**
B 1970 Robb Caledon Shipbuilders, Dundee. **T** 7,093g, 3,612n, 10,238dwt.
D 501.9/152.98 obb, 472.1/143.9 x 73.1/22.28 x 26.4/8.05.
E Sgl scr, oil; 7 cyl Doxford J-type, 2S.SA, 17,500 bhp, 18¼ kts. By Doxford & Sunderland S.B. & E.Co, Sunderland. Controlled from bridge.
H Steel. 2 dks. F 85/25.91. C 687,579/19,470cu g. 8 hatches/ 5 holds.
1970 Mar 24: Launched. Made 20.5 knots on trials. Sept: Delivered to E & B. A break bulk carrier with some modest container capacity. Dec 8: Collided, without severe damage, with the Norwegian steamer *Jark*, A. J. Bonner, Oslo, off the mouth of the Humber. *Jark* had to be towed into Immingham.
1973 Transferred to Ellerman City Liners. Her owners were HLL Shipping Ltd, London. They owned only this trio of ships. All three were adapted to carry 248 containers.
1981 Nov: Sold to Sun Horizon Nav.S.A., Piraeus; owned by Diana Shipping Agencies. R/n *Marianthe*. Served as a unit of the Svedel Line.
1985 Nov 25: Grounded off Turks Island en route Puerto Caballo-Baltimore. Dec 4: Refloated.
1986 Sept 16: Arrived at Kaohsiung and broken up.

621 **CITY OF LONDON (V)**
As 620 except: **B** Upper Clyde Shipbuilders, Scotstoun (the former Chas. Connell's yard). **T** 7,415g, 3,579n. **E** By Barclay, Curle.
1970 Jun 23: Launched. Nov: Delivered to E & B.

1973 Owned by HLL Shipping Ltd, London. Ellerman City Liners managers.
1981 Nov: R/n *Sea Lord* by Paros Shipping Co, Piraeus. Owners P & P Shipping Co (Hellas) S.A.
1988 Broken up at Kaohsiung.

622 CITY OF HULL (II)

As 620 except: **B** 1971. **T** 7,093g, 3,579n, 9,932dwt.
1970 Nov 27: Launched.
1971 April: Delivered to E & B; the final ship constructed for the Company before the merger. M/v on Ellerman-Strick service to the Persian Gulf; quite a memorial to JRE — see 1909 in the Ellerman history!
1973 Owned by HLL Shipping Ltd, London. Ellerman City Liners managers. Operated on the joint P & O-Ellerman service to the Persian Gulf.
1980 May: Sold to Waveney Shipping Corp, Liberia. Greek owned. Associated with City Maritime Ltd, London. R/n *St. John*.
1982 R/n *Seagull* by Jorama Cia. Naviera S. A., Piraeus.
1983 Repaired at Durban after stranding.
1985 Feb: Became *Sea Lady*, Best Maritime S.A., Piraeus.
1988 Sold by auction at Cyprus.

ELLERMAN'S WILSON VESSELS WHICH SERVED WITH ELLERMAN LINES LTD COMPANIES WITHOUT CHANGE OF OWNERSHIP

623 LEPANTO/CITY OF RIPON (I)

B 1915 Russell & Co, Port Glasgow. **T** 6,394g, 4,020n.
D 424.9/129.51 oa, 410.2/125 x 53.5/16.31 x 33.8/10.3.
E Sgl scr, tpl exp, 495 nhp, 180 psi, 3 sgl blrs. 11 kts. By J. G. Kincaid.
H Steel. 2 dks. Flush.
1915 Sept 7: Launched for Thos Wilson, Sons & Co's North Atlantic service. M/v Port Glasgow-New York.
1917 Became a unit of the Ellerman's Wilson fleet.
1934 Transferred to Hall line management; same owner. R/n *City of Ripon*. Hall livery.
1942 Nov 11: Torpedoed by U-160 south east of Trinidad. 57 out of 82 crew lost.

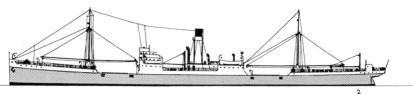

624 URBINO

B 1918 Earles Co, Hull. **T** 5,198g, 3,212n, 8,600dwt.
D 400.4/122.04 x 52.2/15.91 x 28.5/8.68. Dft 26/7.92.
E Sgl scr, tpl exp, 369 nhp. 10½ kts. By builder.
H Steel. 2 dks. F 39/11.88. B 113/34.44. P 49/14.93. (as launched).
1918 Laid down as a war-time Standard A type vessel: *War Seal*. Modified during fitting out, as drawn, F 91/27.74. P 97/29.56.
1919 Delivered to Ellerman's Wilson Line Ltd. Hull-India-Burma service.
1929-33 Laid up in the Gareloch. On one occasion she dragged both anchors but was refloated undamaged.
1934 Taken into Ellerman & Bucknall management. Same owner. Glasgow-South Africa routes.
1937 Outbound Glasgow-Cochin damaged by collision.
1940-44 Feeder service ship Cape Town-South African ports-East Africa-Middle East.
1948-49 Reconditioned by Earles but she suffered from ongoing machinery troubles which did not justify expenditure on new engines.
1954 March: At Glasgow due for overhaul but sold and broken up at Faslane by BISCO.

Vessels managed for the Ministry of War Transport
626 EMPIRE COMFORT 626 EMPIRE COMFORT 627 EMPIRE SHELTER

1,499g. These were specially constructed convoy rescue ships managed by City Line. All three survived the war but they were not commercially viable nor could they be converted for other use. No other details.

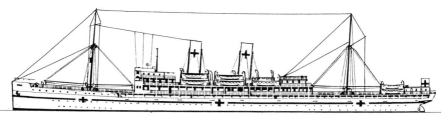

628 EMPIRE CLYDE

B 1925 Ansaldo San Giorgio, La Spezia. **T** 7,515g, 4,205n.
D 447/136.24 oa, 429.3/130.85 x 52.2/15.91 x 36/10.97.
E Tw scr, 2 x 3 DRG turbs, 1,129 nhp, 200 psi, 4 blrs. 15 kts. By Ansaldo at Sampierdarena.
H Steel. 3 + pt 4th dks. **F** 113/34.44. **P** 100 1st, 200 2nd, 1,500 3rd.
1924 Dec 28: Launched as *Leonardo da Vinci* for Transatlantica Italiana S.A. di Nav., Genoa.
1925 May 24: M/v Genoa-Palermo-Boston-New York.
1934 Transferred to Tirrenia. Mediterranean services.
1937 Owned by Lloyd Triestino. South African services with some Far East voyages. Operated as a transport during the Abyssinian invasion.
1941 Feb 11: Captured by the British at Kismayu, Somalia.
1943 Managed by City Line. Converted into a hospital ship as *Empire Clyde*. 300 beds. After the war base hospital ship at Hong Kong.
1948 Jan 1: Taken over by the Admiralty as a permanent hospital ship. R/n *Maine*. Number 54. 411 beds.
1950-53 Korean War hospital ship.
1954 Apr 26: Broken up at Hong Kong.

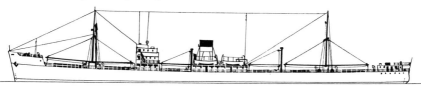

629 EMPIRE FAITH

B 1941 Barclay Curle & Co, Glasgow. **T** 7,061g, 4,244n.
D 432/131.67 oa x 57.4/17.49 x 34.2/10.42.
E Sgl scr, oil, 4 cyl 2S.SA, 3,300 bhp, Doxford. 12 kts. By builder.
H Steel. 2 dks. **F** 25/7.62.
1941 June: Completed as *Empire Faith,* managed by Westcott & Laurence, London, for M.O.W.T.
1946 Acquired by Johnston Warren Lines (Furness Withy & Co), Liverpool R/n *Jessmore*.
1958 Became *Antiope* of Maritime & Commercial Corp. Inc. Panama.
1964 R/n *Global Venture* first by Global Nav. Co, and then re-styled Glory Carriers Inc, Panama. Owned by Wah Kwong & Co (Hong Kong) Ltd.
1971 June 3: Left Hong Kong for scrapping at Kaohsiung.

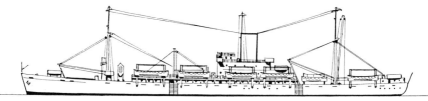

630 EMPIRE GAUNTLET

B 1944 Consolidated Steel Corp, Wilmington, Cal. **T** 7,177g, 4,823n.
D 396.5/120.85 x 60.1/18.32 x 35/10.67.
E Sgl scr, 2 d.r.g. steam turbs. 14 kts. By Westinghouse Elec. & Manuf. Co, Essington, Pa.
H Steel. 3 dks.

1944 Launched as *Cape Comorin*. Type C1-S-AY1 US standard ship for the U.S. War Shipping Administration on lend-lease to U.K. Jan: Completed on bare boat charter to M.O.W.T. as *Empire Gauntlet* taken over and converted into a Landing Ship Infantry. R/n HMS *Sefton, F 123* (as drawn). June: Present at the Utah and Omaha Normandy invasion beach landings. Reverted to supply ship *Empire Gauntlet* with Ellerman City as managers.
1945 Reverted to *Cape Comorin*, U.S. Dept of Commerce, Los Angeles. Spent many years laid up.
1964 Dec: Scrapped at Portsmouth, Va.

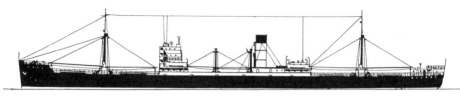

EMPIRE IRVING, EMPIRE PENDENNIS

631 **EMPIRE IRVING**
B 1944 Wm Gray & Co, West Hartlepool. **T** 7,081g, 4,089n, 10,150 dwt.
D 446.3/136.03 oa x 56.2/17.13 x 32.2/9.81.
E Sgl scr, tpl exp, 542 nhp, 220 psi, 12 kts. By Central Marine Eng. Wks, West Hartlepool.
H Steel. 2 dks. F 40/12.19.
1944 June: Completed for M.O.W.T. with Hall Line as managers.
1946 Purchased by Ropner Shipping Co, r/n *Bellerby*.
1960 Sold to Iranian Lloyd, r/n *Persian Cambyses*.
1964 Became *Iranian Trader,* owned by Iranian Shipping Lines with Pan Shipping as managers. Then r/n *Shiraz.*
1970 Sold to Ebrahim Matrood & Essa Zeers Bayrainis, Bahrain. R/n *Sayhet.*
1972 Sold to Gulf Nav. Co and then to Euorasia Carriers Ltd for scrapping. Nov 27: Left Sitra Roads in tow for Gadani Beach and broken up.

632 **EMPIRE PENDENNIS**
Sister to 631 except: **B** 1944 Short Bros, Sunderland. **T** 7,058g, 4,747n.
E By North East Marine Co (1938) Ltd, Newcastle.
1944 June: Completed as *Empire Pendennis* for M.O.W.T. with Ellerman Hall as managers.
1946 Apr: Acquired by Cunard-White Star Ltd. R/n *Vasconia* (as drawn).
1951 Sold to Blue Star Line. Became *Fresno Star.*
1957 Transferred within the Vestey group on bare boat charter to Lamport & Holt. R/n *Millais.*
1960 Jan 1: Became *Grosvenor Navigator,* Grosvenor Shipping Co, Hong Kong.
1966 Sept 9: Arrived at Kaohsiung and scrapped by Sing Chien Yung Steel & Ironworks.

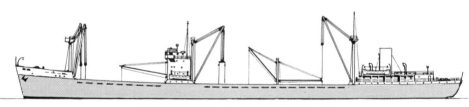

EMPIRE VICEROY, EMPIRE WALLACE

633 **EMPIRE VICEROY**
B 1943 Vickers-Armstrong, Barrow. **T** 7,803g, 4,475n.
D 469.8/143.19 oa x 66.7/20.33 x 31/9.45.
E Sgl scr, 3 DRG turbs, 1,388 nhp, 460 psi, 2 wt blrs. 14½ kts. By Richardsons, Westgarth; Hartlepool. Machy aft.
H Steel. 1 dk. F 39/11.88. B 32/9.75. P 117/35.66. This class of vessel was as designed as 'Strategic Cargo Ships' for awkward loads and had heavy lift derricking. They were direct descendants of Christian Smith's *'Bel* boats'. In some the bridge boat was on gravity davits.
1943 Aug: Completed. Hall Line as managers.
1947 Transferred to Counties Ship Management by M.O.T. The ships did not then fit any of the normal Ellerman trades.
1949 Managed by Pandelis Shipping Co, who purchased her. Same name. They also had her sister *Empire Marshall.*

1954 Sold to Gypsum Carriers Inc, Panama. R/n *Harry Lundeberg*.
1957 R/n *Ocean Carrier;* same owners. They renamed another ship *Harry Lundeberg*.
1973 May 4: Left Los Angeles for Taiwan. July 11: Arrived at Kaohsiung for scrapping.

634 EMPIRE WALLACE

Sister of 633 except: **B** 1946 Greenock Dockyard Co, Greenock. **T** 7,800g, 4,433n.
E One turb driving an electric motor connected to the shaft ie Turbo-electric. By General Electric Co,
Erith. **H** F 59/17.98.
1946 Feb: Completed for the Ministry of Transport with Hall Line as managers.
1947 The Haddon S.S. Co, London, became managers.
1948 Vergocean S.S. Co, managers.
1956 Acquired by Wm Thomson's Ben Line. R/n *Benarty*.
1962 Sold to Harbour Line Ltd, Bermuda. R/n *Elys Harbour*.
1963 Re-engined. 3 cyl oil, 3,310 bhp. 12 kts.
1967 Owned by Unique Development Co. Inc, Monrovia. R/n *Unique Developer*.
1969 Sold to Taboga Enterprises Inc, Panama. Became *Fermenco*.
1971 Same name to Cia. Agropecuaria y Maritima Santa Rosa, Colombia.
1973 Reverted to Taboga ownership.
1974 R/n *Avalon* by Wayne Inc, Panama.
1981 Nov 11: Collided off Barranquilla with *Ciudad de Turbo* and suffered considerable damage. She
was then sold to M. D. Abillo & Cia, Barranquilla, Colombia. R/n *Bahia Colombia*.
1988 Still registered.

EMPIRE SPARTAN See City of Cardiff 592

The Liberty ships (see 119 and 280 for details) were also initially on charter from M.O.W.T.

635 MARINE RAVEN

B 1944 Sun SB & DD Co, Chester, Pa. **T** 11,757g.
D 520/158.49 oa. **E** 2 d.r.g. turbs by Westinghouse. 17 kts.
1944 Jan: This C4-S-B1 standard ship was completed as the first C4 troop carrier for 2,439 men; owned
by the US War Shipping Administration and operated by United States Lines for the US Army. In this
year she made 16 trips to Europe from New York landing troops at the Clyde, Belfast, Newport, Barry,
Swansea and Southampton. She also made three voyages out of Boston to Plymouth.
1945 Lloyd's gives her as being managed by Ellerman but her war history puts her on the New
York-Southampton-Le Havre troop run until July when she switched to New York-Mediterranean
trooping.
1946 Jan: Repatriated German POWs from San Francisco. May 9: Released by the Army. Thus any
management by Ellerman must have been as agents for the handling or directing of the vessel when (if)
she was under British control on a wet boat basis from the United States Lines.
1948 In USMC reserve lay up. She then had a commercial career as *Sophie H, Vasso, Transpacific* and
Vall Moon until:
1976 Feb: Broken up at Gadani Beach.
This entry is, therefore, for record purposes. Further information Ellerman elucidation welcome.

Note during the war, when all ships were under the overall control of the Shipping Controller additional
vessels were handled by the Ellerman group; this arose when Ellerman had a crew available and they
therefore took the voyage irrespective of the owners of the ship. It is not possible to attempt to isolate
such sailings.

636 TAIPOSHAN

B 1901 London & Glasgow Engineering & Iron S. B. Co, Glasgow. **T** 2,143g, 1,356n.
D 290.3/88.48 x 42/12.8 x 15.5/4.72.
E Sgl scr, tpl exp. 10 kts. By builder.
H Steel. 1 + spar dk. F 36/10.97. B 60/18.29.
1901 Oct: Delivered as *Hang Sang* for the Indo-China S.N. Co.
1940 Acquired by Pang Kwok Sui. Taken over and managed for the M.O.W.T. by Ellerman &
Papayanni. R/n *Taiposhan*.
1946 Owned by Tai On S.N. Co, Hong Kong.
1951 Scrapped.

Non-British vessels managed for M.O.W.T.

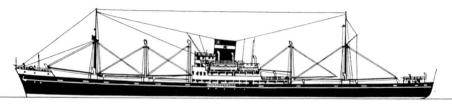

637 ANDREA GRITTI
B 1943 Cantieri Riuniti del Adriatico, Monfalcone. **T** 6,404g, 3,743n.
D 440/134.11 x 60.5/18.44 x 26/7.92.
E Sgl scr, oil. By Fiat, Turin.
H Steel 1 + shelter dk. F 36/10.97.
1943 July: Built for Soc. Italiana di Armamento 'Sidarma', Venice; one of six sister ships. Requisitioned by the Royal Italian Government. Supply ship in the Mediterranean. In September when the Italian armistice was signed the ship came under Allied control with Hall Line as managers. Because Italy was now a co-belligerent (not an Ally) the ship was not given an '*Empire*' name.
1945 Late. Returned to Sidarma as *Andrea Gritti* (Drawing).
1967 Became *Veritas* of Vera Shipping Co, Cyprus.
1971 Aug 12: Arrived at Kaohsiung for breaking up.

M.O.W.T. on bare-boat charter from the Dominion of Canada

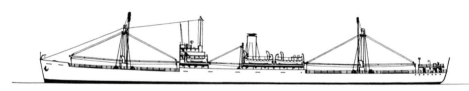

FORT CONSTANTINE, FORT DUNVEGAN, FORT EDMONTON, FORT KILMAR, FORT PROVIDENCE, FORT ST JAMES, FORT TADOUSSAC

638 FORT CONSTANTINE
B 1944 Burrard D.D. Co, South Yard (Vancouver D.D. Co.) Vancouver.
T 7,221g, 4,027n, 10,100 dwt.
D 441.5/134.57 oa x 57.2/17.43 x 34.9/10.63.
E Sgl scr, tpl exp, 4,000 ihp, 2 wt blrs, oil burning. 12 kts. By Canadian Allis-Chalmers, Montreal (Designed by North Eastern Marine Eng. Co. Newcastle).
H Steel. 4 dks. Flush.
1944 Apr 25: Delivered to M.O.W.T. with Ellerman & Bucknall as managers. Known as 'Victory type' (nothing to do with the US Victory ships). The ship was completed as a Stores Issuing Ship, Air, intended to operate with aircraft carriers and forward air bases in the Pacific. In addition to her E & B crew there was a unit, under a Commander, from the Admiralty's Victualling Division.
1949 Transferred to the Admiralty; a Royal Fleet Auxiliary.
1965 Laid up at Plymouth M.O.T. as owners.
1969 Oct 24: Arrived at Hamburg for breaking up by Eckhardt & Co, GmbH.

639 FORT DUNVEGAN
As 638
1944 Apr 14: Delivered; same details as 638.
1949 Transferred to the Admiralty. R.F.A.
1968 Broken up in Taiwan.

640 FORT EDMONTON
As 638.
1944 Sept 13: Delivered. Same details as 638.
1947 Became *Federal Voyager;* Federal & Commercial Nav. Co, Montreal.
1961 Broken up at Chiba, Japan.

641 **FORT KILMAR**
As 638 except: **E** by Dominion Engineering Wks, Montreal.
1944 May 25: Delivered. Same details as 638.
1947 Sold. R/n *Ironside* by Andros Shipping Co, Montreal.
1954 Feb 10: Grounded 3 miles from Nojima Saki, Tokio Bay. Sold for scrap.

642 **FORT PROVIDENCE**
as 638.
1944 July 8: Delivered. Same details as 638.
1948 Became *Eastwater* of Eastboard Navigation Co, Montreal.
1952 R/n *Duneside* of Andros Shipping Co, Montreal.
1953 Owned by Franco Maresca, Genoa. R/n *Mar Libero.*
1959 Sold. R/n *Dugiotok;* owned by Jugoslavenska Tankerska Plovidba, Zadar. Her name was later *Dugi Otok.*
1966 Sold to Prekookeanska Plovidba, Zadar. Same name.
1967 Feb 8: Arrived at Yokosuka for scrapping. Realised $133,000.

M.O.W.T. on bare-boat charter, lend-lease, from the US War Shipping Administration but built, under the Hyde Park agreement, in Canada.

643 **FORT ST JAMES**
as 638 except: **B** 1942. **T** 7,130g, 4,258n, 10,000dwt. **D** 438.5/133.65.
E By Dominion Engineering Wks, Montreal. 3 Scotch blrs. Coal burning.
1942 Jan 29: Delivered. The first ship of the 'North Sands' type, named after J. L. Thompson's North Sands yard where the prototype was built. Differed from the *Fort Constantine* five by having only one pair of lifeboats on the funnel superstructure. Managed by E & B and then Ellerman's Wilson.
1947 Became *Temple Bar* of Lambert Bros. Ltd, London. Temple Bar S.S. Co.
1959 R/n *Nord Sky,* through agents to the Republic of China.
1960 R/n *Hoping Er Shi Shi;* same owners.
1970 The name was spelt *Hoping Er Shi Chi.* On its formation she was transferred to China Ocean Shipping Co.
1978 R/n *Ho Ping 27,* same owners. Trace lost; broken up.

644 **FORT TADOUSSAC**
as 638 except: **B** 1942 Davie SB & Repairing Co, Lauzon, Quebec. **T** 7,129g, 4,259n.
E By Dominion Engineering, Montreal.
1942 Apr 18: Delivered to Canadian Government and transferred to M.O.W.T. with E & B as managers.
1947 Returned to the USA; U.S.M.C. as owners. Laid up.
1959 Broken up at Mobile.

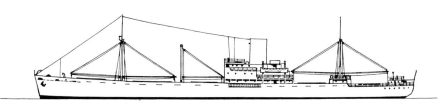

645 **CAPE DOUGLAS**
B 1944 Pusey & Jones, Wilmington, Del. **T** 7,156g, 4,487n.
D 397.3/121.07 x 60.2/18.35 x 25.1/7.65.
E Sgl scr, 2 drg steam turbs by Allis-Chalmers Manufacturing Co, Milwaukee, Wis.
H Steel. 3 dks.
1943 Apr: Launched, sideways. Towed to New York and converted to carry 1,257 troops by Cardinal Engineering Inc.
1944 Jan: Delivered to War Shipping Administration.
1946 March: Laid up by W.S.A.
1947 On bare boat charter to M.O.T. with Ellerman as managers.
1948 Returned to the U.S. Maritime Commission. Laid up in reserve.
1964 Nov: Scrapped at Chesapeake, Va.

Free French ships handled by Ellerman on a mixed wet and dry charter basis.

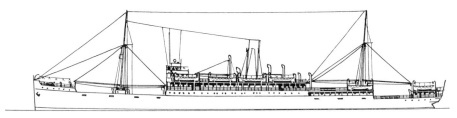

CAP PADARAN, CAP TOURANE

646 CAP PADARAN
B 1922 Ateliers et Chantiers de la Lore, St Nazaire. **T** 8,009g, 4,891n.
D 417.7/127.31 x 55.1/16.79 x 34.4/10.48.
E Sgl scr, 3 drg turbs, 14 kts. By builder.
H Steel. 3 dks. F 45/13.72. B 149/45.41.
P 154 1st, 70 2nd.
1922 Mar 17: Launched as *D'Iberville* for Cie Chargeurs Réunis.
1926 Rebuilt for the Indo-China service. R/n *Cap Padaran*.
1940 June: Remained in Vichy French control after the Franco-German armistice.
1941 Seized by a British warship 200 miles south of Durban. Managed by City for M.O.W.T.
1943 Sept: After the Italian defeat operated as a troopship in the Italian theatre. Dec 9: Torpedoed by *U-596* in the Adriatic.

647 CAP TOURANE
Sister to 646 except: **B** 1923. By builder at Nantes.
1923 Sept 15: Launched as *Jouffroy D'Abbans*.
1925 Rebuilt for the Indo-China service. R/n *Cap Tourane*.
1940-45 Served with the Free French.
1946 Refurbished and returned to Chargeurs Réunis service.
1953 May: Broken up at Zeebrugge.

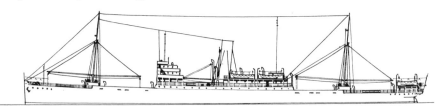

648 D'ENTRECASTEAUX
B 1922 Forges et Chantiers de la Mediterranée, Le Havre. **T** 7,642g, 4,740n.
D 417.8/127.4 x 55.3/16.85 x 34.5/10.52.
E Sgl scr, tpl exp, 416 nhp, 14 kts. By builder.
H Steel. 3 dks. B 147/44.8.
1922 Mar 24: Launched for Chargeurs Réunis.
1941 July 1: Taken at sea by the cruiser HMS *Dunedin*. Ellerman City as managers for M.O.W.T.
1942 Nov 7: Torpedoed by *U-154* in the South Atlantic.

CHARTERS
During the mid-eighties a number of chartered container ships carried 'City' names.
They were:
ELLESMERE PORT-MEDITERRANEAN
649 CITY OF LISBON
B 1985. **T** 3,598g. Launched as *Polaris*; completed as *Eurobridge Beam*.
1980 R/n *Polaris II*.
1983 R/n *Eagle* by Reederei John Lurs K.G. Hamburg.
1985 R/n *City of Lisbon* on charter to Ellerman City Liners.
1986 Became *Manchester City* for Manchester Liners; operated on the same service from Ellesmere Port.

650 CITY OF MANCHESTER
B 1984 **T** 2,778g. Built as *Hasselwerder*. Owned by Gerd Bertels, Lubeck.
1984 R/n *City of Manchester* on charter.
1985 Reverted to *Hasselwerder* off charter.

651 CITY OF OPORTO
B 1979 **T** 1,599g. **1978** Oct 16: Launched as *Royal Prince*, Prince Line; a sister, with *Crown Prince*, of *City of Plymouth* (301).
1984 R/n *City of Oporto*.
1985 Reverted to *Royal Prince* and replaced by another *City of Oporto*.

652 CITY OF OPORTO
B 1981 **T** 1,599g Built as *Nord*. Owned by Friedrich Beutelrock, Lubeck; Hanse-Schiffahrtsgesellschaft.
1985 R/n *City of Oporto* on charter. She replaced *Royal Prince*, Prince Line, on the Ellesmere Port service.
1986 Reverted to *Nord*.

653 CITY OF SALERNO
B 1981 **T** 1,598g. Ex *Nordstar*. Owned by Klaus E. Oldendorff, Hamburg. The ship was registered at Singapore.
1984 On charter as *City of Salerno*.
1985 Reverted to *Nordstar;* owned by Senang Shipping Pte, Singapore (a subsidiary of Oldendorff).

654 CITY OF SALERNO
B 1977 **T** 1,599. **1977** Built as *Peter Knuppel*. Owned by Johs Thode, Hamburg.
1978 Became *Eurobridge Link* on charter to Eurobridge.
1980 Reverted to *Peter Knuppel*.
1982 R/n *Katherine Borchard* on charter to Borchard.
1983 *Peter Knuppel* again. Owned by Hans-Heinrich Knuppel Schiffahrts. K.G.
1985 Became *City of Salerno* on charter.
1986 Reverted to *Peter Knuppel*.

655 CITY OF SALERNO
B 1983 **T** 1,599. Built as *Ocean* for Hans-Hermann Knuppel.
1986 R/n *City of Salerno* on charter. The third ship to cover the berth in continuous service under the name *City of Salerno;* confusing for the historian.
1987 Reverted to *Ocean*.

ELLERMAN CITY LINERS
656 CITY OF LIVERPOOL
B 1982. **T** 18,575g. Owned by Christian F. Ahrenkial, Hamburg. Entered service for Partenrederei 'City of Liverpool'. Bulk carrier.
1985 R/n *Campania* by Navifonds 14 Seeschiffs Anlage Ges. Gmbh & KG, Germany.

657 CITY OF LONDON.
1981 Dec 5: Elder Dempster's *Mentor* (a Blue Funnel name) was renamed *City of London* for one year on charter to Overseas Container Line (then P & O, Ocean and British & Commonwealth now P & O only) when E & B's *City of London* (621) was sold. At the end of the period she reverted to *Mentor* and was laid up in the river Fal. The ship operated for Ellerman Harrison Container Line on the SAECS consortium.